Computer Facial
Animation

Computer Facial Animation

Second Edition

Frederic I. Parke
Keith Waters

A K Peters, Ltd.
Wellesley, Massachusetts

Editorial, Sales, and Customer Service Office

A K Peters, Ltd.
888 Worcester Street, Suite 230
Wellesley, MA 02482
www.akpeters.com

First edition published in 1996.

Library of Congress Cataloging-in-Publication Data

Parke, Frederic I.
    Computer facial animation / Frederic I. Parke, Keith Waters. – 2nd ed.
        p. cm.
    Includes bibliographical references and index.
    ISBN: 978-1-56881-448-3 (alk. paper)
    1. Computer animation. 2. Face. I. Waters, Keith. II. Title.
TR897.7.P37 2008
006.6′96--dc22

                                                                                    2008022175

Front cover: Left image courtesy of R. Fedkiw and E. Sifakis, from [Sifakis et al. 06], imaged by XYZ RGB; right image courtesy of T. Kurihara, adapted from [Kurihara and Arai 91].

Back cover: Images adapted from [Riewe 07].

Printed in India
12 11 10 09 08   10 9 8 7 6 5 4 3 2 1

To *Vicky* for all her love and support

—Fred Parke

To my family—*Susy, Rosey, and Jasper*—and my parents—*Joyce and Lawrence*—whose never failing encouragement over many years allowed me the time and space to write.

—Keith Waters

Contents

Preface

This book is about computer facial models, computer-generated facial images, and facial animation. In particular, it addresses the principles of creating face models and the manipulation or control of computer-generated facial attributes. In addition, various sections in the book describe and explain the development of specific computer facial animation techniques over the past 20 years, as well as those expected in the near future.

In recent years there has been considerable interest in computer-based three-dimensional character animation. Part of this interest is a strong fascination in the development and use of facial animation. There is no single reason for this burst of activity, but it has certainly been fueled by both an emerging computer animation film production industry and the games industry. There has also been a rapid growth of interest within the scientific community. In this context, it has been desirable to develop simulations of surgical procedures, careful and precise observations of computer facial animation, and the production of detailed visualizations of human anatomy.

The first SIGGRAPH tutorials on the *State of the Art in Facial Animation* in 1989 and 1990 provided a vital vehicle to collect and present material from a variety of face-related disciplines. The success of these two courses and the material presented therein prompted the development of this book. Therefore, the text covers much of the material presented in those tutorials, plus a number of topics that originally were not included.

This book was written to meet the perceived need for a text that pulls together, explains, and documents the diverse developments in facial animation. Since the information on computer facial animation is currently quite fragmented, we wish to make this technology much more accessible to a wide range of readers, spanning the spectrum from the merely curious, to serious users of computer animation systems, to system implementers, and to researchers. As a result, the book contains enough depth for serious animators, provides valuable reference for researchers, and still remains accessible to those with little or no sophistication in this area. Our expectation is that this book be used as a text, or as a case-study reference, for courses in computer animation.

Preface to the Second Edition

Much has happened in the development and application of facial modeling and animation in the ten years since the initial publication of this book. As a result, this second edition is intended to incorporate the most important and useful of these new developments, while retaining the core concepts that are still relevant.

Within the animation industry, facial character animation is now taken for granted, and some techniques have become mainstream activities. We believe that the first edition of this book has played a role in shaping that industry by explaining the core principles that underlie most modeling and animation systems used today. This second edition continues to amplify those principles, as well as introducing some newer concepts that have evolved over the past ten years.

Some interesting developments have been in the area of performance-driven face animation, where an actor's performance can be recorded, tracked, and re-animated in three dimensions. The interest in the area resulted in SIGGRAPH courses in 2006. Such techniques are being used extensively in the film industry and are data-intensive operations; gigabytes of data are recorded from multiple high-definition cameras running at high speed for just a few seconds. Additional developments have been in the areas of data-driven facial models and the use of much more sophisticated lighting and rendering techniques, such as ambient occlusion and subsurface scattering. As a result, it is hard to distill and capture all the latest techniques. So instead, we have focused on those competencies that are considered fundamental and have become, or are close to becoming, mainstream.

Acknowledgments

For the first edition, we would like to thank Brad deGraf, Steve DiPaola, Matt Elson, Jeff Kleiser, Steve Pieper, Bill Reeves, Lance Williams, and Brian Wyvill, who participated in the 1989 and 1990 SIGGRAPH Facial Animation tutorials, and who presented much of the material that formed the initial basis for this book.

For the second edition, we would like to thank the following additional contributors whose help made the book that much richer. Cynthia Brezeal for images of Kismet; Zygote Media Group, Inc., for the data used to generate the skull anatomy illustrations in Chapter 3; George Borshukov for imagery used to create Agent Smith for the film *The Matrix Reloaded*; Tony Ezzat for images creating MikeTalk and Mary101; Volker Blanz for images of a morphable model; Ron Fedkiw and Eftychios Sifakis for the Finite Volume face model images; Roz Picard for images of Self-Cam; and Mova for images created from their capture system. Additional images were created by Andy Smith, Jessica Riewe, Jon Reisch, Eric Andraos, and the "Rivalry" team at the Texas A&M University Visualization Laboratory. Images illustrating hair modeling and animation techniques were provided by Florence Bertails, Yosuke Bando, Tom Mertens, Ulrich Neumann, and Yizhou Yu.

Frederic I. Parke
Keith Waters
May 2008

1

Introduction

In recent years there has been dramatically increased interest in computer-based three-dimensional facial character animation. Facial animation is not a new endeavor; initial efforts to represent and animate faces using computers go back more than thirty-five years. However, the recent explosion of activity in character animation has promoted a concurrent interest in facial animation. Our intent is to present the principles of facial animation to enable animation implementors to develop their own systems and environments.

The human face is interesting and challenging because of its familiarity. The face is the primary part of the body that we use to recognize individuals; we can recognize specific faces from a vast universe of similar faces and are able to detect very subtle changes in facial expression. These skills are learned early in life, and they rapidly develop into a major channel of communication. Small wonder, then, that character animators pay a great deal of attention to the face.

Human facial expression has been the subject of much investigation by the scientific community. In particular, the issues of universality of facial expression across cultures and the derivation of a small number of principal facial expressions have consumed considerable attention. *The Expression of the Emotions in Man and Animals*, published by Charles Darwin in 1872 [Darwin 72], dealt precisely with these issues and sowed the seeds for a subsequent century to research, clarify, and validate his original theories.

The value of this body of work, and of others in this field, requires no explanation in the context of facial animation.

The ability to model the human face and then animate the subtle nuances of facial expression remains a significant challenge in computer graphics. Despite a heavy reliance on traditional computer graphics algorithms such as modeling and rendering, facial modeling and animation are still being defined, without broadly accepted solutions. Facial animations often are developed with *ad-hoc* techniques that are not easily extendible and that rapidly become brittle. Therefore, this book presents a structured approach, by describing the anatomy of the face, working though the fundamentals of facial modeling and animation, and describing some state-of-the-art techniques.

1.1   About This Book

Two-dimensional facial character animation has been well defined over the years by traditional animation studios such as Disney Studios, Hanna-Barbera, and Warner Brothers. However, three-dimensional computer-generated facial character animation is not as well defined. Therefore, this book is focused principally on realistic three-dimensional faces.

The purpose of this book is to provide a source for readers interested in the many aspects of computer-based facial animation. In this book we have tried to capture the basic requirements for anyone wanting to animate the human face, from key framing to physically based modeling. The nature of the subject requires some knowledge of computer graphics, although a novice to the subject also can find the book an interesting resource about the face.

Clearly, the field of computer-generated facial animation is rapidly changing; every year, new advances are reported, making it difficult to capture the state of the art. However, it is clear that facial animation is a field whose time has come. The growth of increasingly complex computer-generated characters demands expressive, articulate faces. Most of the techniques employed today involve principles developed in the research community some years ago—in some instances, more than a couple of decades ago.

So why this surge of interest in computer-generated facial animation? There is no single reason, although we can point to several key influences. Perhaps the strongest interest comes from the commercial animation studios, whose insatiable appetite for the latest and greatest visual effect is both enormous and endless. These studios are trendsetters who popularize new animation techniques. DreamWorks and Pixar are examples of such production studios where, for example, the movies *Shrek* and *The Incredibles* were produced. In addition, the advance in realism of video games has demanded expressive facial animation with high levels of realism.

Another key reason is the development of powerful interactive modeling and animation systems, such as Maya and 3D Studio. These systems dramatically ease the development of three-dimensional facial models. Improvements in surface scanner technology, such as optical laser scanners [Cyberware Laboratory Inc. 90], and motion capture systems have enabled many facial modeling and animation approaches based on surface and motion data from real faces. Also, overall advances in affordable computing power have made more sophisticated and computationally intensive modeling, animation, and rendering techniques broadly available.

Another intriguing influence is the advent of believable social agents. The construction of believable agents breaks the traditional mold of facial animation; agents have to operate in real time, bringing along a new set of constraints. While the basic algorithms used to animate real-time characters are concurrent with production animation, new tools have been developed to deal with issues such as lip synchronization and behavior interaction.

1.2 A Brief Historical Sketch of Facial Animation

This section is a brief synopsis of key events that have helped shape the field, rather than a chronological account of facial animation. Most events in facial animation have been published in one form or another. The most popular forums have been the proceedings and course notes of the ACM SIGGRAPH conferences and other computer graphics journals and conference proceedings.[1]

Historically, the first computer-generated images of three-dimensional faces were generated by Parke as part of Ivan Sutherland's computer graphics course at the University of Utah in early 1971. Parke began with very crude polygonal representations of the head, which resulted in a flip-pack animation of the face opening and closing its eyes and mouth. Several of these images are shown in Figure 1.1.

While at the University of Utah, Henri Gouraud was also completing his dissertation work on his then-new smooth polygon shading algorithm. To demonstrate the effectiveness of the technique, he applied it to a digitized model of his wife's face. Parke used this innovative shading technique to produce several segments of fairly realistic facial animation [Parke 72]. He did this by collecting facial expression polygon data from real faces using photogrammetric techniques and simply interpolating between expression poses to create animation. By 1974, motivated by the desire to quickly produce facial animation, Parke completed the first parameterized three-dimensional face model [Parke 74].

---

[1]The reader is encouraged to refer to the Bibliography for a more complete listing.

Figure 1.1.
Several of the earliest three-dimensional face models developed by Parke at the University of Utah in 1971.

In 1971, Chernoff first published his work using computer-generated two-dimensional face drawings to represent a k-dimensional space [Chernoff 71]. By using a simple graphical representation of the face, an elaborate encoding scheme was derived. Also in 1973, Gillenson at Ohio State University reported his work on an interactive system to assemble and edit two-dimensional line-drawn facial images, with the goal of creating a computerized photo identi-kit system [Gillenson 74].

From 1974 through 1978, three-dimensional facial animation development was essentially dormant. However, during this period the development of two-dimensional computer-assisted animation systems continued at the New York Institute of Technology, Cornell University, and later at Hanna-Barbera. These systems supported two-dimensional cartoon animation, including facial animation.

In 1980, Platt at the University of Pennsylvania published his masters thesis on a physically based muscle-controlled facial expression model [Platt 80]. In 1982, Brennan at MIT reported work on techniques for computer-produced two-dimensional facial caricatures [Brennan 82]. Also at MIT in 1982, Weil reported on work using a video-disk-based system to interactively select and composite facial features [Weil 82]. Later at MIT, based on this work, Burson developed computer-based techniques for aging facial images, especially images of children.

In the mid-eighties, developments in facial animation took off once more. An animated short film, *Tony de Peltrie*, produced by Bergeron and Lachapelle in 1985, was a landmark for facial animation [Bergeron and Lachapelle 85]. This was the first computer-animated short where three-dimensional facial expression and speech were a fundamental part of telling the story.

In 1987, Waters reported a new muscle model approach to facial expression animation [Waters 87]. This approach allowed a variety of facial expressions to be created by controlling the underlying musculature of the face. In 1988, Magnenat-Thalmann and colleagues also described an abstract muscle action model [Magnenat-Thalmann et al. 88]. In 1987 Lewis [Lewis and Parke 87] and in 1988 Hill [Hill et al. 88] reported techniques for automatically synchronizing speech and facial animation.

Another groundbreaking animation short was *Tin Toy*, which received an Academy Award. Produced by Pixar, *Tin Toy* was an example of the capabilities of computer facial animation. In particular, a muscle model was used to articulate the facial geometry of the baby into a variety of expressions [Parke 90].

The development of optical range scanners, such as the Cyberware™ optical laser scanner, provides a new wealth of data for facial animation [Cyberware Laboratory Inc. 90]. In 1990, Williams reported the use of registered facial image texture maps as a means for 3D facial expression animation [Williams 90b]. By the late 1990s, large data sets of high quality laser scanned data were being used to create detailed morphable facial models by Blanz and Vetter [Blanz and Vetter 99].

The new wave of enhanced image processing and scanning technology promised to usher in a new style of facial animation. In 1993, Lee, Terzopoulos, and Waters described techniques to map individuals into a canonical representation of the face that has known physically based motion attributes [Lee et al. 93].

Another growth area was in medicine, with a focus on surgical planning procedures and accurate simulation of face tissue dynamics. In 1988, Deng [Deng 88] and later Pieper [Pieper 91] in 1991, used a finite-element model of skin tissue to simulate skin incisions and wound closure. More recently the finite-element approach has been applied to highly detailed biomechanical models of muscle and skin tissue derived from the Visible Human Project by Sifakis, Neverov, and Fedkiw [Sifakis et al. 05].

Through the late 1990s there was a surge of interest in facial analysis from video cameras. This interest was twofold: first, to provide the ability to track the human face to create lifelike characters, and second, to develop the ability to detect facial expression and thereby derive emotional states. There has been some success in both areas. Two popular techniques are model-based [Yuille et al. 89, Blake and Isard 94] and optical flow-based [Black and Yacoob 95, Essa and Pentland 94] techniques.

The late 1990s and early 2000s became a threshold for high-fidelity face capture and rendering for the film industry. Landmark films such as *The Lord of the Rings* (New Line Cinema 2002), *The Matrix Reloaded* (Warner Bros. 2003), *The Polar Express* (Warner Bros. 2004), *Monster House* (Sony Pictures 2006) required face motion capture sessions of actors using markers and head gear. The capture sessions resulted in very large datasets, which had to be processed and rendered. Such techniques are referred to as *data-driven* facial animation and demand blending between more established modeling, rendering, and animation techniques, and alternative approaches [Deng and Neumann 08].

In the more recent past, the ability to create visual surrogates that are authentic enough to deceive observers into thinking they are real people is close at hand. Such techniques will most likekly blend animation, modeling, and control with live captured data. How such surrogates will be used is speculative at this time; however, the film, games, medicine, and virtual online media are likely to be the first beneficiaries. The future is indeed bright for computer facial animation.

1.3   Application Areas

By far the largest motivator, developer, and consumer of three-dimensional facial character animation is the animation industry itself. While the animation studios continue to shape how computers are used in animation, other emerging areas that influence animation are briefly mentioned below.

1.3.1   Games Industry

The games industry has experienced rapid recent development, due in part to increasing processor performance, coupled to more and more powerful graphics coprocessors. Such hardware advances have opened the door to more sophisticated real-time three-dimensional animation software that is different from the techniques employed in film production animation. High quality real-time rendering is now commonplace. For example, texture mapping, as well as many special purpose effects such as hair rendering, skin reflectance mapping, environment mapping, as well as motion dynamics and multi-body interaction, can be rendered on the fly to enhance the realism of game play.

While a maturing games industry has benefited from real-time performance, it also plays an important role in film production, where animated scenes can be blocked in and combined with live action well before final rendering is required. Within the context of facial animation, real-time sequencing and synchronization within the scene can save enormous amounts of time in film production.

It is clear that a number of opportunities for the next-generation facial animation techniques will be at the intersection of real-time performance and off-line, non-real-time production rendering. For the games industry the challenges will be to combine lifelike performances with which players can interact; playing pre-rendered clips of a character will no longer be sufficient to provide a belief that the character is real and engaging. Engaging the player requires some sensing of user actions. For the face in particular, it will be increasingly important for the characters to engage in non-verbal communication, such as eye contact and the eye-gaze behaviors we experience in the real world.

The film industry can afford data-intensive capture and processing sessions to create *one-off* productions. In contrast, the games industry has to create algorithms that are used on the fly to fit the technical constraints of processors and rendering hardware. Nevertheless, compressing the large quantities of capture data down into managable chunks, using principal component analysis (PCA), allows performance data to be used. Such techniques allow performance segments to be seamlessly stitched together into a real-time playback sequence.

1.3.2 Medicine

Computing in medicine is a large and diverse field. In the context of facial animation, two particular aspects are of interest: surgical planning and facial tissue surgical simulation. In both cases, the objective is to execute preoperative surgical simulation before the patient goes under the knife.

Craniofacial surgical planning involves the rearrangement of the facial bones due to trauma or growth defects [Vannier et al. 83]. Because this involves the rigid structures of bone tissue, the procedure essentially becomes a complex three-dimensional *cut-and-paste* operation. Computer models are typically generated from computer tomography scans of the head and the bone surfaces, generated from iso-surface algorithms such as the *marching cubes* [Lorensen and Cline 87]. More recently, the use of detailed data from the Visible Human Project has allowed models of the facial tissues—in particular muscle and skin—to be indentified and modeled [United States National Library of Medicine 94].

For facial tissue simulation, the objective is somewhat different. Here, the objective is to emulate the response of skin and muscle after they have been cut and tissue has been removed or rearranged [Larrabee 86]. Understanding and simulating skin tissue dynamics is the subject of Chapter 8.

1.3.3 Video Teleconferencing

The ability to transmit and receive facial images is at the heart of video teleconferencing. Despite the rapid growth of available communication bandwidth, there remains a need for compression algorithms. One active research area is in model-based coding schemes and, in particular, algorithms applied to facial images [Choi et al. 90].

The components of a very low-bandwidth face video conferencing system are illustrated in Figure 1.2. Each captured frame from video is analyzed

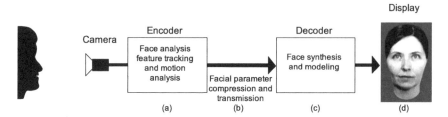

Figure 1.2.
A video teleconferencing protocol. A camera captures moving images of a face:
(a) Face parameters are extracted. (b) The parameters are compressed and
transmitted to a decoder. (c) They are reconstructed. (d) A visual surrogate is
displayed on the receiving end. A two-way system replicates this sequence in the
reverse direction.

by the encoder, with the assumption that the principal object in the scene
is a human face. Computer vision algorithms are then used to extract and
parameterize properties such as the shape, orientation, and motion of the
head and face features.

These few parameters are compressed and transmitted to the decoder,
where a three-dimensional model of the human head is synthesized to create a visual surrogate of the individual. As the head moves from frame
to frame, new parameters are transmitted to the receiver and subsequently
synthesized. This procedure is in contrast to existing video teleconferencing
compression techniques that deal exclusively with compression and transmission of pixel-based image data.

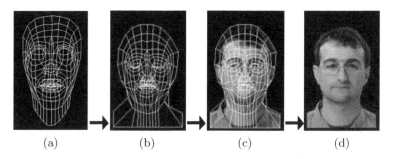

Figure 1.3.
A three-dimensional model created from a single image of an individual,
precisely mapped to a canonical model: (a) the baseline canonical face, (b) and
(c) the topology deformed to match an individual, and (d) the rendered
three-dimensional visual surrogate.

While Figure 1.2 represents teleconferencing in action, there remain a number of key initialization procedures for the encoder and decoder. Figure 1.3 illustrates an example of a three-dimensional canonical model mapped to an individual. As part of the initialization procedure for the encoder, features of the face must be accurately aligned, such that the mouth and eyes open in the correct location with respect to the image texture map.

One of the by-products of mapping images of individuals to canonical representations of the face is that any image can be used to create a novel character. This has resulted in some interesting opportunities to create avatars from animal—or non-animal—images. Re-mapping, or re-targeting as it is sometimes called, is discussed in Chapter 10.

1.3.4   Social Agents and Avatars

A developing area for facial animation is in user interfaces that have characters or agents. The principle of social agents lies in the ability of an agent to interact directly with the user. This ability can be as simple as a reactive behavior to some simple action such as searching for a file, or as complex as an embodiment or characterization of a personal assistant capable of navigating the Internet under voice commands and responding audibly and visually with a resulting find. Some themes include characters that display their activity state through facial expressions.

Ultimately, these agents will understand spoken requests, speak to the user, behave in real time, and respond with uncanny realism. These interfaces often are referred to as *social user interfaces* and are designed to supplement graphical user interfaces. For example, a character will appear to assist when you start a new application. If you hesitate or ask for help, the agent will reappear to provide you with further guidance. In many instances, these characters will be seen as active collaborators, with personalities of their own.

At first sight, building this type of interface appears to be straightforward: construct a character, build a set of behavior rules, and switch the character on. Unfortunately, it is not that simple. It is difficult enough to understand and model human-to-human behavior, let alone human-to-computer behavior. So by endowing a computer interface with some human characteristics, we turn on all our human responses. Most significantly, we expect the interface to behave like a human, rather than a computer. Bearing this in mind, a *useful* social interface, such as a computer-generated humanoid with a face, has yet to be seen. However, many academic and industrial labs are actively developing prototypes.

1.3.5 Social Robots

Robots present a new frontier for experiments to understand what makes us human. Not only is it possible to mimic human responses and behaviors, but new types of robots can serve as human surrogates. Unlike a computer-generated character that is constrained to a two-dimensional display, a physical embodiment of a robot has to move in the real world. This presents engineers with significant additional challenges. Nevertheless, the development of robot agents shares many of the underlying concepts developed for computer-generated three-dimensional characters.

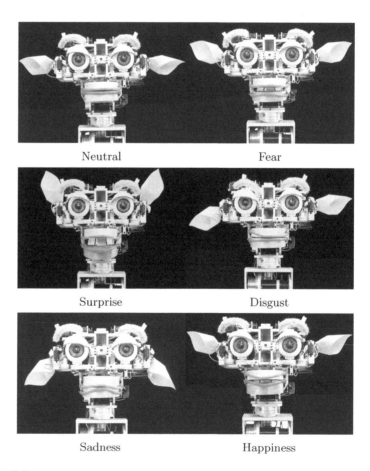

Figure 1.4.
Kismet generating a range of primary facial expressions from [Breazeal 02]. Intermediate expressions are generated by blending the basis facial postures.

Kismet is an early example of a social robot, developed by Cynthia Breazeal at MIT [Breazeal 02]. Kismet is capable of generating a range of facial expressions and emotions, as illustrated in Figure 1.4. While Kismet is an exaggerated non-human character, with large eyes and ears, the design was carefully considered to ensure that it could participate in social interactions matching the robot's level of competence [Breazeal and Foerst 99].

Generating facial expressions for Kismet uses an interpolation technique over a three-dimensional *affect space*. The dimensions of this space correspond to arousal, valence, and stance (a, v, s). An emotional affect space, as defined by psychologists such as Russell [Russell and Fernandez-Dols 79], maps well into Kismet's interpolation scheme, allowing the mixing of individual features of expressions. The specific (a, v, s) values are used to create a net emotive expression P_{net}, as follows:

$$P_{\text{net}} = C_{\text{arousal}} + C_{\text{valence}} + C_{\text{stance}}, \qquad (1.1)$$

where C_{arousal}, C_{valence}, and C_{stance} vary within a specified range using a weighted interpolation scheme. Figure 1.5 illustrates where the expression of disgust can be located with respect to the three-dimensional affect space.

It remains a significant challenge to build an autonomous humanoid robot that can deceive a human into thinking it is real. The design of Kismet as a young, fanciful anthropometric creature with facial expressions that are easily recognizable to humans was carefully considered, ensuring that the expectations for Kismet's behavior were calibrated to its abilities, and therefore, not to fall into a believability trap.

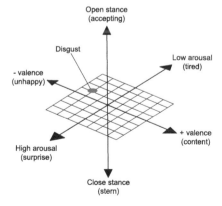

Figure 1.5.
The three-dimensional affect space used by Kismet.

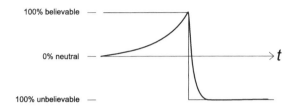

Figure 1.6.
The believability flip. At a certain point in time, when the character is perceived as no longer realistic, a flip occurs, and the character becomes completely unbelievable.

1.4   The Believability Flip and the Uncanny Valley

As the realism of animated characters improve—in terms of their visual and motion fidelity—there comes a point when our perception of a character identifies that something isn't quite right. The character appears *too plastic*, the motion *lacks fluidity*, or the lip-synchronization *looks strange*. At that point, we suspend our belief that the character is real. This is the *believability flip*, as illustrated in Figure 1.6. This turning point has become a critical boundary which many of today's lifelike animated characters are attempting to overcome. This effect is even more pronounced when dealing with virtual surrogates of well known personalities or people we know well. Once the flip occurs, there is no going back. It appears that we re-calibrate with lower expectations and no longer respond to the character in the same way.

It is important to recognize that we have developed a deep and profound understanding of the visual patterns our faces create. This is because we as humans are highly social animals; we benefit from recognizing others in our groups, as well as deciphering emotional states from facial expressions. This has been confirmed by the discovery of cells in our brains that have been identified as exclusively targeting faces. Therefore, overcoming the *believability flip* for virtual surrogates will remain a profound challenge for some time.

The flip—when we realize the character isn't real—varies based on the character; those closest to us are ultimately most familiar and are consequently very hard to synthesize, whereas an unfamiliar person is somewhat easier. In between are personalities that we might observe on television or in the newspapers; they may have some subtle traits that we recognize. Therefore, synthesis complexity is not evenly balanced.

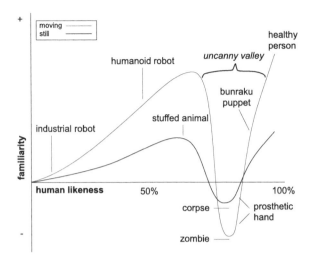

Figure 1.7.
The uncanny valley. (Adapted from [Mori 70].)

In 1970, the Japanese roboticist Masahiro Mori coined the term the *uncanny valley* as a concept of robotics [Mori 70]. It concerns the emotional response of humans to robots, as well as to other non-human entities. The hypothesis states that as a robot is made increasingly human-like in appearance and motion, our human response is increasingly empathetic until a point when there is a reversal and our response becomes strongly repulsive. Figure 1.7 illustrates a familiarity response with respect to human likeness, and the *uncanny valley* is identified by the familiarity reversal.

While the discussion in this section appears to have a scientific basis, it should be recognized that there is little hard evidence either way. The rigorous exploration of human familiarity perception is relatively new, and there is much to learn. It is expected that scientific investigations will be able to shed light on the key components. For example, the formulations of questions on how to measure a synthetic character's performance could lead to some important discoveries about ourselves; this is especially true as computer-generated characters are now capable of exquisite visual fidelity.

1.5   A Turing Test for Faces?

In 1950, Alan Turing, a renowned British mathematician who played a decisive role in the development of the computer during World War II, published a paper on computing machinery and intelligence [Turing 50] to consider the question *"Can machines think?"* He devised an imitation game to test if a machine can converse believably with a human. The test was along the following lines: a human judge engages in a natural language conversation with two other parties, one a human and the other a machine. If the judge cannot reliably tell which is which, then the machine is said to pass the test. Even today, the Turing test remains elusive and begs the question as to if and when a machine will be able to pass the test.[2] Today, computing resources are sufficiently plentiful to expose the problem as one of developing better software algorithms.

While the Turing test is philosophical in nature, there is an emerging need to practically test facial animation systems that attempt to mimic reality. For example, it is intriguing to suggest that an animated visual surrogate might be capable of deceiving us that it is real and thereby could be used as a replacement newscaster presenting the evening news. If so, what would be the criteria for passing such a test, especially in the light of our strong negative human response when we no longer believe the character is real?

1.5.1   A Visual Turing Test

A step toward testing the perception of face synthesis was carried out with Mary101 [Geiger et al. 03] (see Chapter 9 for technical details), where a surrogate was created from video re-synthesis techniques [Ezzat and Poggio 00]. The goal was to test human perception of a talking head to identify a) if people could distinguish between the surrogate and the real video images, and b) the intelligibility of lip-reading.

Figure 1.8 illustrates frames from the tests. At the top are real images while the bottom illustrates frames of the virtual surrogate. The center images show the re-synthesized face components. Their results indicate that a re-synthesized talking head can approximate the video fidelity of a real person. The generation of a virtual newscasters capable of reading the evening news and being perceived as real is within reach. However, many challenges remain before such a surrogate could believably interact with humans.

Speech perception is easier to measure than the realism aspects of a surrogate, in part because there is a direct goal to understanding what was spoken. However, it is a common misconception that *lip reading* is all or nothing—is it possible to lip read or not? In fact, lip reading, more precisely speech reading [Jeffers and Barley 71], varies enormously between people. Individuals who are hard of hearing rely to some degree on visual cues, typically preferring face-to-face conversations to assist a degraded auditory

---

[2]Alan Turing predicted that by the year 2000 computers would have enough memory and processing power to pass the test.

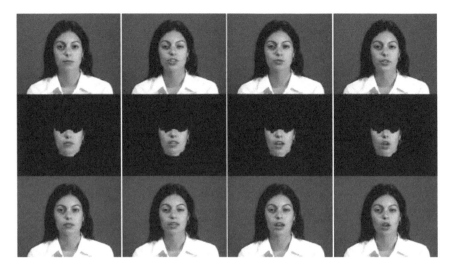

Figure 1.8.
Frames from Mary101 [Geiger et al. 03]. At the top are real image sequences, in the center are re-generated face components, and at the bottom is the final composite.

channel. On the other hand, the profoundly deaf depend exclusively on visual facial cues and therefore demand face-to-face communication, ideally in good lighting and close proximity. The rest of us, with adequate eyesight and hearing, also use facial cues to understand what is being said. This is why we have better comprehension when talking to one another face to face than when talking on the telephone.

As indicated by Mary101, the goal of creating a visually believable surrogate, capable of passing a series of visual perception tests that mimic a real person, can be attained. A visual Turing test for face behavior requires further definition. Perhaps this can be achieved though a set of step-wise face motion tests exercising clearly defined body, head, and face motions and actions.

1.6   Relationship to Conventional Animation

Computer animation is a direct outgrowth of conventional animation, and the Disney Studio has had a significant influence on the animation industry over the years. Most of the hard lessons they learned through trial and error are directly applicable to computer animation, especially character animation. It could be argued that there are few differences between traditional animation techniques and those applied in computer animation, suggesting that computers are merely more powerful tools at the disposal of animators. This being essentially true, we have a great deal to learn from traditional animation.

1.6.1   Disney's Principles of Animation

Frank Thomas and Ollie Johnston outlined twelve principles of animation, which applied to the way Disney Studios produces animation [Thomas and Johnson 81]. These "rules" are widely accepted as the cornerstone of any animation production and can be applied directly to the way computer character animation is produced [Lassiter 87]. What follows are brief descriptions of those principles, which can also be applied to facial animation.

Squash and Stretch

Squash and stretch is perhaps the most important aspect of how a character moves. Objects, such as a bouncing ball, will compress when they hit an immovable object, such as the floor, but they soon come back to their original shape, as illustrated in Figure 1.9. A rule of thumb is that no matter how "squashy" or "stretchy" something becomes, its volume remains relatively the same.

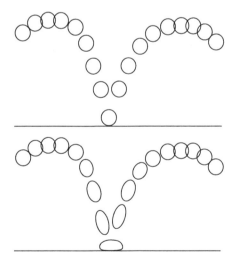

Figure 1.9.
In the motion of a ball bouncing, the ball can appear to have more weight if the drawings are closer together at the top of the arc. In the bottom illustration, a flattened ball on impact and elongation in acceleration and deceleration are the beginnings of squash and stretch.

If a character or object is in motion, it will undergo certain changes within its overall shape. For example, a cat character falling through space stretches in the direction of the fall and squashes, or "splats," when it reaches the ground. The scaling may seem extreme when viewed in a single frame, but in motion it is remarkable how much the squashing and stretching can be exaggerated while still retaining a natural look. This elasticity can be used to imply weight, mass, or other physical qualities. For example, the shape of an iron ball would not be affected by a drop to the ground, whereas a balloon full of water undergoes dramatic shape changes both as it is dropped and when it impacts the ground.

Complex models present complex squash and stretch issues. In a hierarchically defined model, squash and stretch are usually applied differently and at different times to the various model parts to achieve the illusion of mass and weight. Ideally, a flexible model is used, in which the shape of various parts can be appropriately changed by accelerations and impacts.

Anticipation

Anticipation is the act of hinting to the audience what is about to happen. This hint can be a broad physical gesture, or it can be as simple as a subtle change in facial expression. The key idea is not to allow any motion to come unexpectedly, unless that is the desired effect. For example, before a character zooms off, it gathers itself up, draws back in the opposite direction, and then moves rapidly off in the other direction.

These anticipatory moves do not necessarily imply why something is being done, but rather they clarify what is being done. Once a movement has been implied through anticipation, animating a vastly different move can be used to introduce an element of surprise. For example, a car coiling up, ready to shoot forward, but then zooming backward, could be considered a sight gag.

Staging

Staging is the actual location of the camera and characters within the scene. Staging is very important and should be done carefully. Principles of cinema theory come into play in the way that shots are staged. In general, there should be a distinct reason for the way that each shot in the film is staged. The staging should match the information that is required for that particular shot. The staging should be clear, and it should enhance the action. A common mistake in the design of computer-generated films is to make the staging too dynamic, simply because the computer has the capability to do so. As a consequence, the scenes become confusing, or else they distract from the action that is taking place.

One could easily write an entire paper on the meaning and importance of camera angles, lighting, and other film effects. Researching conventional film literature will enhance an animator's understanding of these theoretical film principles and is highly recommended [Katz 91, Arijon 76]. However, the most basic advice for good staging is that the most important information required from a scene should be clear and uncluttered by unusual or poor staging.

Ease-In and Ease-Out

Newton's laws of motion state that no object with mass can start in motion abruptly, without acceleration. Even a bullet shot from a gun has a short period of acceleration. Only under the most unusual of circumstances does the motion of an object have an instantaneous start or stop. *Ease-in* and *ease-out* are the acceleration and deceleration, respectively, of an object in motion. Eases may be applied to any motion or attribute change, including translation, rotation, scaling, or change of color. How an object's motion eases helps define the weight and structure of the object.

An ease is used at the beginning or end of a move to soften the transition from an active state to a static state. Many animation systems offer a choice of eases, a common one being a cosine ease, as illustrated in Figure 1.10 (bottom). The linear motion, as in Figure 1.10 (top), is evenly spaced in time; all motion proceeds in a steady, predictable manner. However, linear motion does not lend itself to interesting animation, and thus it is the least desirable. Nonlinear eases are more widely used; their motion is fluid and more enjoyable. Being able to arbitrarily define eases for every

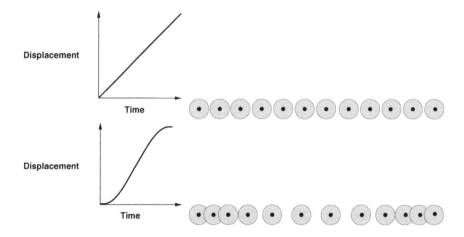

Figure 1.10.
The top profile illustrates a linear time displacement, while the bottom profile shows how the ease-in and ease-out can give the impression of acceleration and deceleration.

action is best. Often, an interactive curve editor is used to graphically edit ease functions using combinations of spline curves, to allow for an infinite number of possible eases. Actually seeing the motion curve dip down to its rest position is sometimes as useful as seeing the animation in preview. The ability to interactively adjust the curves that determine the rate of animation or transition between key poses is crucial.

Follow-Through and Overlapping Action

If all the parts of a character stop or change motion at the same time, the effect is one of extreme rigidity. To impart a sense of fluidity, animators delay the movement of appendages. For example, consider a piece of animation in which a character falls on the ground. Letting the arms lag one or two frames behind the body impact imparts continuity and fluidity to the entire motion. This effect is called *follow-through.*

Overlapping action also is important when moving the camera through an environment or when moving a character through space. Early computer animation was typically comprised of a move, a pause, a rotation, a pause, another move, another pause, and so on. This process quickly becomes tedious. A solution is to start the rotation before the move finishes, overlapping the action, instead of pausing. Follow-through is a common form of overlapping action. Rather than abruptly stopping an action after it has been completed, additional motion eases out along the same path of action. For example, a tennis swing is much more effective if the swing continues after the ball has been hit.

Arcs

Most motion is nonlinear; that is, an object usually follows some curved path. Rather than linearly interpolating from one key frame to the next, passing a curve through the keys gives a more dynamic look to the animation. If animation has been completely interpolated using splines, however, the motion may be too uniform—it will have no punch.

Any "oomph" lost by splining can be regained by editing the motion curves. Again, a function editor that gives an interactive graphic representation is ideal for defining motion curves. Most systems have a number of interpolation functions available to the animator. One issue with cubic interpolating splines is that although they keep slope continuity from key frame to key frame, they also tend to overshoot when confronted with sudden changes in velocity. Since animators usually intend key frames to represent extremes in motion, these overshoots can have undesired results. Feet go through the floor; fingers go through hands. Appropriate interactive control of motion curves is necessary in a production animation environment to allow specification of desired motion without tedious, iterative curve adjustments.

Secondary Motion

Secondary motion is the motion of objects or body parts that depend on primary motion. An example of secondary motion would be the motion of hair or the motion of clothing over the surface of a moving figure. In general, secondary motion is caused by the motion of a primary object. For example, the motions of floppy dog ears would be secondary motions caused by the motion of the dog's head and body.

Exaggeration

Exaggeration involves making the motion more dramatic than one would observe in the real world. If a scene is animated with little or no exaggeration, the motion will be dull and listless. Animators use exaggeration to *sell* the action or the movement of a character.

Exaggeration of motion is not always the way to go, but often exaggeration of motion characteristics is needed to create interesting animation. Exaggeration does not have to impart a cartoon feel to be effective. After the motion has been blocked out, it's up to the animator to decide which movements must be exaggerated to enhance the animation. Live action footage can be used for reference. The live action may be used to rough out the major movements, which are then subtly exaggerated to showcase aspects of the motion.

The exact amount of exaggeration that is required is difficult to judge; however, significant amounts of exaggeration can often be effective. One approach is to push the exaggeration until it is clearly too much and then back off a little.

Appeal

The characters should *appeal* to the audience in some way. This is not to say that the characters need to be cute, but rather that there should be some elements about the characters that make them interesting to watch. The audience should emotionally connect with the characters. They should love the heroine and hate the villain.

2

Face Analysis and Coding

The analysis of faces has a long history, and exactly how the face reflects human emotional states has concerned some noted scientists. One of the first published investigations of facial expression was by John Bulwer in the late 1640s [Bulwer 48, Bulwer 49]. He suggested that one could not only lip read but also infer emotional states from the actions of muscles. Subsequently, in the later part of the nineteenth century, Charles Bell, Duchenne de Boulogne, and Charles Darwin all applied themselves to a more rigorous investigation of facial expression. In the more recent past, Hjortsjö and Paul Ekman applied some further classification to face actions. This chapter reviews some of key aspects of face analysis.

2.1   Charles Darwin's Investigations

Ten years after the publication of Charles Darwin's seminal book *The Origin of Species* [Darwin 72], he published *The Expression of the Emotions in Man and Animals* [Darwin 04]. Although it never received the recognition of his first book, it remains an important departure for modern research in behavioral biology. Darwin was the first to demonstrate the universality of expressions and their continuity in man and animals. Over the next hundred years or so, scientists have classified and refined many of the theories postulated by Darwin at that time.

It is important to understand the significance of Charles Darwin's research within the prevailing scientific climate of the mid-nineteenth century. There was an existing, well-established set of theories, including how human facial expression came to be, which asserted that humans were created though divine intervention. Charles Bell, a leading scientist of the time, suggested that facial muscles are unique in humans to explicitly express emotion to praise and honor their Maker [Bell 33]. Such beliefs were widely supported at that time, with the intention of setting humans apart from other animals. This was not Darwin's thesis, so he produced a calculated rebuke based on his observations of animal behaviors to support his theory that humans and animals were continuous with each other.

Darwin argued, from an observation of dogs, cats, primates, humans and other animals, that facial expressions had clear practical purposes. By illustrating links between expressions and emotions across animals, Darwin was able to weaken the prevailing theological argument and at the same time strengthen his case for expression as a direct consequence of evolution.

Darwin's studies, supported by other naturalists of the nineteenth century, confirmed his conclusion that expression and emotions were important across animal species. While his book on expression of the emotions in humans and animals was intended to support his broader concepts of evolution and natural selection, his probing into *why* expressions were important to humans spawned a great deal more scientific research. One of the most interesting outgrowths was the premise that human facial expressions were universally understood [Fridlund 94].

2.1.1   The Electrophysical Experiments of Duchenne

The most remarkable investigation of facial expression of its time was by Guillaume Duchenne [Duchenne 62]. It is remarkable because he documented his scientific research with the then-new medium of photography in the 1860s. He investigated facial articulation by stimulating facial muscles with moist electrodes that delivered direct "galvanic" current to key motor points on the surface of face. Figure 2.1 illustrates some of the results of his experiments. Isolated muscle contractions were elicited by the careful positioning of the electrodes. Consequently, Duchenne could manipulate and record the activity of facial muscles at will and classify muscles, or small groups of muscles, that could be considered expressive. Armed with this relatively crude tool, Duchenne documented and classified muscles that were expressive, inexpressive, or discordantly expressive. He then published the results in *De la physionomie humaine ou analyse electrophysiologique de l'expression des passions applicable à la practique des arts plastiques* [Duchenne 62].[1]

---

[1]This book was first published in French and has been subsequently translated into English by R. Cuthbertson in 1990 [Duchenne 90].

Figure 2.1.
Photographs from *Mecanisme de la Physionomie Humaine* by Guillaume
Duchenne, 1862. This series of photographs shows Duchenne stimulating
individuals' faces with electrodes.

All researchers in this field, from Darwin to those of the present day,
acknowledge the debt to Duchenne for his remarkable study of facial expression. While there may well be discrepancies between his classification and
more recent research, he essentially defined the field. Table 2.1–Table 2.3
are derived from his classification and his descriptions, which are strongly
correlated to the arts. More recently, Duchenne's approach of transcu-
taneous electrical nerve stimulation has been adopted in performance art
where a performer's face can be controlled via computer programs such as
Text-to-Speech, with some intriguing results [Elsenaar and Scha 02].

Current Name	Name Used by Duchenne
m. frontalis	muscle of attention
superior part of *m. orbicularis oculi*	muscle of reflection
m. corrugator supercilli	muscle of pain
m. procerus	muscle of aggression
m. levator labii superioris alaeque nasi	muscle of crying with hot tears
transverse part of *m. nasalis*	muscle of lust
m. buccinator	muscle of irony
m. depressor anguli oris	muscle of sadness, of disgust
m. mentalis	muscle of disdain or doubt
m. platysma	muscle of fear, fright, and torture, and complimentary to wrath
m. depressor labii inferioris	muscle complementary to irony and aggressive feelings
alar part of *m. nasalis*	muscle complementary to violent feelings
m. maseter	muscle complementary to wrath and fury
palpebral part of *m. orbicularis oculi*	muscle of contempt and complementary to crying
inferior part of *m. orbicularis oculi*	muscle of benevolence and complementary to overt joy
outer fibers of *m. orbicularis oris*	muscle comlementary to doubt and disdain
inner fibers of *m. orbicularis oris*	muscle complementary to aggressive or wicked passions
upward gaze	movement complementary to recollection
upward and lateral gaze	movement complementary to ecstasy and to sensual desire
downward and lateral gaze	movement complementary to defiance or fear
downward gaze	movement complementary to sadness and humility

Table 2.1.
Completely independent expressive muscles. Defined by Duchenne, these muscles are capable of producing expressions by their own isolated action.

Current Name	Name Used by Duchenne
m. zygomaticus major	muscle of joy
m. zygomaticus minor	muscle of moderate crying or weeping
m. levator labii superioris	muscle of crying

Table 2.2.
Incompletely expressive muscles and muscles that are expressive in a
complementary way. Defined by Duchenne, these muscles need the
complemetary activity of other muscles to be expressive.

Primordial Expressions	Muscles That Produce Them
attention	*m. frontalis*
reflection	superior part of *m. orbicularis oculi,* moderately contracted
meditation	same muscle, but strongly contracted
intentness of mind	same muscle, but very strongly contracted
pain	*m. corrugator supercilli*
aggression or menace	*m. procerus*
weeping with hot tears	*m. levator labii superioris alaeque nasi* plus the palpebral part of *m. orbicularis oculi*
moderate weeping	*m. zygomaticus minor* plus the palpebral part of *m. orbicularis oculi*
joy	*m. zygomatic major*
laughter	same muscles plus palpebral part of *m. orbicularis oculi*
false laughter	*m. zygomaticus major* alone
irony, ironic laughter	*m. buccinator* plus *m. depressor labii inferioris*
sadness or despondency	*m. depressor anguli oris* plus flaring of the nostrils and downward gaze
disdain or disgust	*m. depressor anguli oris* plus palpebral part of *m. orbicularis oculi*
doubt	*m. mentalis* plus the outer fibers of *m.orbicularis oris* (either the inferior portion or the two portions at the same time) plus *m. levator labii superioris alaeque nasi*
contempt or scorn	palpebral part of *m. orbicularis oculi* plus *m. depressor labii inferioris* plus *m. transversus* plus *m. levator labii superioris alaeque nasi*
surprise	*m. frontalis* plus muscles lowering the mandible, but to a moderate degree
astonishment	same combinations of muscles and lowering of the mandible, but a stronger contraction
stupefaction	same combinations, maximally contracted
admiration, agreeable surprise	the muscles of astonishment associated with those of joy

Table 2.3.
Synoptic table. Expressions produced by the combined contraction of muscles
that are *incompletely expressive* with those that are *expressive in a
complementary* way.

Primordial Expressions	Muscles That Produce Them
fright	*m. frontalis* plus *m. platysma*
terror	*m. frontalis* plus *m. platysma* and lowering of the mandible, maximally contracted
terror, with pain or torture	*m. corrugator supercilli* plus *m. platysma* and muscles lowering the mandible
anger	superior part of *m. orbicularis oculi* plus *m. masseter* plus *m. buccinator* plus *m. depressor labii inferioris* plus *m. platysma*
carried away by ferocious anger	*m. procerus* plus *m. platysma* and muscles lowering the mandible, maximally contracted
sad reflection	superior part of *m. orbicularis oculi* plus *m. depressor anguli oris*
agreeable reflection	superior part of *m. orbicularis oculi* plus *m. zygomatic major*
ferocious joy	*m. procerus* plus *m. zygomatic major* plus *m. depressor labii inferioris*
lasciviousness	m. transversus plus *m. zygomaticus major*
sensual delirium	gaze directed above and laterally, with spasm of the palpebral part of *m. orbicularis oculi*, the superior portion of which covers part of the iris
ecstasy	same muscles as sensual delirium, but without *m. transverus*
great pain, with fear and affliction	*m. corrugator supercilli* plus *m. zygomaticus minor*
pain with despondency or despair	*m. corrugator supercilli* plus *m. depressor anguli oris*

Table 2.3.
Continued.

2.2 Expression Coding Systems

While Darwin and Duchenne pioneered the study of facial expression, it wasn't until the 1970s that more analytical studies were undertaken. During this period, several systems, or languages, were developed. One of the earliest was the Mimic language, and later in the same decade the most widely used in facial animation, the Facial Action Coding System. Both are described in more detail below in Section 2.2.1 and Section 2.2.2.

2.2.1 Mimic Language

The *Mimic* language developed by Hjortsjö is one of the earliest attempts to investigate and systematize the muscular activities that create the diverse facial expressions [Hjortsjö 70]. Hjortsjö's motivation was to develop a language for describing facial expression. According to Hjortsjö, mimicry includes the play of facial features, gestures, and postures.

In the underlying structure proposed by Hjortsjö, as shown in Figure 2.2, facial expressions are the direct result of both the static structural aspects

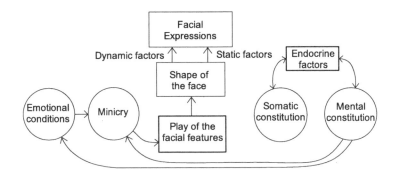

Figure 2.2.
Relationship between facial expression, physical structure, mental condition,
mimicry, and emotional state. (Adapted from [Hjortsjö 70].)

and the dynamic aspects of the face. In turn, the dynamic aspects are
determined by both the mental condition and the emotional state of the
individual. The static aspects also are presumed to be somewhat influenced
by the individual's mental condition, acting through the endocrine system.

The purely static aspects of facial expression are determined by the facial
skeleton and the formation of the soft tissues of the face. The dynamic, living facial expressions are produced by the play of the features—the changes
of form and appearance of the soft facial parts—created by the mimic muscles.

Using one of Hjortsjö's analogies, the soft parts of the face form the
instrument that varies from person to person, while the mimic muscles play
the expression's *melodies*. If the same expressions are played frequently,
they leave visible traces in the form of mimic wrinkles.

The Mimic Muscles of the Face

The mimic muscles are arranged primarily around the facial orifices: the
eye sockets, the nasal cavity, the mouth, and the auditory canals. Some of
these muscles are in the form of circular muscle fibers that contract to close
these openings. Other muscle fibers radiate from the orifice surroundings
toward the openings. Contractions of these fibers open or pull the orifice in
various directions. The mimic muscles never have both the origin and the
attachment to bone; the origin and the attachment are both to soft tissue,
or else the attachment is to soft tissue and the origin is to bone. When the
muscle contracts, the attachment moves toward the origin.

The vast majority of the mimic muscles are associated with the mouth
and eyes. In humans, the muscles associated with the ears have little if

any expressive capability, and the ability to constrict and expand the nasal opening is very limited.

The mimic muscles are innervated by the seventh cranial nerve, the *nervus facialis*. This nerve begins with two small collections of nerve cells located in the brain stem, the *facialis nuclei*. The nuclei are influenced by nerves from the brain cortex and by nerves from the emotional centers of the brain. The cortex nerves correspond to conscious control of facial expression, while the nerves from the emotional centers correspond to unconscious, automatic facial expressions.

A few of the mimic muscles lack direct relation to any orifice. They attach superficially in the skin, often at the location of a skin furrow such as the nasolabial furrow. When contracted, the skin is pulled toward the muscle origin, possibly deepening or displacing a skin furrow. The soft tissue between the origin and attachment of the muscle is also affected. This tissue is pressed together, which may result in displacements, bulges, folds, and furrows. Small depressions or *dimples* can also appear where muscles attach to the skin. Such soft tissue displacements play an important role in expression.

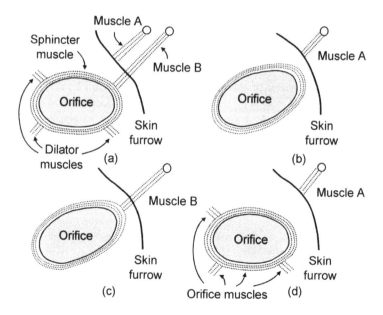

Figure 2.3.
Schematic representation of mimic muscle actions: (a) initial state, (b) effect of furrow muscle, (c) effect of dilator muscle, and (d) effect of furrow muscle and orifice muscles. (Adapted from [Hjortsjö 70].)

The effects of typical mimic muscle actions are illustrated in Figure 2.3. Illustration Figure 2.3(a) shows an orifice and a skin furrow. The orifice is surrounded by a sphincter muscle and a few dilator muscles. The muscle A runs from its origin toward the orifice but does not reach it. It is instead attached to the skin at the furrow. Muscle B runs parallel to muscle A but passes under the furrow and attaches to the orifice. Muscle B is a true orifice dilator. In Figure 2.3, muscle origins are indicated by small circles.

In Figure 2.3(b), only muscle A is acting, which results in the middle part of the skin furrow being pulled toward the muscle origin. This action directly changes the shape of the furrow. The shape of the orifice is indirectly changed by the pull of stretched tissue between the orifice and the furrow. In Figure 2.3(c), only muscle B is acting, pulling the orifice toward the muscle origin. In this case, the middle part of the furrow is indirectly displaced by the compressed soft tissue. In Figure 2.3(d), muscle A is acting and displacing the skin furrow. However, in this case, the orifice is not affected, because the orifice muscles have been activated, holding the orifice in place.

Figure 2.4 shows a schematic view of the mimic muscles. The small circles indicate the muscle origins, and the numbers in the circles correspond

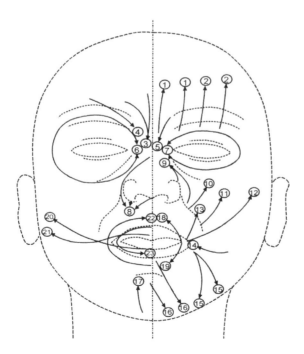

Figure 2.4.
Schematic of the mimic muscles. (Adapted from [Hjortsjö 70].)

to the muscle numbers in the following annotated list. Hjortsjö refers to the actions of these muscles as the *letters* of the Mimic Language. See Chapter 3 for a more detailed discussion of these muscles and their actions.

1. The medial part of the frontalis muscle (*pars medialis frontalis*) raises the inner portion of the eyebrows.

2. The lateral part of the frontalis muscle (*pars lateralis frontalis*) raises the outer portion of the eyebrows.

3. The glabella depressor (*procerus* or *depressor glabelle*) depresses the inner portion of the eyebrows and brings the eyebrows together.

4. The eyebrow wrinkler (*corrugator supercilli*) depresses the middle portion of the eyebrows.

5. The eyebrow depressor (*depressor supercilli*) depresses the inner portion of the eyebrows.

6. The orbital part of the sphincter eye muscle (*pars orbitalis orbicularis oculi*) squeezes the eyes closed. It can depress the eyebrows and raise the upper part of the cheeks. It also creates folds and furrows around the eyes.

7. The eyelid part of the sphincter eye muscle (*pars palpebralis orbcularis oculi*) closes the upper eyelid.

8. The nasal muscle (*nasalis*) reduces the width of the nostrils and deepens the nasal wing furrow.

9. The upper lip and the nasal wing levator (*levator labii superioris alaeque nasi*) pulls up the nasal wings. They raise and deepen the nasolabial furrows and the infraorbital furrow. They may raise the outer part of the upper lip.

10. The upper lip levator (*levator labii superioris*) pulls the outer part of the upper lip up and out. It pulls the upper and middle portions of the nasolabial furrow up and out and pushes the inner cheek up toward the eye.

11. The lesser zygomatic muscle (*zygomatic minor*) pulls the lower part of the nasolabial furrow up and out. It also pulls the corners of the mouth up and out, widening the mouth.

12. The greater zygomatic muscle (*zygomatic major*) pulls the corners of the mouth outward and upward. The lower part of the nasolabial furrow is deepened while being pulled out and up.

13. The levator of the corner of the mouth (*levator anguli oris or caninus*) pulls the corners of the mouth up and raises the nasolabial furrow. It may slightly open the mouth, showing the upper teeth.

14. The smiling mouth (*risorius*) produces a small depression or dimple in the cheeks where it is attached.

15. The depressor of the corner of the mouth (*depressor anguli oris* or *triangularis*) pulls the corner of the mouth down. The depressor deepens the lower portion of the nasolabial furrow and pulls it downward.

16. The lower lip depressor (*depressor labii inferioris*) pulls the lower lip down and somewhat outward, slightly opening the mouth.

17. The chin muscle (*mentalis*) raises the soft parts of the chin, pressing the lower lip upwards. It emphasizes the chin-lip furrow.

18. The incisive muscles of the upper lip (*incisivi labii superioris*) pull the corners of the mouth inward, making the mouth more narrow and rounded. They smooth the lower portion of the nasolabial furrow.

19. The incisive muscles of the lower lip (*incisivi labii inferioris*) pull the corners of the mouth inward, making the mouth more narrow and rounded. They smooth the lower portion of the nasolabial furrow.

20. The lower cheek muscle (*buccinator*) pulls the corners of the mouth outward and slightly up. This muscle deepens the lower part of the nasolabial furrow and pulls it outward and stretches the skin over the chin.

21. The upper cheek muscle (*buccinator*) pulls the corners of the mouth outward and slightly up. This muscle deepens the lower part of the nasolabial furrow and pulls it outward.

Regions	Eyebrow	Glabella Region	Eyelid	Infraorbital Triangle	Nasiolabial Furrow	Nasal Region	Mouth Opening	Chin
Details	Forehead	Root of Nose	Palpebral Fissure	Infraorbital Furrow			Lips	
Muscles								
1,2	*	*	*	o		o		
1	*	*	*					
2	*		*					
3	*	*	o					
4	*	*	*					
5	*	*	o					
6	*	o	*	*	o		o	
7			*					
8						*		
9		o			*	*	o	
10					*	*	*	
11			*		*	*	*	
12			*	*	*	*	*	
13					*		*	
14				*				
15					*		*	
16					*		*	*
17							*	*
18,19					*		*	
20,21				*	*	*	*	*
22					*		*	
23					o	o	*	*

Table 2.4.
Mimic muscle effects.

22. The lip part of the mouth sphincter muscle (*obicularis oris*) constricts the mouth opening. If the red parts of the lips are relaxed, they are pushed out into a funnel shape.

23. The margin part of the mouth sphincter muscle (*obicularis oris*) constricts the mouth opening. It tightens the red parts of the lips, depresses the upper lip, and raises the lower lip. It can also roll the lips in over the teeth.

Table 2.4 presents a summary view of the regions of the face and the facial details affected by the mimic muscles. An * indicates an effect, and an **o** indicates a small effect.

Mimic Co-Movements

The concept of mimicry includes additional expressive movements in the form of gestures and postures that are characteristic manifestations of emotional states. Hjortsjö refers to these movements as the mimic *co-movements*, which include movements of the jaw, the neck, the shoulders, the arms, and the hands. In addition, the eyeballs may be rotated, directing gaze, and pupil dilation may change in response to changes in light or changes in emotional state. None of the co-movement muscles are innervated by the *nervus facialis*.

When the jaw is relaxed, the lower teeth are not pressed against the upper teeth, leaving a small gap called the *freeway space*. The position the relaxed jaws have in relation to each other is called the *rest position*. From this position, the lower jaw can be raised, clenching the teeth. The lower jaw can also be lowered. The lower jaw can also be displaced forward and laterally side to side.

The neck allows the head position to bend and turn relative to the rest of the body. These motions include forward bending, backward bending, lateral tilting, and lateral turning to the right or left. Forward and backward bending can be combined with lateral turning. Lateral tilting may be combined with lateral turning.

Mimic Facial Expressions

The *words* of the Mimic language correspond to facial expressions. These words, or expressions, are formed by combining the *letters* of the language—the actions of the mimic muscles and the mimic co-movements. Hjortsjö describes the facial expressions corresponding to twenty-four emotions. These expressions are arranged in eight groups, as shown in Table 2.5. Figure 2.2 summarizes how these expressions are created using the mimic muscles and a few of the mimic co-movements. An * indicates that the muscle or co-movement contributes to the expression. An **o** indicates that the muscle or co-movement makes a small contribution.

Group	Number	Emotion
	1	precise, resolute, firm, severe
A	2	stern, angry
	3	furious, incensed
	4	mild, smiling, friendly
B	5	happy
	6	hearty laughter
	7	ingratiating smile
C	8	cunning, crafty, slyly smiling
	9	self-satisfied smile
	10	sad, worried, grieved
D	11	mournful, almost in tears
	12	physically hurt, tormented
	13	suspicious
E	14	observing, inquiring, examining
	15	perplexed
	16	surprised
F	17	frightened
	18	panic-stricken, anguished
	19	superior, scornful, ironic
G	20	contemptuous, condescending
	21	arrogant, self-satisfied
	22	disgusted
H	23	nauseated
	24	bitter, woeful, disappointed

Table 2.5.
The mimic expressions.

2.2.2   Facial Action Coding System

The Facial Action Coding System (FACS), developed by Paul Ekman and
Wallace Friesen [Ekman and Friesen 78] in 1978, breaks down facial actions
into small units called *action units* (AUs). Each AU represents an individual
muscle action, or an action of a small group of muscles, a single recognizable
facial posture. In total, FACS classifies 66 AUs that in combination could
generate defined and gradable facial expressions. As a result, FACS has been
used extensively in facial animation over the past decade to help animators
interpret and construct realistic facial expressions. Although not intended
for use in computer animation, this descriptive scheme has been widely used
as the basis for expression control in a number of facial animation systems.

The FACS describes the set of all possible basic AUs performable by
the human face. Example action units are the inner brow raiser, the outer
brow raiser, and the lid tightener. Each action unit is a minimal action
that cannot be divided into smaller actions. According to Ekman, "FACS

Expression	1	2	3	4	5	6	7	8	9	10	11	12	13	14	15	16	17	18	19	20	21	22	23	24
Muscles																								
1				o	*			o	*	*				*	*	*	*	*	*	*	*		*	
2 o	*	*		o	*			o						*	*	*	*			*	*		*	
3 *	*	*									*	*	*									*		
4							*	*								*	*							
5 *	*	*									*	*	*									*		
6			o		*	*	*	o			*										*	*		
7			*		*	*	*	*	o	o	*	*						*	*	*	*	*	*	
8																					*	*		
9				*							*							o	o		*	*	o	
10																		*	*	*		*		
11			*	*	*	*	*	*								o							*	
12				*	*	*	*	*																
13			*	*	*	*	*	*																
14				*	*	*		*																
15	*	*					*	*				o						*	*	*			*	
16 o	*	*			*																	*		
17 o	*	*					*	*			*		*					*	*		*		*	
18,19											*		o	*	*						*			
20,21 o	o	*	o	o	*		o	*		*														
22											*				*		*				*	o		
23 *	*	*				*	o	*			*		*								*			
Positions																								
head forward	o	o	o	o			*	*		*	*			*	*	o	o					*	*	
head back						o			o			*						*	*		o	*		
head tilted				o		*	*	*			*	*	*	*		o					o			o
head turned				o		*	*		*	*	*	*	*			o	o					*		o
teeth clenched	*	*	*						o		*	o								o		*	o	o
jaw dropped				o	*										*	*	*							
looking aside						*	*																	
looking down				o					*	*											*			

Table 2.6.
The mimic muscle basis of the mimic expressions.

allows the description of all facial behavior we have observed, and every facial action we have attempted."

The primary goal of FACS was to develop a comprehensive system that could reliably describe all possible visually distinguishable facial *movements*. The emphasis in the previous sentence is on comprehensive, visual, and movements. FACS deals only with what is clearly visible in the face, ignoring any invisible changes or any changes too subtle for reliable distinction. It only deals with movement and not with any other visible phenomena. FACS is concerned only with the description of facial motions, *not* in inferring what the motions mean.

AU	FACS Name	Muscular Basis
1	inner-brow raiser	*frontalis, pars medialis*
2	outer-brow raiser	*frontalis, pars lateralis*
4	brow raiser	*depressor glabellae,*
		depressor supercilli, corrugator
5	upper-lid raiser	*lavator palpebrae superioris*
6	cheek raiser	*orbicularis oculi, pars orbitalis*
7	lid tightener	*orbicularis oculi, pars palebralis*
8	lips together	*orbicularis oris*
9	nose wrinkler	*levator labii superioris, alaeque nasi*
10	upper-lip raiser	*levator labii superioris,*
		caput infraorbitalis
11	nasolabial-furrow	*zygomatic minor*
	deepener	
12	lip corner puller	*zygomatic major*
13	cheek puffer	*caninus*
14	dimpler	*buccinnator*
15	lip-corner depressor	*triangularis*
16	lower-lip depressor	*depressor labii*
17	chin raiser	*mentalis*
18	lip puckerer	*incisivii labii superioris,*
		incisivii labii inferiouis
20	lip stretcher	*risorius*
22	lip funneler	*orbicularis oris*
23	lip tightener	*orbicularis oris*
24	lip pressor	*orbicularis oris*
25	parting of lips	*depressor labii,* or relaxation of
		mentalis or *orbicularis oris*
26	jaw drop	*masetter;* relaxed *temporal*
		and internal *pterygoid*
27	mouth stretch	*pterygoids; digastric*
28	lip suck	*orbicularis oris*
38	nostril dilator	*nasalis, pars alaris*
39	nostril compressor	*nasalis, pars transversa* and
		depressor septi nasi
41	lid droop	relaxation of *levator*
		palpebrae superioris
42	eyelid slit	*orbicularis oculi*
43	eyes closed	relaxation of *levator palpebrae superioris*
44	squint	*orbicularis oculi, pars palpebralis*
45	blink	relax *levator palpebrae* and then contract
		orbicularis oculi, pars palpebralis
46	wink	*orbicularis oculi*

Table 2.7.
The single facial action units of the Facial Action Coding System.

The use of FACS in facial animation goes beyond what was originally intended. FACS was intended only as a way to *score* or describe facial movements. In a number of facial animation systems, FACS is used as a way to control facial movement by specifying the muscle actions needed to achieve desired expression changes.

FACS was derived by analysis of the anatomical basis for facial movements. Since every facial movement is the result of some muscular action, the FACS system was developed by determining how each muscle of the face acts to change visible appearance. It includes all muscle actions that can be independently controlled.

The first step in developing FACS was to determine those muscles that can be voluntarily *fired* independently, and to determine how each of these muscles changes facial appearance.

The next step was to determine if all the separate muscle actions could be accurately distinguished by appearance alone. There are instances where it is very difficult to differentiate among a set of muscles based on appearance only. In those cases, only one action unit was defined, which might be the result of two or three different muscles. There is not a complete one-to-one correspondence between action units and separate muscles. Also, more than one action unit may be associated with a single muscle, as in the case of the frontalis muscle, which raises the brow. Two different action units, corresponding to the inner brow and the outer brow, are associated with this one muscle. Table 2.7 lists the name, number, and anatomical basis for each action unit.

Table 2.8 lists 11 additional AUs, several of which do not involve any of the facial muscles. FACS also includes descriptors that can be used to measure head and eye position.

FACS is limited to those muscles that can be controlled voluntarily. Any facial muscle not under voluntary control is not included in the FACS approach. The *tarsalis muscle* seems to be the only involuntary muscle of the face, and its effect on appearance is essentially the same as that produced by the *levator palpebrae* muscles.

FACS seems complete for reliably distinguishing actions of the brows, forehead, and eyelids. FACS does not include all of the visible, reliably distinguishable actions of the lower part of the face. The hinged jaw and the flexible lips allow an almost infinite number of actions, which is particularly true for actions associated with speech.

There are a total of 46 action units. Theoretically, it is possible for as many as 20 to combine in a single facial movement. A facial movement also may involve only one action unit. Not all action units can be combined, since some involve opposite actions. Also, some of the actions can conceal the presence of others.

AU	FACS Name
19	tongue out
21	neck tightener
29	jaw thrust
30	jaw sideways
31	jaw clencher
32	lip bite
33	cheek blow
34	cheek puff
35	cheek suck
36	tongue bulge
37	lip wipe

Table 2.8.
Additional facial action units from the Facial Action Coding System.

Example Action Units

AU 10—Upper-lip raiser. The muscles for this action run from roughly the center of the cheeks to the area of the nasolabial furrow. The skin above the upper lip is pulled upward and toward the cheeks, pulling the upper lip up. The center of the lip is drawn straight up. The outer parts of the upper lip also are drawn up, but not as high as the center portion. This action causes an angular bend in the shape of the upper lip. It also raises the cheeks and may cause wrinkling in the infraorbital furrows under the eyes. It deepens the nasolabial furrow and raises the upper part of the furrow, producing a bend in the furrow shape. It widens and raises the nostril wings. If the action is strong, the lips will part.

AU 15—Lip corner depressor. The muscles driving this action unit run from the sides of the chin upward, attaching at points near the corner of the lips. This action pulls the corners of the lips down. It changes the shape of the lips so that they angle down at the corners and are somewhat stretched horizontally. Pouching, bagging, or skin wrinkling may occur below the lip corners. The chin boss may flatten or bulge. This action may produce a medial depression under the lower lip. The nasolabial furrow will deepen and may appear pulled down or lengthened.

AU 17—Chin raiser. The muscle for this action runs from below the lower lip and attaches far down the chin. In this action, the skin of the chin is pushed up, pushing up the lower lip. The skin on the chin may wrench, and a medial depression may form under the lower lip. As the center of the lower lip is pushed up, the shape of the mouth changes to a *frown* shape. If strong, this action may cause the lower lip to protrude.

More recently, FACS has been updated with easy and accessible online media, including improvements on how to score facial expressions [Ekman et al. 02].

2.2.3   Face Coding Standards

The advent of video conferencing systems involves low-bitrate transmission of digital images. The subsequent video encoding techniques logically place an emphasis on people and their faces in the scene. To date, some research has been conducted into both the encoding and decoding of face images, with the intent of creating indistinguishable visual surrogates.

To develop a complete bidirectional system, as illustrated in Figure 1.2, it is necessary to agree first upon the face features to track, second upon the parameters to which those features map, and third upon the geometry of the face model that can be rendered. These are discussed briefly as follows:

Features to track. There are numerous features of the face used in non-verbal communication. At the coarsest level head pose can be determined by rigid six-degrees-of-freedom motion of the skull. The range of motion of the jaw is the second largest motion of the face, followed by the eyes and forehead. The smallest features, and possibly the most salient in non-verbal communication, are the eyes and the tissues surrounding the eyes. Subtle motions of the *obicularis oris* and gaze behavior relay a broad range of expression and emotional intent. Clearly eye contact, gaze direction, eye convergence (focus of attention), eyelid curvature and compression (squinting) coupled to eyebrow behavior have to be captured in detail and then encoded if video teleconferencing surrogates are to faithfully capture an individual.

Feature parameters. The features of the face, such as the lips and eyebrows, display a highly nonlinear motion, because they are controlled by muscles and interact with hard and soft tissue of the skull and skin. As a result, simple linear displacement in three dimensions is unlikely to capture the subtle feature motions, especially for intermediate feature points between those that are encoded. For example, five points on the inner lip margin can only crudely approximate the lips during the production of speech.

Feature mapping. Providing a geometric model onto which tracked features can map requires careful alignment of parameters to a canonical representation of the face. For example, a majority of faces are geometric and dynamically asymmetric. Much of what we recognize to be an individual is described in the way that person's face moves. As a result accurately

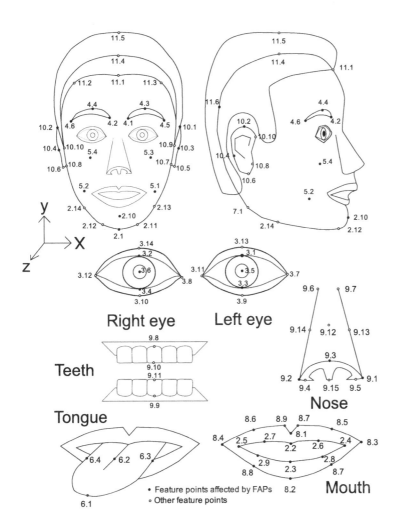

Figure 2.5.
An adaptation of the MPEG-4 FAPs with slight modifications reflecting a more canonical view of the face [MPEG 97]. Some duplicate feature points have been removed for clarity.

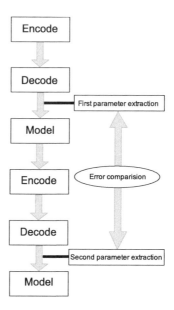

Figure 2.6.
A simple first-pass face coding verification scheme. Re-encoding the first decoding should result in the same parameters being extracted. Such a verification should reveal weaknesses in coding systems.

mapping an individual's features onto a known geometric representation requires a surprisingly large number of feature points.

Figure 2.5 is derived from the Motion Picture Experts Group (MPEG) first publication of the Face and Body Animation (FBA) standard [MPEG 97] with associated Face Animation Parameters (FAPS). Coupled to the explicit face features are 68 parameters that define the range of a canonical face.

To create an MPEG-4 compliant face model, it is necessary to have at least one vertex associated with each standardized feature point of the model, thereby ensuring a very low-bandwidth face coding. This has been the subject of investigation for several years in facial animation (see Chapter 4).

Minimizing the number of features for low-bandwidth transmission is the goal for a video MPEG standard. However, there is a danger that many features of the face and their associated motions may be omitted, either in the encoding or decoding processes. The end result can be a visual surrogate that fails the litmus test of visual fidelity, as described in Section 1.5.1.

The development of tests that verify the results of a coding scheme is within the scope of the MPEG-4 standard. For example, one simple test would be to re-encode the product of the decoder and observe the measured errors. Extracting the same parameters from a secondary encoding would provide a confidence level to the accuracy of the systems, as illustrated in Figure 2.6. Ultimately, verifying the conformance and compliance of any coding systems is key to the development of the most successful standards.

3

Anatomy of the Face, Head, and Neck

The human body has been studied in great detail by artists over the centuries. In particular, the Renaissance artists began the rigorous tradition of figure drawing so they could produce realistic and detailed interpretations of the human form. For example, Leonardo da Vinci would often attend and perform cadaver dissections to understand human form and function [Clayton 92]. His detailed comprehension of anatomy can clearly be seen in his remarkable drawings of the human body. The value of detailed anatomical understanding is reflected throughout fifteenth-century art, and today it remains a foundation of art instruction [Halton 65, Hogarth 81].

One of the objectives in creating three-dimensional computer-generated faces is to design faces that not only appear realistic in static imagery, but also move in animated sequences. Consequently, we can learn a great deal from anatomy in the same way that the artists did who studied the human form to produce realistic interpretations and renditions of the face.

While the artist's perspective is important in computer facial synthesis, twentieth-century medical anatomical reference books provide the most significant insight into human anatomy. The most widely used medical reference manual is *Gray's Anatomy*, which provides precise and detailed anatomical descriptions [Williams et al. 89]. Another particularly insightful reference manual is the *Sobotta Atlas of Anatomy* [Ferner and Staubesand 83]. This manual is graphically illustrated in color, with drawings and photographs. Dissection manuals, such as Cunningham's *Manual of Practical Anatomy, Vol. 3: Head, Neck, and Brain*, offer a different perspective by describing how the face can be taken apart piece by piece [Romanes 67]. Additional medical references include Fried's *Anatomy of the Head, Neck, Face, and Jaws* [Fried 76] and Warfel's *The Head, Neck and Trunk* [Warfel 73]. This chapter makes extensive reference to these anatomy texts and in some parts the descriptions are taken directly from these books. Additional text for this chapter has also been procured from additional sources of other authors. Their contributions are duly acknowledged.

One of the most frustrating aspects of medical reference manuals is the overwhelming quantity of information that is difficult to follow and digest. This chapter attempts to simplify the terminology and describes the anatomical features of the face that are useful for computer modeling. Essentially, the description breaks down into two parts: the facial skeleton and the facial muscles.

In Section 3.2, the individual bones of the skull that make up the skeletal framework of the face are described. This section is followed by Section 3.3, which describes the muscles of facial expression, with their attachments and primary actions. Section 3.3.2 describes the muscles of mastication, followed by a description of the tempromandibular joint. The muscles of the tongue are described in Section 3.5, followed by a brief description of the muscles of the scalp, ear, and neck. The skin and its mechanical properties are described in Section 3.7. Finally, a description of the eyes and eyeballs is given. The reader is encouraged to refer to anatomical references for more complete and comprehensive descriptions.

3.1   Nomenclature

Human anatomy has its own distinctive terminology, based on the assumption that the person is standing erect, arms at the sides, the face and palms directed forward.[1] This posture is known as the *anatomic position*, as illustrated in Figure 3.1. The location of body parts are described in relation to this pose and three imaginary planes:

- *Median plane.* This vertical plane cuts through the center of the body, dividing the body into equal right and left halves. A structure located closer to the medial plane than another is said to be *medial* to the other. A structure lying farther away from the medial plane than another is said to be *lateral* to the other.

---

[1]While this section is rather dry, the reader is encouraged to spend the time to read, digest, and remember these fundamental terms, as all medical references use this type of nomenclature.

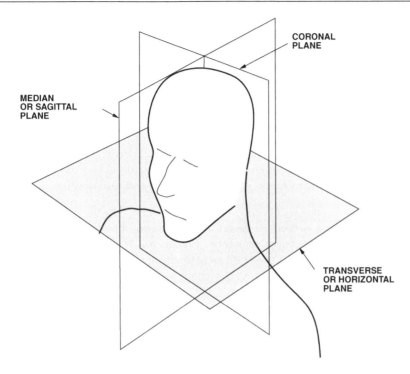

Figure 3.1.
Terminology commonly used in descriptive anatomy.

- *Coronal plane.* This vertical plane divides the body into front and back halves. The coronal plane is at a right angle to the medial plane. The term *anterior* refers to the front of the body; *posterior* refers to the back of the body. A feature is described as anterior (or posterior) to another feature when it is closer to the anterior (or posterior) surface of the body.

- *Transverse horizontal planes.* These planes are at right angles to both the median and coronal planes.

Anatomists need a precise and umabiguious vocabulary to describe parts of the human form because of the volume and sophistication of the consistuent parts. However, for computer animators, graphic artists, and lay readers, these descriptions can be bewildering and frustrating. The following are anatomical terms used in this chapter to detail and describe specific features. The reader may be unfamiliar with these terms; therefore, somewhat simplified descriptions are provided.

- *Superior* and *inferior* refer to relative positions with respect to the upper and lower ends of the body. For example, the lips are superior to the chin but inferior to the eyes. *Superficial* and *deep* refer to the relative distance of structures from the outermost surface of the body. The brain is deep relative to the skull. The lips are superficial to the teeth. *Proximal* and *distal* describe the relative distances from the roots of the limbs or other organs. For example, the ankle is distal to the knee but is proximal to the toes. The tip of the tongue is distal to the root of the tongue. *Ipsilateral* refers to the same side of the body, while *contralateral* refers to the opposite side of the body. The left eye is contralateral with the right eye and ipsilateral with the left ear.

- *Articulating* is used to describe how bones join one another to form composite structures or joints. Sometimes it sounds strange to describe the bones of the skull as articulating with one another, as they are relatively rigid; however, without joints the large bones of the skull would deform as they grow.

- A *complex* is a composite of two or more interwoven parts and can be referred to as complexes, rather than as a collection of the individual constituent parts. This might involve bone, ligaments, cartilage, and skin tissues.

- *Decussate* is used to describe how muscle divide into two or more parts. Typically, the point of division is marked by a crossing that appears in the form of an "X."

- A *foramen* is an opening in the bone. These holes allow other structures, such as blood vessels and nerves, to pass. The Latin word *magnum* is used to describe a large opening.

- A *fossa* is a cavity, hollow, or depression into which other bones fit. These may be deep or shallow concavities, depending on size of the two components.

- A *process* is an outgrowth of bony tissue onto which ligaments, tendons, and other tissues attach. Multiple outgrowths are called *processes*.

3.2   The Skull

The skull is of particular interest for facial synthesis because it provides the framework onto which the muscles and skin are placed. Figure 3.2 illustrates four general views of the skull. In addition, the skull provides

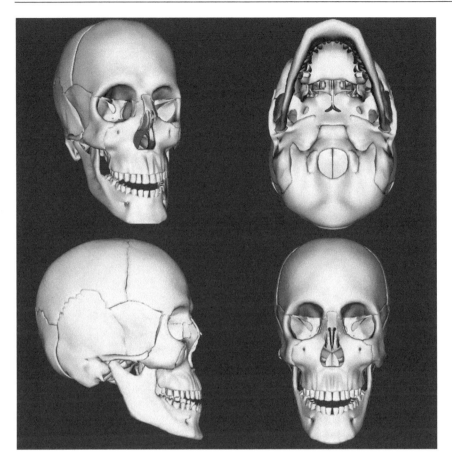

Figure 3.2.
Four views of the skull.

the overall shape of the face as a foundation for artists, as well as forensic anthropologists when reconstructing individuals. From a practical point of view, the skull is a hard protective case for the brain. See Figure 3.3 and Figure 3.4 for frontal and lateral views, respectively.

There are two major components of the skull: the cranium, in which the brain is lodged, and the skeleton of the face. These two regions are illustrated in Figure 3.5(a). The only freely jointed structure of the skull is the mandible, while the other bones are connected with rigid interfaces known as sutures, which allow very little movement between the bones.

The facial skeleton has three major parts: the upper third consists of the nasal bones and the orbits for the eyes, the center third of the maxil-

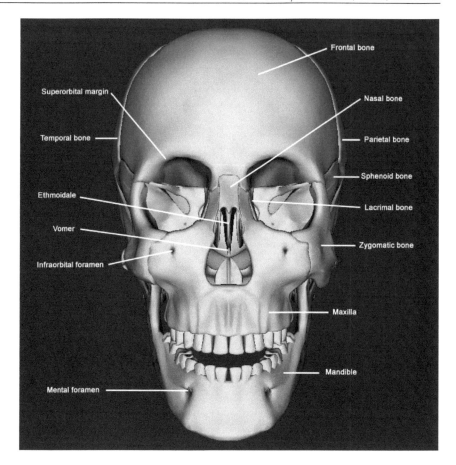

Figure 3.3.
The frontal view of the skull.

lae, the nasal cavities, and nose, while the lower third of the mandible or jaw region. The proportion of each region illustrated in Figure 3.5 varies from male to female as well as from young to old. The variability of human face proportions is important when modeling the face as described in Chapter 4.

3.2.1   Bones of the Calvaria

Frontal bone. The *frontal bone* is a single large, thick structure forming the forehead, illustrated in Figure 3.6, articulating with twelve other bones of the skull. This bone forms the *supercilary arch* and the upper portion of the eye orbits. By the end of puberty, the skull reaches full size and

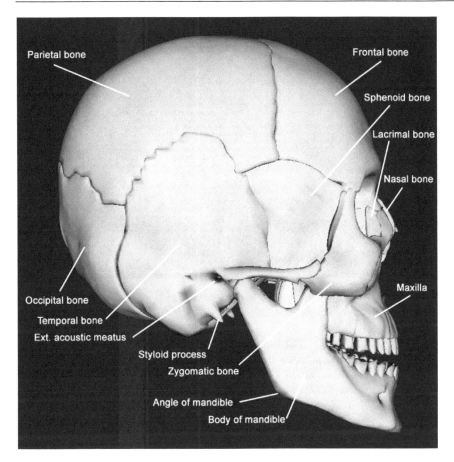

Figure 3.4.
The lateral view of the skull.

the *frontal bone* no longer dominates the facial skeleton proportion, as in infancy. The superciliary arch, also known as the *brow ridge*, is typically more pronounced for males than females, and in early humans such as *homo erectus*, was even more distinct.

Occipital bone. The *occipital bone*, illustrated in Figure 3.7, is a single cup shape forming the posterior of the skull and part of the the cranial base, with a large opening called the *foramen magnum*, through which the spinal cord enters the skull. On either side, flanking the foramen, are the *lateral parts* of the occipital bone. Due to the attachment of muscle, tendon and ligament to the underside of the bone, a large number of rough, uneven markings are evident.

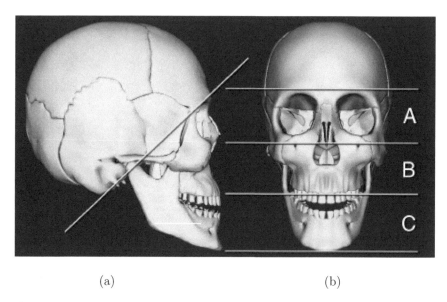

(a)   (b)

Figure 3.5.
The approximate divisions of the skull. (a) Between the skeleton of the face and
the cranium. (b) The anterior (frontal) view illustrates (A) the upper third
consisting of the orbits of the eyes and the nasal bones, (B) the maxillae, and
(C) the jaw region.

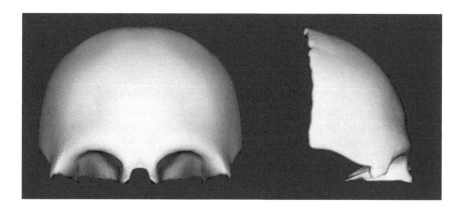

Figure 3.6.
The anterior and lateral views of the frontal bone.

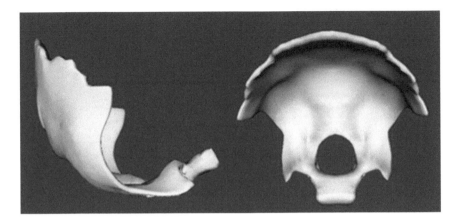

Figure 3.7.
The anterior and transverse views of the occipital bone.

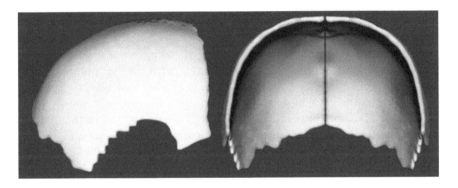

Figure 3.8.
The anterior and lateral views of the parietal bones.

Parietal bones. The *parietal bones*, illustrated in Figure 3.8, are a pair of roughly quadrilateral-shaped bones forming the sides and roof of the cranium. The external surfaces are convex and smooth. Inferiorly, they join the right and left of the great wings of the *sphenoid bone*, as well as the temporal bone. Anteriorly they join the frontal bone. Two curved lines, the *superior* and *inferior temporal lines*, indicate where the outer margin of the powerful temporal muscle attaches.

3.2.2   Bones of the Cranial Base

The *temporal* and *sphenoid bones* form part of the *cranial base*, as illustrated in Figure 3.9 and are located at the sides and base of the skull.

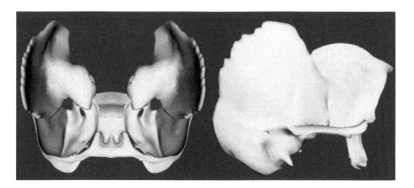

Figure 3.9.
The lateral and internal views of the temporal and sphenoid bones.

Temporal bone. The *temporal bone* consist of five parts: the *squama, petrous, mastoid, tympanic parts*, and *styloid*. For the purposes of skull modeling, it is not necessary to consider each component separately; however, the *squama temporalis*, articulating with the *parietal* bone, has a large, flat portion forming part of the lateral wall of the skull, as well as a fingerlike projection, the *zygomatic process*, articulating with the zygoma to form the *zygomatic arch*. A large opening at the posterior root of the *zygomatic process* forms the opening to the *auditory meatus*, commonly known as the inner ear. The bony projection, the *styloid process*, anterior to the *auditory meatus*, serves as an attachment point for muscle and ligaments. Finally, posterior to the *auditory meatus* is a prominence, the *mastoid*, serving as attachment for the muscles of the neck described in Section 3.6.3.

Sphenoid bone. The *sphenoid bone*, illustrated in Figure 3.9, forms the base of the skull articulating with the facial skeleton, as well as the *temporal* and *frontal* bones. The sphenoid bone is "wedged" between the *frontal* and *temporal* and *occiptial* bones. The central body is paired with greater and lesser wings spreading laterally, giving the impression of the shape of a butterfly. While an important structure of the skull, its external surface exposure to the skull is relatively small and is of little significance for face modeling.

3.2.3   Bones of the Facial Skeleton

The bones of the facial skeleton, as illustrated in Figure 3.2, comprise 14 bones at the front of the skull. Each bone is paired, except for the *mandible* and *vomer*, providing symmetry to the face.[2]

---

[2]To help the reader, the significant bones useful for facial modeling are illustrated. We have also ordered them from most to least proximal, since the deeper bone structures have less influence on the overall face shape.

Ethmoid bone. The *ethmoid bone*, illustrated in Figure 3.10, separates the nasal cavity from the brain. It is located in the center of the face to form part of the nose. The bone consists of four parts: the *cribriform plate*, the *perpendicular plate*, and two lateral masses or *labyrinths*.

Palatine bone. The *palatine bone*, illustrated in Figure 3.10, is located at the back of the nasal cavity and forms part of the floor and walls of the nasal cavity, as well as the roof of the mouth.

Maxillae. Except for the *mandible*, the *maxillae*, illustrated with the *mandible* in Figure 3.11, is the largest of the facial bones located in the lower part (see Figure 3.2 of the facial skeleton, into which the upper teeth are located).

The *maxillae* articulates with the *zygomatic* bones and forms part of the mouth roof and the floor and lateral walls of the mouth, as well as the floor of the eye orbits. The shape of the *maxillae* influences the overall proportion of the face because of its location within the face skeleton and its articulation with nine other bones. The bone consists of the *maxilla body* and four processes: the *zygomatic process, frontal process, alveolar process,* and *palatine process.*

The *maxilla body* provides attachments for a variety of facial muscles, illustrated in Figure 3.11, and anteriorly for the roots of the upper teeth. The *zygomatic process* of the *maxilla* articulates with the *zygomatic bone.* The *frontal process* of the *maxilla* projects backward and upward by the side of the nose. Its smooth lateral surface provides attachments for facial muscles (see Figure 3.15 for details).

The *alveolar process* of the *maxilla* provides the foundation for the teeth on the bone. As a result, it is the thickest part of the *maxilla.*

The *palatine process* of the *maxilla* forms the majority of the roof of the mouth; its inferior surface is concave.

Inferior nasal concha. This bone is a small, long, oval-shaped bone located in the nasal cavity and assists in the flow of air into the nasal passages.

Zygomatic bones. In the facial skeleton, these paired bones are more commonly referred to as the *cheek bones*. They articulate with the *maxilla*, the *temporal*, the *sphenoid*, and the *frontal* bones to form the lateral wall and floor of the eye orbits.

Nasal bones. These are two small bones located side by side in the upper part of the facial skeleton, forming the bridge of the nose, as illustrated in Figure 3.12. Their outer surfaces are convex, while their interior surfaces are concave. Their shape and size have a prominent influence on the overall shape of the nose.

Lacrimal bones. These are two delicate bones, as illustrated in Figure 3.12, and are located at the front part of the medial wall of the eye orbit.

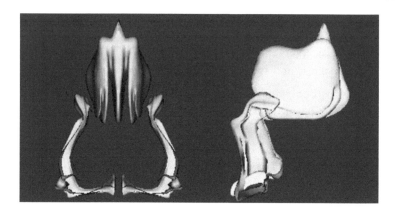

Figure 3.10.
The frontal and lateral views of the ethmoid and palatine bones.

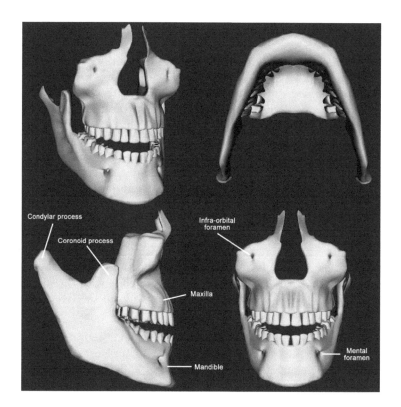

Figure 3.11.
The mandible, maxilla, and teeth.

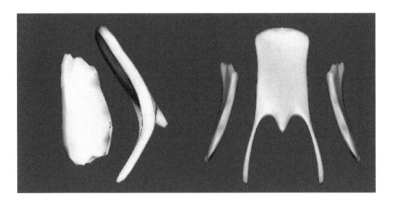

Figure 3.12.
A lateral and frontal views of the nasal and lacrimal paired bones. While small, they provide shape to the bridge of the nose.

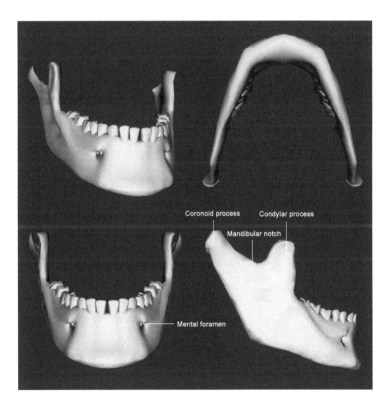

Figure 3.13.
The mandible and teeth.

Mandible. This is a large, strong, heavy bone of the facial skeleton, as illustrated in Figure 3.13. Commonly known as the lower jaw, it is comprised of two prominent *mandibular rami* and the body. The lower teeth are attached in the *avalveolar process.* Two terminal processes are evident on each ramus: the *condyle* and the *coronoid process* to which the large temporal muscle is attached. Two openings called the *mental foramens* provide passage for a nerve called the *mental nerve* that inserts into the lower lip and the skin of the chin. The jaw is a freely jointed bone that has a complex set of motions; for more details, see Section 3.4, describing the temporomandibular joint.

Teeth. There are 16 teeth embedded with long roots into the maxilla and mandible. See Figure 3.14. Children, with smaller jaws, have fewer teeth than adults. These teeth are deciduous, as they are lost over time, to be replaced with permanent teeth. Teeth are used to chew, tear, and scrape food. The molars at the rear of the mouth grind food, while the pincer-like canines grip and the incisors cut food.

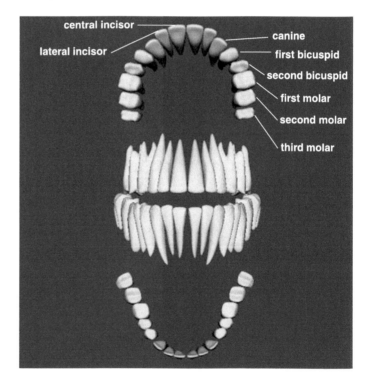

Figure 3.14.
A transverse and frontal view of the upper and lower teeth of an adult. There are 32 teeth in all, 16 in the upper and lower set.

The teeth are the only visible bony surface of the head. Care should be taken when modeling them, especially when considering speech, because they are responsible for shaping the mouth cavity with the tongue and lips to make sounds. For more details, see Chapter 9.

Hyoid bone. This bone contributes to the skeleton of the head and neck and acts as an important functional structure. The hyoid bone is suspended in the neck and lies superior and anterior to the thyroid cartilage (Adam's apple). It serves as the attachment for many muscles that lie in the anterior portion of the neck and as a point of fixation for the accessory muscles of mastication.

Vomer. The vomer is thin and flat, forming the posteroinferior portion of the nasal septum. It is situated in the midsagittal plane of the nasal fossa. It articulates inferiorly with the palatine and maxillary bones. The posterior portion of the anterior superior border meets the perpendicular plate of the ethmoid bone. The anterior portion connects with the cartilaginous septum of the nose.

3.2.4   The Cervical Vertebral Column

The skeletal portion of the neck is known as the *cervical vertebral column*. There are seven cervical vertebrae. The first cervical vertebra is the *atlas*, which serves as the connection of the vertebral column with the skull. The occipital bone of the skull articulates with the atlas. The body of the second cervical vertebra, the *axis*, is fused with that of the atlas. The five remaining cervical vertebrae are joined by movable joints. The neck is flexible at any one of these cervical joints. Fibrocartilaginous pads, the *intervertebral disks*, are spaced between adjacent surfaces of the vertebrae. These pads act as cushions between the articular surfaces.

3.3   Muscles of the Face, Head, and Neck

Most human muscle is associated with some form of motion, because it is usually suspended between two bones or organs. However, some facial muscles, particularly those associated with facial expressions, are attached to bone at one end and at the other to skin. The movable part is known as the *insertion*, while the static end is known as the *origin*.

Muscle activity is stimulated through one or more nerves that cause muscle fibers to contract. These stimulating impulses can also be provided from an external electrical source; for example, in 1862, Duchenne de Boulogne applied electrical probes to the human face to solicit facial expressions by the activation of particular muscles or groups of muscles [Duchenne 62]. He documented his research with 73 photographs of facial expressions, a rare and seminal example of photographs being used for physiological investigation; for more details, see Chapter 2.

3.3.1   The Muscles of Facial Expression

The muscles of the face are commonly known as the muscles of facial expression. Some facial muscles also perform other important functions, such as moving the cheeks and lips during chewing, swallowing, and speech, or constriction (closing) and dilation (opening) of the eyelids. The muscles of facial expression are superficial, and all attach to a layer of subcutaneous fat and skin at their insertion. Some of the muscles attach to skin at both the origin and the insertion, such as the obicularis oris. When the muscles are

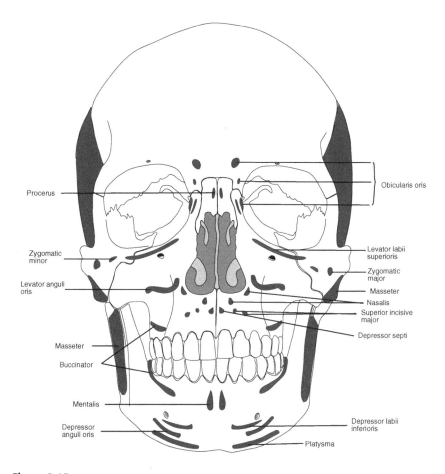

Figure 3.15.
The frontal view of facial muscle attachments.

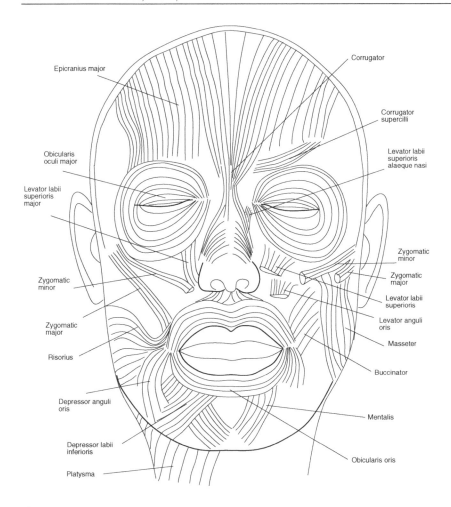

Figure 3.16.
The frontal view of facial muscles.

relaxed, the fatty tissues fill the hollows and smooth the angular transitions so as to allow the general shape of the skull to be seen. The illustrations in Figures 3.16 and 3.18 illustrate the superficial muscles of the face, while Figure 3.19 shows some of the deeper muscles. Finally, Figures 3.15 and 3.17 illustrate the location of facial muscle attachments.

The muscles of facial expression work synergistically and not independently. The muscle group functions as a well organized and coordinated team, each member having specified functions, one of which is primary. These muscles interweave with one another. It is difficult to separate the

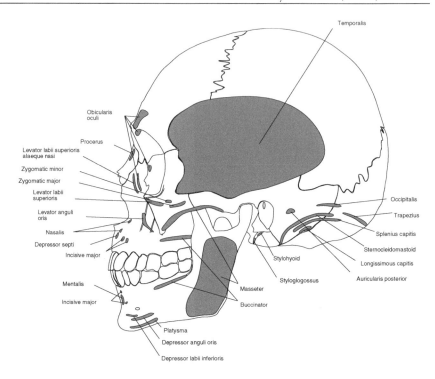

Figure 3.17.
The lateral view of facial muscle attachments.

boundaries between the various muscles. The terminal ends of these muscles are interlaced with each other.

In more general terms, the muscles of facial expression can be grouped according to the orientation of the individual muscle fibers and can be divided into the upper and lower face. Three types of muscle can be discerned as the primary motion muscles: *linear/parallel* muscles, which pull in an angular direction, such as the zygomatic major and the corrugator supercilii; *elliptical/circular* sphincter-type muscles, which squeeze, such as the obicularis oris; and *sheet* muscles, which behave as a series of linear muscles spread over an area, such as the frontalis. The following is a list of the facial muscles with description first, followed by each muscle's primary actions.

Circumorbital Muscles of the Eye

Orbicularis oculi. This muscle circumscribes the entire eye in a concentric fibrous sheet that acts to close the eye. This sphincter muscle arises from the nasal part of the frontal bone and the fibers spread outward to form a broad layer surrounding the eye orbit.

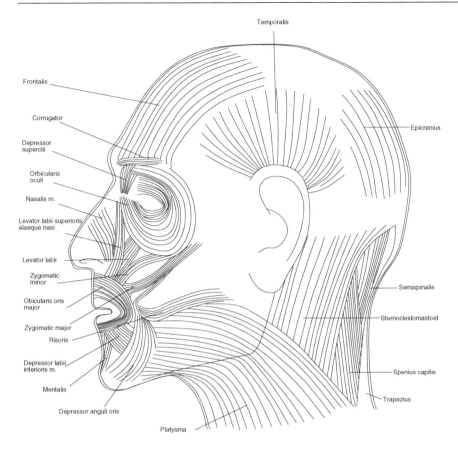

Figure 3.18.
The lateral view of superficial facial muscles.

Action. This muscle plays an important role in the protection of the eye. It firmly closes the eyelids to avoid dust and bright sunlight and to prevent contact of objects against the eye itself. The orbital part can act independently, drawing the skin of the forehead and cheek to the medial angle of the orbit. This activity causes wrinkles radiating from the outer margins of the eye. The palpebral part of the muscle exerts a much finer control over the individual eyelids. This fine control of the eyelids plays an important role in nonverbal communication. The lacrimal part dilates the lacrimal sac.

Corrugator supercilii. This small paired pyramidal muscle is located at the medial end of each brow. Attached to bone at the medial end of the superciliary arch, it ascends laterally, interlacing and blending with the orbicularis oculi.

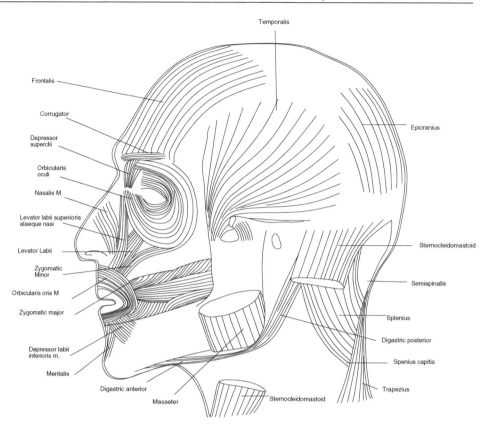

Figure 3.19.
The lateral view of deep facial muscles.

Action. This muscle exerts traction on the skin above the midpart of the supraorbital margin. It draws the brows medially and down, producing (with the orbicularis oculi) vertical wrinkles on the forehead.

Levator palpebrae superioris. This is a thin, flat triangular muscle that arises within the small wing of the sphenoid and in front of the optic foramen. As the muscle advances, it spreads to make up the broad end of the upper eyelid.
Action. When this muscle contracts, it elevates and retracts the upper lid.

Muscles of the Nose

The *procerus, nasalis, depressor septi,* and *levator labii superioris alaeque nasi* are quite rudimentary; however, they act to dilate and constrict the nasal openings.

Procerus. This muscle inserts into the skin between the eyebrows, and its fibers decussate with the frontalis muscle of the brow.
Action. This muscle depresses the medial end of the eyebrow, producing transverse wrinkles over the nasal bridge and root. The action of this muscle aids in reducing the glare of bright sunlight.

Nasalis. The nasalis is a sphincter-like muscle located on either side of the nose. The muscle is divided into two parts: the compressor nasalis and the dilator nasalis. The compressor arises from the frontal part of the maxilla, and slightly superior to the compressor is the origin of the dilator.
Action. This compressor muscle constricts the nostril, while the dilator part flares the nostril. In contraction, the muscle pulls the nostril wings toward the septum and the dilator away from the septum.

Depressor septi. This muscle is attached to the maxilla above the central incisor and ascends to the mobile part of the nasal septum.
Action. This muscle assists the alar part of the nasalis in widening the nasal aperture.

Levator labii superioris alaeque nasi. This muscle is attached to the upper part of the frontal process of the maxilla; it then descends inferolaterally, dividing into a medial slip attached to the greater alar cartilage and the skin over it and a lateral slip prolonged inferolaterally across the vental aspect of the levator labii superioris, and attaches successively to the dermal floor of the upper part of the nasolabial furrow and ridge.
Action. This muscle raises and inverts the upper lip and deepens the nasolabial furrow's superior part; the medial slip dilates the nostril.

Muscles of the Mouth

The numerous muscles of the mouth are important muscles of facial expression, as illustrated in Figure 3.20. The principal muscles are the orbicularis oris, the buccinator, the levator labii superioris alacque nasi, the levator labii superioris, the zygomaticus major and minor, the levator anguli oris, the anguli oris, the depressor labii inferioris, the risorius, and the mentalis. One group opens the lips, and one group closes the lips. The muscles closing the lips are the orbicularis oris and the incisive muscles. The muscles opening the lips are known as the radial muscles, which are divided into the radial muscles of the upper and lower lips, superficial and deep.

Orbicularis oris. This muscle consists of numerous strata of muscular fibers surrounding the orifice of the mouth. It consists in part of fibers derived from the other facial muscles that converge on the mouth. It is the buccinator that forms the deep layer of the orbicularis oris. Some of the fibers decussate at the corners of the mouth, passing over the top of the lip and the underside of the lip. In addition, the levator anguli oris crosses at the

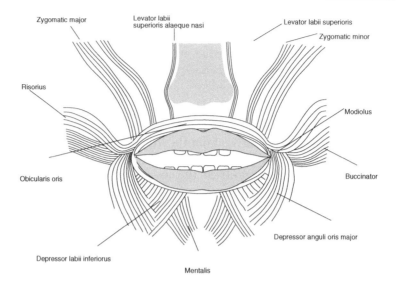

Figure 3.20.
A frontal view of the mouth area, illustrating the principal muscle configuration. The obicularis oris has no skeletal attachment; instead, a variety of muscle fibers interlace with one another, permitting a complex range of lip motion.

corner of the lips and runs around the bottom lip. Likewise, the depressor anguli oris crosses the corner of the mouth and runs around the top lip. Regarding the other muscles, the levator labii superioris, the zygomaticus major, and the depressor labii inferioris intermingle with the muscle fibers just described.

Action. The action of the orbicularis oris produces almost endless control of the lips. The variety of lip shapes are used in speech and nonverbal communication. It is also important in chewing, where it can hold food against the teeth. It also can narrow the lips and force them against the teeth, purse the lips, or protrude the lips.

Buccinator. The buccinator muscle is thin, wide, and flat, forming the major portion of the substance of the cheeks. Its arises both from the maxilla and the mandible opposite the first molar, and from the pterygomandibular raphe. The fibers run forward to blend with those of the orbicularis oris. The medial fibers decussate at the posterolateral to the angle of the mouth, so that the lower fibers run to the upper lip and the upper ones run to the lower lip. The interlacing of the deep buccinator muscles and some of the superficial muscles of the orbicularis oris forms the *modiolus.*

Action. The buccinators compress the cheeks against the teeth, thereby preventing the accumulation of food in the cheek. This muscle works synergistically with the tongue in the process of mastication.

Levator labii superioris alaeque nasi. This muscle originates from the frontal process of the maxilla and passes vertically downward to insert into the skin of the wing of the nose, as well as the orbicularis oris, near the philtrum.
Action. This muscle raises the upper lip, deepening the nasolabial furrows and slightly dilating the nostrils.

Levator labii superioris. This muscle has a wide attachment to the bone of the orbit, zygomatic, and maxilla. It is embedded at the other end into the top lip between the levator anguli oris and the levator labii superioris alaeque nasi.
Action. This muscle raises the upper lip, deepening the nasolabial furrows, like the levator labii superioris alaeque nasi.

Zygomaticus major. This muscle arises from the malar surface of the zygomatic bone and is inserted into the corner of the mouth. The zygomatic major arises on the front surface of the zygomatic bone and merges with the muscles at the modiolus of the mouth.
Action. This muscle elevates the modiolus and buccal angle, as in laughing.

Zygomaticus minor. This muscle originates in the zygoma, in front of the zygomatic major, and inserts into the skin of the upper lip between the modiolus and the nasal wing. The muscle fibers are difficult to distinguish from the zygomatic major.
Action. This muscle elevates the upper lip, sometimes exposing the maxillary teeth, and deepens the nasolabial furrow.

Levator anguli oris. This muscle is slightly deeper than the overlaying zygomatic muscles. It arises from the canine fossa and is inserted into the corner of the mouth, intermingling with the zygomaticus, depressors, and orbicularis oris.
Action. This muscle raises the modiolus and buccal angle, displaying the teeth and deepening the nasolabial furrows.

Depressor anguli oris and depressor labii inferioris. These muscles arise from the mandible, and the fibers converge to the corners of the mouth.
Action. Both of these muscles depress the corner of the lips downward and laterally.

Risorius. This muscle is one of several converging at the modiolos of the mouth. It originates from the fascia over the masseter muscle and passes horizontally to the modiolos of the mouth.
Action. This muscle draws the angle of the mouth laterally and outward.

Mentalis. This muscle originates in the area below the front teeth, and the insertion is in the skin of the chin.

Action. This muscle's action is to elevate the skin of the chin aiding its protrusion/eversion, as in drinking. At the same time as elevating the skin of the chin, it can cause pronounced protrusion of the lower lip.

Levator anguli oris. Also called the caninus muscle, it originates from the canine fossa and inserts into the modoulis node of intertwining muscles at the corner of the mouth.

Action. The function of the caninus is to elevate the modoulis of the mouth in an almost vertical direction.

Depressor anguli oris. This muscle arises from the oblique line of the mandible and the platysma. The muscle inserts into the modoulis of the mouth.

Action. This muscle depresses the modiolus and buccal angle laterally in opening the mouth and in the expression of sadness.

Depressor labii inferioris. This muscle originates from the oblique line of the mandible and passes upward, inserting in the modoulis of the lower lip.

Action. This muscle pulls the lower lip down and laterally in mastication.

3.3.2   The Muscles of Mandible Motion

The movement of the mandible is complex, involving the coordinated action of the muscles attached to it, as illustrated in Figure 3.21. These muscles, like all muscles, work in groups with each other and with other muscles to perform a smooth, balanced, coordinated series of movements of the mandible. Four basic movements of the mandible are:

- *protraction*—pulling the mandible forward so that the head articulates indirectly with the articular tubercle of the temporal bone,

- *retraction*—pulling the mandible backward so that the head moves into the mandibular fossa,

- *elevation*—closing the mouth, and

- *depression*—opening the mouth.

These actions are described in more detail in Section 3.4.

Muscles That Elevate the Mandible

The muscles responsible for elevating the mandible are the *masseter*, the *medial pterygoid*, and the *temporalis*.

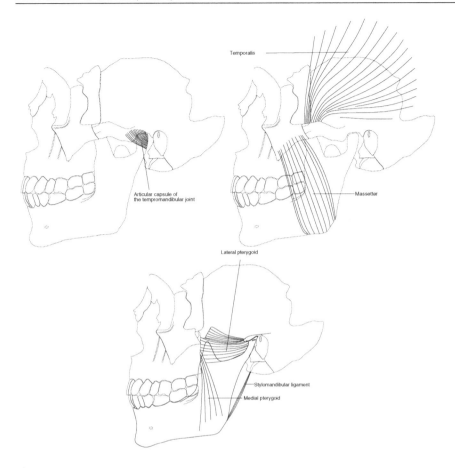

Figure 3.21.
The principal muscles influencing the temporomandibular joint.

Masseter. This muscle is broad and thick, originating on the zygomatic arch and inserting onto the surface of the mandible, as illustrated in Figure 3.21. The deep fibers arise along the length of the zygomatic arch, while the more superficial fibers originate no farther posteriorly than the zygomaticotemoral suture.
Action. This powerful muscle is used to elevate the mandible in mastication. In combination, the masseter works synergistically with other muscles to protract and retract the mandible.

Medial and lateral pterygoid. The medial pterygoid muscle in part originates in the pterygoid fosa and inserts on the surface of the mandible, as illustrated in Figure 3.21. The lateral pterygoid muscle has two heads, one originating on the infratemporal surface of the sphenoid bone, and the other on the lateral surface of the lateral pterygoid plate.

Action. These muscles act to elevate, retract, and protract the mandible. Because of the direction of the muscle fibers, the lateral pterygoid pulls the mandible forward. When the medial and lateral pterygoid muscles on one side contract together, the chin swings to the opposite side. Such movements are important in chewing.

Temporalis. The *temporalis* is a large fan-shaped muscle that arises in the temporal fossa, on the lateral surface of the skull, as illustrated in Figure 3.21. The fibers of the temporalis converge toward the space between the zygomatic arch and the skull, where the muscle inserts onto the coronoid process of the mandible.

Action. Inserting onto the apex of the coroniod process and the dominant vertical orientation of the muscle fibers, the muscle facilitates movement of the mandible. However, because the fibers are longer than the masseter, the temporal muscle is less powerful. Nonetheless, the temporalis is primarily responsible for elevating the mandible, and to a lesser degree, for a retraction due to the lateral orientation of the fibers.

Muscles That Retract the Mandible

The muscles responsible for retracting the mandible are the temporalis described in Section 3.3.2, the digastric, and the geniohyoid. These muscles are located within and beneath the mandible in the upper neck.

Digastric. This muscle is made up to two fleshy parts linked by a tendon. The posterior part originates at the mastoid notch and passes anteriorly and inferiorly to the hyoid bone, where its anterior portion ends in a tendon. The tendon slides through a connective tissue pulley, which is attached to the greater horn of the hyoid bone. The anterior belly arises on this intermediate tendon and passes superiorly and anteriorly to insert on the medial surface of the symphysis of the mandible, near the inferior border.

Action. The paired digastric muscles raise the hyoid bone when the mandible is fixed. In addition, the digastric muscle controls the location of the larynx, an important action when swallowing. When the mandible is raised, the digastric assists in the retraction of the mandible.

Geniohyoid muscle. This muscle originates in the mandible on the back of the symphysis menti, as illustrated in Figure 3.24, and passes posteriorly and inferiorly to the upper half of the body of the hyoid bone.

Action. The geniohyoid muscle acts to elevate the tongue, raising the hyoid bone when swallowing, and depressing the mandible.

Muscles That Protract the Mandible

The muscles repsonsible for protracting the mandible are the lateral ptery-goid, the medial pterygoid, and the masseter, described in Section 3.3.2.

Lateral pterygoid. This muscle originates on the surface of the sphenoid bone, as illustrated in Figure 3.22 and inserts on the anterior surface of the condylar neck of the mandible. Some fibers insert on the anterior surface of the temporomandibular joint capsule.
Action. This muscle acts to open the mandible. In addition, this muscle causes the mandible to shift from side to side when activated in opposition to its contralateral mate.

Muscles That Depress the Mandible

The muscles responsible for depressing the mandible are the digastric, the geniohyoid (described in Section 3.3.2), the mylohyoid, and the platysma.

Mylohyoid. This broad, flat muscle forms the muscular floor of the mouth and is superior to the digastric muscle. Figure 3.27 illustrates the location of the muscle, which originates on the internal aspect of mandible at the mylohyoid line and inserts in two locations, the posterior fibers inserting in the hyoid bone, and the anterior forming a midline raphe, stretching between the symphysis menti and the hyoid bone.
Action. This muscle elevates the tongue and the floor of the mouth. It also elevates the hyoid bone and to some extent depresses the mandible.

Platysma. This is a large, broad sheet muscle that lies just beneath the skin and covers most of the anterior and lateral portion of the neck, as illustrated in Figure 3.18. The muscle originates in the pectoral and deltoid regions of the neck and shoulder and inserts into the mandible, as well as some parts of the mouth.
Action. The action of the platysma is to raise the skin of the neck, as well as drawing down the corner of the mouth. When all the fibers of the neck are contracted simultaneously, the skin of the neck displays significant wrinkling (depending on age) and depresses the lower lip.

3.4   The Temporomandibular Joint

The temporomandibular joint is the articulation between the mandible and the cranium, as illustrated in Figure 3.22. It is one of the few joints in the body that contain a complete intra-articular disk, thereby dividing the joint space into upper and lower compartments. This feature facilitates the combined gliding and hinging movements around a transverse axis that passes between the two lingulae. Both articulating complexes of this joint

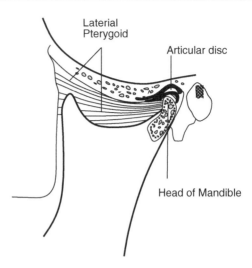

Figure 3.22.
A sagittal view of the temporomandibular joint.

house teeth. The shapes and positions of these teeth influence the function of the temporomandibular joint.

A fibrous capsule encloses the joint. Superiorly, it encircles the glenoid fossa. Below, it attaches to the circumference of the neck of the condyle just beneath the head of the condyle. The inner surface of the capsule is lined by a lubricating synovial membrane.

Inside the capsule is an articular disk. This is an oval plate of fibrous tissue, shaped like a peaked cap, that divides the joint. Its upper surface is sagittally concavoconvex to fit the articular tubercle and fossa, while its inferior concave surface is adapted to the mandibular head.

Three ligaments are associated with the tempromandibular joint: the lateral, the sphenomandibular, and the stylomandibular. Neither the stylomandibular ligament nor the sphenomandibular ligament has any influence upon the movement of the lower jaw.

Lateral ligament. The lateral ligament has a broad attachment to the lower border and tubercle of the zygomatic bone. From here the fibers pass downward and backward, blending with the joint capsule to attach to the lateral and posterior parts of the mandible.

Sphenomandibular ligament. The sphenomandibular ligament is a bond of fibrous tissue arising from the spine of the sphenoid bone and attaching at the lingula of the mandibular foramen. It is located on the medial aspect.

Stylomandibular ligament. The stylomandibular ligament is another fibrous band. It extends from the styloid process to the mandibular angle. Only the temporomandibular ligament limits the joint.

3.4.1 Movements of the Temporomandibular Joint

The motion of the temporomandibular joint (TMJ) can be described as depression, elevation, protraction, retraction, and lateral movement. All of these movements are used to some extent in chewing. The motion of the TMJ is often described as a rotation about a single horizontal axis. However, this is not the case. The complexity of the muscular attachments, coupled with the mechanical structure of the mandible, results in a sliding glide forward as the jaw opens and is illustrated in Figure 3.23(b). The disk, illustrated in Figure 3.23(a), slides on the articular tubercle, and the condyle rotates on the disk when the jaw is opened. When the mandible protrudes, both disks glide forward; rotation of the condyles is prevented by contraction of the elevating muscles of the mandible. A lateral motion of the mandible is the result of one disk gliding forward while the other remains stable. A combination of lateral and protrusion is typically observed in the action of chewing.

Jaw opening is accomplished by contraction of the external pterygoid, digastric, mylohyoideus, and geniohyoideus muscles. Elevation is produced by the masseter, temporalis, and internal pterygoid muscles. The mandible is protruded by simultaneous action of both external pterygoids and the

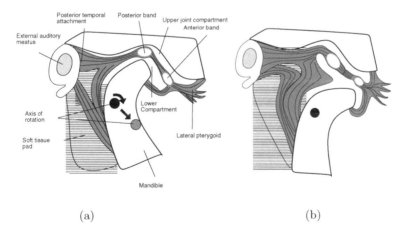

(a) (b)

Figure 3.23.
Sagittal section of the two extreme positions, (a) jaw closed and (b) jaw open, during temporomandibular joint articulation. Notice that the axis of rotation glides forward and downward.

closing muscles. It is retracted by the posterior portion of the temporalis muscle. Lateral movement is accomplished by contractions of the pterygoid muscles.

3.5   Muscles of the Tongue

The tongue is composed entirely of muscles, nerves, and blood vessels as illustrated in Figure 3.24. The muscles of the tongue are divided into two groups, the *intrinsic* and *extrinsic* muscles. The intrinsic muscles lie within the tongue, while the extrinsic muscles originate outside the tongue and attach to other structures and are responsible for positioning the tongue in the mouth.

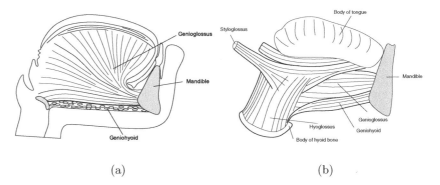

(a)   (b)

Figure 3.24.
A sagittal view of (a) the intrinsic and (b) the extrinsic muscles of the tongue.

Extrinsic Muscles of the Tongue

Each extrinsic muscle is paired to control the tongue's position, as described in Table 3.1.

Muscle	Attachment	Function
genioglossus	mandible	protrudes the tongue
hyoglossus	hyoid bone	depresses the tongue
styloglossus	styloid process	elevates and retracts the tongue
palatoglossus	palatine aponeurosis	elevates the rear of the tongue

Table 3.1.
Extrinsic muscles of the tongue.

Muscle	Description	Function
superior longitudinal	runs along the superior surface	elevates the tongue
inferior longitudinal	runs along the side of the tongue	lateral motion of the tongue
verticalis	runs along the midline of the tongue	broadens the tongue
transversus	divides the tongue along the centerline	narrows the tongue

Table 3.2.
Intrinsic muscles of the tongue.

Intrinsic Muscles of the Tongue

The varying shapes that the tongue can assume are complex; however, this can be easily predicted when considering the contraction of the intrinsic muscles. The intrinsic muscles of the tongue can be subdivided into the longitudinal, transverse, and vertical, as described in Table 3.2.

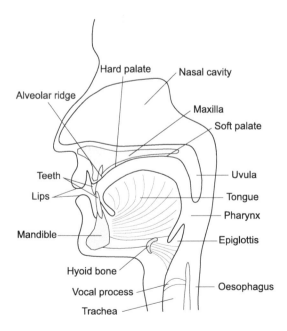

Figure 3.25.
The midsagittal section of the head, showing the tongue and teeth positions.

3.5.1 Tongue Motion

The tongue has an extraordinary ability to modify its shape and position, due in part to its role in chewing (masticastion), deglutition (swallowing) and speech. The tongue is used for manipulating food in the mouth when chewing. In addition, the tongue plays a vital role in shaping the mouth cavity for speech production [Ladefoged 75]. Figure 3.25 illustrates the rest positions of the tongue, teeth, mandible, uvula, and lips, while Figure 9.2 illustrates their positions in the creation of specific speech articulations.

Speech production—in particular the anatomy of acoustic speech—has been the subject of much investigation [Stevens 99]. For a more detailed discussion of speech animation, the reader is referred to Chapter 9.

3.6   The Muscles of the Forehead, Ear, and Neck

This section describes the muscles of the forehead, the vestigial muscles of the ear, and only the large superficial muscles of the neck.

3.6.1   Frontalis

The two thin paired quadrilateral-shaped frontalis have no bony attachment; instead, the fibers emerge from the root of the nose and skin of the eyebrow at one end and run vertically to join the aponeurotca (scalp) below the coronal suture.

Action. The vertical orientation and broad structure of the muscle fibers create horizontal wrinkling when the fibers are contracted. These wrinkles run across the forehead, and the frontalis acts to lift the eyebrows.

The frontalis action can be divided into the inner and outer portions. The inner frontalis raises the medial part of the brow, while the outer frontalis raises the lateral part of the brow. This independent and coordinated set of contracts creates a wide range of wrinkle patterns on the forehead.

3.6.2   Muscles of the Outer Ear

The extrinsic muscles of the ear attach the auricle and the scalp. These muscles are the auricularis anterior, auricularis superior, and auricularis posterior.

Action. The voluntary activation of muscles of the ear can only be performed by some individuals. The auricularis anterior pulls the ear forward and upward, while the auricularis superior draws the ears back. These muscles are more pronounced on other mammals, such as dogs, where the control of the pinna aids in audition by locating sound by turning the ears.

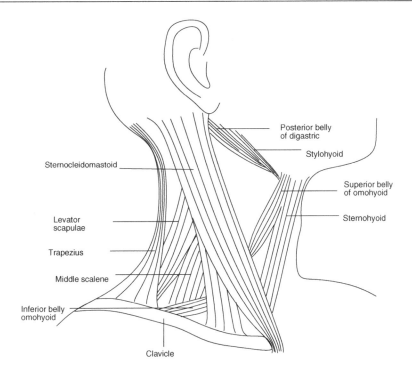

Figure 3.26.
Superficial muscles of the neck.

3.6.3   Superficial Muscles of the Neck

The superficial muscles of the neck are the trapezius, the platysma (described in Section 3.3.2), and the sternocleidomastoid (see Figure 3.26).

Trapezius. The trapezius is a large, superficial triangular muscle covering the back part of the neck and the upper trunk. It arises from the external occipital protuberance, the ligamentum nuchae, the spinous processes of the seventh cervical vertebra, and from the spines of all the thorasic vertebrae. The muscle converges and inserts into scaula.
Action. The wide orientation of the muscle fibers dictates a wide range of actions that includes scapular elevation, adduction, and depression. In addition, when both the right and left trapezius muscles contract together, they pull the head backward.

Sternocleidomastoid. This is a long, large muscle of the neck that originates from the sternal end of the clavicle and inserts into the mastoid process of the temporal bone and the lateral half of the superior nuchal line of the

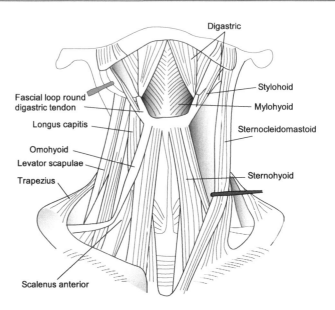

Figure 3.27.
Frontal view of the superficial neck muscles. (Adapted from [Warfel 73].)

occiptal bone. Figure 3.27 illustrates a retracted view of the sternocleido-mastoid that passes obliquely across the neck and is quite pronounced when the head is turned to one side.

Action. When this muscle contracts, the head is turned in the opposite direction, and when both muscles contract, the head is tilted forward. If the head is held static, the action of the muscle causes the clavicle to be raised. The sternocleidomastoid is one of many muscles responsible for movement of the head.

3.7 Skin

The skin covers the entire external surface of the human form and is a highly specialized interface between the body and its surroundings. It has a multicomponent microstructure, the basis of which is an intertwined net-work of collagen, nerve fibers, small blood vessels, and lymphatics, covered by a layer of epithelium and transfixed at intervals by hairs and the ducts of sweat glands, as illustrated in Figure 3.28. While the skin is more or less the same all over the body, the texture and appearance vary with age and should be carefully modeled to reflect its physical characteristics (see Chapter 6 for details).

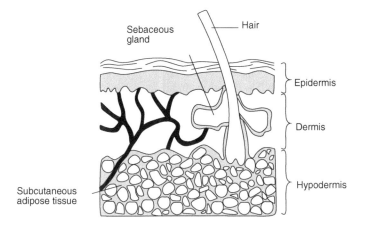

Figure 3.28.
Skin layers.

Facial tissue varies in thickness over the face; around the eyes it is thin, whereas around the lips it is thick. Also, skin texture varies with thickness, giving more of a pinkish color where thin, and a yellowish color where thick. Many factors influence the appearance of skin tissue; thickness, age, and disease are the primary effectors. Between males and females there is a difference in underlying fatty tissue, there being less in men than in women. Skin thickness is less in women than in men, giving a luster to the skin surface of women. Facial wrinkles are caused in part by the loss of fatty tissue as the person grows older, and the loss of elasticity in the skin from aging causes further furrowing and wrinkling.

Human skin has a layered structure consisting of the epidermis, a superficial layer of dead cells, and the dermis, fatty tissue. The epidermis and the dermis, at a finer resolution, have layers within themselves. The mechanical properties of facial tissue are described in more detail in Chapter 8, where a computer model of facial tissue is developed.

3.7.1 The Epidermial Tissue

The epidermis is the outermost layer of skin and is composed mainly of keratin. In this tissue there is a continuous replacement of cells, with a mitotic layer at the base replacing lost layers at the surface.

3.7.2 The Dermal Tissue

The dermis consists of irregular, moderately dense, soft connective tissue. Its matrix consists of an interwoven collagenous network, with varying content of elastin fibers, proteoglycans, fibronectin and other matrix components, blood vessels, lymphatic vessels, and nerves.

3.7.3   The Subcutaneous Tissues

Underneath the dermis lies the superficial fascia, which consists of adipose tissue distributed in a network of connective fibers. This connective tissue is mostly collagen arranged in a lattice with fat cells. The intercelluar amorphous matrix is referred to as the *ground substance*. Beneath the superficial fascia lies the deep fascia, which coats the bones. This layer is formed mainly of aponeuroses, which are flat or ribbon-like tendons.

3.7.4   Skin Lines

The layered structure of skin is non-homogeneous and non-isotropic [Kenedi et al. 75, Larrabee 86]. These features were elaborated in 1861 by Langer, (see Figure 3.29), who made observations on many cadavers. His investigations were based on an earlier observation by Dupuytren (1834) that

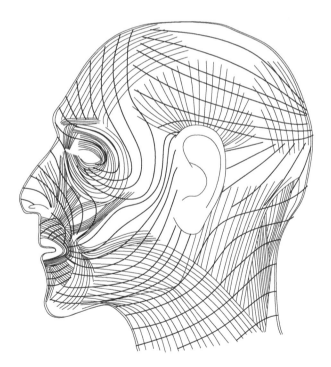

Figure 3.29.
Distribution of Langer's cleavage lines on the face. These lines run approximately perpendicular to the underlying muscle fibers.

a circular puncture on the skin left an elliptical wound. Langer hypothe-
sized that skin is constantly in a state of tension, due to the rhomboidal
arrangement of the dermal fibers. Consequently, if the fibers were dis-
turbed, the tension in the long axis of the rhomboid dominated, deforming
the wound shape. The significance of this investigation was that surgical
incisions should be made parallel to the lines of tension to minimize post-
operative scaring. More recently Kraissl in 1951 described lines of tension
that were usually orthogonal to the line of action of subcutaneous muscle
fibers [Williams et al. 89]. In some cases these lines would run at right angles to Langer lines. However, it is worth noting that Kraissl lines, for the
most part, describe fundamental crease lines on the face.

3.8 The Eyes

The eyes are in reality a separate lobe of the brain, springing from the distal
extremity of the optic nerve. Situated in the skeletal orbits for protection,
the eyes are the end organ of the sense of vision. The positioning of the
eyes in the orbits provides rigid support and sites for muscular attachment.
The muscles permit the accurate positioning of the visual axis under neuromuscular control, to assist in determining the spatial relationship between
the two eyes for binocular vision.

   When creating synthetic computer-generated facial images, careful attention should be paid to the details of the eyes. The eyes should converge
and not stare into space, the pupil should be able to dilate, and the highlight reflection off the surface of the iris and cornea should be modeled with
care. With these basic characteristics, the computer model can maintain
attention, thereby enhancing the realism of the face. See Chapter 7 for more
details on modeling the human eye.

3.8.1 The Eyeball

The eyeball consists of a series of concentric layers, which enclose cavities
filled with separate light-refracting media, as illustrated in Figure 3.30. The
eyeball is about 2.5 cm in diameter but is not perfectly spherical, since the
anterior cornea has a smaller radius of curvature than the rest of the globe.

Sclera. This area is the outermost layer of the eyeball and consists of a
dense, collagenous coat; the posterior five-sixths is the white, opaque sclera,
as shown in Figure 3.31. The point where the optic nerve pierces the sclera
is approximately 3 mm to the nasal side of the posterior pole and slightly
inferior to the horizontal meridian.

Cornea. The anterior sixth of the eyeball is known as the cornea. The
cornea is a thin, bulging, transparent membrane set into the circular gap

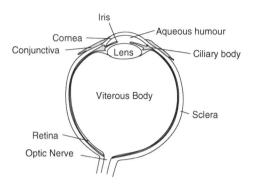

Figure 3.30.
A transverse section through the right eyeball.

at the anterior pole of the sclera, with which it fuses at the sclero-corneal junction. The anterior surface of the cornea is covered with a layer of epithelium which is firmly bound to it, and is continuous with the conjunctiva at the margin of the cornea.

Iris. The iris is an adjustable diaphragm around the central aperture of the pupil. The iris is the mechanism which automatically regulates the amount of light permitted to pass through the lens and is regulated by two sphincter muscles, one to dilate, the other to constrict. It lies anterior to the lens and is separated from the cornea by the anterior chamber. Its circumference is continuous with the ciliary body and is connected to the cornea by the

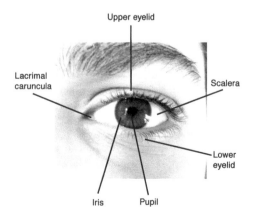

Figure 3.31.
Close-up of the left eye.

pectinate ligament. The iris varies greatly in color and surrounds a central aperture, the pupil. The anterior surface shows faint radial striations.

The accommodation of the lens to near and distant vision is accomplished by the action of smooth-muscle fibers of the ciliary body. These actions may be either automatic or voluntary, providing for unconscious or conscious accommodation.

Retina. The retina is the innermost layer of the eyeball and is, in reality, an expansion of the optic nerve. It consists of ten layers, of which the deepest is the layer of rods and cones. The entire space bounded by the retina, the ciliary body, and the posterior surface of the lens is occupied by the vitreous body, which is filled with a transparent, gelatinous substance.

3.8.2   Eye Motion

When considering the eyes in a computer model, some consideration should be given to the motion of the eyes. In animals this is achieved through a tight coupling of the visual and vestibular systems that in turn control the muscles of the eyes and head. Many eye behaviors are automatic reflex actions that have evolved over thousands of years to provide high-fidelity visual information to the brain. Interestingly, while these motions are exquisitely finessed, we are also highly attuned to observe them in others. For example, we can clearly determine when someone is looking at us in one eye or another when talking to them.

Figure 3.32 and Figure 3.33 show the muscles that control eyeball motion. The oblique and recti muscles coordinate together to precisely move

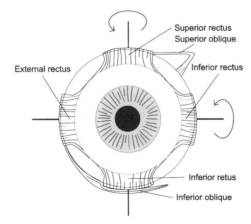

Figure 3.32.
Frontal view of the right eye muscles.

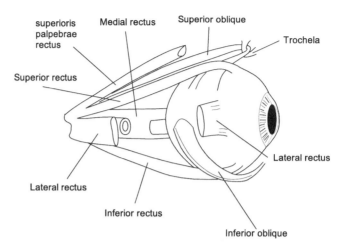

Figure 3.33.
A lateral view of the muscles that control the right eye movement.

the eyes to enable gaze direction, as well as a variety of other motions that are described below.

Vergence

When the eyes focus on an object, they do so by moving each eyeball simultaneously to allow binocular vision. Where the object is in the scene influences how much the eyes converge. A nearby object, a few centimeters from the face, causes extreme convergence, more commonly known as becoming "cross-eyed."

Saccades

These are quick rapid motions of both eyes, triggered by a reflex to fixate and focus on objects, thereby creating a mental image of the scene. Saccades can be extremely rapid, with a peak speed of up to 1000 degrees per second and lasting between 20–200 milliseconds. Blinking is often associated with saccades, and it is suggested that this process "blanks" out the visual information to the brain, which would be a blur. When blinking does not happen, saccadic masking occurs where the eye and brain system conceals the fact that the eyes are moving.

This is an interesting phenomenon that can be demonstrated with a mirror held at arm's length. While observing oneself looking between the eyes, the brain conceals the eye motion, as well as the experience of eye movement. In contrast, an individual observing someone experimenting with the effect can clearly see the eyes moving.

Vistibulo-ocular Reflex

This is the motion of the eyes that keeps the image fixed on the retina when the head moves. As a result, the head moves in one direction while the eyes compensate with a move in the opposite direction. The head is in almost constant motion, and even when very small motions are detected, the vestibulo-ocular reflex continually corrects and compensates.

Optokinetic Reflex

This is an eye reflex created by a stimulus when the head remains still, but the eyes smoothly track an object. Typically, this gives the impression of eye flickering as the eye rapidly returns to track subsequent objects.

4

Modeling Faces

4.1   Introduction

Developing a facial model involves determining geometric descriptions and
animation capabilities that represent the faces of interest. It also involves
the representation of additional attributes, such as surface colors and textures. For our purposes, static models are not useful; the facial models must
be constructed in ways that support animation.

The face has a very complex, flexible, three-dimensional surface. It has
color and texture variation and usually contains creases and wrinkles. As
shown in Chapter 3, the detailed anatomy of the head and face is a complex dynamic assembly of bones, cartilage, muscles, nerves, blood vessels,
glands, fatty tissue, connective tissue, and skin. To date, no facial animation models that represent and simulate this complete, detailed anatomy
have been reported. For some applications, such as medical visualization
and surgical planning, complete detailed models are the ultimate goal. Fortunately, a number of useful applications, such as character animation, can
be accomplished with facial models that approximate only some visual and
behavioral aspects of the complete facial anatomy.

4.1.1   Facial Mechanics

The modeled facial geometry and its animation potential are inseparably
intertwined. The structure of the model determines its animation potential.

The actions a model must perform determine how the model should be constructed. Choices made early in the modeling process determine its animation capabilities.

The mechanics of the face and head are extremely important when constructing these models. The jaw needs to work, the eyelids need to open and close, the eyelids need to stretch over the eyeballs, and the cheeks need to puff and stretch. There are subtle points to consider, as well. When the eyes look from one side to the other, how much of the flesh surrounding the eyes moves? When the mouth opens and closes, how much of the neck is influenced? When the mouth opens, how much do the cheeks move, and how far up the cheeks is there an effect? How is the nose affected? Such details can be the key to a character's age, personality and believability.

The eyes and the mouth are the most expressive areas of the face. They communicate the most information and elicit the greatest emotional responses. Care must be exercised with these regions, so that the necessary details and flexibility are included in the model.

4.1.2 Facial Diversity

Even though most faces have similar structure and the same feature set, obviously there is considerable variation from one individual face to the next. This subtle variation is exactly what makes individual faces recognizable. One of the challenges of facial animation is to develop models that support and allow these variations.

While most of the discussion in this book is centered on the representation of realistic faces, the spectrum of possible representation styles is wide. Artists and illustrators have developed many approaches to depicting the human face. These range from sketches and realistic renderings to cartoons and abstract forms to surrealism—to name just a few. Almost any of these artistic styles might be used as the basis for computer models of the face.

Caricatures

One popular form of facial representation is the caricature. Caricatures typically involve distorting or exaggerating the most recognizable features of a specific face. This often is done in editorial cartoons of famous persons. Brennan developed a computer-based automatic two-dimensional caricature generator [Brennan 82]. By digitizing two-dimensional vector representations of a number of faces and averaging them, a model or description of the normal or average face was developed. Caricatures were then formed by exaggerating the differences of individual faces from the computed normal face. A similar approach can also be applied to three-dimensional faces. Figure 4.1 shows an example of a three-dimensional facial caricature.

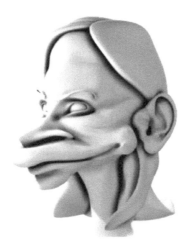

Figure 4.1.
An example three-dimensional facial caricature. (*Courtesy of J. Reisch, Texas A&M Visualization Laboratory.*)

Empathetic Characterizations

In animation we are usually concerned with telling a story, which means getting the audience involved with the characters. This involvement implies that we must develop our facial models so that the audience can establish an emotional response to the character. We want the audience to hate the villain, love the heroine, laugh with the comic, and feel sorry for the unfortunate victim. Developing such empathetic characters is one of the goals of facial modeling.

4.2 Facial Geometry

The goal of the various animation techniques, which are discussed further in Chapter 5, is to control the modeled faces, over time, such that the rendered geometry has the desired shapes, colors, and textures in each frame of the animated sequence. How do we geometrically represent faces in ways that allow both effective animation and efficient rendering?

4.2.1 Volume Representations

One approach to representing faces is to use one of the many volume representation techniques. These include *constructive solid geometry* (CSG), *volume element (voxel) arrays*, and aggregated volume elements such as *octrees*.

CSG is used successfully as the basis for a number of computer-aided mechanical design systems. For these systems, the objects of interest are represented using Boolean set constructions of relatively simple regular mathematical shapes, such as planes, cylinders, and spheres. Unfortunately, realistic faces are not easily represented in this way. Therefore, CSG has not been a popular geometric basis for faces. However, one can imagine a particular style of three-dimensional cartoon faces that might be constructed using CSG techniques.

Volume element, or voxel, representation is a preferred way of describing anatomical structures in medical imaging. These representations may be assembled from two-dimensional data slices of three-dimensional structures. These two-dimensional slices may, for example, be obtained using computer tomography (CT) [Bates et al. 83] or magnetic resonance imaging (MRI) techniques [Hinshaw and Lent 83]. There are numerous examples of this approach being used to create three-dimensional representations of the detailed interior structure of the human head [Farrell et al. 84, Hale et al. 85, Hemmy et al. 83, Cline et al. 87]. Detailed voxel representations typically involve large three-dimensional data arrays, which in turn require large amounts of memory.

There may be a future for voxel models in specific animation areas, such as surgical planning [Brewster et al. 84], where correct detailed understanding of interrelated interior structures is required. However, animation of such models is problematic. Animations based on simple rotations of the voxel data or moving slicing planes through the model are straightforward. However, the structural shape changes usually associated with facial animation are complex and not straightforward for voxel models. Possible animation approaches include interpolation between voxel data sets and the use of freeform deformations similar to those discussed in Section 4.12.6.

Direct voxel models are not usually used for facial animation. However, techniques such as the *marching cubes* algorithm developed by Lorensen and Cline [Lorensen and Cline 87] can be used to extract surface geometry models of the anatomical structures from the voxel data. Animation may then be created using the extracted surface models.

The extracted surfaces usually are constructed to follow specific structure boundaries in the voxel data. These structure boundaries are associated with transitions between regions of specific constant densities within the voxel data.

4.2.2   Surface Representations

Surface primitives and structures are the current preferred geometric basis for facial models. The surface structures used must allow surface shapes and shape changes, as needed for the various facial conformations and expressions. Possible surface description techniques include implicit surfaces, parametric surfaces, polygonal surfaces, and more recently, subdivision surfaces. Parametric surfaces include bivariate Bézier, Catmull-Rom, Beta-spline, B-spline, hierarchical B-spline, and NURB surfaces. Polygonal surfaces include regular polygonal meshes and arbitrary polygon networks. Subdivision techniques generate smooth surfaces based on underlying polygonal forms. The left-most image in Figure 5.3 shows a rendered face modeled with subdivision surfaces.

Implicit Surfaces

One approach is to find an analytic surface or collection of surfaces to approximate the surfaces of the face. An implicit surface is defined by a function $F(x, y, z)$ that assigns a scalar value to each point in x, y, z space [Blinn 82]. The implicit surface defined by such a function is the set of points such that

$$F(x, y, z) = 0.$$

For example, a sphere of unit radius centered at $(0, .5, -.5)$ would be described by the implicit function

$$f(x, y, z) = x^2 + (y - .5)^2 + (z + .5)^2 - 1.$$

Any polynomial function $f(x, y, z)$ implicitly describes an algebraic surface. In particular, quadrics such as ellipsoids, cylinders, cones, and tori can be described as implicit algebraic surfaces.

Given two implicit surface functions $f(x, y, z)$ and $g(x, y, z)$, additional implicit surface functions can be generated by *blending* the two given functions [Woodwark 86]. Some examples of blended implicit functions are Nishimura's *Metaballs* [Nishimura et al. 85] and Wyvill's *Soft Objects* [Wyvill et al. 86].

Although implicit surfaces commonly are expressed analytically, Ricci pointed out that the defining functions could be any procedure that computes a scalar value for every point in space [Ricci 73]. Models constructed with such procedures are called *procedural implicit* models.

The blending and constraint properties of implicit surfaces allow creation of models that would be difficult to build with other techniques. However, interaction with implicit surface models is difficult [Bloomenthal and Wyvill 93]. Real-time display of surfaces is important for interactive design. Implicit surfaces are more challenging to interactively manipulate and display than polygonal or parametric surfaces. Methods that allow a high degree of interactive control over implicit surfaces have yet to be developed. As a result, implicit surfaces are seldom used for facial animation.

Parametric Surfaces

Bivariate parametric functions are used widely to define three-dimensional surfaces. These surfaces are generated by three functions of two parametric variables, one function for each of the spatial dimensions. These functions typically are based on quadric or cubic polynomials.

The most popular of these surfaces, referred to as *tensor-product parametric surfaces*, are defined in terms of control values and *basis* functions. Examples of these include B-splines, Beta-splines, Bézier patches, and non-uniform rational B-spline surfaces (NURBS) [Bartles et al. 87]. These surfaces can be expressed in the form

$$\mathbf{S}(u,v) = \sum_i \sum_j \mathbf{V}_{i,j} B_{i,k}(u) B_{j,m}(v)$$

where $\mathbf{S}(u,v)$ is the parametric surface, $\mathbf{V}_{i,j}$ are the control values, and $B_{i,k}(u), B_{j,m}$ are the basis functions of polynomial orders k and m, respectively. This formulation usually is recast into the matrix representation

$$\mathbf{S}(u,v) = [\mathbf{u}][\mathbf{B}_u][\mathbf{V}][\mathbf{B}_v]^T[\mathbf{v}]^T$$

where $[\mathbf{u}] = [1\,u\,u^2 \cdots u^{k-1}]$ and $[\mathbf{v}] = [1\,v\,v^2 \cdots v^{m-1}]$.

For each surface patch, the parameters u and v vary over the interval $[0.0, 1.0]$. The basis functions $\mathbf{B}_u$ and $\mathbf{B}_v$ are determined by the type and order of the surface. For uniform, bicubic B-splines, $k = m = 4$ and both $[\mathbf{B}]$ matrices are

$$\frac{1}{6}\begin{vmatrix} 1 & 4 & 1 & 0 \\ -3 & 0 & 3 & 0 \\ 3 & -6 & 3 & 0 \\ -1 & 3 & -3 & 1 \end{vmatrix}.$$

For bicubic surfaces, the $[\mathbf{V}]$ matrix is a four-by-four array of control values. The relationship between these control points and the surface they define depends on the surface type. For B-splines these control values are in fact three-dimensional points which are near, but not typically on, the defined surface. For a Catmull-Rom surface the surface will pass through its interior control points [Catmull and Rom 74]. For other surface types, the control values may be points or other geometric entities, such as tangent vectors.

In most implementations, the desired surface is defined and controlled using a large array of control values. Each four-by-four subarray of control values defines one portion or *patch* of the larger surface. These patches join together with specific surface continuity characteristics. The surface continuity is determined by the surface type. Bicubic B-spline surfaces, for example, have $\mathbf{C}^2$ continuity, which means that the surface has second-derivative continuity across the boundaries between the patches. Bicubic Catmull-Rom surfaces have only derivative or $\mathbf{C}^1$ continuity across these boundaries.

A few early facial model implementations, such as Waite [Waite 89] and Nahas et al. [Nahas et al. 88], used bicubic B-spline surface modeling techniques. These models produced faces with smooth curved surfaces that are defined using relatively few control points (typically a 16-by-12 array of control points).

Current interactive three-dimensional modeling and animation systems typically support modeling and animating bi-parametric surfaces. As a result, these surfaces have been widely used to create and animate facial models. This approach does have a few disadvantages:

- The density of control points used does not typically support the detailed surface definition and surface control needed around the eyes and mouth.

- Because of the array structure of the control points, adding detail requires adding complete rows or columns to the control points array.

- Creases in the face are difficult to implement, since they require defeating the natural surface continuity properties.

Hierarchical B-splines. Forsey and Bartels describe a way to increase local detail in B-spline surfaces without the need to add complete rows or columns of control points [Forsey and Bartels 88]. By carefully controlling overlapping boundary conditions, it is possible to locally increase surface detail by overlaying a more detailed surface defined with additional control points only in the region of interest. These additional control points allow more detailed control of the surface in that region. The additional detail is a refinement layered onto the original surface. The added detail is relative to the original underlying surface. When the underlying surface is modified, the added detail follows accordingly. This approach is hierarchical and can be applied repeatedly, adding additional detail onto regions which already have enhanced detail.

Wang's *Langwidere* facial animation system was implemented using hierarchical B-spline surfaces [Wang 93]. In this model, hierarchical refinement was used to add local surface detail, including the interior of the mouth and the eyes and eye sockets. Facial expression animation is controlled using simulated muscle functions to manipulate the hierarchical surface control points.

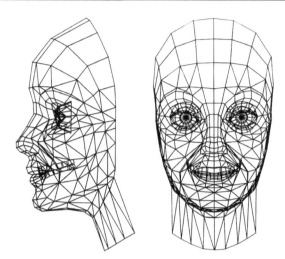

Figure 4.2.
An example polygon topology.

4.2.3   Polygonal Surfaces

Personal computers are now adept at displaying polygonal surfaces and can update modestly complex facial models in real time. Because of this capability, essentially all facial models are displayed using polygonal surfaces. Even the nonpolygonal surface techniques described above are usually approximated with polygon surfaces for display.

Most early and many existing facial models are based on polygonal surface descriptions. These polygonal surfaces may be in the form of regular polygonal meshes or as arbitrary networks of connected polygons, such as that shown in Figure 4.2.

4.2.4   Developing a Polygonal Topology

In this context, *topology* refers to the way the polygon vertices are connected to form the polygonal surface. The regular mesh topology organizes the vertices into a rectangular array. These vertices are then connected with triangular or quadrilateral polygons to form the desired surface. Arbitrary polygonal networks are constructed by connecting vertices, as needed, to form the desired surface. Gouraud's original approach was to directly approximate the surface of a face with an arbitrary network of polygons [Gouraud 71]. This network was constructed by sampling the surface at a number of points and connecting these points to form polygons. No attempt was made to impose a regular structure on the created polygons. The topology shown in Figure 4.2 is an example of an arbitrary polygonal network.

There are a number of things to keep in mind when approximating a face with polygons:

- The polygons must be laid out in a way that allows good approximation of the facial surface shapes. If the same topology is to be used for more than one face, it must allow good surface approximation for each of the faces in the set.

- The polygons must be laid out in a way that allows the face to flex and change shape naturally. If the polygons are not triangles, they should remain approximately planar as the face flexes.

- The polygons must approximate the face for each expression. The polygon topology may need iterative modification until it allows reasonable representation of the face in all of its possible expressions. The eyelids require special attention to ensure that they can open and close naturally. The lips need to be able to take on the needed speech and expression postures.

- The density of surface-defining information should be distributed according to surface curvature. Areas of high surface curvature (the nose, the mouth, around the eyes, and the edge of the chin) need a high density of defining information, whereas areas of lower curvature (the forehead, cheeks, and neck) need less defining information. Higher density also is needed in those areas that require subtle surface control. These areas include the eye region and the mouth, which are the major expressive areas of the face.

- Use the smallest number of polygons consistent with good results. The goal is to have acceptable surface shape accuracy with a minimum number of polygons. A smaller number of polygons allows faster image generation and minimizes the data acquisition problem.

- Polygon edges should coincide with the natural creases of the face (under the eyes, the side of the nose, the edge of the lips, and the corner of the mouth). Polygons should not span these creases.

- Special care is necessary if creases are to be visible in smooth shaded surfaces. Separate normals must be maintained for vertices, along the crease, that are in polygons on opposite sides of the crease. This allows that there will be a shading discontinuity along the crease, and that the crease will be visible.

- Polygon edges must coincide with color boundaries, such as those associated with the lips and eyebrows. Polygons should not span color boundaries. If the model makes use of texture maps, this consideration may not be as important.

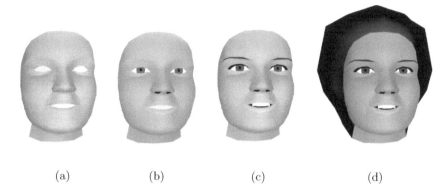

(a)   (b)   (c)   (d)

Figure 4.3.
The effect of facial features: (a) only the facial mask; (b–d) the effect of
additional feature details [Parke 72].

- Since the face is nearly symmetric, we may be tempted to model
  only one side of the face. The other side may then be obtained by
  mirroring or reflecting about the plane of symmetry. This approach is
  not recommended when accurate models of specific faces are desired.
  Much specific personality comes from face asymmetries.

4.3   Face Features

A facial model is usually the sum of many parts and details. Much of the
research on facial animation has focused on techniques for geometrically
defining and manipulating the facial *mask*. A more complete approach is
to integrate the facial mask, facial feature details, the ears, the head and
neck, the interior of the mouth, and hair into models of the complete head.

The facial mask. The facial mask corresponds to the visible external skin
surface of the face and often includes the upper front part of the neck. Many
face models have dealt only with this expressive facial mask, as shown in
Figure 4.3(a). A face mask by itself is not very realistic. It is usually
necessary to add facial features to be convincing. Complete faces include
eyeballs, facial hair (eyebrows, eyelashes, beards, etc.), and the inside of
the mouth, including the teeth, gums, and tongue. The details of the face
are very important in achieving realistic results. Figure 4.3(b–d) shows the
effect that details such as the eyes, eyebrows, eyelashes, teeth, and hair have
on the realism of even a very simple face model.

Eyes. Detailed, dynamic eyes are very important to successful expression
animation. Eye tracking motions, and even pupil dilation changes, add

realism to the animation. Details of iris coloration and reflections from the eyeballs add life to the face. Each eyeball can be approximately modeled as a white sphere with color bands for the iris and pupil. Since only a small portion of the eyeball is actually visible, only the front hemisphere of each eyeball needs to be included in the model.

A better model would include a smaller superimposed reflecting transparent partial sphere as the cornea. An even better model might use texture mapping for the color patterns of the iris and even the blood vessels visible in the whites of the eyes. Sagar et al. developed a very detailed eye model for use in simulating eye surgery [Sagar et al. 94].

Lips. The lips and surrounding tissues are extremely flexible and must be modeled with sufficient curvature density and flexibility to take on the range of possible mouth postures. The lips can also exhibit many small wrinkles and may crease as they take on various shapes. The mouth and lips are instrumental in communicating emotional postures. The lips are also a major component of speech. The lips help form the speech phonemes and their visual counterparts, called *visemes.*

Teeth. The teeth are at least partially visible during many expressions and speech utterances. As a result, including teeth in the facial model is of some importance. The teeth could be modeled in several ways. One of the simpler approaches is that shown in Figure 4.3(c), where each tooth is simply represented by a single forward-facing polygon. A more realistic— and more complex—approach would be to model the detailed shape of each tooth. A third approach would be to texture map teeth images on a simple connected set of polygons used to approximate the upper and lower dental arches.

Other interior structures of the mouth may be visible in some facial postures. These include the gums, the tongue, and the other interior surfaces of the mouth. Including these features increases the fidelity of the facial model.

Tongue. The tongue is visible in many facial postures and is important in distinguishing a number of speech postures. If the tongue is visible, is it between the teeth or touching the roof of the mouth? For several of the speech postures, tongue shape and position are the main characteristics that determine which viseme is being represented. Including even a simple tongue can significantly increase the range of expressions and the ability of the facial model to support speech animation.

Ears. Ears are very individual and are important in capturing and representing *likeness,* that is, representation of a specific individual. They are also difficult to model. Real ears have complex surfaces which require a large number of polygons or complex bicubic surfaces with many control points. In some face models, simple approximations to real ear shapes have been used effectively. In other face models the ears are simply not included, sometimes because they are covered with a hat or hair.

Asymmetries. There is strong temptation to model the face with exact left/right symmetry. This simplifies both the surface definition and the control aspects of face models. However, real faces are not truly symmetric. Asymmetries occur in both conformation and expressions. Structural and expression asymmetries are important characteristics of both realistic and character faces. Much facial personality is the result of these asymmetries.

Hair. Hair, including eyebrows, eyelashes, and facial hair such as beards, is important for realistic facial models. Hair can be an important aspect of a character's personality. Just as in real life, hair and hairstyle can be a significant component in recognizing specific individual characters. Ideally, the hair should behave dynamically in response to head and air current motions.

Hair has been, and continues to be, a challenge for the facial modeler. Polygon or bicubic surfaces are not very good representations for hair, even when texture mapping techniques are used. Several approaches have modeled hair as collections of individual hair strands. Chapter 11 discusses in detail techniques for modeling and animating hair.

4.3.1   Complete Heads

The face should be viewed as an integrated part of a complete head and, in turn, as a part of the complete character. A complete head model includes the face, ears, hair, the back of the head, and the neck. The ability to specify the shape of the head and the conformation of the ears, hair, and hairstyle is important in representing faces of specific people or characters.

Integrating the face, head, and neck into the rest of the body is an important aspect of three-dimensional character animation. The head is connected with the rest of the body through the complex muscle and bone structures of the neck and upper trunk. The dynamics of head and neck motions are discussed in Peterson and Richmond [Peterson and Richmond 88].

4.4   Sources of Facial Surface Data

Regardless of the geometric primitives used, a basic modeling goal is to create descriptions that faithfully represent the desired face or faces. Specifying the three-dimensional surface of a face or any other complex object is a significant challenge.

The following general approaches are used for determining surface shape for face models:

- three-dimensional surface measuring techniques,

- anthropometric modeling,

- interactive surface sculpting,

- assembling faces from components,

- creating new faces by modifying existing faces,

- parameterized models, and

- data based "statistical" models.

Most of the face models discussed in this book rely on measured three-dimensional surface data. Surface measurement can be accomplished using digitizers, photogrammetric techniques, or laser scanning techniques.

4.4.1   Capturing Likeness

To capture likeness, we need to obtain shape and shape change information from real faces. The ability to capture the subtleties of a particular face depends on the density of measured points and the corresponding number of surface polygons or surface patches. It also depends on the accuracy and resolution of the measuring system.

4.4.2   The Time Element

Since faces are dynamic and change over time, it is necessary to *freeze* the desired facial postures. For real faces, this involves holding the face in a desired posture for the duration of the measurement process. Photographic techniques automatically freeze the desired posture at a specific time instant. Physical facial sculptures are another way to freeze facial postures.

4.4.3   Contour Reconstruction

Three-dimensional surfaces can be constructed using digitized two-dimensional contour information from multiple stacked data slices. Surfaces are formed by creating a *skin* of polygons, which connect the contours. Algorithms exist for automatically creating these polygon skins [Fuchs et al. 77]. Information from the contours could also be used as control points for parametric surfaces that approximate or interpolate the contour data.

4.4.4   Three-Dimensional Digitizers

Three-dimensional digitizers are special hardware devices that rely on mechanical, electromagnetic, or acoustic measurements to locate positions in space. The electromagnetically based Polhemus 3Space digitizer has been one of the most widely used devices for this purpose [Pol 87].

These digitizers require physically positioning a three-dimensional probe or locator at each surface point to be measured. The digitizing process requires considerable time if a large number of points are to measured.

The surface points measured may be the vertices of a polygon network or the control points for a parametric surface. Since real faces tend to move and change shape over time, digitizers work best with sculptures or physical models that do not change shape during the measuring process.

4.4.5   Photogrammetric Techniques

These methods capture facial surface shapes and expressions photographically. The basic idea is to take multiple simultaneous photographs of the face, each from a different point of view. If certain constraints are observed when taking the photographs, the desired three-dimensional surface data points can be computed, based on measured data from these multiple two-dimensional views [Parke 74, Sutherland 74]. Since this photographic process *freezes* the facial surface at a given instant of time, it can be used for direct measurement of real faces, as well as for face sculptures.

4.4.6   Laser Scanning Systems

Laser-based surface scanning devices, such as those developed by Cyberware[TM], can be used to measure faces [Cyberware Laboratory Inc. 90]. These devices typically produce a large regular mesh of data values in a cylindrical coordinate system. They can digitize real faces, as well as physical models and facial sculptures. Facial poses must be held constant during the short time interval needed to complete the scanning process. Some versions of these scanning systems can simultaneously capture surface color information, in addition to surface shape data.

Postprocessing of the scanned cylindrical data mesh is often required to extract the specific surface data needed for a particular face model. This postprocessing may include data thinning, spatial filtering, surface interpolation, and transformations from cylindrical to Cartesian coordinate systems.

4.4.7   Standard Form

It is often desireable to put the three-dimensional face data into a standard form, so that all measured faces will have certain common properties. We may, for example, want the symmetry plane of the face to be coincident with the plane defined by the x- and z-axes, with the x-axis pointed toward the front of the face, and the z-axis pointing up. We probably want the origin of the face coordinate system to be located near the center of the head. We also may want the data scaled so that the size of the head is within a specific range.

4.5 Digitizer-Based Modeling

Three-dimensional digitizers involve moving a sensor or locating device to each surface point to be measured. The digitized points may be polygonal vertices or control points for parametric surfaces. These devices require that the positions be measured sequentially. This sequential requirement implies that the total surface digitizing time will depend on the number of points to be measured.

There are several types of three-dimensional digitizers, each based on a different physical measurement technique. These include digitizers based on mechanical, acoustic, or electromagnetic mechanisms.

Mechanical digitizers. Mechanical digitizers rely on positioning a mechanical measuring stylus at the surface points to be measured. The stylus may be attached to a mechanical arm linkage or to an orthogonal set of mechanical tracks. Potentiometers, or shaft encoders, embedded in the mechanism are used to convert the mechanical position of the stylus into electrical signals. These signals are in turn transformed into coordinate values. The mechanical structure of these devices may prevent them from reaching all points on the surface of some objects, such as faces.

Acoustic digitizers. Acoustic digitizers rely on the time of flight of sound pulses to multiple sound sensors. Triangulation based on these propagation times allows spatial locations to be computed. The sound source is usually located at the measuring stylus. At least three sound sensors are located in the measuring environment to receive the sound pulses. Objects in the environment can occlude or distort the sound transmission paths, resulting in measurement errors.

Electromagnetic digitizers. Electromagnetic digitizers, such as the Polhemus 3Space digitizer, work by generating orthogonal electromagnetic fields [Pol 87]. Field sensors attached to the stylus provide signals that can be converted to stylus location *and* orientation. These digitizers do not work well with objects that contain materials, such as metals, that can block or distort the electromagnetic fields.

Digitizer accuracy. The resolution and accuracy of these devices are limited by characteristics of the physical properties being measured and by the accuracy of the sensors. The limitations may be in the form of accumulated mechanical tolerances, distortion of sound waveforms, or the strength and distortion of electromagnetic fields. The Polhemus digitizer, for example, has an accuracy of about .02 inches within a spherical working volume of diameter two feet. To achieve good positional accuracy, the digitized objects should fit within this working volume.

4.5.1   Digitizing Polygonal Surfaces

Kleiser describes the use of a Polhemus digitizer to create polygonal facial models [Kleiser 89]. In this instance, a number of plaster facial sculptures were created for the various facial expressions and speech postures of a specific character. Figure 4.4 shows two of these sculptures.

The same predetermined polygon topology was used to mark each of the face sculptures. Each vertex in the topology is identified. This identification may be in the form of row and column numbers for regular polygonal meshes, or as vertex numbers for arbitrary polygonal networks. For arbitrary networks, the facial topology is recorded by noting how the numbered vertices are connected to form the surface polygons.

The digitizer is used to sequentially measure the vertex positions for each sculpture. The measurements usually are taken in a predetermined order, such as in row or column order or vertex number order. These measurements could be taken in arbitrary order, but doing so requires specifying the vertex order as the digitizing takes place.

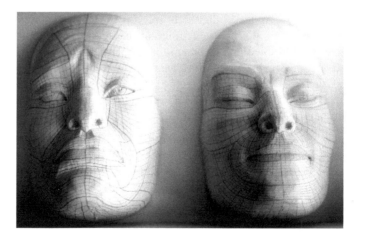

Figure 4.4.
Facial model sculptures. (*Courtesy of J. Kleiser.*)

4.5.2   Digitizing Parametric Surfaces

Reeves [Reeves 90] describes an example of digitizing physical models to define parametric surface face models. In this case the face model was for Billy, the baby character in the film *Tin Toy* [Pixar 88].

The data for Billy's skin was a set of three-dimensional points, along with information that specified how these points were ordered to define the surface. The surface was created by fitting a smooth parametric surface through the digitized data points.

The Digitization Process

A plastic doll head was used to test and debug the digitizing process. The actual Billy prototypes were sculpted in modeling clay. Using clay allowed small changes to the model when necessary. Identifying marks were pressed into the clay surface where desired. The modeling clay allowed these marks to be easily changed when necessary. However, the soft clay also allowed the digitizing stylus to sink into the surface, which made digitizing fine detail difficult and could add error to the resulting data.

Billy's head and body were digitized using a Polhemus 3Space digitizer [Pol 87]. Only one side of Billy's head was digitized. The other side was generated by reflecting the points about the center of the head.

The actual digitizing process was quite simple: position the digitizer stylus at a point on the clay model, hit a foot pedal to record the position, move the stylus to the next position, hit the pedal, etc.

Entering of the connectivity information occurred concurrently. Connectivity was represented as ordered point sets that defined each small surface element. This defining information was entered interactively by requesting a new element and then pointing at the points forming that set, one by one. This procedure is very similar to defining the vertices of a polygon. If control points are defined by point sets organized in rows, a whole row of elements can be automatically specified by identifying the first and last points of the current row and of the previous row.

Surface Fitting

Reeves reports that the initial approach was to fit the data points with triangular Bézier patches. Triangles make it easy to tile a surface that makes transitions from high detail to low detail. Four-sided, five-sided, and *n*-sided patches can be handled easily, since they can be subdivided into three-sided patches.

Unfortunately, the surfaces produced were not smooth. While the triangular Bézier patch interpolates its corner vertices as well as its corner normals and is $\mathbf{C}^1$-continuous across adjoining patches, there is no control

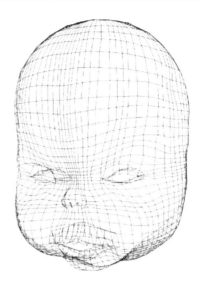

Figure 4.5.
Surface structure for the Billy model. (Adapted from [Reeves 90].)

over what happens interior to the patch. Under some conditions, severe surface undulations can occur.

The next approach tried was to use bicubic Catmull-Rom patches, which are well suited for interpolating data points [Catmull and Rom 74]. Given 16 data points arranged in a four-by-four array, the defined surface patch passes through the four central data points and defines a smooth $\mathbf{C}^1$ boundary, with adjacent patches defined using shared points.

As discussed in Section 4.2.2, four-sided bivariate surfaces such as Catmull-Rom patches are hard to refine. To add detail to the surface, you have to add entire rows or columns of data points. Adding detail in one region also adds it in other regions where it is not needed. The need for relatively fine detail around Billy's mouth and eyes caused unnecessary data points across the bottom of the cheeks, at the top of the neck, and around the ears. As a result, Billy's head, shown in Figure 4.5, was defined by about 2,700 points forming about 2,600 patches. These data took days to digitize. The hierarchical B-spline representation discussed in Section 4.2.2 is one approach to minimizing the number of data points needed for a given surface.

Even using the Catmull-Rom surface, the modeled head was still too wrinkly. Fortunately, applying the concept of *geometric continuity* developed by DeRose and Barsky to the Catmull-Rom surfaces finally achieved acceptable results [DeRose and Barsky 88]. Geometric continuity intro-

Figure 4.6.
Finished frame of Billy from *Tin Toy*. (*Copyright Pixar 1988.*)

duces an additional shape parameter, called $beta_1$, for each curve segment. Reeves used a heuristic developed by DeRose and Barsky to automatically determine $beta_1$ values that smoothed the surface and removed most of its irregularities.

According to Reeves, Billy still had a *north pole* problem, where patches came together at the top of his head, and Billy still had some unwanted surface undulations in the lower cheeks. Figure 4.6 shows Billy in a finished frame from *Tin Toy*, which illustrates the result of this modeling effort.

Modeling Gollum

Following the same basic principles developed by Pixar, Gollum from *The Lord of the Rings*™ is a more recent example of manually creating a surface-based model. Figure 4.7 illustrates the model of Gollum, which was originally sculpted from clay and digitized [Serkis 03]. See Color Plate I for a complete rendered frame of Gollum. The digitized data was used to define and control a subdivision surface model. Gollum animation was achieved using key-framing, such that hundreds of individual facial expressions were created and interpolated to match motion capture data from actor Andy Serkis. For details on motion capture, see Chapter 10.

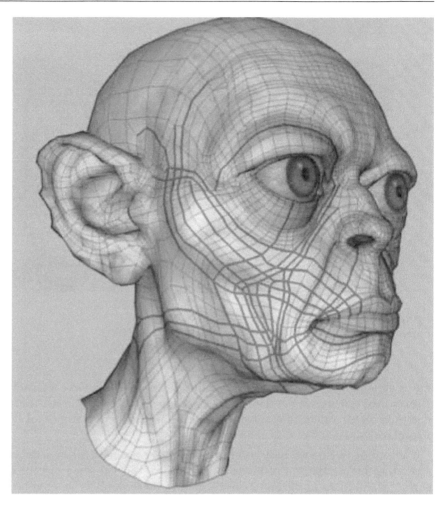

Figure 4.7.
The geometry of Gollum from *The Lord of the Rings*^TM. (*"The Lord of the Rings: The Two Towers" Copyright MMII, New Line Productions, Inc, TM The Saul Zaentz Company d/b/a Tolkien Enterprises under license to New Line Productions, Inc. All rights reserved. Photo by Pierre Vinet. Photo appears courtesy of New Line Productions, Inc.*) See also Color Plates I and II.

4.6 Photogrammetric Measurement

In this section we describe two photographically based approaches to measuring surface position data. The first is procedurally and computationally simple but has limitations and inherent accuracy problems. The second is more robust but is also more procedurally and computationally complex.

For both approaches it is necessary to locate and measure the same surface points in at least two different photographs of the surface. For surfaces such as the face, it is difficult to identify all the needed corresponding points in multiple photographs, unless the surface is somehow marked. One way to do this is to draw or paint a set of points or lines on the surface prior to taking the photographs.

4.6.1 A Simple Photogrammetric Method

For the simple method, we need only one pair of simultaneous photographs for each expression posture. Each pair consists of orthogonal views of the face; one taken from directly in front, and the other taken directly from one side. Once we have a face that has been marked with the desired points, we can capture a number of different poses, expressions, or phoneme utterances simply by taking a simultaneous orthogonal pair of photographs for each pose. Figure 4.8 shows an example pair of photographs.

We establish a three-dimensional coordinate system with a coordinate origin near the center of the head. This coordinate system might be chosen

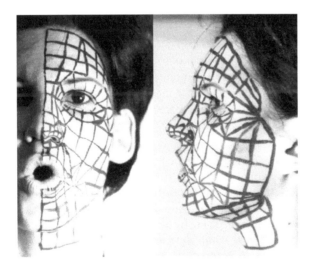

Figure 4.8.
Example image pair for the simple photogrammetric method [Parke 72].

such that two of the coordinate axes lie in the symmetry plane of the face. The three-dimensional position of each surface point is measured directly from the photograph pairs. We get two of the three dimensions from one photo, and two more from the other photo. Of course, it is necessary to maintain correspondence between the points in each image.

One of the dimensions, usually the vertical dimension, appears in both images. It is necessary to scale measurements from one photo to match those from the other photo. This scaling usually is based on measurements in the dimension common to both photos.

This measurement was originally done manually, based on coordinate axes lines drawn directly on prints of the images. A ruler or measurement grid was used to determine the coordinates of each point visible in each view. Later it was possible, and highly desirable, to semi-automate this measurement process using a two-dimensional digitizer such as a data tablet. These days, this process would likely be done with digital images and the measurement would be semi-automated with software that automatically measures selected image locations.

This simple method has significant shortcomings. The photographs are not true orthographic projections, but are in fact perspective projections. Therefore, the images are somewhat distorted. This distortion can be minimized by using long-focal-length lenses.

Some points on the face may not be visible in both views: for example, the inside corner of the eye and the underside of the chin. An estimate must be made for at least one of the coordinates of these occluded points. Clearly, a better method is desired.

4.6.2   A Better Photogrammetric Method

The main objections to the simple method are the perspective distortion and the fact that some of the points may be occluded in one or both of the orthogonal views. The better method, described below, eliminates the perspective distortion and minimizes the occlusion problem.

Theory

A camera may be viewed as a device for projecting a three-dimensional space onto a two-dimensional image space. This mapping can be described mathematically using homogeneous coordinates and the proper transformation matrix, followed by a homogeneous division. If the projection transformation matrices are known, then by using two (or more) photographs of an object, it is possible to compute the three-dimensional position of points visible in at least two photos.

Let $P = [x, y, z, 1]$ be a point whose three-dimensional coordinates are to be found. Let $T1$ be the four-by-three transformation matrix which is used to map the point P into the two-dimensional space of the first photograph.

Let $T2$ be the corresponding transformation for the second photograph. Then,

$$[P][T1] = [P'_1] \qquad \text{for photograph 1}$$
$$[P][T2] = [P'_2] \qquad \text{for photograph 2} \tag{4.1}$$

or

$$\begin{vmatrix} x & y & z & 1 \end{vmatrix} \begin{vmatrix} T1_{11} & T1_{12} & T1_{13} \\ T1_{21} & T1_{22} & T1_{23} \\ T1_{31} & T1_{32} & T1_{33} \\ T1_{41} & T1_{42} & T1_{43} \end{vmatrix} = \begin{vmatrix} x'_1 & y'_1 & h_1 \end{vmatrix} \tag{4.2}$$

and

$$\begin{vmatrix} x & y & z & 1 \end{vmatrix} \begin{vmatrix} T2_{11} & T2_{12} & T2_{13} \\ T2_{21} & T2_{22} & T2_{23} \\ T2_{31} & T2_{32} & T2_{33} \\ T2_{41} & T2_{42} & T2_{43} \end{vmatrix} = \begin{vmatrix} x'_2 & y'_2 & h_2 \end{vmatrix}. \tag{4.3}$$

The coordinates of the point measured in the two-dimensional spaces of the photographs are

$$x_{m_1} = \frac{x'_1}{h_1} \quad x_{m_2} = \frac{x'_2}{h_2}$$
$$y_{m_1} = \frac{y'_1}{h_1} \quad y_{m_2} = \frac{y'_2}{h_2}. \tag{4.4}$$

Therefore,

$$x'_1 = x_{m_1} * h_1 \quad x'_2 = x_{m_2} * h_2$$
$$y'_1 = y_{m_1} * h_1 \quad y'_2 = y_{m_2} * h_2. \tag{4.5}$$

Carrying out the matrix multiplications in Equations (4.2) and (4.3) gives

$$x'_1 = x * T1_{11} + y * T1_{21} + z * T1_{31} + T1_{41}$$
$$y'_1 = x * T1_{12} + y * T1_{22} + z * T1_{32} + T1_{42}$$
$$h_1 = x * T1_{13} + y * T1_{23} + z * T1_{33} + T1_{43}$$
$$x'_2 = x * T2_{11} + y * T2_{21} + z * T2_{31} + T2_{41}$$
$$y'_2 = x * T2_{12} + y * T2_{22} + z * T2_{32} + T2_{42}$$
$$h_2 = x * T2_{13} + y * T2_{23} + z * T2_{33} + T2_{43}. \tag{4.6}$$

Substituting these equations into Equation (4.5), collecting terms for x, y, z, and rewriting in matrix form gives

$$
\begin{vmatrix}
T1_{11} - x_{m_1}T1_{13} & T1_{21} - x_{m_1}T1_{23} & T1_{31} - x_{m_1}T1_{33} \\
T1_{12} - y_{m_1}T1_{13} & T1_{22} - y_{m_1}T1_{23} & T1_{32} - y_{m_1}T1_{33} \\
T2_{11} - x_{m_2}T2_{13} & T2_{21} - x_{m_2}T2_{23} & T2_{31} - x_{m_2}T2_{33} \\
T2_{12} - y_{m_2}T2_{13} & T2_{22} - y_{m_2}T2_{23} & T2_{32} - y_{m_2}T2_{33}
\end{vmatrix}
\begin{vmatrix} x \\ y \\ z \end{vmatrix}
=
\begin{vmatrix}
x_{m_1}T1_{43} - T1_{41} \\
y_{m_1}T1_{43} - T1_{42} \\
x_{m_2}T2_{43} - T2_{41} \\
y_{m_2}T2_{43} - T2_{42}
\end{vmatrix}
$$

or

$$[A][X] = [B]. \tag{4.7}$$

This is an overdetermined system of four equations in the three unknowns x, y, and z. In general, if we have n views with n T matrices, we will have $2n$ equations in the three unknowns. Multiplying both sides of Equation (4.7) by $[A]^T$ gives

$$[A]^T[A][X] = [A]^T[B]. \tag{4.8}$$

This result is a system of three equations that can be solved using standard numerical methods such as Gaussian elimination with partial pivoting [Cheney and Kincaid 80], to give a least-mean-square solution for the three unknowns x, y, and z.

The previous discussion assumes that we know the two transformation matrices, $T1$ and $T2$. To solve for these matrices, we note that each of the T matrices contains 12 element values. If we have 6 *reference points*, whose three-dimensional coordinates are known, visible in each photograph, then we can use the relationships shown in Equations (4.1), (4.4), and (4.5) to construct a system of 12 equations with the 12 unknowns corresponding to the elements of the T matrix. In this case, the known values are the three-dimensional x, y, and z values and the measured two-dimensional x_m and y_m values of the six reference points.

Since we are dealing with a homogeneous system, the matrix T will include an arbitrary scale factor; we are free to set one of the unknown $T_{i,j}$ values to any nonzero value. If we set $T_{43} = 1$, then the system described above becomes one with 12 equations of only 11 unknowns. We can solve this overdetermined system in the same way that we did for Equation (4.8).

Since we get two equations for every reference point, we really need only $5\frac{1}{2}$ reference points to construct the required 11 equations in the 11 unknown T matrix values. On the other hand, if we happen to have more than six reference points, we can certainly include them in the construction of the overdetermined system of equations.

Implementation

For this method, orthogonal views are not required. We are free to place the two cameras so that each sees as many points of the face as possible.

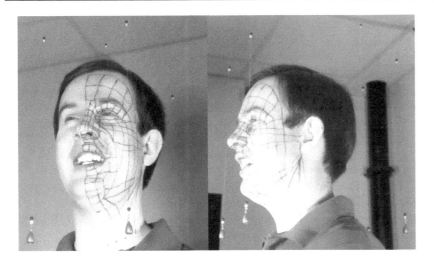

Figure 4.9.
Example photograph pair for the better photogrammetric method [Parke 74].

In fact, this method can be easily extended to more than two cameras. Thus the occlusion problem may be minimized. However, as the camera positions approach each other, the accuracy of the method suffers. The cameras should not be placed close to each other.

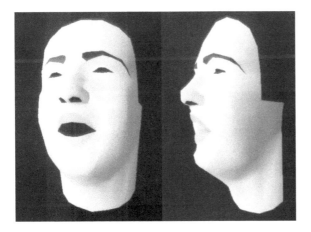

Figure 4.10.
Results from the better photogrammetric method [Parke 74].

This method can also be extended by the use of strategically placed mirrors in the photographed scene. Mirrors, in effect, allow multiple views to be captured within a single photograph. Mirrors can also be used to minimize point occlusions.

One requirement is that we must know the T transformation matrix for each photograph, which generally means including within each photograph at least six reference points whose three-dimensional positions are known.

Figure 4.9 shows an example pair of photographs for this method. The suspended beads act as the reference points. Figure 4.10 shows two views of the resulting measured facial surface.

If the camera position, the three-dimensional face coordinate system, and the two-dimensional photograph coordinate system are all held constant for a series of facial pose photographs, we only need to solve for the T matrices once for the entire series.

4.7   Modeling Based on Laser Scans

Laser-based scanners, such as those produced by Cyberware^{TM}, measure an object by moving a scanning apparatus in a circular path around the object [Cyberware Laboratory Inc. 90]. This action produces a large regular mesh of measured surface values in a cylindrical coordinate system. This mesh typically consists of 512 vertical scan columns, each with 512 measured surface points. Each mesh entry is a range or radius value, indexed by azimuth angle and height.

Figure 4.11.
Scanned surface range data [Waters and Terzopoulos 91].

Figure 4.12.
Scanned surface color data [Waters and Terzopoulos 91].

Figure 4.11 shows a shaded three-dimensional terrain surface based on the range data from such a cylindrical scan. The surface variation at each point is based on the measured range values. The vertical dimension of the image corresponds to height, while the horizontal dimension corresponds to azimuth angle. These cylindrical coordinate data usually are transformed into Cartesian coordinates for use in facial models.

The scanner may simultaneously measure surface color, producing an image of the surface such as that shown in Figure 4.12. This color data set has the same resolution as the range data mesh and is registered point for point with the range data.

4.7.1   Missing Data

One of the problems with laser-based range data is missing data points. For various reasons, the reflected laser beam may be obscured or dispersed so that the sensors see no range or color data for some surface points. Missing points commonly occur on the underside of the chin, in the nostril area, in the pupils of the eyes, and in areas with hair.

To make smooth shading and texture mapping possible, it is necessary to *fill in* the missing range and color data. At least two different approaches have been described for filling in this data.

Lee et al. [Lee et al. 95] used a relaxation membrane interpolation method described in [Terzopoulos 88] to fill in the missing data. Relaxation interpolation creates successively better approximations for the missing data by iteratively using nearest neighbor values. This procedure is analogous to stretching an elastic membrane over the gaps in the surface. This approach also is used to fill in missing color values.

Williams points out that processing digitized range surface data is very similar to processing images [Williams 90b]. Williams suggests restoring surface continuity as follows:

1. The range data mesh is converted to a floating point array with the missing values set to 0.0.

2. A second *matte* array is created and set to 1.0, where valid range data exist, and to 0.0 where gaps exist.

3. In the regions around 0.0 matte values, a small blurring filter kernel is applied to both the matte data and the surface data.

4. Where the blurred matte value increases above a threshold value, the surface sample is replaced by the blurred surface value divided by the blurred matte value.

5. This filtering is recursively applied until no matte values are below the threshold.

The missing data points are thus replaced by smooth neighborhood estimates that gradually grow together. This same approach also can be used to fill in missing color values. This technique reportedly works well for small regions of missing data. It is not expected to work well for missing data regions larger than the filter kernel used.

The scheme may be implemented so that the replacement regions slowly grow outward, smoothing valid data at the missing data boundaries. The matte threshold, region growth, and blur kernel can be varied for different results.

4.7.2 Surface Smoothing

The surface data from laser scanners tends to be noisy. It is often desirable to apply some data smoothing, to suppress noise that could result in spurious surface detail. Williams suggests smoothing the data using a *Turky* or hysteresis blur filter [Williams 90b]. A smooth estimate of the surface at a point is computed using a three-by-three blur kernel with unity gain and a center sample coefficient of 0.0. If the computed estimate differs from the center sample by greater than a threshold amount, the center sample is replaced by the estimate. Williams reports that this filtering process smoothed out a number of spurious surface details.

Filtering the Normals

Surface normals are extremely sensitive to surface perturbations. Williams suggests that the usual methods of computing surface normals for polygon meshes are too local for the noisy, closely spaced data we get from laser

scans [Williams 90b]. It is reasonable to smooth such local normal estimates, or to use normals of a surface somewhat smoother than the one
actually displayed. In this way, satisfactory normal-based shading can be
achieved without smoothing away surface features.

4.7.3   Polar Artifacts

These scanners work in a cylindrical coordinate system, while the head is
roughly spherical. This results in a number of data problems near the top
of the head. The scanned data samples become increasingly sparse near the
top of the head, and the surface is poorly resolved in this region. Because
of the scanning geometry, data near the top of the head are less accurate
and more prone to error.

When filtering is applied to the cylindrical range data mesh, artifacts
may occur near the poles, where sampling errors are greatest. Because sample spacing is far from uniform near the poles, filtering is very anisotropic
in these regions.

One common way to work around these pole-related problems is to ignore
the scanned data near the pole and substitute a separately created *scalp
mesh* that does not suffer from these problems.

4.7.4   Scanned Data Versus Desired Topologies

The scanner produces a large amount of data with constant height and
azimuth spatial resolution. These data are inefficient in terms of capturing
the surface shape. There is usually more data than are needed in some
areas, and perhaps fewer data than are really needed in others. In most
cases, we will want to reduce the data set to a more manageable size.

The data can be automatically *thinned* based on surface curvature. This
reduction is done by throwing away data points in areas of lower surface
curvature or in areas where the surface curvature is below a given threshold
value. This process will generally replace the regular data mesh with an
arbitrarily connected polygon network.

Another approach is to lowpass filter the range data, eliminating higher
spatial frequency information, and then resample the filtered data using a
data mesh with fewer points.

The data points of the scans are not tied to specific facial features and
can shift from one scan to the next. It is difficult to reconcile data obtained
in one scanning pass with data obtained in another scanning pass. We
usually want to use a specific facial surface topology. The scanned data are
not correlated to any specific facial topology.

Interactively Fitting a Topology

To be useful, the data need to be matched to the desired facial topology. One approach is to interactively associate each vertex of a polygon topology with the appropriate corresponding point in the scanned data mesh. For example, we want the polygons forming the lips to be fitted to the scanned data points for the lips.

This procedure might be done by loosely overlaying the desired vertex topology on the scanned data and then scaling, rotating and sliding the entire polygon set around to achieve an approximate match with the scanned data. Each vertex would then be individually adjusted to align with its corresponding data point.

This interactive vertex matching could be done using the range data, or it could be done using the surface color data. It could even be done using both data sets simultaneously. Remember that there is an one-to-one correspondence between the range data mesh and the surface color mesh. To help identify facial features, we might apply an edge-enhancing image filter to the color data or a Laplacian filter to the range data [Lee et al. 93].

The Laplacian filter could be implemented using finite differences of the range data. The Laplacian $l_{i,j}$ at each data point is

$$l_{i,j} = l_{ij}^x + l_{ij}^y,$$

where

$$l_{ij}^x = P(r_{i-1,j} - 2r_{i,j} + r_{i+1,j}),$$

$$l_{ij}^y = P(r_{i,j-1} - 2r_{i,j} + r_{i,j+1}).$$

Here, l^x and l^y are the positive second derivatives of range in the x and y directions, respectively. So, $P(x) = x$ if x is greater than zero and is zero otherwise. These equations assume that the discrete step size is one.

Face Topology Adaptation

Lee et al. propose fitting an adaptive canonical facial polygon network to scanned data using largely automatic techniques [Lee et al. 93, Lee et al. 95]. The canonical network used is designed to provide an efficient surface triangulation with many small triangles in areas of high curvature or high surface articulation and with fewer larger triangles in other areas.

This topology is fitted to the scanned data using the multistep procedure outlined below.

1. Locate the highest range data point within the central region of the face. Globally translate the canonical face network so that the tip of the nose corresponds to this highest point.

2. Locate the chin as the point below the nose with the largest positive range Laplacian.

3. Locate the mouth as the point between the nose and the chin with the highest positive Laplacian.

4. Rescale all vertex positions below the nose based on these located points.

5. Locate the chin *contour* as those vertices lying between the latitude of the nose and the latitude of the chin. Rescale all vertices below the chin contour.

6. Locate the ears as those points near the sides of the head and near the latitude of the nose with Laplacian values greater than a threshold value.

7. Rescale all vertices horizontally to match the ear locations.

8. Locate the eyes as those points with the greatest Laplacian values in the estimated eyes region.

9. Rescale all vertices above the nose to match the located eyes.

In the canonical face network, each vertex pair is connected by a modeled spring. These springs provide forces that are designed to keep the vertices optimally distributed across the surface. Once the network is rescaled as described above, these spring forces are activated. The spring forces adaptively adjust the new network, attempting to minimize network distortions based on the vertex spacing in the original canonical network. The located feature points identified in the steps above are treated as immobile boundary conditions for the adaptation process.

In some cases it may be necessary to interactively adjust some vertex positions after the adaptation step. This adjustment is particularly appropriate for points defining important facial features.

Note that the automated process described above assumes that the facial expression in the scanned data matches the facial expression of the canonical network. Lee et al. discuss extensions to this approach that may be used when the expressions do not match [Lee et al. 93].

Adaptive Meshes

Creating a rectangular mesh model for the entire head from the scanned data is straightforward. A relatively low-density mesh could in effect be overlaid on the scanned data by simply using every tenth data point in azimuth and elevation to form the polygon mesh. However, this mesh completely ignores the distribution of head and facial features. We really want to concentrate

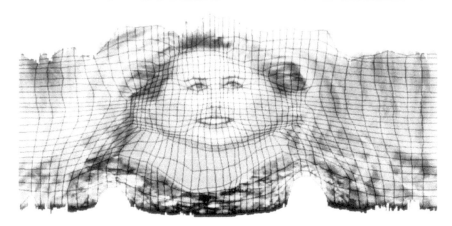

Figure 4.13.
An adapted mesh overlaid on its surface color data [Waters and Terzopoulos 91].

polygons in areas with articulated features, such as the eyes and mouth, and in areas of high surface curvature.

Terzopoulos and Waters describe an approach using *active* meshes to adapt the polygon mesh to the head and facial features [Terzopoulous and Waters 91]. Active meshes adapt to features of interest, increasing vertex and polygon density in those areas. Active meshes include the notion of springs that connect each node to its eight nearest neighbors. As a node is moved, these springs create forces that influence its neighboring points. These points in turn influence their neighbors, and so on. When a point is moved, a new equilibrium configuration for the entire mesh is computed by iteratively simulating the node and spring dynamics.

In adaptive meshes, the mesh nodes or vertices automatically distribute themselves over the data. Each node acts as an *observer* of the data near its location and modifies its spring coefficients, based on what it observes. These spring value changes require computing a new equilibrium configuration for the mesh. From these new positions, the nodes again consider the data near their locations and adjust their spring coefficients accordingly. This process is repeated until the equilibrium configuration becomes stable. Figure 4.13 shows an adapted mesh overlaid on scanned color data.

If the node observations and spring value adjustments are appropriately related to the facial features of interest, the stable adapted mesh will be optimal for representing these features. The observations are typically based on range gradients and feature edge information extracted from the color data. The spring values are adjusted so that the nodes migrate toward features of interest. See [Terzopoulous and Waters 91] or [Waters and Terzopoulos 91] for details.

4.8 Anthropometric Facial Models

Physical anthropologists have developed systems to measure and characterize various aspects of humans, including heads and faces. These include standardized landmarks and measurements and indices for the skull [Steele and Bramblett 88]. Similarly, standardized landmarks, measurements, and indices have been developed for the face [Farkas 94].

These landmarks are specific, consistently identifiable feature locations on the face or skull. Standardized measurements are usually the locations of these landmarks relative to some reference point or plane, or distances between landmark positions. These distances may be straight line distances as measured with calipers or may be distances measured along various curved surfaces of the face or skull. The indices are typically ratios of measured distances.

Using these systems, measured data from various human populations has been collected and analyzed. The measured data for one individual usually varies from the data for another individual. However, data from specific age, gender, or ethnic groups has been collected and analyzed to find average values and ranges of variation for these measures within and between groups.

Computer facial models can be built using the anthropometric measurement schemes and the collected data. DeCarlo et al. have reported a facial model that fits a b-spline surface to the various anthropometric landmark features of the face [DeCarlo et al. 98]. By varying the landmark locations, different facial surfaces are created. Attention to the range of variation within the landmark data and the relationships among the measurements ensures that the created faces are plausible.

Kähler, et al. have reported a model that uses skull measurements and tissue thickness data [Phillips and Smuts 96] to reconstruct facial surfaces [Kähler et al. 03]. In this approach, the underlying skull data is either measured from a real skull or derived from statistical data characterizing skulls. From this data, the shape of the skull can be approximated. Then, at specific landmark positions, statistical tissue thickness data is used to create of set of skin surface locations. The final faces are created by deforming a generic head model to match the landmark skin locations. These approaches are analogous to the work of forensic artists who reconstruct faces from real skulls.

4.9 Sculpting Facial Models

As an alternative to measuring facial surfaces or using anthropometric data, models may be created using operations analogous to those used by sculptors. These methods include assembling sculptures from various component parts and iteratively modifying sculpted surface shapes.

The steady advance in computer processing power and ever more capable graphic processors have enabled the development of very powerful interactive 3D modeling packages such as Maya^{TM} and 3D Studio^{TM}. These packages provide a wide spectrum of tools for designing and manipulating 3D objects and surfaces of all kinds, including representations of faces.

Many, if not most, of the face models currently used in 3D character animation are created using these kinds of systems. These models rely on the skill and creativity of the modeler to sculpt the required face model. This process may be guided by facial anatomy, data scans, or anthropometric data, but it is usually fundamentally driven by aesthetic concerns and creative decisions. Fidelity to real faces may be, but is not usually, of great concern.

Interactive surface editors allow the face modeler to create and modify polygon or subdivision surfaces by interactively manipulating vertex positions, or to create spline surfaces by interactively manipulating surface control points. See [Osipa 03] for discussion of one approach to interactively sculpting and animating face models.

Stereo display. While not widely used, stereo display techniques can be a useful part of such systems. These techniques allow true three-dimensional perception of the surface shapes as they are modified. Stereo display techniques present slightly different views of the surface to each eye. These views correspond to what each eye would see if the surface were a real three-dimensional object. Each eye sees only its view, through the use of various optical techniques such as color filters, polarizing filters, or electro-optical shutters.

4.9.1   Successive Refinement

A common approach is to start with a basic surface shape such as a block or ellipsoid. Then, using polygon surface operations such as dividing polygons, extruding polygons, adding or deleting vertices, beveling edges, cutting holes, etc., the basic shape is iteratively transformed into the desired facial structure. Analogous operations may be used for iteratively refining spline surfaces.

A very early example of this successive refinement approach was described by Elson and is shown in Figure 4.14 [Elson 90]. He describes a successive refinement approach to surface sculpting using interactive modeling tools and techniques based on manipulating winged-edge polyhedral structures and the spatial displacement of the polyhedra vertices. These surface sculpting operations include tools for cutting surfaces into smaller pieces, forming extrusions, and pulling points to locally deform the surface.

For this example, the head began as a cube. Cutting operations were used to rough out the overall shape of the head. Extrusions and local

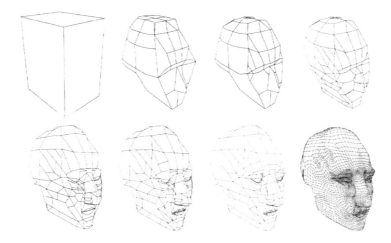

Figure 4.14.
Sculpting a head from a cube. (Adapted from [ELS90].)

surface deformations were used to add features and feature detail. Finally, a *beveling* operation replaced existing edges or vertices with new polygons. This operation was used iteratively, obtaining higher polygon density and smoother surface curvature on each iteration.

4.9.2   Shapes Based on Intensity Painting

Williams describes the use of methods normally associated with digital paint systems to interactively create three-dimensional surfaces [Williams 90a]. The key idea here is to interpret a painted two-dimensional image as a three-dimensional surface, where intensity at each pixel is used as the z depth of the surface at that point. In effect, the intensities of the two-dimensional painting are interpreted as a surface relief map.

The two-dimensional painted images are usually grayscale images. Each grayscale value corresponds to a surface depth value. These images could be initially based on scanned images, such as photographs, and then interactively manipulated to achieve the desired results.

A key aspect of Williams' approach was to provide an interactive three-dimensional view of the painted surface, in addition to the standard two-dimensional view of the intensity image. On current graphics workstations this interactive three-dimensional view could be created in a second screen window using graphics primitives such as vectors or polygons to represent the derived three-dimensional surface.

This approach is limited to single-valued surfaces. It is not possible, for example, to create a single surface to model the entire head using this technique. This limitation may be overcome by painting one surface for the front of the head and another surface for the back of the head. Stitching these two surfaces together forms the complete head.

4.10 Conformation Guidelines

The following facial shape and conformation guidelines, based on work by Kunz [Kunz 89], Halton [Halton 65], and Hogarth [Hogarth 81], are useful in the design of face models. These guidelines are generalizations. Considerable variations occur from one individual face to the next.

Overall Shape and Proportion

- The skull and jaw fit into an egglike shape.

- From the side, the major axis of this egg shape is tilted, with the chin fitting into the narrow bottom. The shape widens at the top to fit the back of the skull.

- The eyes are located halfway between the top of the head and the bottom of the chin.

- The eyes are set back from the front of the face, nested into the eye sockets. The eyes are protected by the front part of the forehead, the cheekbones, and the inner side of the nose.

- The eyes are about one eye's width apart.

- The bottom of the nose is halfway between the eyebrows and the chin.

- The mouth is located one-third of the way from the bottom of the nose to the bottom of the chin.

- The tops of the ears are approximately even with the eyebrows, and the bottoms of the ears are about even with the bottom of the nose.

- The ears are located just behind the midline between the front and back of the skull.

- Lines between the outer corners of the eyes and the tip of the nose form a right angle.

The Eyes and Eyelids

- The eyeball is essentially a sphere. The upper eyelid slides up and down over the eyeball sphere. The lower lid moves very little. The upper eyelid is thicker than the lower.

- The highest point of the upper eyelid is shifted toward the nose. The lowest point of the lower eyelid is shifted away from the nose. The lower lid joins the upper lid at nearly a right angle at the outer corner.

- The eyelids are separated by a pink membrane at the inner corner. At the outer corner, the eyelids come directly together and the upper lid hangs slightly over the lower one.

- The upper eyelid follows the form of the eyeball much more closely than does the lower lid. The edges of both lids are thickened and have a square cross-section. When they close, the two flat surfaces meet. The eyelashes project from the front edges of these flat surfaces. The upper lashes are generally longer and thicker than the lower lashes.

- The lower eyelid is seldom lower than halfway between the eyebrow and the top of the wing of the nose.

The Nose

- The nose is a long wedge-shaped form attached to the forehead with a smaller wedge-shaped form. The nose is thinnest where these two wedges meet and becomes wider toward its bottom.

- Between the eyes, the nose has a concave profile curve between the brow and the narrowest part of the nose. The sides of the nose are steepest here.

- The bottom of the nose is formed by five pieces of cartilage; two form the nostrils, a third separates them, and the remaining two form the tip of the nose. This cartilage allows the lower part of the nose to flex and take on slightly different shapes for various facial expressions.

- The tip of the nose usually slants upward, whereas the nostrils slant down.

- Viewed from below, the nostrils slant towards each other at the tip of the nose.

The Mouth and Lips

- The mouth is the most flexible of the facial features. The upper lip is longer and thinner than the lower lip.

- The upper lip extends out over the lower lip. The upper lip is flatter and more angular. The bottom lip is fuller and rounder. Under the bottom lip there is often a slight indentation.

- The upper lip has three sections; the lower lip has two sections. The center upper lip is directly under the nose; the highest points are close to the center. The lowest points of the lower lip are farther to the sides.

- The shapes of the mouth and lips are influenced by the teeth and the curved shape of the dental arch. A smile or laugh shows the upper teeth clearly. As the corners of the mouth are pulled back, they form a small depression where they meet the cheeks.

The Ears

- Ears are unique to each person and should be modeled with the same care as the rest of the features. The ear has a fleshy lobe at the bottom, but is structured with cartilage elsewhere. The curves and whorls in the center of the ear account for most of the individual differences.

- The ear is somewhat saucer-shaped at its perimeter. The central portion is shaped more like a bowl.

- The ears tend to run parallel to the plane of the side of the head. The outer rim of the ear is curved to catch sound waves.

- From the side, the ear usually slants at the same angle as the nose.

Male versus Female

- Dimensions of male and female heads are essentially the same. However, the angle of the jaw is much less pronounced in women. The distance across the jaw at the throat and the distances from cheekbone to cheekbone and from zygoma to zygoma are less for women. The cheekbones are less prominent and farther behind the chin, and the chin is more pointed in women.

- The head of a man is squared, and its parts project more definitely. The forehead is higher; the zygoma, cheek, and chin bones are more prominent; and the angle of the jaw is squarer and more pronounced. The front of the face at the mouth is flatter.

- In men, the lower third of the face frequently appears longer than the center third of the face.

- In women, the distance from the corner of the eye to the front of the ear is the same as the distance from the corner of the eye to the corner of the mouth. For men, the ear is a little farther back.

- In men, the width across the wings of the nose is equal to or greater than the width of the eye. In women, it is slightly less.

- The mouth is larger in men than women. The indentation under the lower lip is more noticeable in men.

- The height of the brows above the eyes varies considerably. It is mainly in women that the space between eye and brow is of any extent. In men, it is often hidden by the overhanging brow.

- The nose is narrower and the nostrils are more pinched-looking for women. The nostrils often have a dilated appearance in men.

Children

- The overall proportions of the face and the ratio of the face to the rest of the head change dramatically from birth to maturity (at about 15 years of age). At birth, the face takes up a relatively small part of the head; the ratio of facial mass to cranial mass is about 1 to 3.5. The change in this ratio is most rapid in the early years of childhood. By the age of one, the ratio has become 1 to 3; by the age of four, the ratio has become 1 to 2.5. At maturity, the face makes up a much larger portion of the head; the ratio of facial mass to cranial mass is reduced to about 1 to 2.

- Rounded cheeks and smoothness between the brows suggest youth.

- The width across the wings of the nose is even less in children than in women.

- Noses in children are shorter and softer in appearance than in adults. The mouth is also smaller in children.

4.11   Assembling Faces from Simple Shapes

Not all facial models need to be complex, nor do they have to accurately resemble human faces. Sometimes a simple stylized character is better than a complex realistic one. It may be easier to stylize or caricature using simple facial models than with complex models.

Simple facial features can make the face easier to model, easier to animate, and even easier to render. The ways in which simple faces animate are not necessarily determined by the rules of real faces. However, like realistic models, these simple models must be capable of effectively expressing human emotions.

Simple face models can be assembled from basic shapes and can make use of simple control mechanisms. A wonderful example of a character created by assembling simple shapes is Tinny, from the film *Tin Toy* [Pixar 88], shown in Figure 4.15.

Figure 4.15.
Tinny from *Tin Toy.* (*Copyright 1988 Pixar.*)

4.11.1   Simple Facial Shapes

The component shapes can be quite varied and may include basic geometric shapes such as spheres, cylinders, and cones. Other simple shapes might be constructed from simple parametric surface meshes.

Reeves describes what he calls the *bound* shape [Reeves 90]. This shape's outside perimeter is defined by eight points that lie on the surface of a defining sphere and by a central point whose position is the centroid of the eight perimeter points but is offset from the sphere by a given amount. Four bicubic patches are fit to these data to form the bound's surface.

Each defining bound point is defined by its spherical latitude and longitude. The bound also uses four tangent parameters that control how the surface of the bound lifts off the defining sphere.

Constructive solid geometry (CSG) operations may be used with bounds to form facial features. The mouth could be a bound that is sunk into the head using the *difference* operator. The difference operator subtracts the mouth cavity formed by the bound from the head sphere.

The character's eyes might be constructed using overlaying partial spheres or overlaying bounds. The white of the eye might be a bulge on the head defined by a bound. The iris, pupil, and eyelid could also be bounds, but ones which lie just above the surface of the eye.

Reeves also described a simpler shape called a *patchedge* that can be used to form eyes, mouths, and other facial features [Reeves 90]. A patchedge is a single bicubic patch defined by the 16 points arranged in a four-by-four array, as shown in Figure 4.16(a). Patchedge features are animated by controlling the edge control points.

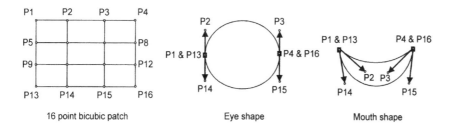

Figure 4.16.
The patchedge structure. (Adapted from [Reeves 90].)

The four left edge points $P1, P5, P9,$ and $P13$ are constrained to be the same point, and the four right edge points $P4, P8, P12,$ and $P16$ are constrained to be another single point. The interior patch points are derived as weighted sums of the edge points. By controlling the tangents formed by the two top edge midpoints $P2$ and $P3$ and the two bottom edge midpoints $P14$ and $P15$, many different shapes can be formed, as shown in Figure 4.16 (middle) and (right). With patchedges, the eye pupils might just be small disks, displaced a small distance above the surface of the iris. Eyelids might be independently animated patchedges, positioned above the eyes, that could close over the eyes or open to reveal them.

Language-Based Modeling

Reeves also points out that the assembly and manipulation of model components can be specified through the use of a modeling language [Reeves 90]. With this approach, the model is actually a program in a special language. Graphic primitives (such as spheres, cones, bounds, patches, and polygons) and operators (such as translate, rotate, and scale) are functions built into the language. The model program is executed to determine the positions and orientations of the graphical objects in the model.

Variables in such a language could include normal variables, which take on assigned values until new values are assigned, and *articulated* variables, which have values associated with keyframes. These articulated values are interpolated between the keyframes using various functions. For an animated model, the program is executed once for each frame time. Changing the model variable values for each frame creates the desired sequence of model postures.

As an example, the model might be a spherical head with simple features. The head could nod back and forth and twist from side to side based on the articulated variables head_{nod} and $\text{head}_{\text{twist}}$. The nose, a small sphere positioned on the head, could be moved around on the surface of the head using additional articulated variables. The two eyes could be positioned anywhere on the head with appropriate articulation variables. The pupils of the eyes, which float just above the surface of the eyeballs, could be articulated with variables that control where the eyes are looking.

4.12   New Faces from Existing Faces

Several approaches have been proposed for creating new faces based on existing faces. These processes include interpolating between existing faces, applying deformations to existing faces, and transforming a canonical face into the faces of specific individuals.

4.12.1   Interpolation for Modeling

Interpolation may be used to specify new faces or face components from previously defined faces. The notion of interpolation is quite simple. In the one-dimensional case, we are given two values and asked to determine an intermediate value. The desired intermediate value is specified by a fractional coefficient α:

$$\text{value} = \alpha(\text{value}_1) + (1.0 - \alpha)(\text{value}_2), \qquad 0.0 < \alpha < 1.0.$$

This basic concept is easily expanded into more than one dimension by simply applying this procedure in each dimension. The idea generalizes to polygonal surfaces by applying the scheme to each vertex defining the surface. Each vertex will have two three-dimensional positions associated with it. Intermediate forms of the surface are achieved by interpolating each vertex between its extreme positions.

Fixed Topology

In the simplest case, the polygonal facial topology must be the same for each face being interpolated. The number of vertices defining the surface and their interconnections must be identical for all faces. If the facial topology is fixed, creating a new face involves just interpolating the vertex positions. Figure 4.17 illustrates the interpolated blending of one face with another.

For this approach to work, a *single* sufficiently flexible topology must be developed that allows representation of a wide range of individual faces. Using such a topology, Parke used the photogrammetric technique described in Section 4.6.2 to collect data for ten different faces [Parke 74]. The topology used was first applied to the plastic head model shown in Figure 4.18. This marked plastic head model served as a storage device for the topology. It was used as a guide each time the topology was applied to a real face, which assured that the topology would be identical from face to face.

Figure 4.17.
Facial interpolation. The center face is an interpolated blend of the left and
right faces.

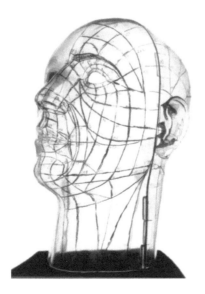

Figure 4.18.
Flexible facial topology storage device.

The data from these ten faces were used to create an animated film showing interpolated transitions from face to face. This film demonstrated that, at least for the faces used, a single topology could allow representation of different faces and would support reasonable interpolated transitions between the faces.

The general interpolation approach can be extended to parametric surfaces. The interpolation would be applied to the control points. Again in the simplest case, the faces being interpolated would have the same surface construction: the same type of surface, the same number of patches, and the same number of control points.

Variable Topology

How do we interpolate between faces if the faces do not have the same topology? The obvious method is to simply add or delete polygons and vertices from one or more of the faces until they have the same topology. However, algorithms to do this for arbitrary polygon networks are not obvious.

Another approach is to convert the arbitrary topology of each face into an $m \times n$ rectangular grid topology [Magnenat-Thalmann et al. 89]. Then interpolate between these grids. Note that in this approach the grid for one face is not required to be the same size as the grid for the next face.

If the grids are not the same size, a corresponding point in the smaller array is determined for each point in the larger array. The implication is that some points in the smaller grid will correspond to more than one point in the larger grid.

Conversion of the arbitrary polygon network into the desired regular grid is done by *resampling* the polygon surface in a specific way. Each of the n columns in the constructed grid surface corresponds to a face *profile* curve created by the intersection of a *slicing* plane with the original polygon network. The m points in each profile column are determined by resampling its profile curve. The number of points, m, in each column is determined by the length of the maximum length profile curve.

4.12.2   *n*-Dimensional Face Spaces

The notion of using interpolation as a way to create new faces can be extended into n-dimensional face spaces. If you have two faces and one interpolation parameter, you can create new faces between the two original faces. If you have four faces and two interpolation parameters, you can then create faces in a two-dimensional face space bounded by the four original faces. Each new face specified by values for each of the two interpolation parameters. If you have eight original faces and three interpolation parameters, a three-dimensional face space is formed. Similarly for 16 original faces and four interpolation parameters, and so on. In theory, arbitrary dimensional face spaces can be formed if enough original faces are available. In practice, forming a specific new face within the face space is challenging and depends on being able to pick the appropriate interpolation values to get the face you want. The range of possible new faces is constrained by the original set of faces. Another way to approach the creation of an n-dimensional *face space* is presented in Section 4.13.

4.12.3   Transforming Canonical Faces

Essentially all human faces have the same basic structure and are similar in shape. This allows the construction of a *canonical* face model. Kurihara and Arai describe a technique for creating specific faces from a single canonical model [Kurihara and Arai 91]. Modeling specific faces consists of transforming the canonical facial model into the desired individual facial model.

The Transformation Method

The canonical facial model shown in Figure 4.19(a) is defined with about 3000 polygons, which were obtained by digitizing a mannequin with a laser scanner. The transformation of this model is defined by a displacement vector for each polygon vertex. Rather than specifying the explicit displacement of each vertex, control points C_j are selected from the vertices. The desired transformations are expressed by displacing these control points.

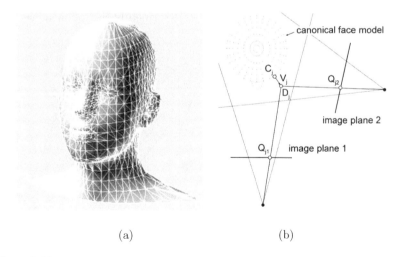

(a)   (b)

Figure 4.19.
(a) The canonical model. (*Courtesy T. Kurihara.*) (b) Determining the destination points. (Adapted from [Kurihara and Arai 91].)

The displacements of the remaining vertices are determined by interpolation of the control-point displacements.

The displacement at each control point is expressed as a three-dimensional vector V_j, which describes the spatial difference between the desired transformed position D_j of the control point and its position C_j in the canonical face, as shown in Figure 4.19(b). The interpolation of these displacement vectors is simplified by projecting the facial surface points into a two-dimensional cylindrical parameter space. A point $P(x, y, z)$ is mapped into $P_s(\theta, H)$ where

$$P_s(\theta, H) = (\tan^{-1}(z/x), y).$$

The two-dimensional θ, H parameter space is triangulated by the control points using Delaunay triangulation [Sibson 78], as shown in Figure 4.20(a). The displacement vector for a given point is based on interpolating the vectors of its three surrounding control points, as shown in Figure 4.20(b).

A total of 58 control points are used for transforming the canonical face. These control points are vertices that are important in specifying the overall shape of the face and the shape and location of facial features such as the eyebrows, the corners of the eyes, and the mouth. Eighteen of these points are manipulated interactively to control facial expression.

The remaining 40 points are used to determine the shape of the face and the shape and placement of the facial features. These points are computed based on photographic measurements, as described in the following section.

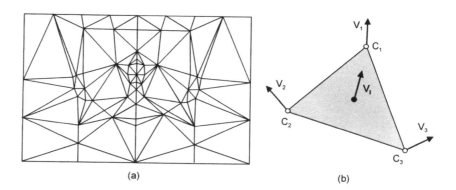

Figure 4.20.
(a) Control-point triangulation. (b) Control-point interpolation. (Adapted from [Kurihara and Arai 91].)

Photographic Transformation Control

While the control points used to create new faces might be interactively manipulated, the creation of a specific facial model can be based on photographs.

The three-dimensional destination points D_j for the C_j control points may be determined from their measured two-dimensional Q_{jk} positions in at least two photographic views of the specific face, as shown in Figure 4.19(b), where the k subscript indicates which photograph. There are no restrictions on camera position and orientation, as long as all the destination points D_j are seen in each view. The D_j positions are determined using the same photogrammetric techniques discussed in Section 4.6.2.

Texture

The canonical model approach discussed in this section depends on texture mapping to supply facial feature details. The texture map is constructed from four photographs of the individual face and head. These photographs are the front, right, left, and back views of the head, as shown in Figure 4.21.

A complete cylindrical texture map, similar to those obtained with a laser scanner (see Section 4.7), is constructed by compositing the information from the four photographs. Each photograph is mapped onto its specific transformed face model and is then projected into cylindrical texture coordinates.

The composited texture, shown in Figure 4.22, is the weighted average of all the projected textures. The weighting function used is based on the *positional certainty* at each surface point. This positional certainty, in turn, is based on the inner product of the surface normal vector and the viewing vector at each point. The weighting function is zero where the positional uncertainty is below a certain threshold value.

Figure 4.21.
Texture source photographs. (*Courtesy of T. Kurihara.*)

Figure 4.22.
Composited texture map. (*Courtesy of T. Kurihara.*)

4.12.4   Growth Transformations

Todd et al proposed that the shape change of the human head as it grows from infancy to adulthood can be modeled using a relatively simple geometric transformation [Todd et al. 80]. The reported work deals only with two-dimensional head profiles. Experimentally, the best growth transformation, referred to as the *revised cardioidal strain transformation*, was specified as

$$R' = R(1 + k(1 - \cos\theta)),$$

$$\theta' = \theta,$$

in polar coordinates. In Cartesian coordinates, R and θ are defined as

$$R = \sqrt{x^2 + z^2},$$

$$\theta = \tan^{-1} x/z,$$

where z is toward the top of the head and x is toward the front of the face. The origin is at the center of the head, and θ is zero at the top of the head. Here, k is a coefficient related to age. The value of k is zero for the infant profile and is increased to generate successively older profiles. Figure 4.23(a) shows the effect of this transformation.

Todd [Todd 80] later indicated that the two-dimensional growth transformation could be extended into three-dimensional spherical coordinates as

$$R' = R(1 + k(1 - \cos\theta)),$$

$$\theta' = \theta,$$

$$\phi' = \phi,$$

where R is the radius, θ is the elevation angle, and ϕ is the azimuth angle. Figure 4.23(b) shows the effect of a three-dimensional growth transformation.

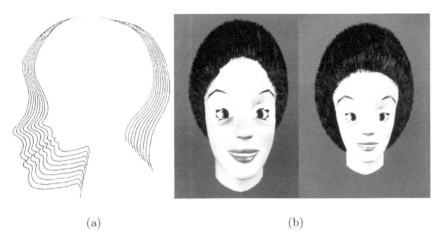

(a)   (b)

Figure 4.23.
Growth transformation. (a) Effect of the two-dimensional transformation.
(Adapted from [Todd et al. 80].) (b) Effect of the three-dimensional
transformation: a mature face and a younger face.

4.12.5   Local Deformations

Local deformations are another way to obtain new faces from existing faces.
A local deformation is a transformation applied to only a portion of an
object, rather than to the entire object. Applying a local deformation requires selecting the region of the object to be transformed and specifying
the transformation to be used.

Magnenat-Thalmann et al. describe five ways of selecting the deformation region of a polygonal model and four transformation methods
[Magnenat-Thalmann et al. 89]. The five selection schemes proposed are
as follows:

- selecting specific vertex numbers,

- selecting vertices within a bounding box,

- selecting vertices within a cylindrical slice,

- selecting vertices with a specific color value, and

- selecting vertices that satisfy set operations between regions specified
  using one or more of the four previous methods.

The four proposed transformation methods are as follows:

- *Percentage to a vertex*—each selected vertex is moved toward a reference point a percentage of the distance between the vertex and the
  reference point.

- *Guided translation*—a translation vector is computed between a point A and a point B, and a specified percentage of this translation vector is applied to all selected vertices.

- *Scaling to a plane*—a scaling is applied to each selected vertex; the magnitude of the scaling is proportional to the distance between each vertex and a specified plane.

- *Variable translation*—a variation factor is used to control transformation within a selected region. If the variation factor is zero, all selected vertices will be transformed in the same way. If the variation factor is 1.0, a vertex at the center of the region will be fully affected while vertices at the edge of the region will not be affected at all. The vertices are modified according to a generalized *decay function* based on position relative to the center of the region [Allan et al. 89].

DiPaola introduced local deformation based on ellipsoidal volumes and warping functions [DiPaola 91]. In this approach, ellipsoidal volumes are used to select the vertices to be transformed. The transformations used are warping or twisting functions of the form $\mathbf{f}(\mathbf{p} - \mathbf{o})$, where $(\mathbf{p} - \mathbf{o})$ is the direction vector from the origin $\mathbf{o}$ of the warping function to the vertex position $\mathbf{p}$. The warping functions that are used decay smoothly to zero, so that they have only local influence.

Each vertex is displaced by the sum of all defined warping functions that have an effect at its location. In DiPaola's system, up to 12 warping volumes

Figure 4.24.
New face created by applying ellipsoidal warping to an existing face. (*Courtesy of S. DiPaola.*)

and functions could be used. Each warping volume could be interactively positioned and scaled.

DiPaola used these warping volume deformations to create character changes such as the large asymmetric cranium and huge chin shown in Figure 4.24. These deformations could also be used to create small subtle changes, such as muscle bulges, brow furrows, and double chins.

4.12.6   Freeform Deformations

Another approach to modifying existing three-dimensional facial models is the freeform deformation (FFD) technique, developed by Sederberg and Parry [Sederberg and Parry 86]. Freeform deformation can be described through the use of a physical analogy. Think of a flexible three-dimensional model immersed in a block of clear, flexible plastic. This block of plastic can be bent or twisted into various shapes. As the plastic block is reshaped, so is the model embedded in it.

The block of plastic in our analogy corresponds to a parametric solid defined by a three-dimensional cubic lattice of control points. As the control points are manipulated, the parametric solid is deformed. As the parametric solid is deformed, so is the embedded model. The basis for the parametric solid is typically a trivariate tensor product Bernstein polynomial.

Freeform deformation is remarkably versatile. It can be applied to various geometric primitives, including polygonal, quadric, parametric, and implicit surfaces, and solid models. Freeform deformation can be applied either locally to only a portion of a model or globally to the whole model. Freeform deformations may be applied hierarchically, with each application modifying the results obtained by previous deformations. Adjoining deformations can be constrained to maintain continuity across their common boundary. Constraints also can be used to control how much the volume of a deformed object changes.

The control points for the freeform deformation described above are arranged in a regular three-dimensional cubic lattice. Coquillart describes extensions that allow alternative control-point structures, such as cylindrical lattices [Coquillart 90]. These extensions allow additional flexibility in the kinds of shape deformations possible.

4.12.7   Stochastic Noise Deformations

Lewis suggests the use of vector-valued solid noise functions to create new models from existing models. The resulting stochastic deformations can be used to create individual *natural* objects based on prototype models [Lewis 89].

Creating new faces with this method involves perturbing existing face models to get additional models that are random variations of the originals.

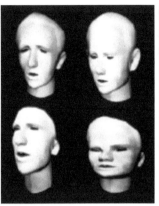

Figure 4.25.
Faces created using stochastic noise deformations: (a) mild deformations,
(b) strong deformations. (*Courtesy of J. Lewis.*)

Three independent scalar solid noise functions are used as the components
of a vector field. This field is used to alter or deform the shape of the original
face model. For polygonal models, each vertex position is perturbed, based
on the solid noise vector field.

The solid noise approach could also be applied to parametric surfaces
and to volume models. For a parametric surface, each control point would
be perturbed.

The characteristics of the solid noise functions may be varied to produce
a range of effects. The noise may be adjusted to create variations that
correspond to those normally seen from one individual face to the next. The
noise could also be adjusted to produce effects associated with caricatures,
or even completely surrealistic faces. Figure 4.25(a) shows deformations
that correspond to normal individual variations; Figure 4.25(b) shows faces
with deformations more like those associated with caricatures.

4.13   Statistical Models

Clearly, there are attributes of facial shapes that distinguish them from
other shapes. What is it that makes a shape *facial*? What is the essence of
face shapes? One approach to answering this question is to build a statistical
model for faces and use the properties of that model to describe what is a
face shape.

4.13.1   A Morphable Model

Blanz and Vetter describe such a model [Blanz and Vetter 99]. They collected laser scan data from 200 individual faces and applied statistical techniques to create a *morphable* face model. Each of the faces in their data set has a mesh of 70,000 data points. Each of these points has an X, Y, Z coordinate location and an R, G, B color value. The geometric data for each face forms a shape-vector $\mathbf{S} = (X_1, Y_1, Z_1, \ldots, X_n, Y_n, Z_n)^T$ and the color data forms a texture-vector $\mathbf{T} = (R_1, G_1, B_1, \ldots, R_n, G_n, B_n)^T$, where n is the number of data points.

If all of the face data sets correspond, that is they are feature aligned with one another, then the morphable model is formed from the shape and texture vectors of all the exemplar faces, as follows:

$$\mathbf{S}_{\mathrm{model}} = \sum_{i=1}^{m} a_i \mathbf{S}_i,$$

$$\mathbf{T}_{\mathrm{model}} = \sum_{i=1}^{m} b_i \mathbf{T}_i,$$

where

$$\sum_{i=1}^{m} a_i = \sum_{i=1}^{m} b_i = 1.0.$$

The morphable model is the set of faces $\mathbf{S}_{\mathrm{model}}(\vec{a})$, $\mathbf{T}_{\mathrm{model}}(\vec{b})$ parameterized by the coefficients $\vec{a} = (a_1, a_2, \ldots, a_m)^T$ and $\vec{b} = (b_1, b_2, \ldots, b_m)^T$. New faces can be created by varying the parameters $\vec{a}$ and $\vec{b}$.

Statistical techniques are used to control the parameter values, such that plausible faces are created. A multivariate normal distribution function is fit to the data as follows. An average shape $\bar{\mathbf{S}}$ and an average texture $\bar{\mathbf{T}}$ are computed. Then the set of difference shape vectors $\triangle \mathbf{S}_i = \mathbf{S}_i - \bar{\mathbf{S}}$ and difference texture vectors $\triangle \mathbf{T}_i = \mathbf{T}_i - \bar{\mathbf{T}}$ are computed.

Then the co-variance matrices for these two difference vector sets are computed. Principal component analysis (PCA) is then applied to the co-variance matrices. This performs a basis transformation to the orthogonal coordinate systems formed by the eigenvectors $\mathbf{s}_i$ and $\mathbf{t}_i$ of the co-variance matrices.

$$\mathbf{S}_{\mathrm{model}} = \bar{\mathbf{S}} + \sum_{i=1}^{m-1} \alpha_i \mathbf{s}_i,$$

$$\mathbf{T}_{\mathrm{model}} = \bar{\mathbf{T}} + \sum_{i=1}^{m-1} \beta_i \mathbf{t}_i.$$

The dimension of the resulting parameter space can be reduced by only including the eigenvectors with the largest eigenvalues. Since this approach is based on a multivariate normal distribution, each of the component parameters α_i and β_i has an expected distribution of values that correspond to plausible faces. There is a σ value determined from the eigenvalue of each eigenvector. Plausible faces are within a few σ of the average face in each of the face space dimensions.

Facial Attributes

Unfortunately, the eigenvector-based model coefficients α_i and β_i do not correspond to intuitive facial attributes. However, intuitive attribute vectors can be derived from the model data. These attributes might be gender, specific expressions, or facial features such as a hooked nose. For a given attribute, we can assign values μ_i to each face, based on the extent that the face exhibits the attribute. For example, assign a value of 1.0 to faces that strongly show the attribute and a value of 0.0 to faces that do not show the attribute at all. Values between 1.0 and 0.0 are assigned to faces with intermediate manifestations of the attribute. We can then compute weighted sums of the difference vectors:

$$\triangle\mathbf{S} = \sum_{i=1}^{m} \mu_i(\mathbf{S}_i - \bar{\mathbf{S}}),$$

$$\triangle\mathbf{T} = \sum_{i=1}^{m} \mu_i(\mathbf{T}_i - \bar{\mathbf{T}}).$$

Multiples of $\triangle\mathbf{S}$ and $\triangle\mathbf{T}$ can then be added to any modeled face to give it more of that attribute. Subtracting multiples of $\triangle\mathbf{S}$ and $\triangle\mathbf{T}$ will reduce that attribute in the modeled face.

Segmented Model

The morphable model can be further enhanced through the segmentation of face subregions, as illustrated in Figure 4.26. The eye, mouth, and nose areas divide the vector space into subregions, and the subsequent linear combination provide a wide variety of potential new face shapes, as illustrated in Figure 4.26.

Matching the Model to an Image

Given the morphable model parameters and a few additional variables that control camera and lighting parameters, it is possible to *fit* the model to match face images. In this process, an initial set of model parameters is selected, along with initial guesses for the camera and lighting parameter values. Using these values, an image of the model face is rendered. This

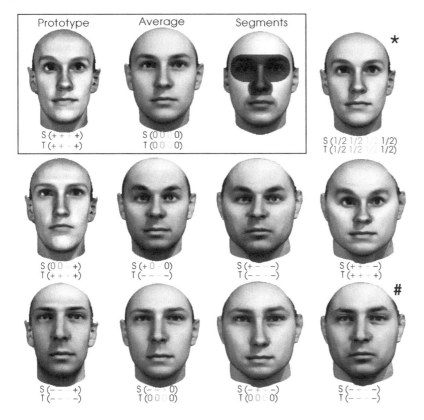

Figure 4.26.
The deviation of a prototype from the average is added $(+)$ or subtracted $(-)$ from the average. A standard morph $(*)$ is located halfway between average and the prototype. Subtracting the differences from the average yields an anti-face $(\#)$. Adding and subtracting deviations independly from shape (S) and texture (T) on each of four segments produces a number of distinct faces [Blanz and Vetter 99]. (*Courtesy of V. Blanz.*)

rendered image is compared with the target face image. A function of the differences between the pixels in the rendered image and the target images is computed. Then an incrementally modified parameter set is selected, and a new rendered image is created. The difference between this new image and the target image is computed. If the new image is better, closer to the target image, the parameter set is again incremented in the same *direction* in the parameter space. If the new image is worse, farther from the target image, the parameters are incremented in a different direction. This process is iterated over and over until the parameters converge to a set of values that produces an image corresponding to the target image. This process uses optimization techniques designed to search the parameter space in a way that rapidly converges to the model parameter set that best matches the target image. If multiple target images for the same individual are available, the process can be modified to find the model parameter values that are the best fit to all images.

4.13.2 A Virtual Sculpture-Based Model

Riewe created a similar model, but rather than basing it on scans of real persons, she based her model on data from virtual sculptures [Riewe 07]. Starting from a generic polygon face model, sixteen artists were asked to interactively sculpt the model into whatever face shapes they desired. The only constraint was that they not alter the orientation or the polygon topology of the face. Each artist was asked to create a neutral expression and three additional facial expressions for their sculpture. This produced a data set of 64 faces. For this project, surface texture data was not used; only surface geometry data was considered.

Following the process developed by Blanz and Vetter, the average face was computed. Then the co-variance matrix formed by the differences between the individual faces and the average was determined. Then principal component analysis was used to determine the desired face space parameters. Only the first 15 principal components were used for this model.

An interactive interface was developed to allow exploration of this 15-dimensional face space. A set of sliders facilitated interactive control of the coefficients of the component vectors. The scale of each slider was computed to allow only variation within a range of -3.0σ to $+3.0\sigma$ for each component.

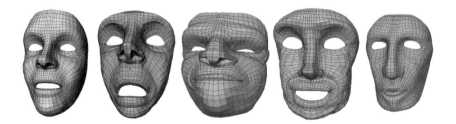

Figure 4.27.
Images from a virtual-sculpture-based morphable model. Adapted from [Riewe 07]. The left-most is the average face, the next face is 3.0σ along the first principal component, the center face is -3.0σ along the second principal component, the next face is -2.8σ along the fifth principal component, and the right-most face is -2.8σ along the sixth principal component.

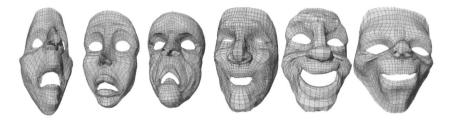

Figure 4.28.
Expression variation from a virtual-sculpture-based morphable model. (Adapted from [Riewe 07].) The left three faces have *fear* added, while the right three faces have *joy* added.

Figure 4.27 shows the average sculpted face and four face variations created by this model.

As in the morphable model, attribute vectors were developed by associating attribute weighting values with the various data set faces. Using these attribute values and the differences of the corresponding faces from the average face, a vector in the face space was computed for each attribute. For the virtual sculpture model, the attributes considered included gender and emotional expressions. Figure 4.28 shows faces with fear or joy attributes applied. For each of these faces, a facial conformation was first specified, using the principal component parameters, and then an expression attribute vector was added.

4.14 Parameterized Conformation Models

Another approach, related to many of the approaches described previously in this chapter, is the use of parameterized facial models. In fact, parameterized models can be implemented using many of the techniques discussed in this chapter. The basic idea for a parameterized model is to create a desired face or facial expression based on some number of controlling parameter values. If the model supports *conformation* parameters, it can be used to generate a range of individual faces.

The conformation parameters might include control of overall head and face proportions and the relative proportions and spacing of individual facial features. The range of possible individual faces generated by the model depends on the number and type of control parameters and the permissible value range for each parameter. Such parameterized models are not necessarily bound to the constraints imposed by measured data from real faces or available anthropometric data. These models can be as stylized or surrealistic as desired. Chapter 7 presents a more detailed discussion of parameterized models.

5

Facial Animation

5.1   Fundamental Animation Techniques

There are a number of approaches to facial animation. These include key framing using shape interpolation or blend shapes, performance-driven animation, parameterized models, and pseudomuscle-based, muscle-based, and language-driven animation [Parke 91b].

The goal of the various animation techniques is to manipulate the surfaces of the face over time, so that the faces have the desired poses and expressions in each frame of the animated sequences. This process involves directly, or indirectly, manipulating the surface polygon vertices or the surface control-point positions over time.

Interpolation is perhaps the most widely used of the techniques. In its simplest form, it corresponds to the *key-framing* approach found in conventional animation. The idea behind key-frame or *key-pose* animation is that the desired facial expression is specified for a certain point in time and then again for another point in time some number of frames later. A computer algorithm then generates the frames in between these key frames.

Key-pose animation requires complete specification of the model geometry for each key facial expression. This specification makes it a labor-intensive approach.

Performance-based animation involves measuring real human actions to drive synthetic characters. Data from interactive input devices such as

Waldos [deGraf 89], data gloves, instrumented body suits, and laser- or video-based motion-tracking systems are used to drive the animation. See Chapter 10 for a detailed discussion of performance animation techniques.

In the parameterized modeling approach, sets of parameters are used to control to control facial expressions [Parke 74]. A parameterized model may use region interpolations, geometric transformations, and mapping techniques to manipulate the features of the face. See Chapter 7 for more detail on parameterized models.

With pseudomuscle-based facial animation, muscle actions are simulated using geometric deformation operators. Facial tissue dynamics are not simulated. These techniques include abstract muscle actions [Magnenat-Thalmann et al. 88] and freeform deformation [Sederberg and Parry 86].

In the muscle-based approach, Platt and Badler used a mass-and-spring model to simulate facial muscles [Platt and Badler 81]. Waters developed a face model that includes two types of muscles: linear muscles that pull, and sphincter muscles that squeeze [Waters 87]. Like Platt and Badler, he used a mass-and-spring model for the skin and muscles. However, Waters' muscles have directional (vector) properties.

Terzopoulos and Waters applied physical modeling techniques to the control of facial expressions [Terzopoulos and Waters 90]. Facial muscle actions are modeled by simulating the physical properties of facial tissue, including the muscles. See Chapter 8 for more details about muscle-based animation.

5.2   Control Parameterizations

A unifying theme proposed in this chapter is that, from the animator's point of view, facial animation may be viewed as the manipulation of a set of control mechanisms or control parameters. It is argued that all currently used or anticipated facial animation schemes may be viewed as *parameterizations*. The animation control schemes may then be viewed as control parameterizations. Animation becomes the process of specifying and controlling parameter values as functions of time.

The development of facial animation may be viewed as two *independent* activities: the development of control parameterizations and associated user interfaces, and the development of techniques to implement facial animation based on these parameterizations.

For any animation model, control interfaces or *control handles* for the animator are very important. The goal is to provide a wide range of natural and intuitive poses and expression control.

From the animator's point of view, the interesting questions are:

1. What are the parameters?

2. Are the parameters adequate and appropriate?

3. How are the parameters actually manipulated?

The animator usually is not interested in the implementation algorithms or details, but rather in the animation functionality provided. The animation system may be viewed as a *black box* with, hopefully, a useful, predictable interface that allows the animator to produce the desired results. The animator really does not care how the black box works, only that it does work and provides appropriate functionality.

From the implementer's point of view, the interesting questions are:

1. What parameters should be provided?

2. What user interface to these parameters should be provided?

3. What algorithms and techniques should be used to actually implement the system?

Most development work has concentrated on specific techniques for implementing facial animation. Relatively little work has been done on establishing guidelines for control functionality and animator interfaces. Questions concerning *optimal* and *complete* control parameterizations remain mostly unanswered. The functionality provided by each implementation has been influenced primarily by the characteristics of the particular implementation techniques or environment, rather than by an attempt to fulfill a well-understood set of functionality and interface goals.

There are two major control parameter categories. The more often addressed category concerns control of facial poses and expressions. The other category concerns control of individual facial shape or conformation. Conformation control is used to select or specify a particular individual face from the universe of possible faces and is discussed in Chapter 4. Pose and expression control is concerned with changes of facial posture and expression and is the primary topic of this chapter. In the ideal case, these two categories are *orthogonal*: conformation is independent of expression, and expression is independent of conformation.

As we shall see, the development of *complete* low-level parameterizations enables the development of higher levels of control abstraction.

5.3   Interpolation

Interpolation is one way to manipulate flexible surfaces such as those used in facial models. Interpolation is probably the most widely used technique for facial animation. As shown in Chapter 4, the notion of interpolation is quite simple. In the one-dimensional case, we are given two values and asked to determine an intermediate value where the desired intermediate value is specified by a fractional interpolation coefficient α.

$$\text{value} = \alpha(\text{value}_1) + (1.0 - \alpha)(\text{value}_2) \quad 0.0 < \alpha < 1.0 \quad (5.1)$$

This basic concept is easily expanded to more than one dimension by applying this simple procedure in each dimension. The idea generalizes to polygonal surfaces by applying the scheme to each vertex defining the surface. Each vertex will have two three-dimensional positions associated with it. Intermediate forms of the surface are achieved by interpolating each vertex between its two extreme positions.

5.3.1 Key Expression Interpolation

Among the earliest, and still widely used, schemes for implementing and controlling facial animation is the use of key expression poses and interpolation. Parke first demonstrated the use of this approach to produce viable facial animation [Parke 72]. The basic idea and the control parameterization for interpolations are very simple and also very limited.

The idea is to collect, by some means, geometric data describing the face in at least two different expression poses. Then a single control parameter, the interpolation coefficient, is used as a function of time to change the face from one expression into the other. A basic assumption underlying the interpolation of facial surfaces is that a single surface topology can be used for each expression. If the surface topology is fixed, manipulating the surface shape involves only manipulating the vertex positions.

Figure 5.1.
Interpolation between expressions [Parke 74].

To change the face from one expression to another is a matter of moving each surface control point a small distance in successive frames. The position of each point is determined by interpolating between the extreme positions.

Can a single surface topology be mapped onto a wide range of facial expressions? Will the transitions between these expressions be reasonable? To answer these questions Parke collected data for a number of real facial expressions [Parke 74]. The topology used is the one shown in Figure 4.18. This simple topology uses about 300 polygons defined by about 400 vertices.

Using this data, an animation was created, showing that a single topology would allow both representation of many expressions and reasonable interpolated transitions between the expressions. Figure 5.1 illustrates an interpolated transition between two expressions. The middle image is an interpolation between the two key poses.

Bilinear Expression Interpolation

Expression interpolation can be extended in several ways. More than two expression poses may be used. For example, if four expressions are available, then two interpolation parameters may be used to generate an expression which is a *bilinear* blend of the four key poses. If eight expressions are available, then *three* interpolation parameters may be used to generate a *trilinear* expression blend.

n-Dimensional Expression Interpolation

Four interpolation parameters and 16 key expressions allow blending in a four-dimensional interpolation space. Interpolation in higher dimensional expression spaces is possible, but probably is not useful to the animator, since interpolation in these higher dimensional expression spaces is not very intuitive.

Pairwise Expression Interpolation

Another way of exploiting multiple expression poses is to allow pairwise selection of the poses from a library of expressions and to use a single interpolation parameter to blend between the selected poses. This method requires specifying three control values: the starting pose, the final pose, and the interpolation value.

Again, if many expression poses are available, they could be selected four at a time and used as the basis for bilinear expression blending. They could even be selected eight at a time as the basis for trilinear expression interpolation. The possible variations on these interpolation schemes seem quite open-ended; however, the usefulness of these approaches is not established.

Facial Region Interpolation

Another useful extension to expression interpolation is to divide the face into a number of *independent* regions. Separate interpolation values may then be applied to each region. This approach extends the control parameter space in an intuitive way. An example of this approach, presented by Kleiser, is to divide the face into an upper region and a lower region [Kleiser 89]. The upper region is used primarily for emotional expression, while the lower region is used primarily for speech expression. This division allows some *orthogonality* between emotion and speech control. Special care is exercised in manipulating the surface along the boundary between the regions.

Nonlinear Interpolation

Since the face is governed by physical laws, its motions are not linear, but tend to accelerate and decelerate. The *linear* aspect of linear interpolation refers to the fact that the interpolated value is computed using a linear function of the two endpoints. There is, however, no restriction on the way we manipulate the α interpolation coefficient as a function of animation frame time. The α value may be a nonlinear function of time. Parke found that functions based on cosines of fractional time intervals were useful acceleration and deceleration approximations [Parke 72].

In addition, the vast collection of parametric curve, surface, and volume specification techniques, such as B-splines, beta-splines [Bartles et al. 87], and so on, might be used as the basis for generating nonlinear expression blends. The key-pose vertices would provide the geometric basis for the control points required by these techniques.

Limitations of Interpolation

The interpolation schemes outlined above have limitations. First, the range of expression control is directly related to the number and disparity of expression poses available. An expression that falls outside the *bounds* of the key-pose set is unattainable—except perhaps by extrapolation, an inherently risky approach. Also, each key pose requires an explicit geometric data collection or data generation effort. For a large set of poses, this is a daunting task. If different individuals, as well as various expression poses, are to be included, the number of key poses needed may be very large. In all but the simplest cases, providing intuitive, orthogonal control parameters to the animator is difficult.

5.4   Facial Rigging

The animator's task is to manipulate the model's controls to bring the face to *life*. A rich, interactive environment that supports the animator in this activity is highly desired. Interactive animation tools consist primarily of motion control tools and motion preview tools.

Facial rigging is the process of creating the animation controls for a facial model and the animator's interface to those controls. One early example is a system developed by Hanrahan and Sturman, which allowed the animator to establish functional relationships between interactive input devices and control parameters [Hanrahan and Sturman 85].

For example, in this system the animator might define a functional link between an input dial value and a control parameter. The dial value, RSMILE, might affect the right corner of the mouth by pulling it up and back as the dial value increases. This system provided great flexibility in defining the functional links between the input values and the generated control values.

Modern interactive animation systems provide a wide variety of ways for linking user interactions to animation actions.

5.4.1 Use of Articulated Joints

One widely used approach is to embed within the face model an articulated *joint* hierarchy. Each joint corresponds to the articulated connection between two skeletal segments or *bones*. These joints are manipulated by varying their orientation angles.

For the face, this joint structure might consist of several joints for the neck, connected to a joint for the jaw and a joint for the skull. The joint for the skull might in turn be connected to joints for the eyeballs. The joint for the jaw might in turn be connected to a joint for the tongue.

Influences are established between the surface vertices or control points and one or more of these joints. As the joints are manipulated and their orientation angles adjusted, the associated surface points are rotated along with the joints. The influence between a specific surface point and a given joint is usually a *weighting* value. Some surface points close to the joint might be completely influenced by it, moving exactly as it moves. Other points might be only partially influenced by a joint, only moving a percentage of its motion. Each surface point is likely to have a different weight or influence from a given joint. Some points on the surface may be influenced by several joints.

Establishing the joint structure and determining the surface point weighting values for the joints is a part of the rigging process. For examples of this approach see [Osipa 03].

5.4.2 Use of Blend Shapes

Another widely supported approach is the use of *blend shapes*. Blend shapes are a form of surface shape interpolation. Here the surface is sculpted into

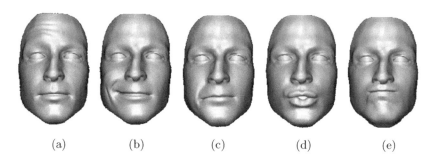

(a)   (b)   (c)   (d)   (e)

Figure 5.2.
Blend shapes used to mimic muscle actions: (a) right brow raiser, (b) right lip corner puller, (c) right lip corner depressor, (d) lip pucker, (e) chin raiser. (*Courtesy of A. Smith, Texas A&M Visualization Laboratory.*)

two or more shapes. One of these is the base shape, while the others are called target shapes. The differences between the base and target shapes are represented as vector sets. Each vector set corresponds to the difference between the base shape and one of the target shapes. Each vector in a blend shape is the difference in location between a point in the base shape and its corresponding point in the target shape. When a blend shape is applied to the base shape, it takes on the target shape for that blend. If the blend shape is only partially applied, the base shape moves partially toward the target shape. This allows interpolation between the base and target shapes. This interpolation is controlled by a blending coefficient. If the coefficient is 0.0, the surface has the base shape. If the coefficient is 1.0, the surface takes on the target shape. For values between 0.0 and 1.0, the surface takes on a shape between the base and target shapes.

For a given blend shape, perhaps only a few of the surface points are affected. That is, for a given blend shape, some of the surface points may have zero length vectors. This means that the positions for these points are the same in both the base and target shapes. Also, a given surface point may be affected by more than one blend shape. If more than one blend shape is applied to a surface, each surface point will be moved, based on the sum of the point vectors for each blend shape, weighted by their respective coefficients.

Figure 5.2 illustrates the use of blend shapes. In this example, each of the blend shapes shown was sculpted to mimic the effect of a particular facial muscle.

5.4.3   Use of Clusters

A *cluster* is a group of points that are associated with a coordinate transformation. This transformation might be a scale, a translation, a rotation,

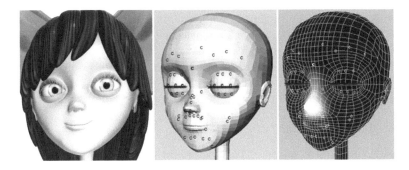

Figure 5.3.
Use of clusters: (left) rendered face model, (middle) cluster locations, (right) weighting of one cluster near the tip of the nose. (*Courtesy of Texas A&M Visualization Laboratory.*)

or a combination of these. Clusters allow groups of surface points to be scaled, translated, and rotated relative to a defined cluster origin location. The effect of a cluster transformation on a given point in the cluster is determined by a *weighting* value. Different points in the cluster typically have different weighting values, or weights. The point weights allow the effects of a cluster transformation to vary across the set of cluster points. Typically, the effect of the cluster transformation is greatest near the origin of the cluster and tapers off further away from this origin. The right-most image in Figure 5.3 shows this tapered weighting for one of the clusters near the end of the nose. In this figure, white corresponds to maximum weight, while black corresponds to zero weight. Gray values correspond to weights between maximum and zero.

In Figure 5.3, the left-most image shows a finished rendering of the face model shown in the center image. The center image shows the location of the clusters used in this model.

For the face model shown in Figure 5.3, cluster-based deformation was used to control facial expressions. About 50 clusters were created for the facial mesh. For this model, the polygon mesh shown controlled a subdivision surface used for the final rendering. The clusters were used to control the following facial features: eyelashes, eyelids, nose, upper lip, lower lip, neck, brow, jaw, and cheeks. Typically, several clusters were used to control the shape of each feature. For example, the eyelids not only open and close, but the shape of each eyelid can take on varying shapes based on three clusters that influence the shape of that eyelid.

5.4.4 Use of Functions

Joints, blend shapes, and clusters establish specific relationships between the control parameters and their effect on surface points. Many animation systems also allow the rigging to make use of arbitrary functional relationships between control parameters and their effect on surface points. This is done by developing sets of equations that manipulate various surface points, based on control parameters. These manipulations can be most anything that can be specified as a functional relationship between the control parameter values and the desired effect on the surface points.

5.4.5   The User Interface

Usually, the control values or parameters for the joint angles, blend shape weights, cluster transformations, and functional expressions are set at specific times or key frames of the desired animation. The parameter values at other frame times are derived from these key frame values using some form of linear or spline interpolation.

An interactive *curve editor* is often provided as part of the animation system. The curve editor allows the animator to manipulate the interpolation curves used in transitioning from one key frame to the next. Usually, the curve editing can be applied on each parameter individually. In fact, different parameters may have different sets of key frame times.

GUI Interfaces

So how are the key frame parameter values set? One approach would be to simply type in the parameter values for each key frame. This approach can be quite tedious and ignores the power provided by graphical user interfaces or GUIs. In a GUI, graphical icons or other graphical devices are provided as a way to control parameter values. As an icon or device is interactively manipulated, control parameter values are changed.

Figure 5.4 shows the graphical interface used to control the model shown in Figure 5.3. This face-shaped GUI was designed so that the graphical control devices appear in a layout corresponding to the placement of facial features. In this GUI, two graphical devices are used; one is the slider, the other is the control box.

Manipulating a slider typically controls a single control parameter. Manipulation within a box typically controls two parameters simultaneously. Moving the box locator horizontally changes one parameter, while vertical motions change another parameter.

Usually, GUI controls implement limits on the range of values that can be applied to the parameters. These limits prevent the animator from selecting values that are outside the plausible range for the specific model.

Often, the GUI locators do not directly manipulate the control parameters, but rather manipulate several parameters through the use of mapping expressions. For example, in the upper eyelid boxes shown in Figure 5.4, moving the locator in the vertical direction opens and closes the eyelid, while motion in the horizontal direction changes the shape of the eyelid. The

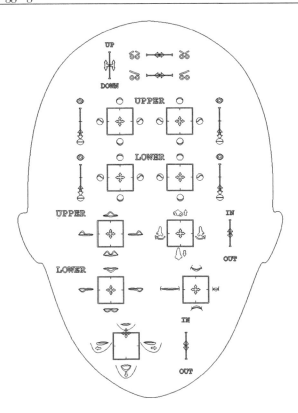

Figure 5.4.
Example GUI interface. (*Courtesy of Texas A&M Visualization Laboratory.*)

opening and closing, and the shape changes, are controlled by a number of parameters that simultaneously manipulate three clusters. The cluster control parameters are derived from the control box locator motions through the use of expressions that map the locator position to specific parameter values.

Similarly, the right mouth control box can create a smile or a frown, and can also control the width of the mouth. Simple sliders are used to raise and lower the eyebrows, and to change their shapes.

The creation of the graphical icons and manipulators, and establishing the correspondence between the manipulators and the control parameters, are part of the facial rigging process. The example shown is but one of a number of possible interface design paradigms. The key issues are establishing the appropriate surface controls and providing the animator with an effective, efficient, and intuitive interface.

5.5   Performance-Based Animation

Performance-based animation involves using information derived by measuring real human actions to drive synthetic characters. Performance-based animation often uses interactive input devices such as Waldos [deGraf 89], data gloves, instrumented body suits, and laser- or video-based motion-tracking systems.

Two performance-based approaches are discussed here: expression mapping and model-based persona transmission. Additional approaches to performance animation are discussed in Chapter 10.

5.5.1   Expression Mapping

The expressive facial animation developed by Bergeron, Lachapelle, and Langlois for their 1985 animation *Tony de Peltrie* can be viewed as an early form of performance animation [Bergeron and Lachapelle 85].

The first step in the process was to digitize twenty different expression and phoneme poses directly from a real person. This step was done using photographic digitizing techniques.

A correspondence was made between the neutral expression (E_0) of the real face and the neutral face of the character to be animated. Because the number of points defining the character face was larger than the number of points defining the real face, a one-to-n point correspondence was used. For each point of the real face, a correspondence to several points in the character face was defined. However, each point in the character's face had only one corresponding point in the real face.

Once this correspondence was defined, character expressions were computed, using a function that mapped real face expressions to the character. This function was based on the differences between real face expressions. The difference between the neutral expression and the target expression ($E_T - E_0$) of the real face was added to the neutral character expression. The difference for each point in the real face was added to its corresponding point group in the character. In this way, the exaggerated features of the animated character were driven from the real face expressions by expression mapping. An amplification factor was used to increase or decrease the magnitude of the added differences.

A library of standard key expressions was computed by applying expression mapping independently to five areas of the face: the left and right eyebrows, the left and right eyelids, and the rest of the face, including the mouth. A three-dimensional curved interpolation algorithm was then used to generate intermediate expressions between key character expressions [Kochanek and Bartels 84]. The key expressions used were from the standard library or were created as needed by combining standard expressions or by exaggerating existing expressions.

5.5.2   Model-Based Persona Transmission

Parke [Parke 82] suggested that a convincing synthetic representation of a person's face could be used to create a synthetic videophone if sufficiently powerful analysis techniques were developed, capable of matching the motions of a synthetic image to those of an actual person. Such a system could operate over very low data rate channels, even over the standard telephone network [Welsh et al. 90, Welsh 91]. This concept was introduced in Chapter 1 and is described in more detail here.

The image analysis and image synthesis aspects of this scheme are equally important. The image analysis needs to automatically extract all of the relevant parameters from the source image in real time. This analysis includes tracking head movements and identifying facial features and feature shapes. This extracted information is then transmitted to the remote image synthesis system to produce the corresponding synthetic facial images.

Success depends on generating convincing real-time synthetic faces. Real-time implementations of any of the animation techniques described in this chapter could be used to synthesize the necessary facial representations.

Image Analysis

To match the synthesized image to the posture and expression of the real face, the boundaries of the head and shoulders, as well as the positions and shapes of the facial features, must be determined.

One analysis approach is an algorithm developed by Nagao for locating the eyes and mouth in a facial image [Nagao 72]. A large, cross-shaped image mask is convolved with the facial image, which has the effect of low-pass filtering the image and applying a Laplacian or second-derivative operator. The output image is thresholded to produce a binary image. Thresholding isolates negative peaks in image luminance and effectively produces a line sketch of the face. The line elements in the image are referred to as *luminance valleys* [Pearson and Robinson 85].

The algorithm then scans this image from top to bottom, searching for the two vertically oriented luminance valleys corresponding to the sides of the head. The area between these sides is searched for the symmetrically located eyes. The positions of the eyes determine the orientation axis of the face. The algorithm then searches for luminance valleys corresponding to the bottom of the nose, the lips, and the chin.

Snake-based algorithms also have been used for locating the boundaries of the head and shoulders [Waite and Welsh 90]. A snake is an energy-minimizing spline guided by external constraint forces and influenced by image content so that it is pulled toward features such as lines and edges. Snakes can also be useful for estimating local feature motion. For example, lip tracking is shown in [Kass et al. 88]. In addition, feature motion vectors can be extracted using hierarchical block matching [Bierling 88].

An additional source of information about mouth shape comes directly from speech. The speech track may be analyzed to determine which sequence of mouth shapes should be displayed [Morishima et al. 89].

5.6   Facial Expressions

For the animation approaches described in the previous sections, we did not need much understanding of the underlying structure and expression capabilities of the face. To continue our study, we need to look more carefully at the expressive character of the face, and to understand in more detail the expressive structure of the face.

5.6.1   The Universal Expressions

Research in facial expression has concluded that there are six *universal* categories of facial expressions that are recognized across cultures [Ekman 89]. These categories are sadness, anger, joy, fear, disgust, and surprise, as shown in Figure 5.5. Within each of these categories there may be a wide range of expression *intensity* and some variation in expression details.

Faigin presents an excellent discussion, from an artist's point of view, of these expressions and their variations [Faigin 90]. Faigin describes each expression category and its variations in terms of the appearance of three facial regions and their associated facial wrinkles. The three expressive regions are the eyebrows, the eyes, and the mouth.

Sadness

In simple sadness, the inner portions of the eyebrows are bent upward. The skin and soft tissue below the eyebrow are piled up above the upper eyelid. The eyes are slightly closed because of downward pressure from the tissue above the eyelid and because of upward motion of the lower eyelid. In simple sadness the mouth is relaxed. Sadness is illustrated in Figure 5.5(a).

The wrinkles associated with sadness include horizontal folds across the brow, trace vertical lines between the eyebrows, oblique folds above the upper eyelid, and a smile-shaped fold under the lower lip.

Sadness has many intensities and variations, including open-mouthed crying, closed-mouth crying, suppressed sadness, nearly crying, and looking miserable. These variations may include completely lowered eyebrows, tightly shut eyes, a square-shaped open mouth, a bulge on the chin, and a very pronounced nasolabial fold.

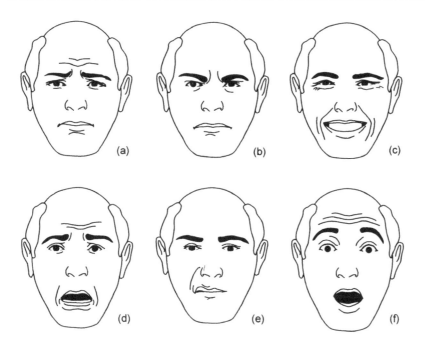

Figure 5.5.
The universal expressions: (a) sadness, (b) anger, (c) joy, (d) fear, (e) disgust, and (f) surprise.

Anger

In simple anger the inner corners of the eyebrows are pulled downward and together. The lower edge of the eyebrow is at the same level as the upper eyelid. The eye is wide open, but pressure from the lowered brow prevents the white of the eye from showing above the iris. The mouth is closed, with the upper lip slightly compressed or squared off. Anger is illustrated in Figure 5.5(b).

The wrinkles for anger include horizontal folds above the upper eyelids and vertical lines between the eyebrows.

Variations of anger include shouting rage, rage, and sternness. These variations may include tightly compressed lips with a chin bulge, or an open mouth with a sneering upper lip and a straight lower lip, showing both the upper and lower teeth.

Joy

In simple joy, the eyebrows are relaxed. The upper eyelid is lowered slightly and the lower eyelid is straight being pushed up by the upper cheek. The mouth is wide, with the corners pulled back toward the ears. If the mouth is closed, the lips are thin and pressed tight against the underlying bone. If the mouth is open, the upper lip is straight, showing the upper teeth; the lower lip is straight in the middle and angled near the corners. Joy is illustrated in Figure 5.5(c).

For joy, the wrinkles create "crow's feet" at the corners of the eyes, a smile-shaped fold under the lower eyelid, dimples, and a deep nasolabial fold from nose to chin.

Variations on joy include uproarious laughter, laughter, open-mouthed smiling, smiling, stifled smile, melancholy smile, eager smile, ingratiating smile, sly smile, debauched smile, closed-eye smile, false smile, and false laughter. False smiles and false laughter are indicated by diminished crow's feet at the corners of the eyes and by only slight or absent folds under the lower eyelids.

Fear

Fear can range from worry to terror. In fear, the eyebrows are raised and pulled together. The inner portions of the eyebrows are bent upward. The eyes are alert. The mouth may be slightly dropped open and stretched sideways. Fear is illustrated in Figure 5.5(d).

The wrinkles associated with fear include horizontal brow folds, vertical lines between the eyebrows, dimples above the eyebrows, and oblique folds above the upper eyelids.

In worry, the lips are squeezed tightly together, and the lip margins disappear. There is a bulging below the lower lip and over the chin. In terror, the eyes and mouth are wide open. The upper lip is relaxed, while the lower lip is stretched wide and tight, exposing the lower teeth. The nasolabial fold becomes straight and shallow. Bracket-shaped folds appear to the sides of the lower lip.

Disgust

Disgust ranges from disdain to physical repulsion. In disgust, the eyebrows are relaxed. The eyelids are relaxed or slightly closed. The upper lip is raised into a sneer, often asymmetrical. The lower lip is relaxed. The nasolabial fold is deepest alongside the nose. Disgust is illustrated in Figure 5.5(e).

In disdain, the eyelids may be partly closed, with the eyes looking down. For physical repulsion, the eyebrows are lowered, especially at the inner corners. The eyes may be mostly shut in a squint. The upper lip is raised in an intense sneer, which may show the upper teeth. The lower lip is slightly pushed up. There are vertical lines between the brows, crow's feet and lower eyelid creases, wrinkles from the inner corner of the eye across the bridge of the nose, and a chin bulge.

Surprise

In surprise, the eyebrows are raised straight up, as high as possible. The upper eyelids are open as wide as possible, with the lower eyelids relaxed. The mouth is dropped open without muscle tension to form an oval shape. In surprise, horizontal folds are formed across the brow. Surprise is shown in Figure 5.5(f).

5.6.2   Expressions of Physical States

There are many expressions that are not directly related to emotion. Faigin describes additional expressions associated with physical states such as pain and sleepiness. Faigin asserts that many of these expressions are also universally recognized. Faigin's list includes pain, exertion, drowsiness, yawning, sleeping, singing, shouting, passion, intensity, attention, perplexity, shock, and the facial shrug.

5.7   Parameterized Models

Motivated by the difficulties associated with the key-pose animation, Parke developed *direct parameterized* models [Parke 74, Parke 82]. The desire was to create an encapsulated model that would generate a wide range of faces and facial expressions, based on a fairly small set of input control parameters. The goal was to allow both facial expression and facial conformation to be controlled by the parameter set values.

The ideal would be a model that allowed any possible faces, with any possible expressions to be specified by selecting the appropriate parameter value set. The models created to date are certainly less than this ideal, but they do allow a wide range of expressions for a fairly wide range of facial conformations.

The challenge is to determine a *good* set of control parameters and to implement a model that uses these parameters to generate the desired range of faces and expressions. For the parametric models that have been developed, the parameter sets are fairly primitive and low level. The implementation approach has been to apply operations such as rotation, scaling, position offsets, and interpolation in combination to local regions of the face.

These models were experimentally derived to represent the visible surface features of the face, based on observation and a general reference to the underlying structures. The control parameters provided include:

- *Expression*—eyelid opening, eyebrow arch, eyebrow separation, jaw rotation, mouth width, mouth expression, upper-lip position, mouth corner position, and eye gaze.

- *Conformation*—jaw width, forehead shape, nose length and width, cheek shape, chin shape, neck shape, eye size and separation, face region proportions, and overall face proportions.

About 10 expression parameters allow the animator to specify and control a wide range of facial expressions. About 20 parameters are used to control a limited range of facial conformation. A detailed discussion of parameterized models is included in Chapter 7.

5.8   Pseudomuscle-Based Animation

The complex interaction between facial tissue, muscles, and bones, and between the muscles themselves, results in what are commonly called "facial expressions." It is evident that these interactions produce an enormous number of motion combinations. The idea, for the pseudomuscle approaches, is not to exactly simulate the detailed facial anatomy, but rather to develop models with only a few control parameters that emulate the basic face muscle actions.

5.8.1   Abstract Muscle Actions

Magnenat-Thalmann et al. developed a pseudomuscle-based model in which the parameters control *abstract muscle action* (AMA) procedures [Magnenat-Thalmann et al. 88]. This approach is based on empirical models and not on physical simulation.

The AMA procedures are similar to, but not the same as, the FACS action units. However, the FACS action units were used as the guide for constructing the muscle procedures. The action of each of these procedures is typically more complex than the action of a single parameter in the direct parameterized approach discussed above. The AMA procedures work on specific regions of the face. Each AMA procedure approximates the action of a single muscle or a group of closely related muscles.

For example, the vertical jaw action is responsible for opening the mouth. It is composed of several motions: lowering the corners of the mouth, lowering the lower lip and parts of the upper lip, and rounding the overall lip shape.

A partial list showing the most important of the 30 AMA procedures is given in Table 5.1. These AMA procedures are *not* independent, so the ordering of the actions is important.

This model allows facial control by manipulating the parameter values for the *low-level* AMA procedures, and also by manipulating composite parameters at a higher *expressions* level. *Expressions* are formed by controlling the AMA procedures in groups. Two classes of expression level controls were developed: *emotions* and *phonemes*.

close upper lip	close lower lip
right eyelid	left eyelid
right zygomatic	left zygomatic
move right eyebrow	move left eyebrow
left lip raiser	right lip raiser
move right eye horizontal	move left eye horizontal
move right eye vertical	move left eye vertical
right risorius	left risorius
mouth beak	
vertical jaw	
compressed lip	

Table 5.1.
The most important of the 30 AMA procedures.

5.8.2   Freeform Deformations

Freeform deformation (FFD) is a technique for deforming solid geometric models [Sederberg and Parry 86]. It can be used to control shape change for surface primitives of any type or degree, such as planes, quadrics, parametric surface patches, or implicitly defined surfaces. As discussed in Section 4.12.6, FFDs correspond to shape deformations of imaginary parallelepipeds surrounding the surface or object of interest. The appropriate analogy is the deformation of a clear, flexible plastic in which embedded flexible objects also are deformed. FFD involves a mapping from one three-dimensional space to another, using a trivariate tensor product Bernstein polynomial. Deformations are specified by moving the lattice of control points from their initial positions.

Chadwick et al. describe a technique to simplify the task of specifying and controlling muscle actions, based on deforming skin surfaces using freeform deformations [Chadwick et al. 89]. Freeform deformations provide a powerful basis for implementing pseudomuscle facial action procedures.

Rational Freeform Deformations

Rational freeform deformations (RFFDs) are an extension to basic FFDs, which use rational basis functions in the formulation of the deformation. The rational basis functions incorporate weights for each control point in the parallelepiped control lattice.

Rational FFD's weights provide additional degrees of freedom when manipulating the deformations. When the weights at each control point are unity, the RFFDs are equivalent to the basic FFDs.

5.8.3   Facial Animation using RFFDs

Kalra et al. describe interactive techniques for simulating facial muscle actions using rational freeform deformations [Kalra et al. 92]. Each particular muscle action is controlled by the displacement of the lattice control points for an RFFD defined in a facial region of interest.

To simulate the facial muscle actions, surface regions corresponding to anatomical regions of the desired muscle actions are defined. A parallelepiped control volume is defined around each muscle region. The muscle deformations corresponding to stretching, squashing, expanding, and compressing the surface region of interest are simulated by interactively displacing the lattice control points and by changing the weights assigned to each control point.

Interpolation is used to determine the deformation of points lying within the boundary areas between adjoining pseudomuscle regions.

Displacing a control point is analogous to actuating a muscle. The resulting deformations can closely match the natural muscle actions. However, specifying the displacement of the control point is simpler than simulating the muscle.

5.9   Muscle-Based Facial Animation

The detailed anatomy of the head and face is a complex assembly of bones, cartilage, muscles, nerves, blood vessels, glands, fatty tissue, connective tissue, skin, and hair, as discussed in Chapter 3. To date, no facial animation models based on this complete detailed anatomy have been reported. However, several models have been developed that are based on simplified models of facial bone structure, muscles, connective tissue, and skin. These models provide the ability to manipulate facial expression based primarily on simulating the characteristics of the facial muscles and facial tissue. A detailed look at the properties of human skin is presented by Pieper [Pieper 89].

Platt and Badler developed an early dynamic face model in which the polygonal vertices of the face surface (the skin) were elastically interconnected with modeled springs [Platt and Badler 81]. These vertices also were connected to the underlying bone structure of the model using simulated muscles. These "muscles" had elastic properties and could generate contraction forces. The face expressions were manipulated by applying muscle forces to the elastically connected skin mesh. The muscle actions used were patterned after the Facial Action Coding System action units.

Waters developed a dynamic face model that includes two types of muscles: linear muscles that pull, and sphincter muscles that squeeze [Waters 87]. Like Platt and Badler, he used a mass-and-spring model for the skin and muscles. However, Waters' muscles have directional (vector) properties that are independent of the underlying bone structure. These vectors make the modeled muscles independent of specific face topology. Each muscle has a zone of influence. The influence of a particular muscle is diminished as a function of radial distance from the muscle attachment point. The muscle control parameters of this model also are based on the FACS.

Extensions to the Waters model have been reported [Terzopoulos and Waters 90]. The same FACS-based control parameterization is retained, but the facial tissues are now modeled using a three-layer deformable lattice structure. These three layers correspond to the skin, the subcutaneous fatty tissue layer, and the muscles. The bottom surface of the muscle layer is attached to the underlying bone. A detailed discussion of muscle-based facial models is included in Chapter 8.

5.10 Language-Based Animation

Language-based approaches to facial animation are used in the form of animation sequencers, animation scripting languages, and true animation programming languages.

5.10.1 Animation Sequencers

An animation sequencer is a program the takes as input a list of parameter or action descriptors and outputs a time-ordered list of animation control values. One set of values is generated for each frame of the animation. Sequencers allow fairly easy manual specification of many concurrent parameter or motion changes.

For each frame of a sequence, the sequencer scans its list of control action descriptors, checking the current frame number against the frame range of each descriptor. If the current frame is within the range of a descriptor, the sequencer computes the correct control values to output for the descriptor for this frame. The control value computations usually are based on interpolation or spline curve-fitting techniques.

Parke used a control parameter sequencer to control the animations produced with his early parameterized model [Parke 74]. In this case, each parameter descriptor consisted of the parameter name, the beginning frame, the ending frame, the initial parameter, the ending parameter value, and the interpolation method to be used between the beginning and ending frames of this descriptor. Time gaps could be left in the specifications for a given parameter. The sequencer simply output the last computed value for that parameter for frames between input specifications.

Magnenat-Thalmann et al. used a similar multitrack-based sequencer [Magnenat-Thalmann et al. 88]. Each of the independent *tracks* is a chronological sequence of key values for a given parameter. Each key value consists of a track ID, a frame value, and an intensity value. The track ID corresponds to the AMA parameter, and the intensity value is similar to the parameter value in Parke's sequencer. An interpolation scheme was used to compute AMA intensity values between the key values.

This system was extended to include an *expression* track, in addition to the thirty AMA parameter tracks. Expression key values include an expression identifier. This identifier specified which predefined AMA-based expression group to use during a given time span. With this extension, it is easy to define, for example, eye and eyebrow movements in an expression corresponding to a phoneme. This approach was used for the film *Rendez-vous à Montreal* [Magnenat-Thalmann and Thalmann 87].

These early animation sequencers were not interactive. The parameter descriptors came from files created using text editors. However, the sequencer concept can be made interactive by applying interactive curve-fitting techniques to the various control value tracks.

5.10.2   Animation Languages

The language approach to animation can be very powerful. Reeves, for example, describes an animation programming language developed at Pixar [Reeves 90]. A face animation model could actually be a program in this special programming language. To animate the face, the time-dependent animation program is executed for the sequence of desired frame times. Many of the simple characters in early Pixar films were modeled and animated using this language.

Graphical primitives, such as spheres, cones, patches, and polygons, and operators, such as translate and rotate, are defined as built-in functions in the language.

Variables in the language come in two forms: variables that take assigned values (and retain them until new values are assigned) and *articulated* animation variables. Articulated variables are never assigned. They take values that are based on key-frame values. The key-frame values are interpolated over time, using various kinds of splines.

For example, a very simple facial model could be a head that is a sphere with its base sitting at the origin. This head could nod back and forth and twist from side to side with the $head_{nod}$ and $head_{twist}$ articulated variables. The nose could be a small sphere that lies on the surface of the head. The nose could move around on the surface of the head with the $nose_{ud}$ and $nose_{lr}$ articulated variables. Two eyes could be positioned anywhere on the head with appropriate articulation variables. In addition, each eye might have a pupil that is positioned to float just above the surface of the eye.

5.11   Abstraction-Layered Facial Animation

Kalra et al. describe a facial animation system based on layered abstractions [Kalra et al. 91]. A high-level language provides simple, general, extensible synchronization mechanisms. These mechanisms hide the time specifications.

   Facial animation in this system is based on multiple specification layers. Successively higher layers define entities in more abstract ways, starting with phonemes and working up through words, sentences, expressions, and emotions. The highest layer allows abstract manipulation of the animated entities, with assured synchronization of eye motion and emotions with the word flow of sentences.

5.11.1   The Abstraction Layers

This approach is decomposed into five layers. The highest layers are the most abstract and specify *what to do*; the lowest layers describe *how to do it*. Each level is an independent layer, with its own inputs and outputs. The five defined layers are:

   Layer 0: abstract muscles
   Layer 1: minimal perceptible actions
   Layer 2: phonemes and expressions
   Layer 3: words and emotions
   Layer 4: synchronization of emotions, speech, and eye motions

Layer 0: Abstract Muscles

This level corresponds to the most basic facial modeling and animation system. This implementation is based on the abstract muscle action procedures developed by Thalmann et al. [Magnenat-Thalmann et al. 88] (see Section 5.8). At this basic level, the facial animation is based on a set of independent parameters that control specific abstract muscle emulations. Each abstract muscle has parameters such as the minimum value, the maximum value, and the current contraction value.

Layer 1: Minimal Perceptible Actions

Each minimal perceptible action (MPA) is a basic facial motion parameter. The range of each motion is normalized between 0 and 1 or between -1 and $+1$ (see Table 5.2). MPA specifications have the following general form.

$$< \text{MPA name} > \quad < \text{framenumber} > \quad < \text{intensity} >$$

   Each MPA has a corresponding set of visible facial features such as movement of the eyebrows, the jaw, the mouth or other motions that occur as a result of contracting muscles associated with the region. MPAs also

MPA Name	Value Range
raise_eyebrow	-1 to 1
squeeze_eyebrow	0 to 1
move_horizontal_eye	-1 to 1
move_vertical_eye	-1 to 1
close_upper_eyelids	-1 to 1
close_lower_eyelids	-1 to 1
stretch_nose	-1 to 1
raise_nose	0 to 1
raise_upper_lip	0 to 1
puller_lower_lip	0 to 1
puller_corner_lip	0 to 1
lower_corner_lip	0 to 1
stretch_corner_lip	0 to 1
mouth_beak	0 to 1
zygomatic_cheek	0 to 1
puff_cheek	-1 to 1
nod_head	-1 to 1
turn_head	-1 to 1
roll_head	-1 to 1

Table 5.2.
Minimum perceptible actions.

include nonfacial muscle actions such as nods and turns of the head and movement of the eyes.

Layer 2: Facial Snapshots

Snapshots correspond to specific phonemes or expressions. A snapshot is made up of one or more MPAs. The basic MPAs are combined to form the higher level expressions, such as anger, fear, and surprise.

One can create natural expression snapshots, as well as some unnatural and idiosyncratic snapshots. The intensity of an expression is directly determined by the intensity of its MPAs. A strong or feeble expression can be created by appropriately changing the intensities of the contained MPAs.

Facial snapshots representing expressions and phonemes can be created interactively. Users can construct and save static expressions to form a library of expressions. Newly designed expressions may be added to the predefined expression database.

Expression editing is, by design, independent of the low-level realization of muscles and their actions. With this independence, the low-level implementation of an expression could be as simple as rotation or scaling of a region, or as complex as a 3D finite-element model of the region. It would be possible to use entirely different implementation models for each MPA, without effecting high-level control.

Once defined, a snapshot has the following form:

< framenumber >   < snapshot >   < intensity >

Several snapshots may be active at the same time. This synchronous activity allows specifying a phoneme ànd a smile for the same time interval.

Phonemes. A phoneme snapshot defines the position of the mouth and lips during a particular sound emission. A phoneme is defined by a set of interacting minimal perceptible actions, such as:

```
[snapshot      pp=>
     [action     raise_sup_lip      30%]
     [action     lower_inf_lip      20%]
     [action     open_law           15%]
]
```

Expressions. An expression snapshot is a particular posture of the face. These postures are generated using minimal perceptible actions in the same way as phonemes. The basic expressions, as well as variants, may be specified as snapshots.

Layer 3: Sequences of Snapshots

Words and emotions are defined as sequences of snapshots.

Words. A word may be specified as a sequence of component phonemes. A dictionary is used to store the phonemes for each word.

One problem is determining the duration of each phoneme, relative to the average duration of the phoneme, based on its current context. Duration is influenced by the phonemes prior to and following the current phoneme. Several heuristic methods have been proposed by researchers of text-to-speech synthesis [Allen et al. 87]. This system is able to generate the correct sequence of phonemes for a given time interval by using specifications such as:

```
How are you (pause 200 ms) Juliet?
```

Additional commands may be used to control the intensity, duration, and emphasis of each word. Pauses may be added to control rhythm and intonation of the sentence.

Emotions. Emotions are defined as time-dependent changes in facial expression. The time-dependent behaviors are specified using *expression intensity envelopes.* The intensity envelopes are defined using time-based functions [Ekman 77]. Each envelope has four stages:

- *Attack*—transition between the absence of the expression and the maximum expression intensity.

- *Decay*—transition between maximum intensity and stabilized expression intensity.

- *Sustain*—duration of the active expression.

- *Release*—transition back to the quiescent state.

For each emotion, the sequence of expressions and the durations of the expression stages are specified.

Generic emotions. Each specific emotion has an average overall duration. However, time variation is context sensitive. For example, a smile may have a five-second average duration, but it may last as long as thirty seconds in some situations. The duration of each emotion stage is not equally sensitive to the time expansion. Expanding the overall duration of the emotion envelope expands the attack and release stages proportionally less than the sustain stage. A duration sensitivity factor is associated with each stage.

Duration distributions are used to specify each generic emotion. For example, a stage duration may be defined as 5 ± 1 seconds, based on a uniform distribution, or an intensity level may be defined as 0.7 ± 0.05, based on a Gauss distribution.

Once a generic emotion is introduced in the emotion dictionary, it is easy to produce an instance by specifying its overall duration and magnitude.

Layer 4: Synchronization Mechanisms

There is a need for synchronizing various facial actions: emotions, dialogue, and eye motion. In this layer, language formalisms are introduced for specifying the starting time, the ending time, and the duration-independent action.

5.11.2   High-Level Script Language

The high-level script scheduler is a formalism for specifying the synchronization and the dependence between the various actions. An action is invoked as part of a specific sequencing with a specific execution duration, as follows:

```
while   < duration >   do   < action >
```

Action Durations

Action durations may be specified in several ways: no specification (use the default value), relative duration, absolute duration, or relative to another action.

Action Sequencing

Actions may be sequenced as follows:

- $[A][B][C]$—Action C follows action B, which follows action A.

- $[A][\text{fork } B][C]$—Actions B and C both follow action A, in parallel.

- $[A] \cdots [\text{fork } B] \cdots$—Action A continues while action B is started and runs in parallel with action A.

- $[A][\text{end fork } B][C]$—When action A ends, wait for the end of action B before starting action C.

- $[A \cdots [\text{end fork } B] \cdots]$—Action A continues after parallel action B ends.

Action Synchronization

This system provides several types of action synchronization. These types include *actor synchronization*, *emotion synchronization*, and *sentence synchronization*.

Actor synchronization. The use of actor names allows the actions of several actors to be synchronized.

```
[actor JULIET while
    [        [say   "What's the time?"]
           [actor ROMEO while
                 [say "It's midnight..."]
           ]
           [say "Oh, it's late..."]
    ]
]
```

Emotion synchronization. The following statements generate a sequence of facial emotions for an actor. The emotions are assumed to be in the emotion dictionary.

```
[emotion FEAR]
[emotion ANGER while
        [say "Aghh"]
]
```

Sentence synchronization. Word flow may be synchronized with expressions to form expressive sentences. Each word is considered an independent action, with a starting time and a duration. It is possible to execute an expression action between words.

```
[say "My name is Juliet"
     [emotion WINK]
    "and yours?"
]
```

5.12   The Billy Animation

This section discusses an animation example that illustrates a few of the concepts presented in this chapter. This example is based on Reeves' description [Reeves 90] of animating the Billy baby face in Pixar's animation *Tin Toy* [Lassiter 87].

To animate Billy's face (see Figures 4.5 and 4.6), a muscle-based model similar to the model proposed by Waters [Waters 87] was used. Muscles were embedded in the surface model of Billy's head. As each muscle contracted, it pulled on the data points around it and moved the skin surface. The amount of contraction for each muscle over time was animated using keyframing and splining tools.

Two kinds of muscles were implemented: the linear and elliptical sphincters. A linear muscle was defined by two points: a bone attachment point that always remained stationary, and a skin attachment point that would contract isotonically when the muscle operated. Other parameters for each linear muscle defined its zone of influence. A conical zone of influence with a circular cosine dropoff function was defined for each muscle.

The sphincter muscles pulled skin toward or away from a central point, rather than tugging in a direction. Sphincter muscles were used around the mouth to purse the lips, and around the eyes. A single point defined the center of the muscle. Three additional points defined the three axes used in establishing an ellipsoidal zone of influence. A circular cosine dropoff function was used to blend between maximal displacement at the center of the region and zero displacement at the edge of the region.

A total of 43 linear muscles and four sphincter muscles were used in Billy's face. The placement of the muscles was based on the illustrations shown in the Facial Action Coding System manual [Ekman and Friesen 78].

The muscle model, which supported linear and radial displacement, was not appropriate for the jaw or the eyelids. The skin in these areas is constrained by contact with another object, the jaw bone or the eyeball. When the skin moves in these areas, it is pulled over the object and moves rotationally or in an arc, instead of linearly. A third kind of muscle, called a rotational muscle, was developed for these regions. Its zone of influence was defined using a partial torus centered about a point. A second point was used to specify the orientation of the torus. A third point specified the axis about which the torus points rotated. When the rotational muscle was actuated, all data points originally lying within the partial torus were rotated around the axis as a group by the same amount.

A relaxation mechanism was implemented to smoothly disperse some of the rotation movement to neighboring points. This relaxation step was responsible for moving points on the upper lip, cheeks, and neck in reaction to the jaw opening or closing.

Higher levels of control, called *macro muscles*, were developed. A macro muscle controls several low-level muscles. The amount of muscle contraction was weighted for each low-level muscle within a macro muscle. Thirty-three macro muscles were developed for Billy, but, only twelve of them were used for most of the film. The macro muscles saved time by encapsulating commonly used actions. However, the animator retained complete control of the underlying low-level muscles when needed.

The Billy facial and body model lacked one important characteristic: the skin was flexible but didn't simulate real tissue. The skin did not droop due to gravity or wobble due to inertia. This made Billy seem as if he were made of flexible stretchy plastic, rather than skin.

5.13   Creating Good Animation

As introduced in Chapter 1, Thomas and Johnston outlined the animation principles developed by Disney Studios [Thomas and Johnson 81]. These principles may be applied directly to computer character animation as discussed by Lasseter [Lassiter 87]. The principles that make great conventional animation great are those that can make computer character animation great. These principles insure that the animation is effective and truly communicates.

These principles cross the boundaries of animation technique and focus on the areas of story, design, and execution. Animation that lacks any of these aspects will suffer. Animation, computer or conventional, that succeeds at all of these levels will be successful.

5.13.1   Does It Communicate?

Successful animation implies much more than just moving objects from point A to point B. The primary goal of animation is communication. The fundamental test of good animation is how well it communicates. It must communicate the intended message clearly, creatively, and logically. Effective animation elicits a response from the viewer. It informs, captivates, and entertains. In short, it communicates!

Story or Content

The story or content is of fundamental importance in the success of an animation. Content largely determines the enjoyment the audience receives from the animation. Even if the concept is visually abstract, you are still telling a story. The story must be strong enough to justify the incredible time and energy required to produce the animation. If the content is trivial, the animation is not worth doing.

Design

Design in animation is very important. Since every element in an animation must be planned, considerable emphasis should be placed on the production design. Animation is really a form of cinematography. All cinematic approaches, techniques, and philosophies come into play. Design includes the determination of composition, balance, and color, as well as film structure, in terms of sequences, scenes, cuts, and pacing. Dynamic camera angles and creative editing procedures are all part of the process.

Characters should be designed so that they can accomplish the actions that the story requires. The character design must be appropriate for the sophistication of the software and hardware available. Characters should be designed so that they look and behave as three-dimensional entities.

Execution

Execution is very important and should be done well. The story and the design should allow good execution. The story and design should not overpower the available techniques and resources. It is easy to have story and design concepts that are beyond the capabilities of available resources.

5.13.2   Use of Conventional Animation Techniques

Observing the motion of an object or character, seeing the essence of its movement, and then knowing the best way to represent it, are the most basic skills of an animator.

Animation is the art of making the inanimate come to life. Computer animators, like conventional animators, strive to bring life to the screen by creating effective image sequences. The principles of conventional animation can be used to enhance the quality of computer-generated animation.

Computer animation may borrow many of the techniques of conventional animation. It also may borrow the thinking process, as well. Useful conventional animation techniques include the use of storyboards, a structured approach to animation production, and the use of pencil tests.

The Storyboard

Creating a storyboard is one way to communicate the combination of motions, events, and unfolding information of a story in a time sequence. It is a series of images, often simply drawings, by which the designer communicates the story concepts through visual choreography.

The purpose of the storyboard is to visually understand what is happening in the story and in the scenes. What precedes this shot? What comes after this shot? How does this shot fit within the scene and within the story?

Designing or choreographing computer animation via storyboards can save many hours and many production dollars. Concepts and ideas can be sketched, discussed, and revised prior to initial modeling and animation on the computer.

What we are trying to accomplish with a storyboard is to turn the story into a sequence of actions with specific timing. These actions, simple or sophisticated, must communicate the intended message clearly and creatively.

The Structured Animation Approach

The production of computer animation, like conventional animation, is usually structured, with each scene composed of multiple scene elements.

The animation may be created one element at a time, which allows flexibility in producing it. Elements can be added, and existing elements can be enhanced, to arrive at the final animation. Changes in one element do not require redoing the entire animation, just recombining the scene elements.

The structured approach can be applied to production activities as well. The production effort may be decomposed into multiple interlocking activities. Each activity accomplishes a part of the overall animation production process.

Pencil Tests

In conventional animation, quick pencil tests are used to evaluate animation sequences prior to creating the finished animation. The same basic idea is used in computer animation. A low-effort animation test is often done before investing in the final animation rendering.

For example, animation can be created using low-resolution models rendered as low-resolution images. When the tested animation is finalized, the low-resolution model motions are applied to high-resolution models, creating the high-resolution images of the final animation.

5.13.3   Hints for Animating Simple Facial Models

Reeves provides several animation hints, based on conventional animation techniques, that can make simple facial models more interesting and more alive [Reeves 90].

- Motions and poses should not be symmetric. For example, make one eye slightly larger than the other. Turn one corner of the mouth down more than the other. When blinking the eyes, blink one eye a frame or two before the other.

- If the character talks, do not strain to attain perfect lip sync. It is most important to capture the ebb and flow of the dialogue.

- Caricature may be done by *cheating* facial expressions. For example, swing the mouth around the head so that it is almost below where the ears would be if there were ears. This action allows the camera to see the expression on the mouth, while also showing a profile of the head.

- Exaggeration is a form of cheating. For example, when a character is shocked, his eyes might change scale three times in four frames: from normal size, to 1/4 normal, to three times normal, and back to normal again. Cheats like these, while not anatomically correct—and hence sometimes quite difficult to do with complex facial models—are very powerful in establishing the character and showing emotion. This is the power of animation, computer-assisted or not, over live action. It can create alternate realities!

5.14   Control Parameterizations Revisited

A number of facial animation techniques have been reviewed. Each of these has an associated control parameterization. In most cases, the control paradigm for the implementation is intimately related to its underlying techniques. The control of facial animation may be viewed as control parameterization and control interface issues. The development of control parameterizations and the development of animation system implementations should be *decoupled*. Parameterization research should focus on developing high-quality interfaces and parameterizations, and implementation research should focus on developing optimum techniques for modeling faces and generating facial expressions based on these parameterizations.

5.14.1   Ideal Parameterizations

The ideal parameterization and interface allows the animator to *easily* specify any individual face, with any speech and expression sequence. This is in fact the definition for a *universal parameterization*, one that enables all possible individual faces and all possible expressions and expression transitions. No implemented facial parameterization to date is even close to being universal.

The FACS system seems the best current basis for low-level expression parameterization, but it is probably not ideal from the animator's viewpoint.

Input and guidance from animators is certainly needed in the development of good, useful parameterizations. The focus should be on developing powerful control parameter sets that are motivated by the needs of the facial animator, *not* based on the characteristics of a particular implementation scheme.

Developing a truly *universal* parameterization appears very difficult and may not be possible. However, developing useful, broadly applicable parameterizations is feasible and very worthwhile.

5.14.2   Quality of Control Parameterizations

Assuming that truly universal parameterizations are not possible, at least in the near term, what are the metrics for judging the quality of a control parameterization? Attributes such as control range, complexity, number of parameters, intuitiveness, naturalness, and powerful interfaces immediately come to mind. Certainly an important measure is the range of possible faces and expressions that can be specified. How much of the universe of faces and facial expressions is covered by the parameterization? Judgment of this aspect is somewhat application-dependent. For example, if the application requires animation of only one specific character, conformation control is not an issue.

Intuitive and natural parameters, the number of parameters, and parameter complexity are all directly related. The number of parameters provided and the overall complexity of the parameterization should be just sufficient. Unnecessary parameters or parameter complexity should be avoided. Ease of use will be strongly coupled to how natural and intuitive are the parameters and the interface to those parameters.

Subtlety and orthogonality also are measures of parameterization quality. Subtle variations in expression and conformation often are needed. The ability of a parameterization to support these subtle variations is highly desired. Mutual independence of the parameters is also an issue. The change in one parameter value should have minimal and predictable interaction with other parameters. Change in one parameter value should not require reworking the other parameter values. This feature is particularly true for the interactions between expression and conformation parameters, and between speech and expression parameters.

Another measure of an effective parameterization is its capability to serve as the basis for higher levels of control abstraction. As in the case of speech animation, the construction of control parameters at the phoneme level, or at higher levels of abstraction built on top of the basic parameterization, should be possible.

5.14.3   High-Level Control Abstraction

A major focus of future efforts should be on the development of powerful models with the effective low-level parameterizations discussed above. The availability of such models would greatly facilitate development of very capable character animation systems. The development of complete low-level parameterizations enables the development of higher levels of control abstractions. Several high-level control abstractions are outlined below.

Speech-Driven Level

Much facial animation is related to speech. One particularly useful higher-level control abstraction would be at the speech level. A second-level speech parameterization would be in terms of phonemes and perhaps emotions. The phoneme-level parameters would in turn control the low-level lip shape deformation parameters.

Animating the face directly from a speech soundtrack is an intriguing concept. It involves analyzing the speech to identify the various phonemes and pauses and their durations. At a higher level, it involves analyzing the speech for emotional content as well. These concepts are discussed in more detail in Chapter 9.

Behavior-Driven Level

An area of considerable interest is the development of animation techniques that operate at the behavior level. At this level, the animator/director expresses the desired actions in terms of high-level *behaviors*, rather than in detailed low-level motions. Work in this area has concentrated on activities such as legged locomotion and grasping objects. The underlying detail-control parameters for these particular activities are well defined and well understood.

The ability of the animator to specify facial actions in terms of high-level behaviors is certainly desired. An example would be the ability to simply supply dialogue text, along with emotional directions, and have the face *act out* the scene.

Another example would be the ability to specify a character's *personality* and have the animation system ensure that the facial actions conform to the specified personality traits. Work in this area is just beginning.

Story-Driven Level

Takashima et al. outline the development of a story-driven animation system [Takashima et al. 87]. This system is an example of animation control at a very high level of abstraction. It is limited to simple children's stories. However, it does demonstrate a useful framework of such systems. This framework is based on three major activities: story understanding, stage direction, and action generation. Story understanding and stage direction are largely knowledge-based AI activities. Behavior-driven animation systems, as discussed above, would be a part of the action generation activity. One can envision future story-driven systems that include synthetic facial *acting*, rather than just facial animation.

6

Facial Image Synthesis

Once we have created a facial model and determined how we want it to move, the next step is to actually generate the sequence of facial images that form the desired animation. The generation of synthetic images has been the focus of intense research and development over the last forty years. There is a vast body of literature on synthetic image generation, and a wide range of synthesis techniques exist. It is not the intent of this chapter to provide in-depth discussion of image synthesis, but rather to introduce the major aspects of image synthesis, to provide pointers into the literature, and to highlight aspects that are particularly relevant to facial images.

6.1 Synthetic Images

At the lowest level, computer-created synthetic images are simply large rectangular two-dimensional arrays of image fragments called *pixels*. Each pixel of the array has the same size and shape. Each pixel has a *color value*. When one of these color value arrays is displayed on an appropriate device, such as a color monitor, we perceive an image. The task of image synthesis is to compute the correct color value for each pixel in the desired images.

The size of the pixel array and the range of color values for each pixel determine the maximum visual information an image can represent. Common sizes for images range from a few hundred to a few thousand pixels in each dimension. Color values range from a few bits to as many as 48 bits per pixel. Colors are typically represented as triples of 8-bit values; one 8-bit value for each of three primary color components (usually red, green, and blue, or RGB).

6.1.1 The Image Synthesis Tasks

Image synthesis includes three major tasks:

- transforming the geometric model and model components into the viewing coordinate system,

- determining which surfaces are visible from the viewing position, and

- computing the color values for each image pixel, based on the lighting conditions and the properties of the visible surfaces.

6.1.2 Coordinate Transformations

The various components making up the scene to be synthesized may be defined in a number of different coordinate systems. Coordinate system transformations are used to move objects from one coordinate system into another. The transformations used include operations such as translation, rotation, and scaling [Foley et al. 90].

These transformations may be defined as sets of equations that operate on coordinate values defined in one system to create new coordinate values in another system. It is often convenient to express these operations using matrix notation. For example, the rotation of a three-dimensional point could be expressed as

$$
\begin{vmatrix} X' \\ Y' \\ Z' \end{vmatrix} = \begin{vmatrix} R_{11} & R_{12} & R_{13} \\ R_{21} & R_{22} & R_{23} \\ R_{31} & R_{32} & R_{33} \end{vmatrix} \begin{vmatrix} X \\ Y \\ Z \end{vmatrix},
$$

where X', Y', Z' are the coordinates of the rotated point, $R_{11}, \ldots, R_{33}$ are the terms specifying the desired rotation, and X, Y, Z are the original point's coordinates. The rotation terms are based on sines and cosines of the rotation angle.

Note that the rotation of a point within a coordinate system is exactly the same as the opposite rotation of the coordinate system itself.

Homogeneous Coordinates

We typically make use of four-dimensional homogeneous coordinates and coordinate transformations when describing and manipulating geometric models. The three-dimensional point X, Y, Z becomes the point $X, Y, Z, 1$ in a four-dimensional homogeneous system.

Homogeneous coordinates and transformations provide several advantages. All coordinate transformations of interest can be easily expressed using four-by-four transformation matrices. These matrices can be multiplied together to express complex transformations. For example, the following matrix expression is used to specify a coordinate transformation involving translation, scaling, and rotation:

$$
\begin{vmatrix} X' \\ Y' \\ Z' \\ 1 \end{vmatrix} = \begin{vmatrix} R_{11} & R_{12} & R_{13} & 0 \\ R_{21} & R_{22} & R_{23} & 0 \\ R_{31} & R_{32} & R_{33} & 0 \\ 0 & 0 & 0 & 1 \end{vmatrix} \begin{vmatrix} S_1 & 0 & 0 & 0 \\ 0 & S_2 & 0 & 0 \\ 0 & 0 & S_3 & 0 \\ 0 & 0 & 0 & 1 \end{vmatrix} \begin{vmatrix} 1 & 0 & 0 & T_1 \\ 0 & 1 & 0 & T_2 \\ 0 & 0 & 1 & T_3 \\ 0 & 0 & 0 & 1 \end{vmatrix} \begin{vmatrix} X \\ Y \\ Z \\ 1 \end{vmatrix}.
$$

The same transformation, after multiplying the matrices, may be expressed as

$$
\begin{vmatrix} X' \\ Y' \\ Z' \\ 1 \end{vmatrix} = \begin{vmatrix} R_{11}S_1 & R_{12}S_2 & R_{13}S_3 & R_{11}S_1T_1 + R_{12}S_2T_2 + R_{13}S_3T_3 \\ R_{21}S_1 & R_{22}S_2 & R_{23}S_3 & R_{21}S_1T_1 + R_{22}S_2T_2 + R_{23}S_3T_3 \\ R_{31}S_1 & R_{32}S_2 & R_{33}S_3 & R_{31}S_1T_1 + R_{32}S_2T_2 + R_{33}S_3T_3 \\ 0 & 0 & 0 & 1 \end{vmatrix} \begin{vmatrix} X \\ Y \\ Z \\ 1 \end{vmatrix}.
$$

As we see, the result of concatenating several transformations may also be expressed as a four-by-four matrix. And, as we shall see below, the perspective viewing transformation can also be expressed as a four-by-four matrix.

Modeling Transformations

Different parts of a geometric model often are defined in different coordinate systems. Coordinate transformations are then used to put the various pieces together to form the complete model. Modeling transformations include: scaling to change object size, rotation to change object orientation, and translation to change object location. The coordinate system of the complete model or the complete scene is called the *world* coordinate system.

For example, when modeling the face, each eye usually is defined in its own coordinate system. This separation allows the eye to be rotated independently of the head and then translated into its proper location within the head.

Note that the order of transformations is important. Rotating an object and then translating it usually has a very different result than translating the object and then rotating it.

Viewing Transformations

In addition to assembling the components of a three-dimensional scene, coordinate transformations are used to put the assembled scene into the desired viewing coordinate system. This process is sometimes referred to as the *look-at, look-from* problem. The viewing system usually is specified by establishing the viewing position and the viewing direction in the world coordinate system.

The world coordinate system is translated so that the look-from position becomes the viewing system origin. Then the coordinate axes are rotated so that the Z-axis (the depth axis) is pointed toward the look-at position. Then additional transformations may be applied so that the X and Y axes of the viewing system correspond to the X and Y axes of the desired image or display screen. These additional transformations may include switching from a right-handed to a left-handed coordinate system and rotating around the Z-axis so that the viewing system is oriented to give the desired image [Foley et al. 90].

Perspective

We often want our images to have perspective similar to that which we see in the real world. In perspective, objects appear smaller as they move away from us.

To achieve simple perspective, we again make use of homogeneous coordinates. We first transform the scene elements already in the viewing coordinate system by a perspective transformation. We then project the resulting homogeneous point positions into a three-dimensional screen space by dividing X', Y', and Z' by the homogeneous W coordinate as shown below:

$$\begin{vmatrix} X' \\ Y' \\ Z' \\ W \end{vmatrix} = \begin{vmatrix} 1 & 0 & 0 & 0 \\ 0 & 1 & 0 & 0 \\ 0 & 0 & 1 & 0 \\ 0 & 0 & 1/d & 0 \end{vmatrix} \begin{vmatrix} X \\ Y \\ Z \\ 1 \end{vmatrix},$$

$$X_s = X'/W,$$

$$Y_s = Y'/W,$$

$$Z_s = Z'/W.$$

Here, d is the distance from the viewing system origin to the image projection plane. And, X_s and Y_s are the projected image coordinates, while Z_s is a function of the distance from the viewer to the point.

Simple perspective is only one of many possible viewing projections [Foley et al. 90]. In general, a perspective viewing projection maps a four-dimensional homogeneous space into a three-dimensional space. Ignoring the depth dimension maps this space into a two-dimensional image space.

Perspective transformations more complex than the one shown above may be used. But the basic notion of a perspective transformation in homogeneous four-dimensional space, followed by a homogeneous division, (thus projecting the points back into a three-dimensional screen space), remains the same. A sometimes more useful perspective transformation is to substitute $tan(\alpha)$ for the $1/d$ term in the transformation shown above. The angle α is one-half the desired field of view [Newman and Sproull 79].

6.2   Visible Surface Determination

Since our facial models are merely mathematical surfaces and not real objects, we must explicitly determine which surfaces are actually visible from a given viewpoint. The development of visible surface algorithms has been an area of research since the early days of computer graphics. Many such algorithms have been developed [Foley et al. 90, Joy et al. 88].

6.2.1   Visible Surface Algorithm Taxonomies

Several taxonomies have been proposed for classifying the many visible surface algorithms. The first of these was proposed by Sutherland et al. [Sutherland et al. 74]. This taxonomy classifies ten visible surface algorithms, based largely on three criteria: whether the algorithm operates in image space or object space, the sorting order used, and the sorting algorithms used.

Grant has proposed other taxonomies based on the type of sampling used, the type of geometric subdivision used, and the sorting order used [Grant 88]. The sampling types include continuous sampling and point sampling. The geometric subdivision types include: object-based, space-based, scan plane, scan line, and screen area.

Image Space/Object Space

For object space algorithms, surface visibility is computed prior to being projected into screen space. The visibility computations are done at the precision used to represent the geometric primitives. Examples of object space algorithms include those proposed by Roberts [Roberts 63] and Appel [Appel 67].

For image space algorithms, surface visibility is computed in the screen coordinate system after being projected from the world coordinate system. Visibility computations are typically done only for each pixel, and only at the precision needed for a valid screen space solution. Most of the algorithms described below are image space algorithms.

Sorting Order and Algorithms

The sorting operations and the sorting order used are one way to classify the approaches to visible surface computation. The sorting operations used include bucket sorting and bubble sorting [Knuth 69]. Bucket sorting partitions a set of objects into a predetermined number of groups. Bucket sorting may be used to sort polygon edges into scan line groups, based on the minimum Y value of each edge. Bubble sorting orders members of a set by iteratively exchanging neighboring elements until the elements of the set are in the desired order. Bubble sorting may be used to add a new element to an already sorted list simply by appending to the end of the list. The new element is then exchanged with its neighbors until it is positioned so that the augmented list is completely sorted again.

Sorting orders used by visible surface algorithms include depth sort first, Y sort first, and its corollary, X sort first. In each of these approaches, additional sorting along the other dimensions is usually used to complete the visibility determination.

6.2.2   Use of Coherence

Visible surface algorithms often make use of various forms of scene and image coherence to minimize the amount of work needed to complete the visibility computation [Foley et al. 90]. For example, *object coherence* might be used to reduce the sorting effort. If one object is completely separated from another object in one or more dimensions, it is not necessary to compare all of the components of one object with all of the components of the other object.

Since properties usually vary smoothly across surfaces, *surface coherence* allows the use of incremental techniques to compute variation of these properties across the surface. *Edge coherence* means that a surface edge can only change visibility when it crosses another edge or when it penetrates another surface.

Scan line coherence means that the visible spans along one scan line are likely to be very similar to the visible spans in adjacent scan lines. *Area coherence* means that adjacent groups of pixels are often covered by the same visible surface. *Depth coherence* means that adjacent areas of a single surface typically have similar depth values, while adjacent areas of different surfaces typically have significantly different depth values.

Frame coherence means that the visible surfaces in one frame of an animation are usually very similar to the visible surfaces in adjacent frames.

6.2.3   Depth Sort Algorithms

Several algorithms make use of the depth-first sorting order. These algorithms include the Painter's algorithm, the Newell algorithm, and the binary space partition (BSP) algorithm. The BSP algorithm uses a spatial partitioning scheme to determine depth. The Newell algorithm uses sorting in addition to depth sorting to completely determine visibility. The Painter's algorithm uses no sorting beyond the initial depth sort.

Painter's Algorithm

For the Painter's algorithm, the surfaces in the scene are sorted or ordered into a depth priority list. The surfaces are then rendered into an image buffer in reverse priority order. The lowest priority surface, or the surface farthest away, is rendered first. As the scene is rendered or *painted* from back to front, the correct visibility image is formed.

Newell Algorithm

The algorithm due to Newell, Newell, and Sancha [Newell et al. 72] first sorts all polygons based on the farthest Z depth coordinate of each polygon. If polygons overlap in X or Y and also in Z depth, one or more of the polygons is split so that a definite polygon ordering in Z can be achieved.

The depth-ordered list of polygons is scan converted from back to front. The scan conversion used does not require an image buffer, but rather makes use of an X-sorted list of visible span segments for each image scan line. As each polygon is converted into scan line segments, the segments are added to the segment lists for the scan lines. The scan line segment lists are sorted in X. Where these segments overlap in X, the previously established depth ordering of the polygons is used to determine visibility.

BSP Trees

The binary space partitioning algorithm developed by Fuchs, Kedem, and Naylor [Fuchs et al. 80, Fuchs et al. 83] creates a tree-structured spatial partitioning of the scene. Each node in the partitioning tree corresponds to a plane that divides the scene space into two half-spaces. Additional nodes in the subtrees correspond to additional planes that further partition the scene. The tree is extended until all surface primitives are uniquely partitioned. The leaf nodes of the tree correspond to the partitioned surface primitives. It may be necessary to subdivide surfaces to create a valid spatial partitioning.

The depth priority for the scene from a particular viewpoint is determined by traversing the partitioning tree. At each node, a test is made to determine on which side of the partitioning plane for that node the viewpoint is located. The result of this test determines which subtree at that node is traversed first. A complete traversal of the tree for a given viewpoint results in a visibility priority list for the scene. The traversal order for one viewpoint will likely be different than the order for another viewpoint. Different traversal orders create different visibility lists.

6.2.4   Scan Line Algorithms

Scan line algorithms typically first sort the scene polygons based on their
Y values. Starting at the top of the image, polygons are added to an active
polygon list based on the scan line Y value. Polygons are maintained on
the active list as long as the current scan line intersects the polygon.

For each scan line, a set of spans, from the active polygons, is ordered
in X. Where these spans overlap, visibility is determined based on Z
depth. A number of scan line algorithms have been developed, including
those by Wylie et al. [Wylie et al. 67], Romney et al. [Romney et al. 69],
Watkins [Watkins 70], Bouknight [Bouknight 70], and Bouknight and Kelley [Bouknight and Kelley 70]. These algorithms differ primarily in the
ways they sort the polygons in Y, the ways they X-order the scan line spans,
and the ways they resolve depth where the spans overlap in X. There are
also some differences in how image coherence is exploited.

Area Subdivision Algorithms

Rather than subdividing the scene based on image scan lines, Warnock
recursively subdivides the scene into smaller and smaller areas [Warnock 69].
The algorithm starts by considering the entire scene. If the scene is *simple
enough*, it is rendered. If it is too complex to render directly, it is cut into
four smaller regions by dividing it in half in both the X and Y dimensions.
Each smaller region is then considered. If the region is simple enough it
is rendered. If not, it is divided again into four smaller regions. This area
subdivision is continued until each region is simple enough, or until the size
of the region reaches the size of the image pixels.

The "simple enough" criteria varies with implementation. "Simple
enough" means that the visible complexity of the region can be directly
rendered by the implementation. Typical examples include the cases where
only the background is in the region, where only one polygon covers the
region, where only one visible polygon covers the region, and so on.

6.2.5   Z-Buffer

The *depth buffer* or *Z-buffer* algorithm is probably the simplest and by far
the most widely used visibility algorithm. Because of its simplicity, it is easy
to implement in either software or fast dedicated hardware. The Z-buffer
scheme is built into the hardware of essentially every modern graphics card.

For each pixel in the image, a record is kept of the current distance from
the closest surface to the viewpoint. This collection of depth distances is
referred to as the Z-buffer [Catmull 74]. The color of the closest surface at
each pixel is also stored in an image buffer.

As each surface primitive is rendered, the Z-depth value and the surface
color value are computed for each pixel within the primitive. If the newly

computed Z value at a pixel is closer to the viewer than the stored Z value, the new Z value and the new color value for this pixel are stored in the buffer. After all surface primitives are rendered, the image buffer will contain the final rendered image.

The Z-buffer is inherently a point sampling algorithm and suffers from the aliasing problems outlined in Section 6.6. Carpenter describes an extended form of the Z-buffer called the A-buffer [Carpenter 84]. The A-buffer keeps a list of visible objects for each pixel. A 32-bit coverage mask is used to record which part of the pixel is covered by each visible object. Complex coverage comparisons are implemented using Boolean operations. The A-buffer provides better images with reduced aliasing, at an increased computational cost.

6.2.6 PRMan

Another approach is the one used in Pixar's PRMan renderer [Apodaca and Gritz 00]. In this approach, each image pixel has a number of sample points randomly distributed in the image area corresponding to the pixel. At each of these sample points, a list is kept of image fragments overlapping its location. These image fragments are typically computed by interpolating between surface shading points. Each image fragment has a depth, a color, and an opacity. When all image fragments have been rendered, each fragment list is composited, based on depth, opacity and color. Final image pixels are then computed using a two-dimensional filter, which integrates the contributions of all sample points within the area of the pixel filter. This approach can produce very high quality images with minimal aliasing. Quality is controlled by the number of samples per pixel, the integrating filter used, and the number of shading points computed for each surface primitive.

6.3   Surface Shading

The computed colors for the image pixels are determined by the surface properties of the visible surfaces and the modeled lighting conditions.

6.3.1   Surface Properties

Surface shading properties may include color, texture, displacement, reflectivity, refraction, and opacity or transparency.

Surface Color

Color is a modeled attribute associated with each surface. Color may be uniform across a surface, or it may vary across the surface. For polygonal surfaces, color may be assigned as a vertex attribute, allowing each vertex to have a different color. Color values across the surface between these vertices are then determined, using color interpolation.

A particular color can be described by specifying its location in a three-dimensional color space. A number of different standard color spaces might be used. Probably the most common is the RGB color space, in which each color has a specific value in red, green, and blue. Other color spaces include the HSV (hue, saturation, and value) color space and the YIQ color space used in analog NTSC color television.

Colors that are difficult to specify in one color space may be easy to specify in another. For example, skin tones are much easier to specify in the HSV space than in the RGB space. Transformations exist that can convert colors defined in one space into the equivalent colors in another space [Smith 78].

Texture Maps

Another way to specify colors that vary across a surface is to use a *texture map* [Catmull 74]. A texture map is simply a two-dimensional color pattern. This pattern can be synthetically generated, or it can be from an image.

A *UV* parameter coordinate system is introduced to associate the texture map with the modeled surface. The texture map is defined in the two-dimensional *UV* coordinate system. For polygonal surfaces, each vertex has an assigned *UV* texture coordinate. For points on the surface between vertices, the *UV* texture coordinates are interpolated. For bi-parametric surfaces, the *UV* coordinates are simply the surface parameter values.

Each *UV* coordinate pair corresponds to a specific location in the texture space. The color for each point on the surface is determined by finding the *UV* value for that point and then looking up the corresponding color value in the texture map.

Since the texture map is essentially a two-dimensional array of color values, it has values defined only for discrete *UV* values. This means that *UV* interpolation across textured surfaces can result in *UV* values that fall between these discrete values. When this happens, bilinear interpolation may be used to compute the texture value. The fractional portions of the interpolated *UV* values are used as interpolation coefficients to find the required texture color from the four closest surrounding values in the texture map. Higher quality texturing may involve applying convolution filters to the region of the map being sampled.

Williams introduced the *mipmap* concept of repeatedly prefiltering the texture map to obtain multiple representations of the texture data [Williams 83]. Each filter repetition results in a texture map with less detail and lower spatial frequencies. Aliasing effects (see Section 6.6) can be minimized by selecting the appropriate texture representation level. Aliasing can be further reduced by using trilinear interpolation. Trilinear interpolation involves bilinear interpolation in each of two adjacent representation levels, followed by interpolation between the levels. The interpolation within each level is as described above and is based on the fractional UV values. The two representation levels used, and the interpolation coefficient between the levels, are determined by the screen size of UV increments across the surface. As the surface becomes smaller on the screen, more heavily filtered versions of the texture map are used.

Volume textures. The concept of texture maps can be extended to three-dimensional volume textures [Perlin 85, Peachey 85, Perlin and Hoffert 89]. Here, each location in space has a three-dimensional UVW texture coordinate. These coordinates specify locations in a three-dimensional texture array or are used as variables in a three-dimensional texture function. For objects defined with surfaces, the three-dimensional texture is usually only evaluated on the visible surfaces.

The texture coordinates may be embedded in the space containing the model, or the texture space may be attached to the object. If the texture is embedded in the space, the texture of the object will change as it moves through the space.

Texture maps provide a relatively simple and computationally inexpensive way to dramatically increase the perceived surface detail. This can be used for faces to provide variation in skin color and skin surface details. Texture maps can also be used to provide detail for features such as eye irises, lips, and perhaps approximations to facial hair, such as eyebrows.

Opacity and other maps. Opacity, or transparency maps, are very similar to texture maps, but rather than containing color values, they contain opacity or transparency values. This provides an effective way to vary transparency or opacity across skin surfaces or other facial features. Additionally, other surface properties such as specularity and diffuse reflection can be controlled through the use of addition maps that contain information to manipulate these properties across the surfaces.

Bump maps. As we will see, the surface normal is fundamental to reflection calculations, and the normal is also fundamental in shading calculations. Blinn proposed the use of surface normal *variation* as a way of specifying additional surface shading complexity [Blinn 78]. Variation in the surface normals can be used to create wrinkled or bumpy-looking surfaces. The underlying surface geometry is not changed, just the surface shading calculations, which are based on the modified surface normals.

Bump maps are one way to specify the desired surface normal variations or perturbations. The bump map is defined in a UV space similar to that of a texture map. The bump map entries are accessed using the UV values associated with modeled surfaces. Interpolation techniques may be used for bump maps, just as for texture maps.

Bump maps are often vector valued arrays. Each UV coordinate in the map has a vector value. These vectors are used to modify the surface normal vectors.

Displacement maps. Displacement maps are in many ways similar to bump maps. However, rather than manipulating surface normal vectors, displacement map values are used to actually displace the surface location of the points being shaded [Cook 84]. After the surface shading points are displaced, new surface normals are computed-based on the new surface geometry. Bump maps and displacement maps are often a convenient way to create bumps, wrinkles, and creases on the face.

6.3.2   Reflection Properties

Light reflection properties are associated with the modeled surfaces. These properties are usually specified in terms of diffuse reflection, specular reflection, and transparency.

Diffuse. Diffuse light reflection is actually a subsurface property. Light falling on the surface penetrates below the surface, is internally reflected multiple times, and eventually re-emerges from the surface. Diffuse reflection can be modeled using Lambert's law, which states that the amount of diffuse light leaving the surface seen by the viewer depends only on the angle between the surface normal and the direction of the light source illuminating the surface:

$$I = I_s K_d \cos \theta,$$

where I is the diffuse reflected light, I_s is the intensity of the light source, K_d is the diffuse reflection coefficient of the surface material, and θ is the incident angle of the light. The color of diffuse reflected light is primarily a property of the surface material.

Subsurface scattering. Many renderers now have the ability to model the subsurface diffusion of incident light in more detail than is embodied in the Lambert's law approach. For many materials, such as human skin, subsurface light diffusion can result in light re-emerging from the surface some distance away from its entry location, or even re-emerging on the back side of the modeled structure [Hanrahan and Krueger 93]. This effect can be pronounced in thin structures such as the ears and nostrils, especially when backlit.

Specular. Specular light reflection occurs at the surface of the material. It is the kind of reflection that we see from the surface of a mirror or polished chrome. The specular reflection a viewer sees depends on her location relative to the light source and the orientation of the surface. Light incident on a specular surface will be reflected along a vector that is determined by the incident light vector and the surface normal vector. The reflection vector will be in the plane defined by the incident vector and the normal vector. The reflection vector is the incident vector mirrored about the normal vector.

The amount of specular reflection the viewer sees depends on the angle between the reflection vector and the vector from the surface to the viewer's position. For a perfect reflector, the viewer's position must lie directly on the reflection vector to see the reflected light. For less-than-perfect reflectors, which include most specular surfaces, the viewer will see some reflected light even if not positioned directly on the reflection vector. As the angle between the viewing vector and the reflection vector increases, the amount of light seen decreases. This relationship can be expressed as

$$I = I_l K_s \cos^p \gamma,$$

where I is the amount of reflected light, I_l is the intensity of the incident light, K_s is the specular coefficient of the surface, γ is the angle between the viewing vector and the reflection vector, and p is an exponent that determines how rapidly the light falls off as the viewer moves away from the reflection vector. The color of specular reflected light depends on the type of surface material. For metal surfaces, specular color is primarily a property of the surface. For many surfaces, such as plastics, the specular color is primarily a property of the light source.

Reflection maps. Blinn and Newell extended the notion of specular reflection to include reflection maps [Blinn and Newell 76]. A reflection map is essentially a panoramic wraparound image representing the peripheral part of a modeled scene. Vectors going from the viewer position toward the modeled surfaces are specularly reflected. The directions of these reflected vectors are used to access elements of the reflection map. The directions of the reflected vectors are usually specified in terms of azimuth and elevation angles. What the viewer sees reflected from the surface depends on where the reflection vector points in the reflection map. As with texture maps, interpolation or filtering of the map elements may be used to compute the values returned from the reflection map.

Opacity. Opacity is a measure of how much light is transmitted through a material. An ideal transparent material would let all light falling on one side pass through to the other side. Most transparent materials attenuate light transmission to some extent. The attenuation may be color- or wavelength-dependent. Opaque materials transmit no light.

Careful modeling of transparency also includes refraction of the light as it enters the material at one surface and as it leaves the material at another surface.

The Eye as an Example

The eyeballs are an example that illustrates the texture, reflection, and transparency concepts. Texture mapping is a very effective way to represent the complex color patterns in the iris of the eye. These patterns would be very difficult to model using just geometry. Texture mapping could also be used to represent the detailed blood vessel patterns visible on the white of the eye.

Because the surface of the eye is wet, light reflected from the eye is predominantly specular. However, diffuse reflection does contribute significantly. Diffuse reflection is the dominant factor in determining the colors of the iris.

A detailed model of the eye depends on transparency to model the lens of the eye. Light passes to and from the interior of the eye, and to and from the iris, through the lens. Specular reflection from this transparent curved surface creates the dominant highlights we expect to see on the eyes.

6.4   Lighting

Lighting in a synthetic scene is controlled by placing light sources in the modeled environment. Scene lighting can be determined in terms of direct lighting or global lighting or illumination. Direct lighting only considers light falling on surfaces directly from light sources in the environment. Global illumination considers light falling on surfaces directly from the light sources, but also light reflected from, or refracted through, other surfaces in the environment.

6.4.1   Direct Lighting

Direct lighting considers light coming directly from sources such as ambient lights, directional lights, local lights, and spotlights.

Ambient light. Ambient light is a nondirectional, nonlocational source of light. Ambient light is used to approximate the light in a scene due to reflections between the various surfaces. Ambient light intensity usually is specified for the entire scene. Each modeled surface will typically have an ambient light reflection coefficient to determine how much ambient light it will reflect.

Directional lights. Directional light sources are located at an infinite distance in a specific direction. Since these lights have only a direction and not a specific location, some lighting calculations are simplified for directional lights.

Local lights. Local lights have a specific location in the scene. Lighting calculations are more complex for local lights, since the relevant lighting vectors vary across surfaces and throughout the scene.

Spotlights. Spotlights are local lights, but with bounds on the direction of the light. The light is constrained to be within a cone or other cross-sectional shape around a specified direction vector. The size of the bounding shape is a part of the spotlight specification. Light coming from a spotlight often has a fall-off function such that the light is strongest near the light's direction vector and weaker toward its shape boundary.

Direct shadows. Shadows in directly lit scenes fall into two broad classes: those that occur simply because no light happens to illuminate some portion of an object, and those that are caused by an object blocking light that would otherwise fall onto the surface of another object.

The first kind of shadowing may occur even in very simple scenes containing just one object. Those surfaces that are on the side of the object away from all light sources will be in shadow.

Cast shadows are created when objects are positioned between light sources and other objects. For a given single light source, the cast shadow problem is essentially the same as the visible surface problem, but from the point of view of the light source. Surfaces that are not visible to the light source will be in a shadow cast from that light source.

Shadow maps. Shadow maps, developed by Williams, are a common approach to computing cast shadows [Williams 78]. A shadow map contains depth information for the scene, from the point of view of the light. When rendering the scene, this depth information is used to determine if a surface point being shaded is in shadow for that light. If the distance from the light to the shading point is greater than the corresponding depth value in the shadow map, the surface is in shadow at that point.

6.4.2   Global Illumination

Global illumination takes into account the light in an environment that reflects from or through other surfaces before falling on the current shading point. A number of global illumination techniques have been developed. These include ray tracing, radiosity, photon mapping, ambient occlusion, and image-based lighting.

Ray Tracing

Ray tracing, first proposed by Kay [Kay 79] and Whitted [Whitted 80], combines visible surface determination, lighting, shadows, and surface shading into a single algorithm. A simple ray-tracing algorithm applies a recursive procedure to each image pixel to find its color.

This procedure creates a directed line segment or ray from the viewer's eye through the center of each screen pixel. For each pixel, this line is tested to see if it intersects any surfaces in the modeled scene. If so, information about the first surface encountered is stored and new rays are created. One of the new rays is the surface reflection of the original ray. Another new refracted ray is created if the surface is transparent.

Each of these new rays is tested to see if it intersects any surfaces in the scene. Each time a ray intersects a surface, new rays are spawned. The rays are organized in a tree structure. When a ray fails to intersect any surface, a default color value is assigned to that node in the tree, and no new rays are spawned.

When all spawned rays for a given pixel are completed, the ray tree is traversed from the leaf nodes back to the original pixel node. Node color values are computed as the tree is traversed. Node colors are determined by the shading model in effect for the surface at that node, which includes the contributions of reflected and refracted rays from that node. The final result is a single color value for the pixel. This color is based on what the original ray and its descendants encountered in the scene. Ray tracing is good for representing scenes that contain objects with shiny specular or transparent refractive surfaces.

Ray tracing is a simple concept, but it requires significant computation. In the simplest implementations, each ray must be tested against every surface to find possible intersections. When intersections are found, the new rays also must be exhaustively tested. Spheres are a favorite modeling primitive for ray tracing because intersection, reflection, and refraction calculations are fairly simple for spheres.

A number of optimizations have been proposed to increase the efficiency and reduce the cost of ray-tracing calculations [Glassner 84, Kay and Kajiya 86, Glassner 89].

Distributed ray tracing. The simple ray-tracing algorithm outlined above is inherently a point sampling algorithm and as such is subject to spatial aliasing artifacts (see Section 6.6). One approach to reducing aliasing is to trace several rays for each pixel and use a weighted sum of the results. For example, each pixel could be subdivided into 4, 9, or 16 subpixels; each subpixel corresponds to one traced ray.

Cook, Porter, and Carpenter proposed a scheme in which a number of rays are traced for each pixel [Cook et al. 84]. Instead of spacing the rays based on a regular subpixel array, however, the rays are distributed randomly throughout the pixel area. The number of rays traced may be adaptively adjusted. When the summed pixel color converges to a stable value, additional rays are not computed, since they are probably not needed.

Radiosity

Rather than approximating the light due to reflections between objects in the scene with an ambient light term, Goral et al. [Goral et al. 84] and Nishita and Nakamae [Nishita and Nakamae 85] proposed explicitly modeling these interactions using mathematics originally developed to model radiant heat flow. This *radiosity* approach models the steady-state light energy transfer between the light sources and the surfaces in the scene. Radiosity models diffuse inter-reflections between the surfaces.

The result of this complex calculation is independent of viewer position and remains constant for a given scene. If some aspect of the scene lighting or surface placement is changed, the radiosity solution must be recalculated. However, since the calculation is iterative, the previous solution usually provides a good starting point for determining a new solution.

Photon Mapping

In photon mapping, discrete packets of light, the light photons, are simulated. These light packets are emitted from the environment light sources and are reflected and refracted by the various scene surfaces. How the photons are affected by the surfaces depends on the properties of the surface. For some surfaces, the photons that hit stick to the surface, for other surfaces the photons are reflected, for still others they are refracted. More typically, some of the photons stick, while others are reflected or refracted, based on surface properties and a probability function. Eventually all of the photons end up sticking to some surface or are lost from the scene, having encountered no sticking surface [Jensen 01].

This photon tracking process creates a three-dimensional map of the light energy in the scene containing the final location, intensity, and incident direction of all of the photons. The surface shading process then accesses this information to determine the light relevant to each shading point. A three-dmensional filter is typically used to integrate the light energy from the photons in the region around the shading point.

Ambient Occlusion

Ambient occlusion is a kind of global shadow calculation and is computed by casting rays into the environment. Ambient occlusion is an approximation that assumes that light is arriving at a surface point from many directions, having been reflected from many scene surfaces or coming from a surrounding light source, such as the sky.

At each shading point, a number of rays are sent out into the environment in random directions. For each ray that encounters a surface, a hit is recorded. Usually the length of these rays is limited to only allow hits relatively close to the shading point. The computed ambient occlusion at

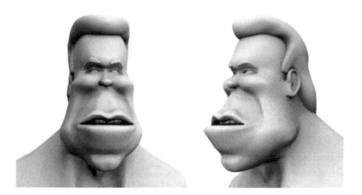

Figure 6.1.
Ambient occlusion applied to a face model. (*Courtesy of E. Andraos, Texas A&M Visualization Laboratory.*)

each shading point is the number of hits divided by the total number of rays sent out. This fraction is used as a coefficient or filter to diminish the surface shade at that point. This produces a shadowing effect that depends on how much of the scene is blocked or occluded by objects close to the shading point. Figure 6.1 shows ambient occlusion applied to two views of a caricature face model.

Image-Based Lighting

In image-based lighting, discrete light sources are replaced by a wraparound image of the surrounding environment, including any light sources such as the sun. These wraparound images may be computed or may be formed by merging a number of photographs, each of them a different view into an environment. These images are often high dynamic range images (HDRI), as discussed below.

The shading calculations for image-based lighting are often quite similar to those used for ambient occlusion. At each shading point a number of rays are cast in random directions into the environment. Rays that do not encounter scene objects will intersect the surrounding environment image. The color or light information at these intersections is integrated to form all or part of the light used in the shading calculations.

High dynamic range images. Conventional photographs and computer images have a limited dynamic range. Film and conventional display devices can only capture and display images with limited dynamic range. Dynamic range refers to the span between the darkest and lightest values in an image, and the number of bits used to represent this intensity span. A typical computer display device can only present images with about 8 bits of information in each of three color channels. While gamma functions are often used to encode this information in a nonlinear way, these devices cannot present the wide range of light values present in most natural scenes.

High dynamic range images allow much wider ranges of intensity information, typically encoding this information as 32-bit floating point values, rather than as 8-bit integer values. High dynamic range images are often created using specialized software to merge conventional photographs, each taken with different exposure settings. The different exposure settings allow each photograph to capture a different portion of the dynamic range of the scene.

6.5   Polygonal Shading Models

While much more elaborate geometric modeling and shading techniques are available, many face models use polygonal surfaces with fairly simple shading. Several shading models have been developed to fill in the pixel color values for polygonal surfaces. These include flat shading, smooth or Gouraud shading, and Phong shading. These techniques are directly supported in the hardware of most graphics cards.

6.5.1   Flat Shading

For flat shading, one color value is computed for each polygon. This color value is based on a single surface normal vector for the entire polygon. Flat shading produces surface shading discontinuities at the boundaries between adjacent polygons. The shaded surface appears *faceted*.

6.5.2   Gouraud Shading

In Gouraud shading a color value is computed for each polygon vertex [Gouraud 71]. Pixel color values between the vertices are computed using linear interpolation. The color value at each vertex is based on a surface normal vector for that vertex. Usually the normal vector at a vertex is computed by summing the normal vectors for all polygons that share that vertex. Since shared vertices have a common normal vector, they will usually have a common vertex color. Gouraud shading eliminates first-order shading discontinuities between adjacent polygons, and the surface appears smooth. Most of the facial images shown in Chapter 7 make use of Gouraud shading.

6.5.3   Phong Shading

Phong Bui-Tuong extends the Gouraud approach to interpolate the vertex surface normals across the polygons [Phong 76]. The vertex normals are computed as in the Gouraud approach. However, a new normal vector is interpolated and renormalized for every pixel. This pixel normal vector is then used to compute the pixel color.

The Phong approach requires significantly more computation but produces better surface shading. Phong shading minimizes the higher-order shading discontinuities between adjacent polygons. Phong shading allows effective specular highlights; Gouraud shading does not.

6.5.4   The OpenGL Shading Model

A typical polygonal shading model is the one used in OpenGL [Neider et al. 93]. This model is directly supported by the hardware in most graphics cards. In this model, a surface color is determined for each polygon vertex. The pixel colors between vertices are determined using Gouraud shading (recent OpenGL implementations also support Phong shading in hardware).

The surface color at each vertex is the sum of three components: a surface material emission component, a global ambient light component, and the sum of contributions from all specified light sources. This sum is expressed as

$$\text{color}_{\text{vertex}} = \text{emission} + \text{ambient}_{\text{global}} + \sum \text{light}_{\text{sources}}. \qquad (6.1)$$

Each of these components has contributions in three primary colors: red, green, and blue. The resulting color values are *clamped* or limited to be in the range [0,1.0]. This model does not include any cast shadow calculations and does not incorporate light reflected from objects onto other objects.

6.5.5   Emission Term

The emission term is the simplest. It models light coming from self-illuminating objects, i.e., objects that *glow*. It is a triplet of RGB light values associated with the object.

6.5.6   Ambient Component

The scene ambient component is calculated by multiplying a scene ambient light term by the ambient material property at the vertex:

$$\text{ambient}_{\text{global}} = \text{ambient}_{\text{light}} * \text{ambient}_{\text{material}}. \qquad (6.2)$$

This calculation is done for each of the RGB color contributions:

$$\begin{aligned} R_{\text{ag}} &= R_{\text{al}} * R_{\text{am}}, \\ G_{\text{ag}} &= G_{\text{al}} * G_{\text{am}}, \\ B_{\text{ag}} &= B_{\text{al}} * B_{\text{am}}. \end{aligned} \qquad (6.3)$$

6.5.7 Contributions from the Light Sources

The contributions of all light sources are summed together. For each light source, its contribution is computed using ambient, diffuse, and specular terms, an attenuation factor, and a possible spotlight effect, as shown below:

$$\text{light}_n = \text{attenuation}_n * \text{spotlight}_n * (\text{ambient}_n + \text{diffuse}_n + \text{specular}_n). \quad (6.4)$$

This computation is done for each of the RGB components.

The attenuation factor for a *local* light is based on the distance between the light source and the vertex, and on three attenuation coefficients:

$$\text{attenuation} = 1/(K_c + K_l d + K_q d^2), \quad (6.5)$$

where d is the distance, K_c is a constant attenuation coefficient, K_l is a linear attenuation coefficient, and K_q is a quadratic attenuation coefficient.

If the light source is *directional* rather than local, the attenuation factor is set to 1.0. A directional light source is located at infinity in a particular direction.

If the light is not a spotlight, the spotlight term is set to 1.0. If the light is a spotlight, but the vertex is outside the illumination cone of the light, the spotlight term is set to 0. If the light is a spotlight and the vertex is inside the cone of illumination, the spotlight term is calculated as follows:

$$\text{spotlight} = \max(v \cdot t, 0)^{\text{spot}}, \quad (6.6)$$

where $v \cdot t$ is the dot product of the two vectors, v is the unit vector that points from the spotlight to the vertex, and t is the unit vector in the direction the spotlight is pointing.

This dot product varies as the cosine of the angle between these two vectors. Objects directly in line with the spotlight get maximum illumination, while those off the spotlight axis get less illumination. The cone of illumination is determined by checking the dot product value against the cosine of the spotlight's cutoff angle. The *spot* exponent determines how fast the spotlight illumination falls off as an object moves away from the center line of the spotlight.

The ambient term for each light is the product of the light source ambient term with the ambient term of the surface material:

$$\text{ambient} = \text{ambient}_{\text{light}} * \text{ambient}_{\text{material}}. \quad (6.7)$$

The diffuse contribution for each light is computed as follows:

$$\text{diffuse} = \max(l \cdot n, 0) * \text{diffuse}_{\text{light}} * \text{diffuse}_{\text{material}}, \quad (6.8)$$

where $l \cdot n$ is the dot product of the unit vector l, which points from the vertex to the light source, and the unit surface normal vector n, at the vertex. The diffuse$_{\text{light}}$ term is a property of each light, while the diffuse$_{\text{material}}$ term is a property of the surface material.

If $l \cdot n \leq 0.0$ for a light, there is no specular component for the light.

If there is a specular component for the light, it is computed as shown below:

$$\text{specular} = \max(s \cdot n, 0)^{\text{shininess}} * \text{specular}_{\text{light}} * \text{specular}_{\text{material}}, \qquad (6.9)$$

where $s \cdot n$ is the dot product of the unit vector s and the unit surface normal vector n, at the vertex. The unit vector s is formed first by adding the vector from the vertex to the light source and the vector from the vertex to the viewpoint, and then by normalizing the result. The specular$_{\text{light}}$ term is a property of each light, whereas the specular$_{\text{material}}$ term is a property of the surface material. Shininess is also a property of the surface material. It determines how shiny the surface is. Chrome has a high shininess value, and felt has a low shininess value.

6.5.8   Shading Languages

The OpenGL shading model discussed above is an example of the kind of shading model often built into a graphics API. This approach presents a fixed shading model, with limited opportunity to customize the resulting shading. Variation is limited to adjusting a few shading coefficients and the placement and kinds of lights used.

Many modern rendering environments support very flexible approaches to shading [Hanrahan and Lawson 90]. For example, Pixar's Renderman environment provides a shading language that allows users to implement essentially any shading algorithms they wish [Apodaca and Gritz 00]. This approach supports the development of custom surface, displacement, volume, and light shaders.

Also, many recent graphics cards support languages for implementing algorithms, including shading algorithms, directly at the graphics hardware level.

6.6   Aliasing

It is important to remember that the pixels of the image array are representations of small image areas, and not simply point locations in the image. A fundamental flaw in most early image synthesis algorithms was that they simply point sampled the projected scene data when determining the color value for each pixel. This approach, while computationally attractive, does not take into account basic sampling theory and thus results in various objectionable image artifacts, such as jagged *stairstep* edges and pixel scintillations in animations.

6.6.1 Spatial Aliasing

Sampling theory tells us that for point sampling to faithfully represent the sampled signal, we must sample at a rate more than twice the highest frequency in the signal. If we fail to do so, the high-frequency components in the signal will not be correctly represented and will appear to be signal components of lower frequency. This misrepresentation is called *aliasing* [Crow 76, Foley et al. 90].

For images, the frequencies of interest are the image spatial frequencies. High spatial frequencies are associated with sharp edges and image detail. Blurry or fuzzy images have relatively low spatial frequencies.

Convolution

The correct way to determine the value for a pixel is to *convolve* the projected two-dimensional scene information with a sampling filter function that preserves the spatial frequencies that can be represented in the image and eliminates the spatial frequencies that cannot be represented [Gonzales and Wintz 87, Foley et al. 90]. The filter functions are continuous two-dimensional weighting functions. *Convolution* involves a two-dimensional integration of the projected scene information multiplied by the filter function. This integration is done for each pixel in the image, with the sampling filter aligned to that pixel.

There are many possible filter functions. Some have finite extent, and some have infinite extent. Some filters do a good job of rejecting unrepresentable frequencies, while others do not. An example of an infinite-extent filter is the function $\sin(x)/x$, where x is the radial distance from the center of the current pixel. It is also the ideal filter function. One simple finite-extent filter is the *box* filter, which has the value 1.0 in the region

Figure 6.2.
Cross-sections of several image filter functions: (left) the *box* filter, (middle) the *triangle* or *tent* filter, and (right) the *Gaussian* filter.

corresponding to the area of the pixel and has a value of 0.0 everywhere else. The box filter gives much better results than simple point sampling, but it is far from an ideal filter. Better finite-extent filter functions include the *triangle* or *tent* filter, and the *Gaussian* filter, as shown in cross-section in Figure 6.2. These filters usually cover an area larger than the pixel.

The size and shape of the filter function have a dramatic effect on the spatial frequency characteristics of the produced image and on the perceived quality of the image. For example, a wide Gaussian filter will produce soft, fuzzy images with relatively low spatial frequencies.

Super Sampling

As you would expect, the convolution-based approach to image synthesis can be enormously expensive. As a result, a number of computationally less expensive techniques have been developed which, while not theoretically correct, give good *approximate* results. These techniques include *super sampling* and *stochastic super sampling* [Cook 86]. Both approaches approximate the convolution integration by summing a number of weighted point samples in and around the region of each computed pixel. In stochastic super sampling, the locations of the point samples are randomly selected; in super sampling, the point sample locations are on a fixed grid. The weightings used for the point samples may be uniform or may vary, based on functions similar to the convolution filter functions.

Area Sampling

Another approach is to determine the area coverage for all visible surface fragments within each pixel region. Catmull did this determination for polygons by clipping the scene polygons along polygon boundaries and along pixel boundaries [Catmull 78]. This action produces a set of polygon fragments for each pixel. Using essentially a box filter, the color for each pixel is computed by summing the color contributions of all visible polygon fragments within the pixel. The contribution of each fragment is formed by weighting its color with the area it covers in the pixel.

6.6.2   Temporal Aliasing

Aliasing can also occur because of poor *temporal* sampling. Each image in an animation represents a finite time span, not just an instant of time. If the time duration of animation images is ignored, temporal aliasing will occur.

Motion blurring is the most obvious manifestation of temporal sampling. Temporal sampling is accomplished in film cameras because the shutter is open for a finite duration while exposing the film. A similar time-dependent sampling occurs in video cameras.

For synthetic images, the correct solution involves a combined temporal and spatial convolution of the image information. This convolution involves a three-dimensional integration of the temporally changing projected scene information, multiplied by a three-dimensional filter function. The third dimension here is time. This solution requires truly heroic amounts of computation.

Temporal super sampling offers a computationally tractable approach. Multiple spatial samples are computed at multiple times within each animation frame. These samples, regularly distributed in both space and time, are summed to form the value for each image pixel. A weighting function, similar to the three-dimensional filter function of the convolution, may be applied to the samples when forming the pixel sums.

Temporal super sampling may be extended to stochastic temporal super sampling. In stochastic temporal super sampling, multiple samples randomly distributed in both time and space are summed to determine each pixel value. A weighting function, similar to the three-dimensional filter function of the convolution, may be applied to these random samples when forming the pixel sums.

6.7   Generating Synthetic Human Skin Texture

For synthetic actors, detailed surface structure should be considered in rendering human skin. While surface texture information may be obtained from photographs or created with a computer painting system, it would be useful to directly generate synthetic human skin textures.

Early work in synthetic skin-like textures includes the work of Miller, Kaufman, and Nahas et al. Miller created reptile skins using bump map and color map techniques [Miller 88b]. Kaufman created reptile skin patterns using a high-level texture synthesis language [Kaufman 88]. Nahas et al. described a method for creating skin texture using texture data obtained from laser scans [Nahas et al. 90].

Ishii et al. developed a synthetic texture generation model specifically for human skin [Ishii et al. 93]. This model has two components: a skin geometry model and a skin reflection model. The geometry model creates detailed three-dimensional skin structures consisting of small furrows and ridges. Reflection is based on a multilayer skin model. In this case, the reflection model is based on the optical features of real skin, which has a number of distinct layers. Light absorption and scattering occur within each skin layer. Light reflection and transmission occur at the boundaries between skin layers.

6.7.1   Skin Surface Geometry

Skin surface consists of four elements: ridges, furrows, hair follicle openings, and sweat gland openings. The furrows and ridges are the dominant geometric features that determine the appearance of the skin. The configuration of these features determines our overall impression of the skin surface. Skin furrows cross the skin surface like a net. Skin ridges lie within the domains produced by the furrows. Hair grows from the follicles, which are located in the furrows. Sweat gland openings are located on the ridges.

In the model proposed by Ishii et al., the overall two-dimensional pattern of the skin is generated using a Voronoi pattern. Variation of furrow shapes is created using pseudofractal subdivision. For some skin surfaces, such as around the wrist, the configuration of furrow and ridge patterns is anisotropic.

The three-dimensional curved ridge surfaces are defined and controlled using Bézier curves. The hierarchical structure of ridge polygons is described recursively. The hierarchical three-dimensional ridge surfaces are the basis for bump-mapped skin surface images.

Pattern Generation

Voronoi division is used to divide the skin surface into initial polygons representing the skin furrow pattern. For natural-looking furrow variations, pseudofractal subdivision is applied to the polygon edges.

Ridge pattern variations are created by changing seed point positions in the Voronoi division and the subdivision deformation magnitude. Pattern anisotropy is created by expanding or contracting vertex positions in particular directions. Figure 6.3 shows results of the Voronoi division and the subdivision methods. Figure 6.4 shows the effect of changing the seed points. The magnitude of perturbation increases from left to right. The

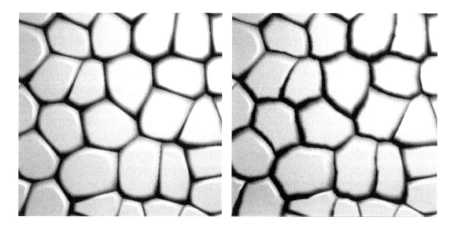

Figure 6.3.
Voronoi division and pseudofractal subdivision results. (*Courtesy of T. Ishii.*)

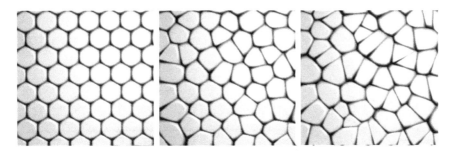

Figure 6.4.
Effect of seed point perturbation, increasing from left to right. (*Courtesy of T. Ishii.*)

fundamental configuration of seed points is a triangular lattice, and the placement perturbation is based on uniform random numbers.

Hierarchical Skin Structure

The skin ridges have a hierarchical structure that determines the skin surface pattern. Small polygons are formed inside the initial polygons, and these small polygons in turn have smaller ridges. This hierarchical structure is created by applying a Voronoi division to each polygon to generate smaller polygons. This polygon division is recursively executed until the desired hierarchical structure is generated. Ishii et al. indicate that three levels are sufficient. Figure 6.5 shows the effect of the hierarchical levels.

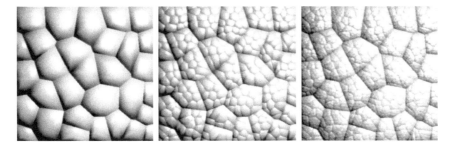

Figure 6.5.
Effect of hierarchical levels: (left) one level, (middle) two levels, (right) three levels. (*Courtesy of T. Ishii.*)

Skin Ridge Shape Definition

The shape of each ridge component in the hierarchy is defined by its base polygon. Each ridge component has a curved three-dimensional surface, whose height increases from its sides to its center. See Figure 6.6.

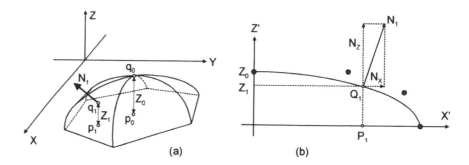

Figure 6.6.
(a) Ridge shape. (b) Ridge shape cross-section.

Cubic Bézier curves are used to define these shapes. Assuming that the base polygon is on the XY plane and the point $P_1(x_1, y_1, 0)$ is on the polygon, we can determine both the height from P_1 to a point $Q_1(x_1, y_1, z_1)$ on the component surface and the normal vector at Q_1, as follows.

First, define a coordinate system for the ridge component by:

- defining the origin at the center point P_0 of the base polygon,

- defining the X'-axis along the direction from point P_0 to point P_1, and

- defining the Z'-axis in the direction perpendicular to the base polygon.

Second, specify the half cross-sectional shape of the ridge component with a cubic Bézier curve defined by four control points in the $X'Z'$ plane.

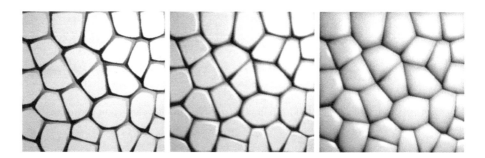

Figure 6.7.
Effect of Bézier curve slopes: (a) discontinuous surface derivatives, (b) steep slope with continuous surface derivatives, (c) a mild slope. (*Courtesy of T. Ishii.*)

The height Z_1 from the base polygon to the ridge component surface and the normal vector S_1 on the surface can be derived from the defined Bézier curve, as shown in Figure 6.6. Different surface shapes can be formed from the same base polygons by changing the control points defining the Bézier cross-sectional curves. The overall surface shape of the skin is formed by compositing the surface shapes of the hierarchy levels.

Figure 6.7 shows the effect of changing the Bézier curve control points, in turn controlling the ridge surface slopes.

6.7.2 Shading Calculation

The shade value of each point on the surface is computed by determining its normal vector. For each point, the base polygons in each hierarchical level are determined. (See Figure 6.8(a).) The parent-child relationship can be efficiently used to find these polygons. For each base polygon, the height and normal vectors at this point are determined using the scheme described above. The height and normal vectors at each level are composed to determine the height and the normal vector for the skin surface at this point. Figure 6.8(b) illustrates this process. The composite normal information forms the bump map used to shade the skin surface.

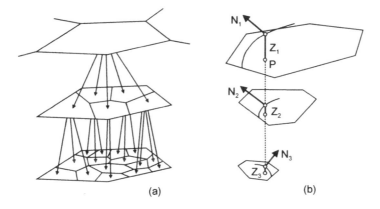

Figure 6.8.
Hierarchical skin structure. (a) Hierarchy of base polygons. (b) Composition of height and normal vectors.

6.7.3 Skin Texture Control Parameters

The following are the geometry control parameters for the Ishii et al. model.

- *Placement of the seed points.* Three types of placement are used: triangle lattice, square lattice, or random lattice. The placement may

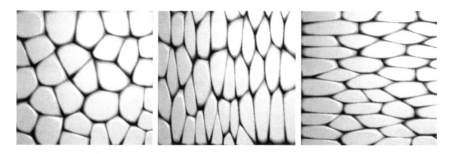

Figure 6.9.
Effect of anisotropic skin structure. (*Courtesy of T. Ishii.*)

be perturbed using random values. Figure 6.4 shows the effect of changing the seed points.

- *Pseudofractal variation of the base polygon edges.* This variation is controlled by specifying the largest distance between the deformed edge and the original edge. The effect of pseudofractal edge variation is shown in Figure 6.3.

- *Anisotropic scaling.* For anisotropic ridge configurations, the base polygon vertices are transformed using asymmetric scale values. Figure 6.9 shows the effect of isotropic structure, vertical asymmetry, and horizontal asymmetry.

- *Number of hierarchy levels.* Figure 6.5 shows the effect of the number of hierarchical levels.

- *Bézier curve control points.* For each hierarchical level, the control point parameters include the number of the curve segments and the placement of the four control points for each segment. Figure 6.7 shows the effect of changing the Bézier curve control points, in turn controlling the ridge surface slopes.

6.7.4 Skin Surface Reflection

Real skin surface consists of the epidermis, the dermis, and the subcutaneous regions. The epidermis, in turn, consists of the horny layer, the granular layer, the thorny layer, and the basis layer, as shown in Figure 6.10.

Skin cells are generated in the basis layer by cell division. These cells move upward and change into thorny cells, granular cells, and horny cells. When horny cells reach the top of skin surface, they are washed or worn off. This is the *keratinization* process of epidermis cells.

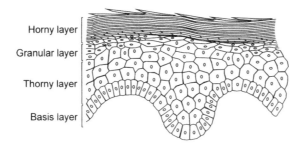

Figure 6.10.
Layers of the epidermis.

Usually, the word *skin* is used to refer to the horny layer. The horny layer itself has a multilayer structure: the sebaceous layer, a number of horny cell layers, and a number of intercellular substance layers (see Figure 6.11). Horny cell layers and intercellular substance layers alternate. The optical characteristics of the skin depend on the number of horny cell layers, the thickness of each layer, and the skin moisture content. The number of horny cell layers is usually about 14. Normal appearance of skin surface depends on normal keratinization and proper moisture in the horny layer.

The Ishii et al. reflection model is based on the optical properties of the horny layer. This model includes absorption and scattering within each horny layer, reflection and refraction at the boundaries between layers, and multiple reflections among the horny layers. This model also includes light reflection at the surface boundary between the air and the first horny layer. The *glossy* appearance of the skin surface is determined by specular reflection, whereas the *soft* appearance of the skin is determined by diffused reflection.

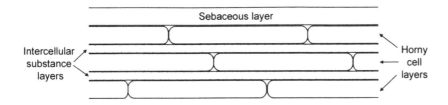

Figure 6.11.
Structure of the skin horny layer.

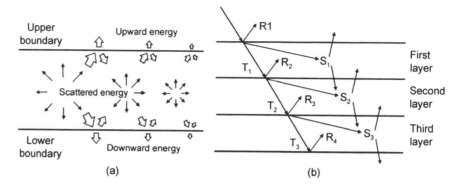

Figure 6.12.
(a) Multiple scattering of light within each layer. (b) Multiple light reflection among the horny layers.

Multiple Light Reflections

It is assumed that the horny layers are essentially parallel (see Figure 6.11). Parallel light enters a layer from its upper boundary. Part of this light is absorbed or scattered within the layer. Light arriving at the lower boundary is divided into reflected light and transmitted light, according to a boundary reflection factor.

Each layer has three modeled light components: parallel light reflected upward from the upper boundary, parallel light transmitted downward at the lower boundary, and the light scattered within the layer.

The scattered light is divided into upward energy and downward energy. These energies are reflected multiple times within a single layer, as shown in Figure 6.12(a). Upward scattered light is divided into transmitted light and reflected light at the upper boundary, based on an upward reflection factor. Downward scattered light is treated similarly. The reflected scattered light turns into new scattered light within the layer.

Four factors are defined for the combined multiple reflections within each layer. These are the reflection factor, the transmission factor, scattered light transmission up, and scattered light transmission down. These factors are applied iteratively from the first layer to the last layer, and from the last layer back to the first layer, as shown in Figure 6.12(b).

The parameters that control the appearance of synthesized skin surface are

- the total number of modeled layers, which affects both the glossy and soft appearance,

- the thickness and scattering coefficients, which affect soft skin appearance, and

- the refraction indices, which affect glossy skin appearance.

Refraction indices, absorption coefficients, and scattering coefficients change with horny layer moisture content.

6.7.5 Rendering Calculations

For the Ishii et al. model, skin rendering consists of two parts: calculating a table of light reflection energies, and rendering the skin images. After assigning the number of layers and setting values for thickness, refraction index, absorption coefficient, and scattering coefficient for each layer, light reflection energies are calculated. The table of reflection energies is computed, based on the incidence angle of light at the skin surface. This table enables quick image shading calculations.

For different skin colors, the reflection energies have different values. The reflection energies are calculated for wavelengths that represent the red, green, and blue color components. The diffusion factor value also varies with wavelength.

Figure 6.13 shows several synthetic skin textures created by combining the skin surface geometry model with the skin surface reflection model.

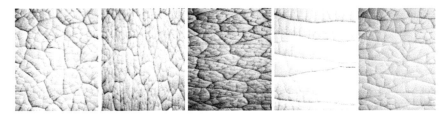

Figure 6.13.
Five skin surface textures synthesized with the Ishii et al. model. (*Courtesy of T. Ishii.*)

6.7.6 Vascular Skin Color Effects

Skin color is partially determined by the flow of blood to and through the skin. Changes in physical and emotional state can affect this blood flow [Kalra and Magnenat-Thalmann 94]. Increased blood flow is associated with physical exertion and emotions such as joy and anger. Decreased blood flow is associated with emotions such as shock and fear.

Increased blood flow causes the skin to appear flushed. Decreased blood flow causes the skin to become more pale. Skin temperature also is reflected in skin color. Hot skin, either from exertion or from being in a hot environment, is associated with increased blood flow and redder skin. Cold skin is associated with decreased blood flow and paler skin. Physical well-being is associated with *rosy* or *glowing* skin, whereas illness is associated with skin pallor.

Although changes in skin color generally apply to the entire face, some areas may be more affected than others [Patel 95]. The cheeks, ears, neck, lips, and forehead may be more or less affected. For example, the blushing associated with embarrassment is usually more noticeable on the cheeks and ears.

6.8   Lighting the Face: Lessons from Portrait Photography

The task of the portrait photographer is to capture optimal facial images. This is done by arranging the pose, selecting the camera placement, and controlling the lighting. Lighting the face is one of the most important aspects [Kodak 61]. There are important lessons to be learned from portrait lighting that can be directly applied to the creation of synthetic facial images.

There are two broad classes of portrait lighting: *directional lighting* and *diffused lighting* [FPC 63]. Directional light includes bright sunlight and artificial light sources such as floodlights and spotlights. Directional lights create distinct highlights and shadows. With directional light, the relative positions of the face, the light sources, and the viewpoint are critical. If the face turns, or if the positions of the lights change, the lighting effect is changed. With directional lights, the interplay of light and shadow on the face can be used to achieve many effects. Lights can be used to emphasize form and texture or to flatten them out.

Light and shadow can be used to emphasize or de-emphasize facial features. Lighter areas in an image are perceived as coming forward, and darker areas are perceived as receding. Highlights on the forehead, nose, chin, and cheeks, along with shadows on the neck and sides of the face, can help create a three-dimensional appearance to the face.

Diffused light is relatively soft and even. It is truthful lighting. It reveals all facial features with equal emphasis. It includes light from a single large light source, light from multiple distributed light sources, light reflected from light-colored surfaces, daylight from a window or skylight, and the light of a gray overcast day. With diffused light, the relative positions of the face, the light sources, and the viewpoint are not critical. Diffused light does not allow the control of light effects that can be achieved with directional lights.

A basic principle of directional portrait lighting is that there should be one dominant light source, with all other light sources subordinate. The placement of this main or key light in relation to the face and to the camera is a primary consideration.

Figure 6.14.
Single-source symmetry plane, full face lighting (side views) from left to right:
light high above the viewpoint, light above the viewpoint, light at the viewpoint,
light below the viewpoint.

6.8.1 Single-Source Lighting

The simplest lighting situation is the use of a single directed light source.
The lighting effect produced is critically dependent on the relative position of the light source, the viewpoint, and the position and orientation of
the face. A number of lighting combinations and the resulting effects are
described below.

Full Face—Viewpoint Directly in Front of the Face

For these poses, the viewpoint or camera position lies on the symmetry
plane of the face, directly in front of the face, looking at the full face.

Light on the symmetry plane of the face. The single light is located in front
of the face, on the symmetry plane of the face, and shines in the direction of
the face. The variations here are primarily in the height of the light source
relative to the face and the viewpoint position. These lighting set-ups are
shown in Figure 6.14.

- *Light high above the viewpoint.* The cheeks and forehead appear
  rounded. The eyes disappear into the shadows of the eye sockets.
  A shadow from the nose is cast down onto the mouth. The face has
  an overall gloomy, tragic look. The cast shadow of the head is not
  usually visible on the background.

- *Light above the viewpoint.* This lighting strongly shows the structures
  of the face. The height of the light should be adjusted so that a
  catchlight—a tiny reflection of the light source—is visible on each eye.
  These catchlights add *life* to the face. The nose shadow shouldn't quite
  touch the upper lip. Slight adjustments in the height of the light can
  significantly change the overall lighting effect.

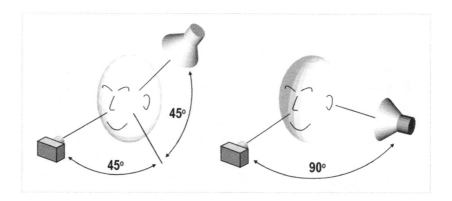

Figure 6.15.
Single-source full face side lighting: (left) light 45 degrees to the side and 45 degrees above the viewpoint; (right) light directly to the side of the face.

- *Light at the viewpoint.* This placement produces lighting that is not very interesting. It flattens facial curvature and washes out facial textures and wrinkles. The head may cast a visible shadow on the background.

- *Light below the viewpoint.* The nose and other facial features cast shadows upward. The eyes catch a lot of light, and the face looks unusual. This lighting can lend an air of mystery and is often used in mystery and horror movies.

Light 45 degrees to the side, 45 degrees above. Here the light source is moved 45 degrees to one side of the face and raised, so that the light is falling on the face at a 45-degree angle from above. This placement provides a flattering illumination of the face, which emphasizes the cheekbones. With the light position properly adjusted, a triangle of light will fall in the upper cheek opposite the light. There should be a reflection from the light visible in both eyes. The result is the classic 45-degree portrait lighting, which can also be used with the head turned partially to the left or right. This set-up is shown in Figure 6.15(left).

Light directly to the side of the face (90 degrees). Moving the single light directly to the side of the face creates a very dramatic effect. One side of the face is lighted, while the other side is completely in shadow. The light can be adjusted in height, but it is usually at the same height as the face. This set-up is shown in Figure 6.15(right).

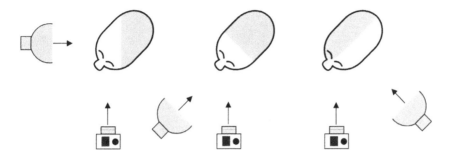

Figure 6.16.
Three-quarter pose lighting set-ups (top views) from left to right: short lighting, butterfly lighting, broad lighting.

Three-Quarter Pose

In this pose, the face is turned slightly away from the viewpoint. The light usually is located somewhat above the face. The height of the light is adjusted so that it creates a catchlight in both eyes, as seen from the camera. The exact height of the light also may be adjusted to flatter particular facial structures. For example, prominent cheeks can be de-emphasized by lowering the light. A short nose appears longer when the light is raised.

There are three categories of lighting for this pose, each determined by the side-to-side placement of the light. These lighting set-ups are shown in Figure 6.16.

- *Short lighting.* The light is located on the side of the face away from the camera, fully illuminating the side of the face away from the camera. This placement emphasizes facial contours and makes the face appear narrower.

- *Butterfly lighting.* The light is placed directly in front of the face and casts a butterfly-shaped shadow under and in line with the nose. This placement is used most successfully with normal-width faces. It may highlight the ears, making them undesirably prominent.

- *Broad lighting.* The light is on the side of the face toward the camera, fully illuminating the side of the face toward the camera. This placement de-emphasizes facial texture and makes narrow faces appear wider.

Facial Profiles

For facial profiles, the camera is positioned directly to one side of the head. The single light may placed in various positions.

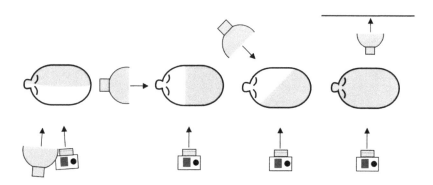

Figure 6.17.
Lighting for profiles (top views).

- Placing the light close to the viewpoint is often the most effective profile lighting.

- Placing the light so that it points directly at the front of the face flattens the curvature of the face, but emphasizes the jaw line with a strong shadow.

- Moving the light farther from the camera produces a partial back-lighting effect. Most of the head will be in shadow, but light does hit some areas of the face. The effect is dramatic, and the contour of the profile is strongly emphasized.

- A complete profile silhouette is obtained by moving the light completely behind the head and turning it to only illuminate the background. No light falls directly on the face.

These lighting set-ups are shown in Figure 6.17. In addition, the single-light set-ups previously described may be used with the viewpoint simply moved to the side of the head.

6.8.2 Multiple-Source Lighting

Most portrait lighting set-ups use multiple lights. The main or key light corresponds to the single-source lighting discussed above. In addition to the main light, there may be one or more fill lights, a background light, one or more hair lights, and perhaps a back light. The basic multiple source lighting set-up is shown in Figure 6.18.

- *The main or key light* generally is located higher than the face and about 45 degrees to one side of the face. It can be in either the *short*

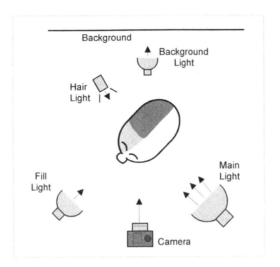

Figure 6.18.
The basic multiple-source lighting set-up (top view).

or *broad* light position, as discussed above. The main light can be
a diffuse or direct light source, depending on the desired effect. A
diffuse main light will minimize facial texture.

The main light should be positioned so that:

- the far cheek is illuminated with a triangular highlight,
- the nose shadow extends downward toward the far corner of the
  mouth, and
- prominent catchlights appear at about the 11 o'clock or 1 o'clock
  position on the eyes as seen from the camera position.

- *The fill light* is placed on the side of the face opposite that of the
  main light. It usually is placed at about the same height as the viewpoint. Its exact side-to-side placement can be used to control facial
  highlights. If this light is positioned too far to the side, it may cause
  unwanted shadows from the cheeks across the mouth. Varying the
  intensity ratio between the main light and the fill light can be used
  to create various effects. This intensity ratio is usually about 3 to 1.
  The ratio can range from as low as 2 to 1 to as high as 6 to 1.

- *The background light* is used to illuminate the background, providing
  tone and color separation between the face and the background. It
  can also provide additional visual interest to the background. This

light usually is placed behind the head, midway between the head and the background. It is placed so that it is not visible from the viewpoint.

- *The hair light* adds detail and highlights to the hair. If the head has no hair, this light is not needed. It is placed high above and slightly behind the face. It can be placed directly overhead or to one side or the other. It should be placed so that it does not shine directly on the face, causing distracting highlights. The intensity of this light is adjusted depending on the color and refection properties of the hair. Dark hair in general will require more light. Multiple hair lights may be used.

- *The back light* is used to partially outline the silhouette of the head or shoulder, separating them from a dark background. It is usually a spotlight placed slightly above and behind the face. It is usually, but not always, on the same side of the face as the main light.

Wraparound Lighting

Sometimes two fill lights are used, rather than just one. By positioning the second fill light about halfway between the main light and the normal single fill light, a pleasant wraparound lighting effect is obtained. The height of the second fill light is usually midway between the height of the main light and the height of the first fill light. The middle fill light helps blend highlight and shadow areas. There is gradual transition from light to dark, which gives the face a more rounded appearance.

6.8.3   Use of Makeup

Makeup is used to modify the properties of the skin or the facial hair. These modifications change skin or hair color or change skin reflection characteristics. The purpose of makeup is to emphasize or de-emphasize facial features. Features may be de-emphasized by making them darker or putting them in shadow. Features may be emphasized by making them lighter.

Makeup can be used to change the apparent contours of features such as the cheekbones. Makeup also can be used to change the color and shape of the eyebrows, the color of the eyelashes, and the shadows around the eyes. Lipstick can be used to change the shape, color, and reflection properties of the lips.

6.9   Animation Rendering and Perception

There is a strong correlation between the characteristics of the human visual system and the methods used to create animation. All film and video media rely on the ability of the human visual system to form a coherent view of dynamic scenes from a rapid sequence of essentially *still* images. The basic frame rates used for these image sequences are the result of compromises based on visual perception characteristics and economics. Human visual system characteristics determine the lower bound on these rates, while technical and economic realities set the upper bound. A frame rate that is too low to sustain the perception of smooth, flicker-free motion is not acceptable. It is also unacceptable for economic and perhaps technical reasons to choose a frame rate so high that it does not further enhance perceived image quality and motion.

Experience and experimentation have determined that 30-Hz-interlaced video is near the lower bound of acceptability. Video frame rates in excess of about 80 Hz contribute very little to perceived quality. For film, a rate of 24 frames per second, with projectors that show each image multiple times, is near the lower acceptability bound. Film systems based on frame rates up to 60 per second have seen limited use. Essentially, all computer and conventional animation is produced for either the 30-Hz video (25-Hz in some countries) or the 24-Hz film standards.

Animators have long had at least an intuitive understanding of additional visual perception characteristics. For example, if the action is slow, a new image is not needed at every frame time. A frame may be held for 2, 3, 4, or even 6 frame times.

If the action is very fast, intentionally blurring the moving portions of the animated images works well. In computer animation, correct temporal sampling blurs the moving parts of the images. These methods and other effective animation techniques work well, because they match human visual perception characteristics [Madsen 69].

Research over the past few decades has demonstrated that human visual perception is supported by two major neurological systems which operate in parallel. These two perception channels are referred to as the *sustained* and the *transient* systems [Kulikowski and Tolhurst 73, Tolhurst 75, Lennie 80]. The sustained system has poor temporal response but has good spatial resolution. It is specialized for pattern and detail detection. The transient system has poor spatial resolution but has good temporal response. It is specialized for motion detection.

The visual system seems designed to give highest priority to moving objects. Motion and scene changes impair the perception of detail, which is the result of a stimulus-masking phenomenon. This masking occurs both backward and forward in time, because the activity of the sustained channel is preempted by the faster transient channel in route to the deeper visual processing areas of the brain [Breitmeyer and Ganz 76]. An abrupt motion will mask detail perception for about 250 milliseconds.

Perception experiments also indicate that the visual system is relatively insensitive to high-spatial-frequency color information [Glenn et al. 85]. It is much more sensitive to high-spatial-frequency luminance information.

Rendering for single still images and rendering for animation sequences are not necessarily optimized in the same ways. Rendering systems designed for animation can take advantage of the temporal characteristics of the visual perception system. Computational economies can be obtained by computing spatial detail only when and where it actually can be perceived in the animation [Parke 91a].

7

Parameterized Face Models

As discussed in Chapter 5, there are many approaches to facial animation. For example, in key-pose animation, the desired shape articulations are specified at various time points. An interpolation algorithm is then used to generate the necessary poses for the in-between frames. However, using this approach, each key pose must be completely specified. Even with current interactive modeling systems, developing the required three-dimensional key-pose descriptions is a challenge. As the number of key poses needed becomes large, this approach quickly becomes daunting.

Motivated by the large effort required by key-pose, interpolation-based animation, Parke developed a *parameterized* face model [Parke 74]. This model originated as an extension to key-pose animation. The desire was to create an encapsulated model that could generate a wide range of faces and facial expressions, based on a small set of input control parameters. With an appropriate parameterized model, animation sequences can be produced with relatively little effort. The value of parameterized models to the animator is that she only needs to manipulate a limited amount of information—the parameters—to create a sequence of animated images.

This chapter describes the development of an early parameterized model and later, several derivative parameterized models. This early model was implemented with relatively primitive techniques. With the development of better, more complete facial parameter sets, and the application of more sophisticated surface modeling and image synthesis techniques, parameter-

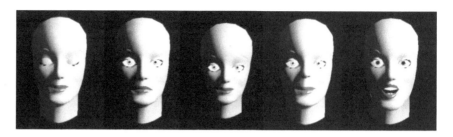

Figure 7.1.
Faces created using a parameterized model.

ized models can now allow much better facial animation. While current techniques allow much more sophistication, this model still has relevance. Direct derivatives of this model are still being used, and many of the techniques embodied in it are useful in simple, low-complexity face models, such as those used in computer games and avatars.

The ideal parameterized model would be one that allowed any possible face with any possible expression to be specified by merely selecting the appropriate parameter value set. A parameterization that enables all possible individual faces and all possible expressions and expression transitions is referred to as a *complete* or *universal* parameterization.

The ad hoc parameterized face model described here certainly falls far short of this ideal, but it does allow a wide range of expressions for a fairly wide range of individual facial conformations. Several faces generated using this parameterized model are illustrated in Figure 7.1.

7.1   Parameterized Model Concepts

There are three basic ideas involved in the creation of parameterized graphic models. One is the fundamental concept of parameterization. Another is the development of appropriate descriptive parameter sets. The third is the development of processes that transform the parameters into the desired facial geometry, which in turn is used to create the desired facial images.

7.1.1   The Basic Parameterization Concept

Consider a class of objects for which individual members have identifiable differences. If the differences between member objects can be associated with a set of differentiation or specification criteria, then individual members of the class can be described or specified by these criteria values. These criteria are the *parameters*.

A *complete* set of specification criteria or parameters is one that allows every member of an object class to be specified by selecting an appropriate set of parameter values. If certain members of the class can be differentiated, but not uniquely described, by parameter values, the parameter set is not complete. In a complete set, every possible unique member of the class can be described by a unique n-tuple of parameter values. Some parameters might have values from finite discrete sets, while others might have values from bounded or unbounded continuous ranges.

A simple example of this notion is the class of objects called *cubes*. The description or specification for a particular cube consists of a set of parameter values, such as the length of its edges, the color of each face, its weight, material, etc. If the set of parameters is complete, one can specify every possible cube by specifying the appropriate n-tuple of the parameter values. However, even for such simple objects, it may be difficult to develop truly complete parameterizations.

7.1.2   The Synthesis Model

Given a parameterization scheme, the remaining task is to develop a synthesis process to produce images based on the parameter values. Figure 7.2 illustrates the major components of animator interaction with such a model. It has two major parts: the parameterized model and the image synthesis routines.

At the heart of the process are the data, functions, and algorithms that form the parameterized model. This model takes as its input the parameter values specified by the animator. It produces as output a set of graphic description primitives, such as vector or polygon descriptors. These graphics primitives are passed as input to the synthesis routines that actually create the images.

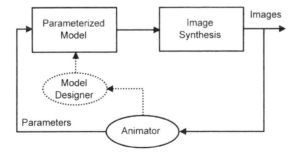

Figure 7.2.
Animator interaction with a parameterized model.

In an interactive implementation, the animator can interactively adjust the parameter values to achieve the desired images or poses. Ideally, the model designer, the model implementor, and the animator interact closely in determining the actual parameterized characteristics of the model.

Part of the model development process is determining the type of images to be produced. These types might be simple vector images generated using line segment descriptions. At the other end of the complexity spectrum, they might be images based on textured bicubic surfaces rendered using complex surface shading and lighting models [Catmull 74]. For simple models, a typical choice is to use polygonal surfaces rendered using fairly simple lighting and surface shading rules [Gouraud 71].

7.2   Facial Parameterization

Given this conceptual framework, developing the desired parameterized model consists of two distinct tasks:

- developing an appropriate set of parameters, and

- developing the parameterized model to implement this parameter set.

The first step is to determine the appropriate set of facial parameters. We would, of course, like to develop a complete parameter set for creating and specifying any possible face with any possible expression. However, the feasibility of developing such a complete parameterization is an open question.

If a complete parameterization is not practical or even possible, can useful parameterized models be developed? Are the parameters appropriate and efficient? Are they the correct parameters? Are they natural and intuitive to use? Do they meet immediate needs? Can the needed range of faces and expressions be generated using the chosen parameter set? Furthermore, can useful parameter sets be developed for which the number of parameters is relatively small?

No implemented facial parameterization to date is even close to being complete. The challenge is to determine a *good* set of control parameters and then to implement a model that uses these parameters to generate the desired range of faces and/or facial expressions. Several useful parameterizations, using only a few parameters, have been demonstrated [Parke 74, Parke 82].

7.2.1   Developing Facial Parameter Sets

How are facial parameter sets developed? One approach is to simply observe the surface properties of faces and to develop *ad hoc* parameters that allow specification of these observed characteristics.

A second approach involves studying the underlying facial structures or anatomy and developing a set of parameters based on this anatomy (see Chapter 3). The models developed by Platt and Badler [Platt and Badler 81] and Waters [Waters 87], for example, were developed based on simple models of the underlying anatomical structures that control facial expression.

A hybrid approach to developing a facial parameter set blends these two approaches. In the hybrid approach, parameters are based on structural understanding wherever possible and are supplemented as necessary by parameters based on observation. The parameterized model described below falls into this hybrid category.

Input and guidance from animators is certainly needed in the development of good, useful parameterizations. The focus should be on developing powerful control parameter sets that are motivated by the needs of the animator.

7.2.2 Expression Versus Conformation

There are two broad categories of parameters: those that control the conformation, or shape, of an individual face, and those that control the face's expression, or emotional aspects. To some extent these two sets overlap, but conceptually they can be considered distinct. Control provided by the early parameterized model includes:

- *Expression parameters.* These parameters, including eyelid opening, eyebrow arch, eyebrow separation, jaw rotation, mouth width, mouth expression, upper-lip position, mouth corner position, and eye gaze, allow the animator to specify and control a range of facial expressions.

- *Conformation parameters.* These parameters, including jaw width, forehead shape, nose length and width, cheek shape, chin shape, neck shape, eye size and separation, face region proportions, and overall face proportions, are used to control a limited range of facial conformation.

The most general parameterized models are those that allow a wide range of both facial conformation and facial expression. However, models that allow variation only in conformation or only in expression are often useful. For example, the animation of a specific character may only require variation in facial expression. Such limited models often have the advantage of simplicity and efficiency.

Most facial models have focused only on expression control. The early work by Parke [Parke 74] and DiPaola's extensions [DiPaola 89, DiPaola 91] also included conformation control as part of the parameterization.

7.2.3   Expression Parameters

Of primary importance in expression are the eyes and the mouth [Madsen 69, Faigin 90]. Therefore, most of the expression parameters relate to these areas. The *best* expression parameter set remains undetermined.

With only a few parameters, it is possible to develop a model that allows interesting expression animation that can be matched to a spoken soundtrack [Parke 74]. Parameters that have been successfully used in past and current models are discussed below.

Expression parameters useful for the eyes include eyelid opening, pupil size or dilation, eyebrow shape and position, and the direction in which the eyes are looking. Useful expression parameters for the mouth include jaw rotation (which strongly influences mouth shape and opening), width of the mouth, mouth expression (smiling, frowning, etc.), position of the upper lip, and positions of the corners of the mouth.

Other useful expression parameters include the orientation of the face and head with respect to the neck and the rest of the body. The ability to orient the head, to turn and tilt it, was not included in early models and was obvious by its absence.

Facial Action Coding System

The muscle-based *Facial Action Coding System* (FACS) notation developed by Ekman and Friesen is one possible foundation for expression parameterizations [Ekman and Friesen 78]. The FACS actions are based on the activity of facial muscles (see Chapter 2). The actions can occur separately or in combination to form expressions. The FACS system appears to be the most complete single basis for developing low-level expression models.

7.2.4   Conformation Parameters

Changes in the conformation of faces, those aspects that vary from individual to individual and make each person unique, require a distinct set of parameters.

Conformation parameters control the relative size, shape, and positioning of the facial features. A few conformation parameters, such as the overall height-to-width aspect ratio of the face, apply globally to the face. These global parameters include a transformation, suggested by Todd et al. [Todd et al. 80] that attempts to model facial growth (see Section 4.12.4). Other conformation parameters may control skin and feature colors and textures.

The variations in facial structure from one individual to another are less understood than the ways in which a given structure varies from one expression to another. Sources of conformation information include facial anatomy, physical anthropology, and those art disciplines concerned with realistic human form representation. Conformation principles from sculpture and portraiture can be useful. The notions of distortion and exaggeration from conventional character animation can also play a role. The development of truly complete conformation parameter sets appears to be difficult. An interesting step in this direction is discussed in Section 4.13.

7.2.5   Quality and Scope of Control Parameterizations

As discussed in Chapter 4, the *quality* of a parameter set refers to the appropriateness and efficiency of the parameters. *Scope* refers to the range of possible faces and expressions that can be generated using the chosen parameter set.

Assuming that truly universal parameterizations are not available, at least in the near term, what are the metrics for judging the quality of a control parameterization? Attributes such as range of control, complexity, parameter set size, intuitiveness, naturalness, and control interfaces immediately come to mind. Are the parameters the correct parameters, and are they natural and intuitive to use?

Certainly an important measure is the range of possible faces and expressions that can be specified. How much of the universe of faces and facial expressions is covered by the parameterization? Judgment of this aspect may be application dependent. If, for example, the application only requires animation of one specific character, then conformation control is not an issue.

Complexity, number of parameters, and intuitive and natural parameters are all directly related attributes. The number of parameters provided and the overall complexity of the parameterization should be just sufficient. Unnecessary parameters or parameter complexity should be avoided.

Subtlety and orthogonality are also measures of parameterization quality. Subtle variations in expression and conformation are often needed. The ability of a parameterization to support these subtle variations is highly desired. Mutual independence of the parameters is also an issue. The change in one parameter value should have minimal and predictable interaction with other parameters. Change in one parameter value should not require reworking the other parameter values. This is particularly true for the interactions between expression and conformation parameters, and between speech and expression parameters.

Another measure of an effective parameterization is its capability to serve as the basis for higher levels of control abstraction. In the case of speech animation, for example, the construction of control parameters at the phoneme or higher levels of abstraction built on top of the basic parameterization should be possible.

7.3   Implementation of a Parameterized Model

Formal procedures for developing models that generate facial images based on a parameter set do not currently exist. The model [Parke 74] described in this section was developed with little theoretical basis and only limited attention to facial anatomy. It was experimentally derived to represent the visible surface features of faces, based on observation and a general understanding of the underlying structures.

This model produces faces constructed of three-dimensional polygonal surfaces. The faces are manipulated through the use of parameters that control procedural shaping functions, interpolation, translation, rotation, and scaling of the various facial features.

This early parameterized facial model has many shortcomings by today's standards. However, it is viable and illustrates one approach to parameterized models. It has been widely distributed and has been sufficiently robust to serve as the basis for subsequent use by other researchers. It has served as the basis for additional work in speech animation [Lewis and Parke 87, Wyvill et al. 88]. This model and its descendants have proved useful to psychologists interested in expression and communication, including the study of multimodal visual speech communications [Cohen and Massaro 90, Cohen and Massaro 93, Cohen and Massaro 94].

This model is both data- and parameter-driven. Data files define the polygon topology and the extreme vertex positions used for the interpolation-based shape changes. The parameter values are entered interactively or, for animated sequences, from command files. The model generates polygon descriptors, which in turn drive polygon rendering routines. Models of this complexity can easily be animated in real time on current personal computers.

7.3.1   Polygon Topology

For this model, image generation is based on polygonal surfaces. The facial mask is one polygonal surface mesh, and each eyeball is another; the teeth are separate polygons. As shown in Figure 7.3(a), the polygon topology for the facial mask is an arbitrary network, rather than a regular grid. The polygonal connections, or topology, of each surface remain constant, but the three-dimensional position of each vertex can vary according to the parameter values, eye orientation, and face orientation. As the vertex positions change, the polygonal surfaces flex and stretch, allowing the face to change shape.

This topology is the result of trial-and-error experience. It contains about 300 polygons defined by about 400 vertices. The polygons are sized and positioned to match the features of the face. There are many small polygons in areas of high curvature and fewer, larger polygons in the flatter regions.

Skin Creases

For smooth shaded polygon meshes, skin creases are a way of adding detail to the facial model without adding polygons. The skin creases are specified in the input data and are not directly controlled by the parameters. Skin creases are generated by controlling the way vertex normals are calculated at the desired skin crease locations. Normals on one side of the crease are computed independently of the normals on the other side of the crease resulting in a shading discontinuity along the crease. The crease vertices are shown in Figure 7.3(a) as small circles.

Single Topology Assumption

A basic assumption underlying the parameterized face model is that a single facial polygon topology can be used. If the facial topology remains fixed, manipulating the face shape or pose only involves manipulating the vertex positions.

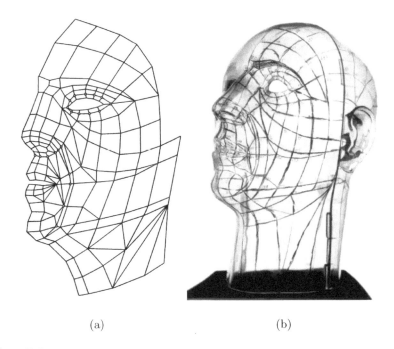

(a)   (b)

Figure 7.3.
(a) Data collection facial topology. (b) Plastic model topology storage device [Parke 74].

Figure 7.4.
Transition from one face into another [Parke 74].

From earlier work [Parke 72] it was known that a fixed topology would allow a specific face to change expression. To determine if a single sufficiently flexible topology could reasonably model different faces, ten different faces were digitized, using the technique described in Section 4.4.5. All ten data sets used the polygonal topology shown in Figure 7.3(a).

This topology was first applied to a plastic model of the head. This model, shown in Figure 7.3(b), served as a storage device for the topology. The plastic model was used a guide each time the topology was applied to a real face, which assured that the topology would be identical from face to face.

Data from the ten faces were used to create an animation that showed transitions from face to face. This animation demonstrated that, at least for the faces used, a single topology would allow representation of many faces and reasonable transitions between faces. Figure 7.4 shows a transition between two of these faces.

7.3.2   Model Data

The parameterized model is based on data measured from the plastic head shown in Figure 7.3(b). Since this head is symmetric, only one side of the face was measured. Except for the eyes, one side of the face is a mirror image of the other side.

Manipulation techniques were then developed to transform this static data into a dynamic, parametrically controlled facial model. These manipulation techniques included procedural functions, interpolation, translation, rotation, and scaling of the various facial features.

7.3.3   Interpolation Basis

Providing useful shape control is crucial to successful face models and facial animation. The polygonal surface approach *requires* that each vertex position be explicitly specified for each facial shape. Recognition that interpolation is a good way to specify flexible polygonal surfaces was a key factor in the development of this early face model.

Interpolation generalizes to polygonal surface shapes by applying it to each vertex defining a surface. Each vertex has two or more three-dimensional positions associated with it. Intermediate forms of the surface are achieved by interpolating each vertex between its associated positions. For interpolation to work, the surface topology must be fixed. That is, the number of vertices defining the surface and their interconnection must be identical in all forms of the surface.

7.3.4 Operations

For this model, operations, such as interpolation, are applied independently to local regions of the face, rather than globally to the entire face. Figure 7.5 gives an overview of the model structure. The parameters affecting the various features are shown. An * indicates the use of interpolation to implement that parameter.

Five operation types were used to determine vertex positions from the parameter values. Although sometimes applied globally to the face, instances of these operations are in most cases applied independently to specific facial regions. These operations are usually order dependent; the operation results depended on a specific order in applying the operations.

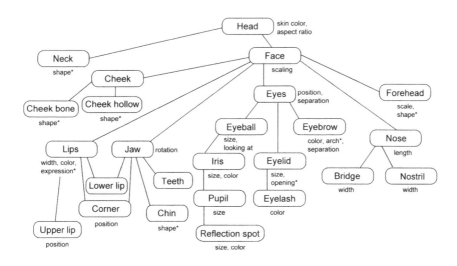

Figure 7.5.
Structure of the parameterized model [Parke 74].

- *Procedural* construction was used to model the eyes. The eyeball procedure accepts parameters for eyeball, iris, and pupil size, and for the color of the iris, the eye position, and the eyeball orientation. It then procedurally generates the polygon descriptors needed for the desired eyes.

- *Interpolation* is used for most regions of the face that change shape. These regions include the forehead, the cheekbones, the neck, and the mouth. Each of these areas is independently interpolated between defined extreme shapes, as specified by a parameter value. For a given vertex in one of these regions, two extreme positions are defined. Parameter values control interpolation between the extreme positions.

- *Rotation* is used to open the mouth by rotating the lower portion of the face around a jaw pivot axis. The effect of this rotation is tapered or weighted from the lower jaw up to the middle of the cheeks.

- *Scaling* controls the relative size and placement of facial features. For example, the chin's prominence and the widths of the nose, jaw, and mouth are controlled by scaling. These scale factors are applied only to vertices within specified regions of the face.

- *Position offsets* control the length of the nose, the corners of the mouth, and the raising of the upper lip. Position offsets move collections or regions of vertices as a group. The effect of some offset operations is tapered or weighted to blend into surrounding regions.

Using current modeling systems, the rotation, scaling and offset operations would mostly likely be done using *clusters*. Operations corresponding to the shape interpolations would likely be implemented using *blend shapes*. The procedural construction operations would likely be done using an embedded language such as MAYA's embedded language MEL capability.

7.3.5 Eyes

The eyes are arguably the most important part of a facial model. Walt Disney once commented that the audience watches the eyes, and that is where time and money must be spent if the character is to be convincing.

The initial step in developing this model was the creation of realistic eyes. This development was done in two steps: first the eyeballs and then the eyelid mechanism.

The Eyeball Model

The eyeballs are modeled as partial spheres. The eyeball sphere is created using concentric bands. The center band forms the pupil, while several

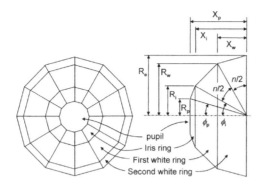

Figure 7.6.
Construction of the eyeball [Parke 74].

surrounding bands are used to model the iris. The outer bands form the
white of the eye. Several parameters are devoted to controlling the size and
spacing of the pupil and iris bands, as well as the iris colors. In a more
modern implementation, these polygon bands would likely be shaded with
texture maps.

The eyeballs are created by a procedure called for each eyeball instance.
This procedure models the eyeball as a polygonal approximation to a hemisphere, as shown in Figure 7.6. This hemisphere consists of a 12-sided pupil
polygon surrounded by three rings of 12 quadrilaterals each. The first of
these rings forms the iris, while the other two form the white of the eye.
The decision to use 12 polygons per ring was a compromise between eyeball
complexity and the desire for the pupil and iris to appear nearly circular.

The following relationships are used in the construction of the eyeballs:

$$\phi_i = \sin^{-1}(R_i/R_e),$$

$$\phi_p = \sin^{-1}(R_p/R_e),$$

$$n = \pi/2 - \phi_i,$$

$$R_w = R_e \sin(\phi_i + n/2),$$

$$X_w = R_e \cos(\phi_i + n/2),$$

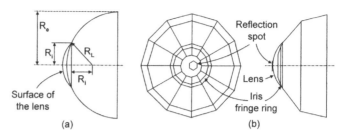

Figure 7.7.
(a) The eyeball lens. (b) The reflection spot and the iris fringe [Parke 74].

$$X_i = \sqrt{R_e^2 + R_i^2},$$

$$X_p = \sqrt{R_e^2 + R_p^2},$$

where R_e is the radius of the eyeball, R_i is the radius of the iris, and R_p is the radius of the pupil.

To achieve more realistic eyes, a reflection of the light source is included on each eye. Eye reflections are almost always visible over some portion of the pupil or iris. These visible reflections are due to the fact that the eyeball is not really spherical, but has a smaller partial sphere, the lens, superimposed on it, as shown in Figure 7.7(a). Here, R_L is the radius of the lens. The reflection spot is modeled as a six-sided polygon tangent to the surface of the eye lens and is free to move over the lens surface, as shown in Figure 7.7(b). The exact positions of the reflection spots depend on the position and orientation of the eyes within the head, the location of the light source, and the location of the viewer relative to the head.

Further realism is obtained by adding an additional ring of polygons to each iris. This ring is used to add a color fringe around the iris, as shown

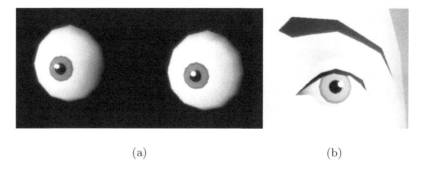

Figure 7.8.
(a) The eyeballs with iris fringes and reflection spots. (b) Eyeball positioned within the face [Parke 74].

in Figure 7.8(b). Figure 7.8(a) shows a rendering of the eyeballs produced by the eyeball procedure.

7.3.6 The Eye Tracking Algorithm

Real eyes have the ability to look at or track objects in their environment. An eye tracking capability is included in this model. Like real eyes, the left and right eye track independently. The orientation angles of each eye depend on the position being looked at and the position of the eyes within the head.

The eyeballs generated by the procedure are centered at the origin of the eye coordinate system with the X-axis passing through the center of the pupil. The desired orientation angles are those that will rotate each eyeball, so that it will be looking in the desired direction when positioned in the face.

Referring to Figure 7.9, we see that each eye has two orientation angles, α and β. These angles are computed independently for each eye. The following equations are used to determine these angles:

$$\alpha_R = \arctan((Y_T - Y_R)/(X_T - X_R)),$$

$$\alpha_L = \arctan((Y_T - Y_L)/(X_T - X_L)),$$

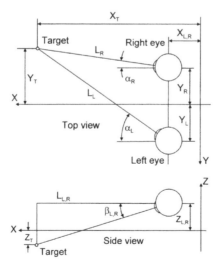

Figure 7.9.
Eye orientation angles [Parke 74].

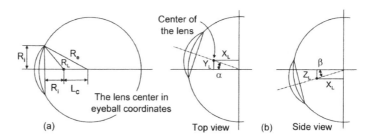

Figure 7.10.
(a) The lens center in eyeball coordinates. (b) The rotated lens center [Parke 74].

$$\beta_R = \arctan((Z_R - Z_T)/L_R),$$

$$\beta_L = \arctan((Z_L - Z_T)/L_L).$$

where

$$L_R = \sqrt{((Y_T - Y_R)^2 + (X_T - X_R)^2)},$$

$$L_L = \sqrt{((Y_T - Y_L)^2 + (X_T - X_L)^2)}.$$

7.3.7 Eyelids

The eyes are installed by generating eyeballs of the size needed and then positioning them in the head coordinate system. The eyelids are fit over the eyeballs using a *spherical mapping* technique.

The eyelids are fit by computing the spherical coordinates (origin at the center of each eyeball) of the eyelid polygon vertices. The spherical radius coordinate of each eyelid vertex is then adjusted to be slightly larger than the radius of the eyeball. The ability to open and close the eyelids is implemented by combining a variation of the spherical mapping technique with linear interpolation.

Figure 7.11 shows the eyelid polygon structure used. The vertices enclosed by the dashed line are involved in opening and closing the eyelid. These vertices are defined in only two dimensions, width and height. The third dimension is obtained by projecting the vertices back onto a sphere slightly larger than, and centered on, the eyeball.

The edges of the eyelids are modeled as a thin strip of polygons, whose inner vertices are projected back onto a slightly smaller sphere.

Using two sets of two-dimensional vertex data values, one for wide open eyes and one for closed eyes, intermediate eyelid openings can be interpolated. Projecting the interpolated two-dimensional vertices back onto

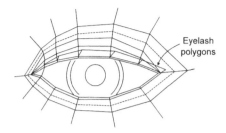

Figure 7.11.
Two-dimensional eyelid topology [Parke 74].

the eyelid sphere produces the desired eyelid opening. The eyelid opening parameter controls the two-dimensional interpolation. This process is analogous to real eyelids, where two membranes are stretched across a spherical surface. This procedure is illustrated in Figure 7.12. The result of fitting the eyeballs into the face is shown in Figure 7.8(b).

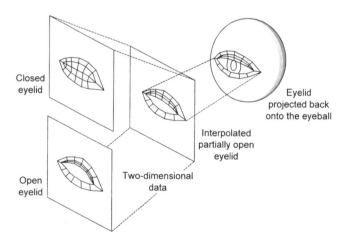

Figure 7.12.
The eyelid mechanism [Parke 74].

Eyelashes

The eyelashes are modeled as a set of five polygons, as shown in Figure 7.11. These polygons are included as part of the upper eyelid. Like the eyelid polygons, they are only defined in two dimensions. The inner vertices of the eyelashes are projected back onto the same sphere as the main eyelid vertices. However, the outer eyelash vertices are projected onto larger spherical surfaces.

In the early model, these polygons were assigned a single eyelash color. In a current implementation, these polygons would likely be assigned a texture map with transparency, This would allow a better approximation to the actual eyelash structures.

7.3.8   Eyebrows

The dynamic expression properties of the eyebrows are implemented using a combination of interpolation and translation. Two sets of shape data for the eyebrow vertices are specified. The eyebrows are varied from high to low arch by interpolating between these two data sets. An additional parameter uses translation to vary the separation of the eyebrows across the bridge of the nose.

7.3.9   Eye Region Parameters

Table 7.1 lists the parameters that affect the eye region of the face model. Iris, iris fringe, and reflection spot colors are additional model parameters. Figure 7.13 shows the effect of varying only two of these parameters: eyelid opening and eyebrow arch.

Parameters	
(interpolated)	
eyebrow arch	eyebrow separation
eyelid opening	eyeball size
(fraction of eyeball size)	*(fraction of iris size)*
iris size	iris fringe size
reflection spot size	pupil size

Table 7.1.
Eye region parameters.

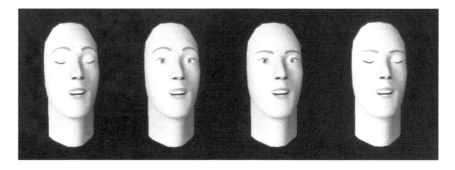

Figure 7.13.
Effect of eyebrow arch and eyelid opening parameters [Parke 74].

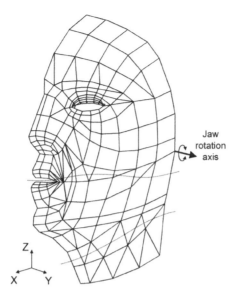

Figure 7.14.
Vertices affected by jaw rotation [Parke 74].

7.3.10   Mouth and Jaw

The mouth is opened by rotating the vertices of the lower part of the face about a jaw pivot axis. Jaw rotation is necessary for the mouth to assume its various speech and expression postures. This rotation is tapered or weighted. The vertices along the jaw are rotated by the full amount specified in the rotation parameter, but the rotation applied to those points above the jaw and below the mouth tapers, so that the amount of rotation gradually diminishes for points higher in the face. While the lower lip rotates, most of the the upper lip does not; therefore, the mouth opens.

The vertices located between the dashed lines in Figure 7.14 are the vertices affected by jaw rotation. The jaw axis of rotation is parallel to the Y-axis and passes through the indicated jaw pivot point. The lower lip, lower teeth, and corner of the mouth rotate with the jaw. Positive jaw rotation has the effect of opening the mouth.

The center points of the lower lip are rotated with the jaw. Other points along the lower lip are rotated by amounts that taper toward the corners of the mouth. Vertices closer to the corners rotate by smaller amounts. The corners of the mouth rotate by one-third of the jaw rotation. This scheme gives a fairly natural oval-looking mouth.

Another parameter allows the upper lip to be raised and lowered. The effect of this translation is tapered from the center of the lip to the corners of the mouth. The center vertices receive the full effect, while the corner vertices are not affected.

The mouth can vary in shape by interpolating between two expression data sets. These data sets represent two expression extremes, such as *smile* and *neutral*.

The model has several additional mouth manipulation parameters. A scaling factor is used to control the width of the mouth. A translation parameter allows the lips to move forward, away from the teeth. Another parameter controls the thickness of the lips at the corner of the mouth. Three translation parameters allow the corners of the mouth to move in all three dimensions. A translation parameter is used to tuck the lower lip up under the front teeth—the position assumed by the mouth when forming the *f* and *v* sounds. The teeth are modeled as 32 four-sided polygons arranged along an approximation to the dental arch.

7.3.11 Mouth Region Parameters

Table 7.2 lists the parameters affecting the mouth region of the face model. Figure 7.15 show the effects obtained using three of these parameters: jaw rotation, upper-lip position, and mouth expression.

Parameters	
jaw rotation	mouth width
mouth expression	mouth corner width
X corner displacement	upper-lip position
Y corner displacement	forward lip offset
Z corner displacement	"*f*" tuck

Table 7.2.
Mouth region parameters.

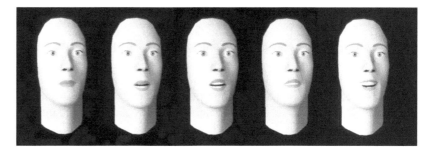

Figure 7.15.
Effect of jaw rotation, upper-lip position, and mouth expression [Parke 74].

7.3.12   Conformation Parameters

A set of parameters is included in the model that allow the face to change in conformation. Conformation is used here to mean those features of the face that vary from one individual to another, as opposed to features that change from expression to expression.

Although the following parameterization is clearly not complete, it does allow a variety of facial conformations within the implied limits. These parameters are implemented by means of interpolation, scaling, and translation.

Parameters Implemented by Interpolation

The shape of the chin and neck are modified using interpolation. The forehead shape can be varied from sloping to bulging. The cheekbone can range from not noticeable to very pronounced. The hollow of the cheek can change from convex to concave.

Parameters Implemented by Scaling

Three parameters determine the overall *aspect ratio* of the face and head by scaling the entire head in each of the three dimensions.

Two parameters are used to control the width and height of the eyelids. Varying the values of these parameters controls the shape and size of the eyelids.

The nose is affected by two scaling parameters. One controls the width of the bridge of the nose. The other determines the width of the lower portion of the nose, including the nostrils.

Three scale parameters are used to control the vertical proportions of the face. One parameter scales the region from the chin to the mouth. Another parameter scales the region from the chin to the eyes. The third parameter scales the region above the eyes.

Additional parameters scale the width of the cheeks and the width of the jaw. The effect of the jaw scaling is tapered. The maximum effect is applied to the lower forward point of the jaw. The scaling effect diminishes toward the upper rear of the jaw.

Parameters Implemented by Translation

It is possible to move the chin up and down, as well as forward and back in relation to the rest of the face. The lower portion of the nose can be moved forward, backward, up, or down. The eyebrows also may be displaced up or down.

Table 7.3 lists the conformation parameters and their value ranges. Figure 7.16 illustrates the effect of several conformation parameters.

Parameters	
(*Scaling*)	(*Interpolation*)
head X-scale	forehead
head Y-scale	cheekbone
head Z-scale	cheek hollow
chin-to-mouth	chin shape
chin-to-eye	neck shape
eye-to-forehead	
eyelid X-scale	(*Translation*)
eyelid Z-scale	chin X-offset
jaw width	chin Z-offset
cheek width	end-of-nose X-offset
nose bridge width	end-of-nose Z-offset
nose nostril width	eyebrow Z-offset

Table 7.3.
Conformation parameters.

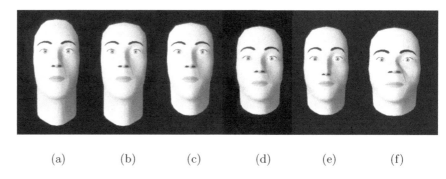

(a)   (b)   (c)   (d)   (e)   (f)

Figure 7.16.
The effect of several conformation parameters: (a) the initial face; (b) changed forehead shape; (c) changed neck shape and jaw scale; (d) changed chin-to-mouth scale, changed chin-to-eye scale, and increased vertical scale; (e) end of the nose moved down, horizontal scale decreased, and the cheekbones slightly more prominent; (f) increased horizontal scale, raised and widened end of nose, narrowed bridge of nose, lowered eyebrows, more prominent cheekbones, and more concave cheek hollows [Parke 74].

Additional Parameters

A number of additional parameters affect the face or its environment. These parameters include the position of the eyeballs within the head, where the modeled eyes are looking, where the light source is located, where the viewer is located and where she is looking. Other parameters control the field of view, the colors of facial features, and the shading model used.

7.3.13   Parameter Ordering

Several regions of the face are affected by many parameters. The results of applying the parameter-controlled operations are dependent on the order in which the operations are performed. The ordering depends on the specific implementation of a given parameterized model.

7.4   Animation Using the Parameterized Model

A parameterized model allows the animator to create facial images by simply specifying the appropriate parameter values. Animation is reduced to varying the parameter values over time. A sequence of images can be created by specifying the parameter values for each image in the desired animation sequence.

The challenging part of this task is to determine how the values must change over time to achieve a desired effect. The solution usually involves varying several parameter values simultaneously over any given time period.

7.4.1   Key Framing in Parameter Space

Key framing can be applied to the parameter values required to specify the face poses, rather than directly to the face poses. For each parameter, a time-tagged set of values is specified. At each frame time of the animation sequence, a function is evaluated for each parameter. This function is usually a simple interpolation based on the time-tagged key parameter values. The interpolation could be linear or could use an ease-in or ease-out function, or both.

7.4.2   Speech Animation

One of the main goals for this early model was to support speech animation. Speech animation was achieved by manipulating the facial parameters so that the facial expression and lip motions matched a spoken soundtrack. Madsen indicates that the capabilities listed below are required for lip animation [Madsen 69] (see Chapter 9 for a detailed treatment of speech animation).

- Open lips for the open vowels—a, e, and i.

- Closed lips for the accent consonants—p, b, and m.

- An oval mouth for u, o, and w.

- Tucking the lower lip under the front teeth for f and v.

- The ability to move between these lip positions as required.

A number of the parameters described in the previous sections are used for speech animation. These parameters include jaw rotation, mouth width, lower-lip tuck, upper-lip raising, moving lips forward from the teeth, and manipulation of the corner of the mouth. Manipulation of the eyebrows, eyelids, and the mouth expression is used in conjunction with the speech parameters to convey emphasis and emotion.

Fewer than ten parameters are needed to do a reasonable job of speech animation. The parameters found most effective for facial expression and speech animation are listed in Table 7.4.

Figure 7.17 shows two more recent parameterized models that are direct descendents of the original model. These models are intended for expressive speech animation and do not include any conformation change capability.

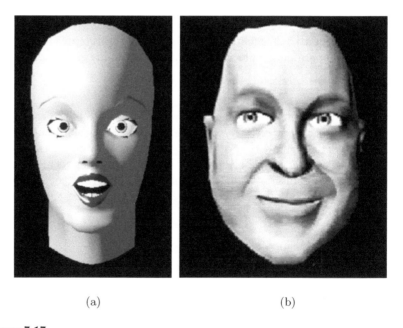

(a)   (b)

Figure 7.17.
Two more recent parameterized models. (b) This version was designed as an interactive avatar.

Lip Animation Parameters
jaw rotation
upper-lip position
mouth width
Expression Parameters
mouth expression
eyebrow arch
eyebrow separation
eyelid opening
pupil size
eye tracking

Table 7.4.
Speech parameters.

7.5 Parameterized Model Extensions

DiPaola, Pearce, and Cohen have each created extended versions based on the original Parke model. These extensions are discussed in this section. Possible future extensions are also presented.

7.5.1 DiPaola Extensions

DiPaola created a second-generation parameterized model based on the early model described above [DiPaola 89, DiPaola 91]. This implementation is sometimes referred to as the Facial Animation System (FAS). It was designed to integrate into an early production animation system.

This model was extended to include about 80 parameters for controlling the face, head, and facial hair. Like the earlier model, the operations controlled by the parameters include interpolation, translation, rotation, and scaling applied to particular regions of the face or head. These operations usually taper their effect on vertices near the region boundaries. More of the parameters in this model control procedural operations than in the earlier model. The development of the parameter operations was based primarily on visual results achieved.

Broader Range of Facial Types

One of the main attributes of this extended system is its ability to specify and animate a wider range of facial types. This system deals with faces outside the range of realistic human conformation. It includes conformation parameters that allow stylized humanoid faces, caricatures, and cartoon-like faces, as well as realistic faces.

Parameters controlling localized deformation functions, such as those described in Section 4.12.6, are examples of the procedural operations used to extend the range of facial types. An example is shown in Figure 4.24.

Global and local squash and stretch parameters have been added to the model. The squash and stretch parameters, patterned after squash and stretch in conventional animation, preserve the volume of the face and head.

If an animator chose to scale the eyes to half the size of the head, the eye scale parameters would also have to influence neighboring regions, such as the forehead and the cheek regions. This capability is supported by this model. Broadening other parameters in this way adds additional flexibility. It also adds algorithmic complexity.

Since different facial types are just extreme variations in facial conformation parameters, different facial types can morph into each other by simply interpolating the conformation parameter values.

Asymmetry

Natural-looking faces need to be asymmetrical. If the topology of the facial model is asymmetric, the model will continue to be asymmetric even when symmetric expression parameters are applied to it. However, asymmetric expression parameters are also desired.

Most expression parameters for this model are implemented as dual asymmetric parameters, with left and right side components. The left component affects the left side of the face, while the right component affects the right side of the face. These components can also be used in a mode where both are changed as one symmetric parameter.

Additional Expression Parameters

Puffed upper cheeks were added as a necessary companion to closed or squinted eyes. Flared nostrils were added as a complement to many mouth positions, including the angry mouth expression. Neck rotations were added to allow appropriate head gestures.

Eyes

The eyes are capable of being scaled in all directions, producing, among other shapes, large elongated oval eyeballs. For this distortion to work, the neighboring facial areas need to accommodate as required. The skin surrounding the eyeballs stretches appropriately. The eyelids close naturally, no matter how the shape of the eyes is exaggerated. DiPaola's model is designed so that most of these compensations occur automatically. Therefore, specific accommodation parameters are not needed, and the eye control parameters need only include eyeball scales, eyelid positions, and eyeball rotations.

The eyeball is modeled as a high resolution sphere. The iris and pupil are modeled with a second, smaller sphere that intersects the larger eyeball sphere. This added curvature closely approximates the curvature of the real human eye. With this complex curvature, reflections are rendered over the iris most of the time.

Texture mapping was used to define the iris and pupil area. This texture was derived from a photograph of an actual eye.

Complete Heads

The early parameterized models included only the face and the front of the neck. This DiPaola model is more complete, including the ears, the back of the head, and facial hair.

Ears

Ears are very individual and are important in representing individual likenesses. They are also challenging to model. Ears have complex shapes, with higher surface curvature than most other regions of the head. To model them well requires a large number of polygons or complex bicubic surfaces, with many control points.

The amount of data needed to represent detailed ear curvature can be large and may be out of proportion to the importance of the ears in the overall model. Overly detailed ears may actually draw attention away from the rest of the face.

The obvious solution, of lowering the modeled detail of the ears, can result in overly simplified, very unnatural ears. The compromise used in this model is to model the ears with a relatively low resolution polygonal surface. Skin creases corresponding to curvature boundaries are then used to emphasize ear surface curvature.

Facial Hair

Facial hair includes the eyebrows, and a mustache or beard, if present. The facial hair is modeled with *hair globs*. These hair globs are small, irregularly shaped polygonal surfaces. The shapes of these surfaces are intended to mimic small tufts of hair. The hair globs are procedurally positioned and automatically aligned to the topology of the face. The hair globs flex and move with the face as it is animated.

Paths are defined on the face where the hair is to be located. These paths pass through points tied to the topology of the face. The type of hair glob and the number of globs for each path are specified. The hair globs are automatically positioned and aligned along the defined paths. Additional parameters are implemented to animate the hair regions independent of the face motions.

Eyebrows

Eyebrows are extremely expressive, capable of achieving a wide range of poses. In the case of cartoons and caricatures, the variety of eyebrow shapes is almost limitless.

The eyebrows in this model are created using hair globs. Several parameters are used to create the overall eyebrow shapes by controlling a number of facial points. A cubic spline is passed through these points, defining a smooth eyebrow shape. Hair globs of the necessary size and orientation are positioned at intervals along this shape.

Neck

In addition to rotation parameters, the neck has parameters controlling its length and width. These parameters aid in attaching the face to an independent body model.

Matching Facial Animation with Body Animation

This facial model was combined with a full body model that was animated using a key-frame system. The body model was first animated with a dummy place holder head, rather than with the detailed facial model. To coordinate the facial animation with the completed body animation, the hierarchical head transformation information from the body animation was read into the facial animation system. This made it possible to transform the face into the proper positions and orientations needed to match the body animation.

Interactive Control and Real-Time Playback

This facial model incorporates interactive control and real-time playback, much like a *track-based* key-frame animation system. As with a key-frame animation system, the animator can create key poses, choose interpolation schemes, edit parameter value tracks, and preview animation in real time. The major difference for the facial system is that parameter values, rather than hierarchical transformations, are saved, interpolated, and applied to the model.

In addition to using entire key poses or individual parameter tracks, facial *region* tracks can be used. Region tracks are composed of parameter groups for specific facial regions.

The use of facial expression libraries is supported by this model, which allows reuse of previous expression descriptions and animation sequences.

7.5.2   Pearce Extensions

Pearce re-implemented and extended the original model to directly support phoneme-based speech animation [Pearce et al. 86]. The main extension was to provide phoneme-based control, which was done by mapping phoneme specifications into parameter value sets. This mapping also included time duration information. Transitions between sequential phonemes therefore included not only the parameter values for each phoneme, but also information about how the parameter values changed over time during the transition.

These transitions are specified using nonlinear interpolation. The transition timing between phonemes is dependent on the specific phoneme sequence.

7.5.3 Cohen Extensions

To support work in *visible speech*, Cohen implemented a number of extensions to the original parameterized model [Cohen and Massaro 90, Cohen and Massaro 93]. These included additional lip and tongue parameters, the use of skin texture mapping, and skin transparency.

Additional Lip and Tongue Parameters

To allow better speech articulation, four additional lip control parameters were added to the model:

- Raise the lower lip.

- "Roll" the lower lip.

- Adjust lip thickness.

- Jaw thrust—translate the jaw forward or backward.

Two of the original lip parameters were modified to have more global effects. Raising the upper lip also raises some of the facial area above the lip. When the lips protrude, the cheeks are pulled inward.

Since the tongue is important for representing detailed speech articulation, a simplified tongue was added, along with four tongue shape and position control parameters. This tongue was modeled as a polygonal mesh surface. These tongue control parameters are:

- tongue length,

- tongue width,

- tongue thickness,

- tongue angle.

Image Mapping

The implementation was extended to support the mapping of two-dimensional facial images onto the polygonal surface of the face. These images are typically obtained from video sequences. The images are scaled and centered to match the face model. In addition, the face shape conformation parameters are adjusted to conform to the shape of the facial images.

Once the image is scaled and centered and the face conformation is adjusted to achieve the best match between the image and face surface shape, the image is *attached* to the polygonal surface. The mapped image then moves with the parameter-controlled surface articulations.

Skin Transparency

An additional parameter was used to control the transparency of the polygons representing the skin of the face. Transparency makes speech articulations inside the mouth visible.

7.5.4   Extensions

Several extensions to direct parameterized models are discussed below.

Use of Parametric Surfaces

A lesson learned from the early parameterized models is that the polygon data density for the facial surfaces was too sparse. Higher polygon density is needed to represent the subtle shape variations associated with subtle expression and conformation changes. The data density certainly needs to be increased in the major expressive areas of the face, the eyes, and the mouth.

The use of subdivision or bicubic surfaces presents an attractive alternative to the polygonal approach. With such representations, the facial control parameters would manipulate surface control points, rather than manipulate the surfaces directly.

Better Parameterizations

The goal is to provide natural and intuitive parameters that allow a wide range of conformation and expression control and flexibility.

Better parameter sets are needed. This need is particularly true for the conformation parameters, but it is also true for the expression parameters.

One area of improvement might be the more effective use of parameter-controlled procedural construction and manipulation of facial features.

Another possibility would be to include automatic *secondary actions* in the model. This addition could possibly reduce the size and complexity of the parameter set for a given level of capability. The effect of each parameter would be extended to support any secondary actions associated with its main function.

Higher-Level Parameterizations

Parameters for the original model are specified at a fairly low level, such as width of mouth, upper-lip position, etc. There is an obvious need for parameterizations specified at higher levels of abstraction. Examples of higher level parameters might be age, ethnic type, speech phonemes, etc. Such parameters would allow facial conformation and animation control at a much higher level.

The high-level parameterizations might be built on top of existing or future lower-level parameterizations. They could be implemented using groups of operations similar to those used in the current low-level parameterized models.

At an even higher level would be parameterizations more like the *language* used by directors in guiding live actors. These parameters might include ones controlling overall expression, mood, and attitude.

Non-Humanoid Faces

Facial models in general, and parameterized models in particular, have generally been limited to humanoid faces. However, conformation parameters might be extended to include non-humanoid faces, such as primates. They might be extended to include animal faces, and even fanciful or alien creature faces.

.

8

Skin and Muscle-Based Facial Animation

The detailed anatomy of the head and face is a complex assembly of bones, cartilage, muscle, nerves, blood vessels, glands, fatty tissue, connective tissue, skin, and hair, as described in Chapter 3. To date, facial animation, based on this level of anatomical detail, is hard. However, it is possible to reduce the complexity of the anatomy and mechanical properties to construct a simple animated model of the face. These models manipulate facial expression based on the physical characteristics of facial muscle and skin.

Recently, simulating skin tissue dynamics has received attention, particularly in surgical planning, where it is desirable to visualize the effects of surgery before the actual operation. Some of these techniques have been applied to facial animation to enhance the dynamic behavior of facial models, in particular skin tissue deformations, that produce subtle deformations such as furrowing. Therefore, this chapter focuses on some of the techniques that people have addressed to date.

8.1 The Mechanics of Facial Tissue

A description of facial tissue was described in Section 3.7, so this chapter focuses on the mechanics of facial tissue. Skin tissue deformation under applied loads has been the subject of a number of biomedical investigations

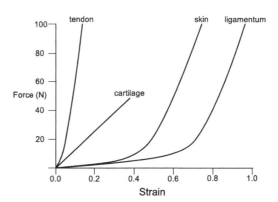

Figure 8.1.
Force-deformation relations for a selection of excised human tissues tested in uniaxial tension.

[Rose et al. 78, Kenedi et al. 75, Harkness 77, Wright 77, Larrabee 86]. These investigations adopt an engineering point of view, similar to that taken by researchers in material science and continuum mechanics [Atkin 80]. What is evident from the experiments on living tissue is that there is a greater complexity displayed than that exhibited on structural materials for construction and manufacturing.

As a unit, soft tissue is *viscoelastic* in its responses to *stress*, the force of load, and *strain*, the deformation or stretch. The result is that it has properties of both an elastic solid and a viscous liquid. The elastic nature of soft tissue refers to its storage of energy and tendency to return to its rest shape when the load is removed. The relationship between load and deformation is nonlinear, even in the range of deformations commonly encountered in living subjects. Figure 8.1 illustrates the relationship between stresses and strains in soft tissue under typical uniaxial tension.

Tissue is viscous, such that the internal forces generated due to a deformation are dependent not only on the amount of deformation but also on the rate of deformation. The viscoelastic nature of soft tissue additionally displays the following phenomena:

- *Hysteresis* refers to a change in the response of the material under cyclic loading and unloading, as illustrated in Figure 8.2.

- *Stress relaxation* is the reduction in the force opposing a deformation held constant in time.

- *Creep* is the increase in strain over time in a material under the influence of a constant load.

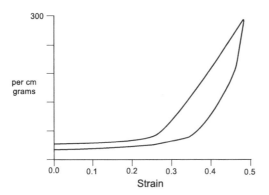

Figure 8.2.
Loading versus unloading force elongation curves of a skin patch. The
separation of the two curves illustrates a hysteresis effect.

- *Preconditioning* is when repeated applications of the same load result
  in different deformation responses.

The mechanical properties of skin are the result of the interaction of
two cellular bases: elastin and collagen. The behavior of elastin, which is a
major component of blood vessels, is very similar to an ideal rubber with an
essentially linear stress/strain response over a wide range of deformations.
Collagen, the material of tendons, has a much stronger stress response to
applied load and has a more limited range of deformation. The low stress
response to small strains may be due to the stretching of elastin, since the
collagen is arranged in a deformable lattice structure. The sudden increase
in stress may be due to the stretching of collagen once it is aligned with
the deformation. The pattern of the collagen lattice is not symmetric and
tends to form contour lines of fibers with common orientation. These lines
correspond to lines of anisotropic deformation of the skin, called Langer's
lines [Warwick 73], as illustrated in Figure 3.29.

The fat cells and the ground substance, which are composed mostly of
water, account for the viscous properties of skin. They also account for the
behavior of the tissue under compression, where the collagen lattice on its
own would merely collapse. Instead, since the water in the fat and ground
substance is incompressible, they are forced outward, perpendicular to the
line of compression. This phenomenon is called the *Poisson effect*. Extension of the tissue also causes contraction along the plane, perpendicular to
the line of extension.

The composition of the soft tissue of the face changes with age
[Gonzalez-Ulloa and Flores 65]. In the dermis of a newborn, there is a large

proportion of collagen compared to the amount of elastin, but this ratio inverts in old age, so that elastin is present in much higher concentrations than collagen. In addition, skin becomes thinner with age, due to the reduction of adipose tissue. Folds form along lines of the skin adherence and muscle insertion, causing characteristic wrinkle lines.

8.1.1 Biological Solids

When considering a computer model of a biological solid, it is useful to consider some basic engineering principles. In particular, forces are defined to be applied per unit area and can be related either to the original cross-sectional area or to the deformed cross-sectional area. A force, or stress, placed on a material acts in a specific direction, and therefore is defined as a stress vector.

When a material is deformed, the change in length is defined in terms of strain. Take for example the material illustrated in Figure 8.3. This material is deformed from an original length L_0 to an elongated state L. A variety of ratios can then be used to represent this change in length $\lambda = \frac{L}{L_0}$, with the corresponding strain measures:

$$e = \frac{L - L_0}{L_0}, \qquad E = \frac{L - L_0}{L};$$

$$e = \frac{L^2 - L_0^2}{2L^2}, \qquad \xi = \frac{L^2 - L_0^2}{2L_0^2}.$$

These strains are all roughly equal for very small deformations, but become different under larger deformations.

A deformable material often is defined as a Hookean elastic solid following Hooke's law: $\sigma = Ee$, where σ is stress, E is a constant known as Young's modulus, and e is strain. Hooke's law can be exactly applied to materials with linear stress/strain relationships. When defining a three-dimensional solid, multiple elastic constants are required. However, the equations can be simplified for materials that are isotropic (equal stress produces equal

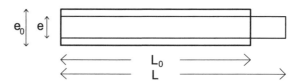

Figure 8.3.
A material of length L_0 elongates to a length L while the width changes from e_0 to e.

displacement in any direction) rather than anisotropic materials, characterized by directional variations. When considering a two-dimensional isotropic material, further simplifications can be made. Only two elastic constants need be defined: E or Young's modulus, and v or *Poisson's* ratio, which is the ratio of the contraction of the surface in one direction when it elongates in the other.

Whereas elastic materials can be realized as Hookean solids, liquids can be realized as Newtonian fluids. Liquids traditionally are modeled according to the principles of hydrodynamics, where a viscous liquid obeys Newton's law:

$$\sigma = \frac{\eta de}{dt},$$ (8.1)

where η is viscosity, e is strain, and t is time.

Many biological materials combine both elastic solid and viscous liquid behavior and subsequently are called viscoelastic. The properties of viscoelastic materials have already been described as hysteresis, stress relaxation, and creep. By using both Hookean and Newtonian laws, models of viscoelastic materials can be simulated. Essentially, these materials are a combination of a linear spring with a Young's modulus E and a dashpot with a viscosity η. As a result, the spring creates a deformation proportional to the load, while the dashpot becomes a shock absorber producing a velocity proportional to the load. These two basic components can be combined in a variety of ways to simulate viscoelastic materials [Terzopoulos and Fleischer 88b]. Two simple combinations are the Maxwell and Voight, as illustrated in Figure 8.4, that have been used to describe the effects of muscle and tendons. For example, Hill's muscle model, illustrated in Figure 8.5, was developed by the observation of isolated frog muscles [Gasser and Hill 24].

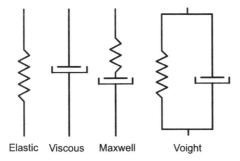

Elastic   Viscous   Maxwell   Voight

Figure 8.4.
Mechanical models for viscoelastic soft tissue.

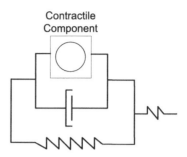

Figure 8.5.
Hill's muscle model consisting of a contractive component and a parallel viscous
unit coupled to additional elastic units.

8.2   The Mechanics of Muscles

Muscles are the principle motivators of facial expression, such that when a
muscle contracts, it attempts to draw its attachments together. For facial
muscles, this action usually involves drawing the skin toward the point of
skeletal subsurface attachment.

Muscle fibers come in many lengths, sometimes stretching the whole
length of the muscle, and are usually 10 to 100 microns in diameter. The
muscle fibers are composed of still smaller elements called myofibrils that
run the whole length of the fiber. Each myofibril is about 1 to 2 microns
thick. As a result, a single muscle fiber contains hundreds to several thousands of myofibrils.

Along the longitudinal axis of each myofibril is a repeating pattern of
filaments called *sarcomeres*. The sarcomere is the actual functional unit of
contraction in the muscle. Sarcomeres are short—only about 1 to 2 microns
long—and contract developing tension along their longitudinal axis. It is
this shortening, in series, of many sarcomeres that creates the shortening
of a single muscle fiber; the subsequent overall shortening of a muscle is
created by the contraction of many fibers in parallel.

At the most fundamental level, two contractive proteins, actin and
myosin, form the filaments within a sarcomere. In cross-section, they are
packed hexagonally with six thin myosin filaments surrounding each thick
actin filament. A theory of sliding filament muscle contraction was developed by Huxley in 1954, by the careful observation of isolated frog muscle
[Huxley and Niedergerke 54]. Essentially, he observed that during muscle
contraction, the actin filaments were drawn into the A-bands, between the
myosin rods, as illustrated in Figure 8.6.

Effectively, muscles behave like tunable springs, such that forces generated by them are a function of length and level of neural activation

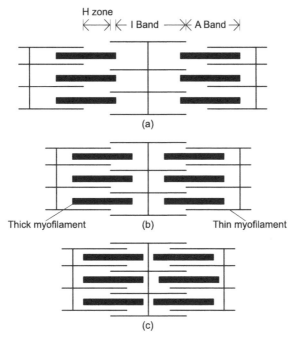

Figure 8.6.
A schematic diagram illustrating the changes (a), (b), (c) in myosin and actin banding patterns observed by Huxley.

[Bizzi et al. 82]. By attributing spring-like and viscous qualities, a displacement becomes proportional to force and stiffness. This result is simply a restatement of Hookean and Newtownian laws in a biological context.

8.3   A Muscle Model Process

The anatomical and mechanical characteristics described so far illustrate the complexity of the systems we are attempting to model. One approach is to ignore many of the physical attributes and simply mimic the primary biomechanical characteristics of facial tissue displacements by a geometric distortion function. This procedure is by far the most computationally inexpensive solution and produces reasonable results.

What follows is the description of the three primary muscle types: *linear*, *sphincter*, and *sheet* [Waters 87]. Linear muscle and sheet muscle are described as *linear muscle vectors*, whereas the sphincter muscle is described as an *elliptical contraction*.

8.3.1   Muscle Vectors

Muscle vectors, as the name suggests, follow the major direction and insertion of muscle fibers. Whereas real muscle consists of many individual fibers, the computer model assumes a single direction and attachment. With this simplifying assumption, an individual muscle can be described with direction and magnitude in both two and three dimensions; the direction is toward a point of attachment on the bone, and the magnitude of the displacement depends upon the muscle spring constant and the tension created by a muscular contraction.

In linear or parallel muscle, the surrounding skin is contracted toward the static node of attachment on the bone, until, at a finite distance away, the force dissipates to zero. In sphincter muscle, the skin tissue is squeezed toward an imaginary center, like the tightening of a string bag. This squeezing can be described as occurring uniformly about a point of contraction. Sheet muscle is a broad flat area of muscle fiber strands and does not emanate from a point source. As a result, it contracts to a localized node, rather than to a group of separated muscle fiber nodes. In fact, the muscle is a series of almost parallel fibers spread over an area.

The behavior of the linear, sphincter, and sheet muscles results from low-level muscle fiber contractions. Therefore, the requirement of the muscle model is to compute the displacement of surface nodes to new locations, thereby emulating real skin deformation.

8.3.2   Linear Muscle

For the linear muscle, it is necessary to compute how adjacent tissue, such as the node $\mathbf{p}$ in Figure 8.7(b), is affected by a muscle vector contraction. It is assumed that there is no displacement at the point of insertion in the bone, and that maximum deflection occurs at the point of insertion into the skin. Consequently, a dissipation of the force is passed to the adjoining tissue, both across the sectors $\mathbf{A}$ and $\mathbf{B}$ in Figure 8.7(a).

To compute the displacement of an arbitrary node $\mathbf{p}$ in Figure 8.7(b), located on the mesh, to a new displacement $\mathbf{p}'$ within the segment $v_1 p_r p_s$ toward v_1 along the vector p, v_1, the following expression is employed:

$$\mathbf{p}' = \mathbf{p} + akr\frac{\mathbf{pv_1}}{||\mathbf{pv_1}||}. \tag{8.2}$$

Here the new location $\mathbf{p}'$ is a function of an angular displacement parameter

$$a = \cos(a2), \tag{8.3}$$

where $a2$ is the angle between the vectors $(\mathbf{v_1}, \mathbf{v_2})$ and $(\mathbf{v_1}, \mathbf{p})$, D is $||\mathbf{v_1}-\mathbf{p}||$, and r is a radial displacement parameter, such that

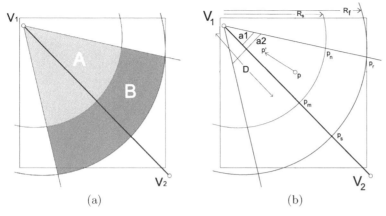

Figure 8.7.
The linear muscle description: (a) The two zones **A** and **B** in which two
different displacement are calculationed. (b) The parameters required to
calculate the displacement of node **p** to **p**$'$.

$$r = \begin{cases} \cos(\frac{1-D}{R_s}), & \text{for } \mathbf{p} \text{ inside sector } (\mathbf{v}_1\mathbf{p}_n\mathbf{p}_m\mathbf{p}_1), \\ \cos(\frac{D-R_s}{R_f-R_s}), & \text{for } \mathbf{p} \text{ inside sector } (\mathbf{p}_n\mathbf{p}_r\mathbf{p}_s\mathbf{p}_m), \end{cases} \qquad (8.4)$$

and k is a fixed constant representing the elasticity of skin. By varying the
contraction factor of the muscle, the displacement of skin will appear to

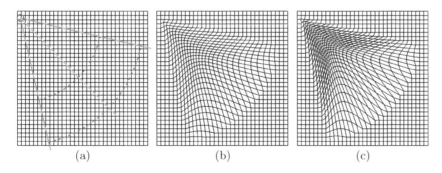

Figure 8.8.
A progressing sequence of muscle contraction with a linear cosine activity. The
mesh is a regular lattice of 20 x 20 units, and the contraction factor is (a) 0.3,
(b) 0.5, and (c) 0.7.

move along the main axis of the muscle toward the root of the vector, as illustrated in Figure 8.8.

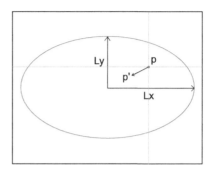

Figure 8.9.
The sphincter muscle description.

8.3.3   The Sphincter Muscle

Unlike the linear muscle model, a sphincter muscle contracts around an imaginary central point. As a result, the surface surrounding the mouth is drawn together, like the tightening of material at the top of a string bag.

Essentially, the sphincter muscle is elliptical in appearance, surrounding the mouth. The muscle consists of other muscles that surround the mouth opening; for more anatomical details, see Chapter 3. With reference to Figure 3.20, the overall shape of the muscle can be simplified to a parametric

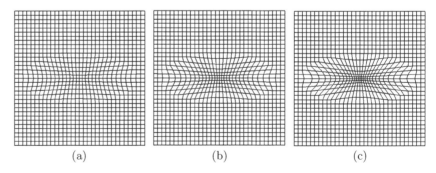

(a)   (b)   (c)

Figure 8.10.
A progressing sequence of sphincter muscle contraction with a cosine activity. The eliptical parameters are: lx is 18.0 and ly 7.0 with a mesh size of 20 × 20 units with 42 increments. Muscle contractions are (a) 0.3, (b) 0.6, and (c) 0.9.

ellipsoid with a major and minor axis, lx representing the semimajor axis, and ly the semiminor axis about an imaginary epicenter c, as illustrated in Figure 8.9. To compute the displacement of node $\mathbf{p}$ to $\mathbf{p}'$ in Figure 8.9, the following equation is used:

$$f = 1 - \frac{\sqrt{ly^2 p_x^2 + lx^2 p_y^2}}{l_x l_y}. \qquad (8.5)$$

Figure 8.10 illustrates three images of a progressive sphincter muscle contraction.

8.3.4   Sheet Muscle

Sheet muscle consists of strands of fibers that lie in flat bundles. An example of this type of muscle is the frontalis major, which lies on the forehead and is primarily involved with the raising of the eyebrows.

Whereas a linear muscle has a radial component, a sheet muscle neither emanates from a point source, nor contracts to a localized node. In fact, the muscle is a series of almost parallel fibers spread over an area, as illustrated in Figure 8.11(a). The computation of a node $\mathbf{p}$ can then be defined, in reference to Figure 8.11(b), as

$$d = \begin{cases} \cos(1 - \frac{L_t}{R_f}), & \text{for } \mathbf{p} \text{ inside Zone } A, \\ \cos(1 - \frac{L_t}{R_f} * (\frac{V_i}{V_l} + V_f)), & \text{for } \mathbf{p} \text{ inside sector Zone } C. \end{cases} \qquad (8.6)$$

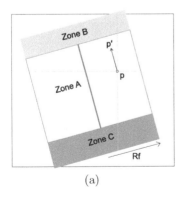

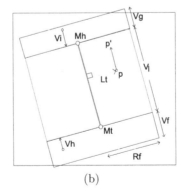

(a)   (b)

Figure 8.11.
The components of a sheet muscle: (a) The three zones **A**, **B**, and **C** into which a node $\mathbf{p}$ can fall. (b) The parameters used to compute the displacement of a node $\mathbf{p}$ to $\mathbf{p}'$, depending on in which zone the node falls.

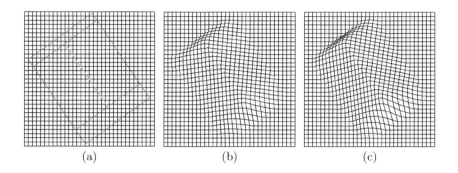

(a)   (b)   (c)

Figure 8.12.
A progressing sequence of sheet muscle contraction based on a cosine activity.
Mesh size is 20×20. Contractions are (a) 0.3, (b) 0.7, and (c) 0.9.

Figure 8.12 illustrates the contraction of a sheet muscle influenced by an increasing contraction.

8.3.5   Varying the Elastic Properties

The linear, sphincter, and sheet muscles use a cosine function as a first-order approximation to the elastic properties of skin. While this approach produces adequate results, it is evident that the elasticity of skin varies with age and from person to person [Gonzalez-Ulloa and Flores 65]. By replacing the cosine function with a nonlinear interpolant, or power function as illustrated in Figure 8.13, it is possible to vary the elasticity of the mesh and thereby emulate the lower elasticity of skin as it ages.

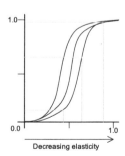

Figure 8.13.
Smooth nonlinear interpolation splines as a first approximatation to lower skin elasticity.

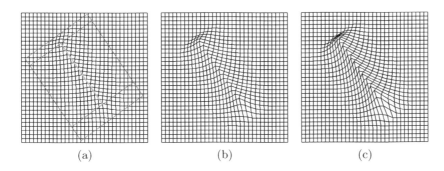

Figure 8.14.
An increasing sheet muscle activity raised to a power of 3 illustrates the reduced elasticity of skin.

A power function increases the falloff to zero at the boundaries of the muscle vectors. Figure 8.14 illustrates the function raised to a power of 3. Such a technique allows a more flexible approach to the modeling of the primary muscle vectors. For a more direct approach, splines can be empolyed in the derivation of the interpolation coefficients.

8.4   Modeling the Primary Facial Expressions

Extensive research by psychologists of nonverbal communication has established a basic categorization of facial expressions that are considered generic to the human race [Ekman 73]. Ekman, Friesen, and Ellsworth propose happiness, anger, fear, surprise, disgust/contempt, and sadness as the six primary effect categories [Ekman et al. 72]. Other expressions, such as interest, calm bitterness, pride, irony, insecurity, and skepticism can be displayed on the face, but they have not been as firmly established as fear, surprise, disgust and sadness.

The Facial Action Coding System (FACS), developed by Ekman and Friesen [Ekman and Friesen 78], psychologists of nonverbal communication, is a widely used notation for the coding of facial articulation (for more details, see Chapter 2). FACS describes 66 muscle actions (some muscle blends), which in combination can give rise to thousands of possible facial expressions. These discrete units can be used as fundamental building blocks or reference units for the development of a parameterized facial muscle process.

What follows in the next sections describes the synthesis of the six primary facial expressions: surprise, fear, disgust, anger, sadness, and happiness.

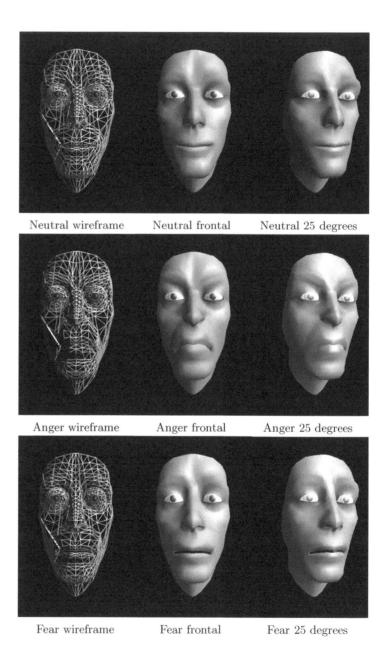

Neutral wireframe   Neutral frontal   Neutral 25 degrees

Anger wireframe   Anger frontal   Anger 25 degrees

Fear wireframe   Fear frontal   Fear 25 degrees

Figure 8.15.
Neutral, anger, and *fear* expressions created from the muscle model process.

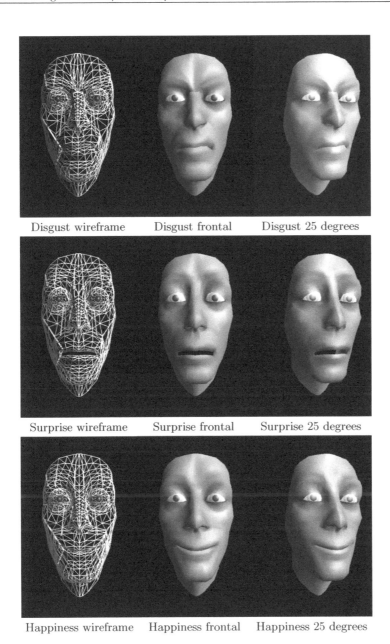

Disgust wireframe   Disgust frontal   Disgust 25 degrees

Surprise wireframe   Surprise frontal   Surprise 25 degrees

Happiness wireframe   Happiness frontal   Happiness 25 degrees

Figure 8.16.
Disgust, surprise, and *happiness* expressions created from the muscle model
process.

8.4.1   Surprise

Surprise is perhaps the briefest expression. In the upper face, the brows are curved and raised (AU1 + AU2). There are no distinctive muscle actions in the midsection of the face. The jaw drops, causing the lips and teeth to part. The more extreme the surprise, the wider the jaw becomes (Figure 8.16 and Color Plate III).

8.4.2   Fear

Fear varies in intensity from apprehension to terror. In the upper face, the brows appear raised and straightened (AU1 + AU2 + AU4). The eyes are tense during fear, with the upper lid raised and the lower lid tense. In the midsection of the face, the corners of the lips may be drawn backward (AU20), tightening the lips against the teeth. In the lower face, the teeth usually are exposed by the downward pull of the lip (AU15 and/or AU16) (Figure 8.15 and Color Plate III).

8.4.3   Disgust

Disgust is an expression of aversion, such as the taste of something you want to spit out. In the upper face there could be a lowering of the brows (AU4); however, the primary cues to the expression are found in the midregion of the face around the nose and upper lip. Usually the upper lip is raised (AU9 and/or AU10), drawing up the flanges of the nose. The lower lip may be drawn downward or raised (AU17) (Figure 8.16 and Color Plate III).

8.4.4   Anger

In the emotional state of anger, a person is most likely to harm someone purposefully. The brows are drawn down and together (AU2 + AU4), while the eyes stare in a penetrating fashion, with the eyelids wide (AU5). In the midregion of the face, the flanges of the nose can be drawn upward (AU10). In the lower face region, there can be two distinctive types of motion: the lips closed hard against the teeth (AU24), or the lips parted to bare teeth (AU25) (Figure 8.15 and Color Plate III).

8.4.5   Happiness

Happiness is a positive emotion and can vary in intensity from mildly happy to joy or ecstasy. In the upper face, the brows hardly change, while the eyelids are slightly compressed by the cheek, which is up (AU6). The most prominent action is the raising of the corners of the lips, which widens the mouth into a broad grin (AU12). This action usually is combined with deepening nasolabial folds (AU11) (Figure 8.16 and Color Plate III).

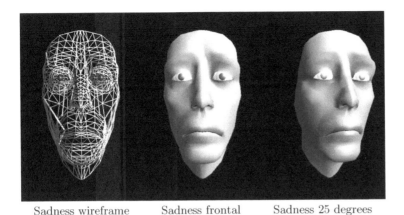

Sadness wireframe   Sadness frontal   Sadness 25 degrees

Figure 8.17.
Sadness expression created from the muscle model process.

8.4.6 Sadness

Sadness is endured stress, and unlike surprise, it is often prolonged in duration. In sadness, the inner portion of the brows are drawn together and raised (AU1 + AU2 + AU4). The eyes usually are cast downward and the lower eyelids slightly raised. The mouth displays subtle motions that are akin to the expression of disgust, where the corners of the mouth are pulled downward (AU15) (Figure 8.17 and Color Plate III).

8.5 Parametric Surface Patches

The polygon is one of the basic primitives in every computer graphics system. In most cases, a sequence of polygons is sufficient to approximate a curved surface. However, obtaining satisfactory smoothness, especially when considering the face, often requires large amounts of data. Furthermore, even with continuous Gouraud or Phong shading models, undesirable visual artifacts can arise, such as Mach banding [Gouraud 71].

Chapter 4 described a variety of representations capable of producing continuous surfaces and thereby reducing such artifacts. A popular representation is the class of parametric surfaces such as B-splines, NURB surfaces, Catmull-Rom splines, Beta-splines, and hierarchical B-splines. These representations produce faces with smooth, curved surfaces, using relatively few control points.

While the parametric representation is attractive from a facial modeling point of view, it does complicate the manipulation of the surface for facial animation. The next three sections describe a variety of approaches taken to date to overcome the issues that arise in facial animation.

8.5.1   Bicubic B-spline Patches

The ideal layout for B-spline patches is a regular lattice of control points, which was employed by Waite to model and animate the face with a muscle model [Waite 89]. The muscles were coordinated with the Facial Action Coding System to create a facial expression editor.

To achieve an animated face, Waite determined the activation regions of the face aligning muscles, or small groups of muscles, to the Facial Action

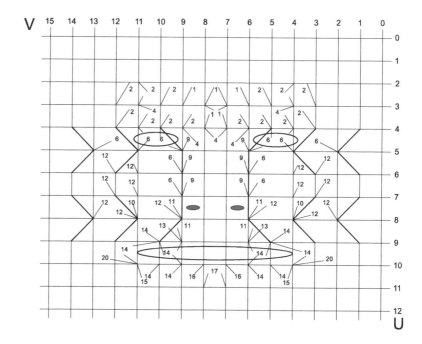

Figure 8.18.
A B-spline face patch. The U, V Facial Action Coding Unit mappings for the left side of the face are as follows:
AU1 Left=(3,9)(3,8)(4,9)(4,8), AU2 Left=(3,11)(3,10)(4,11)(4,10),
AU4 Left=(2,11)(2,8)(3,10)(3,9)(4,9)(4,8)(3,11),
AU6 Left=(4,12)(4,11)(4,10)(4,9)(5,9)(5,11)(5,13)(6,9)(7,9),
AU9 Left=(5,9)(6,9)(7,9), AU10 Left=(8,10), AU11 Left=(8,9)(9,9),
AU12 Left=(9,11)(10,11)(8,9)(8,11)(8,13)(7,12)(7,11)(6,11)(6,12),
AU13 Left=(9,9), AU14 Left=(9,10)(9,9)(10,10)(10,9),
AU15 Left=(9,11)(10,11), AU16 Left=(10,9)(10,8),
AU17 Left=(10,8)(10,7)(11,8)(11,7), AU20 Left=(9,11)(10,11)

Coding System. The result was a 15 by 12 rectangular face patch, as illustrated in Figure 8.18. Within the face patch, five holes were trimmed out to represent the eyes, nostrils, and mouth. Furrow lines, such as the nasiolabial and infraorbital furrows, were created by doubling up control points, thereby lowering the continuity at that location by one factor. Finally, the mappings between the action units and the u, v space of the patch were defined.

Perhaps the biggest limitation of this approach is that the face does not conform to a rectangular geometry configuration and has to be deformed into a face shape.

8.5.2 Bicubic and Catmull-Rom Splines with a Muscle Model

In the animation of *Tin Toy* [Reeves 90], the geometry of the baby's face was constructed from four-sided bicubic Catmull-Rom patches.[1] The complete geometry for the face consisted of some 6,000 three-dimensional node vectors, far too many to control in an animation sequence.

The animation of the face was achieved by a muscle-based model similar to Waters' [Waters 87]; two kinds of muscles were implemented: linear and elliptical sphincters. A linear muscle was defined by two vectors: a bony attachment and a skin attachment. The sphincter muscles were used around the mouth to purse the lips and around the eyes. In this case, a single point defined the center of the muscle contraction, and three other points defined the axes from which an ellipsoid zone of influence was created. In both cases, a cosine function was used to blend between the maximal displacement at the center of the region of the ellipse and the edge of the linear muscle.

While having 50 muscle controls was a significant reduction in the total number of parameters in the face, further reduction was necessary for the animators. This reduction was achieved by creating macro muscles. A *macro muscle* is a single control that when contracted, causes several low-level muscles to contract. The amount of contraction is weighted by a scaling factor for each low-level muscle. For example, a contraction of 1 on the left brow macro muscle pulls 0.3 on the left1a, 0.5 on left1b, and 0.8 on left2a. A total of 33 macro muscles were defined, and approximately 12 were in use for most of the animation. While the macro muscles saved time by encapsulating commonly used actions, the animator retained complete flexibility, because the underlying low-level muscles could be tweaked as well. Figure 4.5 illustrates the geometry, and Figure 4.6 shows a rendered frame of the baby displaying an expression.

A cubic B-spline patch is defined by 16 control points. While spline patches can define almost any arbitrary surface, only so much detail can be defined from the original 16 control points. To increase detail, more

---

[1]Additional work done to improve smoothness contraints with shape parameters for each curve segment is derived from [DeRose and Barsky 88].

control points can be added in a hierarchy to allow detail to be added only where desired [Forsey and Bartels 88]. This is achieved by overlays of more finely subdivided spline patches that conform to the surface to be refined. As a result, changes to a single control point affect the surface up to two control points distant. For example, a single central control point will affect a grid of 5×5 control vertices. By increasing the size of this grid, one line of control points on each side at each subdivision, the refined surface can be guaranteed to conform smoothly to the underlying control points at all times, creating a single continuous surface with continuity on both first and second derivatives.

8.5.3   Gradient-Based Muscles

One of the problems with the muscle model is that node displacements do not curve around the surface, which is most noticeable in areas of high curvature [Wang 93]. To overcome this limitation, it is possible to calculate the surface derivative in the direction defined by the muscle vector, as illustrated in Figure 8.19, resulting in the sequence of expressions illustrated in Figure 8.20. The point displacement is then scaled by the direction derivative, as well as the relative strain rate along the projected vector, to produce the final result.

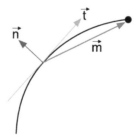

Figure 8.19.
Gradient-based displacement. Vector $\vec{n}$ is normal to the surface, $\vec{t}$ is the tangent vector, and $\vec{m}$ is the normal direction of displacement of the muscle model.

8.6   Physical Models of Facial Tissue

The purely geometric nature of prior facial models ignores many of the complexities of the human facial tissue, as described in Chapter 3. This is understandable when one considers the granularity and detail involved.

One of the largest assumptions of the geometric approach is to consider the skin as an infinitesimally thin surface with no underlying structure,

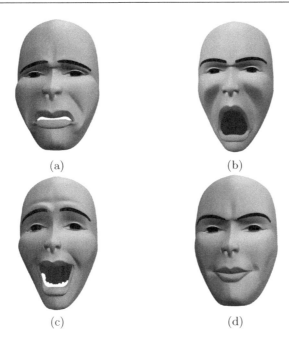

(a)　　　　　　　　　　　　(b)

(c)　　　　　　　　　　　　(d)

Figure 8.20.
Animated hierarchical B-spline model. (*Courtesy of D. Forsey.*)

on which deformations are generated by geometrically manipulating the surface. Consequently, attempts to mimic many of the subtle facial tissue deformations, such as wrinkles and furrows, are spurious.

8.6.1 A Tension Net

The simplest approach to skin tissue emulation is a collection of springs connected in a network, or tension net, described in [Platt 80]. In this model the skin is represented as a warped plane of skin nodes, connecting neighbors by arcs, as illustrated in Figure 8.21. The arcs have elastic material properties that make them behave like Hookean springs, where the extension is proportional to the force divided by the spring constant k:

$$\text{extension} \propto \text{force}/k. \tag{8.7}$$

Forces are generated by synthetic muscles. In this model, muscles are collections of fibers connected at one end to skin and at the other to bone. While real muscle consists of many individual fibers, for simplicity this model considers only one or two macroscopic fibers per muscle, as illustrated in Figure 8.21. One arc, that is a macroscopic fiber, consists of two

Figure 8.21.
A brow patch of a tension net model. The solid square represents the bone
attachment, the solid circle a muscle node, and the open circle the skin node
attachment.

parts: the tail, which connects to bone, and the head, which connects to
a skin node. When a simple muscle fiber contracts, a force is applied to
a muscle node in the direction of its tail (bone attachment). This force
causes a displacement of the muscle node. The force is then reflected along
all arcs adjacent to this node; these reflected forces are then applied to their
corresponding adjacent nodes. In this way, an applied force is propagated
out from the initial node, across the face.

The spring lattice approach to facial expression modeling has a distinct
advantage over a purely geometric technique, because the displacement of
one node can influence all the other nodes in the surface. Consequently,
muscle forces "blend" together, providing a unified approach to facial expression modeling. Furthermore, the inherent nature of springs helps maintain some geometric integrity, allowing the surface to dimple and bulge,
which is characteristic of facial tissue. The tension net is a variation of a
discrete deformable model, which will be described in the following section.

8.6.2 A Deformable Lattice of Skin

Deformable models are physically models of nonrigid curves, surfaces, and
solids [Terzopoulos and Fleischer 88a]; often, the fundamental element is
the spring connected to point mass nodes [Greenspan 73]. Models with
diverse topologies can be constructed by allowing springs to share nodes; the
elements may be chained together to form deformable curves, or they may
be assembled into more complex composite units, which are the building

Figure 8.22.
The fundamental building block of two nodes m_i, m_{i+1} connected by a spring
with a resting length of l_k that is extended by e_k.

blocks of deformable surfaces and solids. What follows is a description of a
basic discrete deformable model.

Nodes

In the most fundamental form, a single node i can be described where
$i = 1, \ldots, N$ has a point mass m_i and a three-space position $\mathbf{x}_i(t) = [x(t), y(t), z(t)]'$. The velocity of the node can be described by $\vec{v}_i = d\mathbf{x}_i/dt$,
and its acceleration by $\vec{a}_i = d^2\mathbf{x}_i/dt^2$.

Springs

A single spring unit k, which connects two nodes x_i and x_{i+1}, has natural
length l_k and stiffness c_k, as illustrated in Figure 8.22. The actual length
of the spring is $||\vec{r}_k||$, where $\vec{r}_k = \mathbf{x}_i - \mathbf{x}_{i+1}$ is the vector separation of the
nodes. The deformation of the spring is $e_k = ||\vec{r}_k|| - l_k$, and the force the
spring exerts on a node can be described as

$$\vec{s}_k = \frac{c_k e_k}{||\vec{r}_k||} \vec{r}_k. \tag{8.8}$$

The spring force is a nonlinear function of node positions, because $||\vec{r}_k||$
involves roots of sums of squares.

8.6.3   Integration

The discrete Lagrange equation of motion for the dynamic node/spring
system is the system of coupled second-order ordinary differential equations

$$m_i \frac{d^2 \vec{x}_i}{dt^2} + \gamma_i \frac{d\vec{x}_i}{dt} + \vec{g}_i = \vec{f}_i, \qquad i = 1, \ldots, N, \tag{8.9}$$

where

$$\vec{g}_i(t) = \sum_{j \in \mathcal{N}_i} \vec{s}_k \tag{8.10}$$

is the total force on node i due to springs connecting it to neighboring nodes
$j \in \mathcal{N}_i$, and where $\vec{f}_i$ is a net force acting on node i, which may include

application-dependent driving forces and forces due to boundary conditions and constraints. The quantity γ_i is a velocity-dependent damping coefficient for dissipating the kinetic energy of the deformable lattice through friction.

To simulate the dynamics of a deformable lattice, we provide initial positions $\vec{x}_i^0$ and velocities $\vec{v}_i^0$ for each node i for $i = 1, \ldots, N$ and numerically integrate the equations of motion forward though time. At each time step $\Delta t, 2\Delta t, \ldots, t, t + \Delta t, \ldots$, we must evaluate the forces, accelerations, velocities, and positions for each node. A simple and quick time-integration procedure is the explicit Euler method [Press et al. 86].

8.6.4 Layered Tissue Models

Having described the basic mathematics of discrete deformable models, we can now construct a variety of geometric structures to represent soft objects, in particular skin tissue. Figure 8.23(a) and (b) illustrate some basic stable geometric configurations for spring lattices that can be used to construct skin lattices. Geometric stability is an important consideration because the springs only connect nodes without any angular integrity. To compensate, cross-structing springs are added, thereby maintaining each unit's three-dimensional shape coherence.

For facial tissue, an idealized discrete deformable skin lattice structure is illustrated in Figure 8.24. Each line in the figure represents a biphasic spring. The springs are arranged into layers of pentahedral and hexahedral elements cross-strutted with springs to resist shearing and twist-

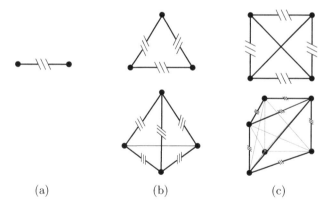

(a)   (b)   (c)

Figure 8.23.
The fundamental building units of a deformable skin lattice model. The top row represents two-dimensional configurations, while the bottom row are three-dimensional composite lattice structures: (a) the fundamental unit, (b) a tetrahedral element, and (c) a hexahedral element.

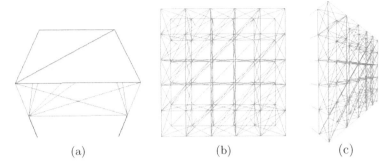

(a)　　　　　　　(b)　　　　　　　(c)

Figure 8.24.
An idealized three-dimensional facial tissue model. (a) A single three-dimensional volume unit based on the hexahedral element described in Figure 8.23. (b) Top view. (c) Three-quarter view showing the tetrahedral elements and their attachment to the subsurface.

ing stresses. The springs in the three layers—representing cutaneous tissue, subcutaneous tissue, and the muscle layer—have different stiffness parameters, in accordance with the nonhomogeneity of real facial tissue. The topmost surface of the lattice represents the epidermis (a rather stiff layer of keratin and collagen), and the spring stiffnesses are set to make it moderately resistant to deformation. The springs underneath the epidermis form pentahedral elements, which represent the dermis. The springs in the second layer, which contains hexahedral elements, are highly deformable, reflecting the nature of subcutaneous fatty tissue. Nodes at the bottom of the second layer represent the fascia, to which the muscle fibers that run through the hexahedral elements in the third layer are attached. Nodes on the bottom-most surface of the lattice are fixed onto the bone surface.

Figure 8.24 illustrates three views of an idealized slab of skin tissue constructed from three-dimensional tetrahedral elements. Each layer has varying visco-elastic behavior, and the lower layer can be either rigidly attached or mobile. Figure 8.25 illustrates a patch of 12×12 units with the application of a textured skin surface. Figure 8.26 illustrates the progressive animation of an idealized deformable skin lattice under deformation of a single muscle contraction.

Translating an idealized slab of tissue into a facial topology is a nontrivial task. To automate the facial model assembly, the procedure starts with the triangular facial mesh, whose nodes and springs represent the epidermis. First, it projects normal vectors from the center of gravity of each triangle into the face, to establish subcutaneous nodes, then forms tetrahedral dermal elements by connecting them to epidermal nodes us-

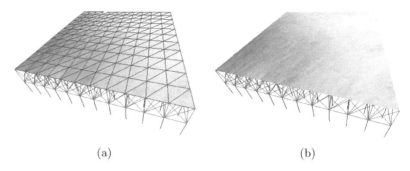

(a)   (b)

Figure 8.25.
A 12×12 lattice constructed from a regular series of base hexahedral volume units. (a) The complete wireframe lattice; (b) the surface wireframe removed revealing a textured skin patch.

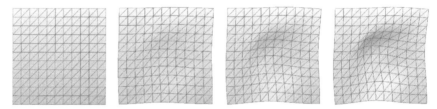

Figure 8.26.
An idealized three-dimensional facial tissue slab animated with a single muscle contracting from the center to top left. Notice that the increasing deformation causes buckling and creasing of the surface as the elements preserve the volume structure.

ing dermal springs. Second, it forms subcutaneous elements by attaching short, weak springs from the subcutaneous nodes downward to muscle layer nodes. Third, it adds the muscle layer, whose lower nodes are constrained, anchoring them in static skeletal bone. Finally, it inserts the muscle fibers through the muscle layer from their emergence in "bone" to their attachments at muscle layer nodes. Figure 8.27(b) illustrates a facial topology after the automatic assembly. The synthetic tissue includes about 960 elements with approximately 6,500 springs in total. The physics-based face model then can be simulated and rendered at interactive rates.

To incorporate both volume preservation and skull penetration forces, a variation of the scheme described above was developed, such that they could be added to Equation (8.9) [Lee et al. 95]. In this model, a volume preservation force is computed for each element, represented as a discrete set of nodes:

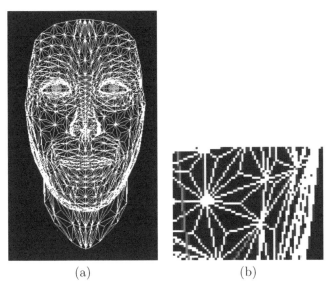

(a)   (b)

Figure 8.27.
A wire frame of the skin layer construction: (a) the tetrahedral dermal elements generated automatically from the surface topology, and (b) a closeup of the cheek region of the face.

$$\mathbf{q}_i^e = k_i(V^e - \tilde{V}^e)\mathbf{n}_i^e + k_2(\mathbf{p}_i^e - \tilde{\mathbf{p}}_i^e), \qquad (8.11)$$

where V^e and $\tilde{V}^e$ are the rest and current volumes for the element e; $\vec{n}_i^e$ is the epidermal normal for the node i; $\vec{p}_i^e$ and $\tilde{\mathbf{p}}_i^e$ are the rest and current nodal coordinates for i with respect the center of gravity of the element; and k_1, k_2 are scaling force constants.

As mentioned in Section 8.5.3, it is important to maintain the curvature aspects of the facial tissue as it slides over the underlying skull. To model this effect, there has to be an underlying geometry for the skull which can be either estimated, or computed as an offset to the surface geometry [Lee et al. 95]. Once again the additional force can be added to Equation (8.9). The penalizing force can be computed as follows:

$$\mathbf{s_i} = \begin{cases} -(\mathbf{f}_i^n \cdot \mathbf{n}_i)\mathbf{n}_i & \text{when } \vec{f}_i^n \cdot \mathbf{n}_i < 0, \\ 0 & \text{otherwise,} \end{cases} \qquad (8.12)$$

where $\vec{f}_i^n$ is the net force on the facial node i, and $\vec{n}_i$ is the surface normal at that node.

The result of using a physically based approach with range data collected from a Cyberware^{TM} scanner is illustrated in Color Plate V.

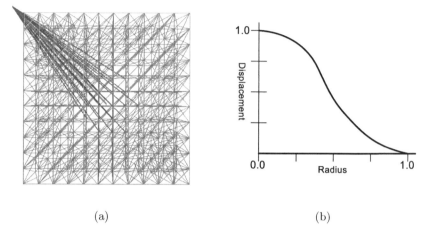

(a)   (b)

Figure 8.28.
(a) A three-dimensional lattice with muscle fiber attachments. (b) The nonlinear force function for muscle fibers, as a function of a radial displacement for the muscle insertion.

8.6.5   Muscles

Muscles that apply forces to the tissue lattice run through the second layer of the synthetic tissue, as illustrated in Figure 8.28. Muscle fibers emerge from some nodes fixed onto the bone at the bottom of the third layer and attach to mobile nodes on the upper surface of the second fascia layer.

Let $\vec{m}_i^e$ denote the point where muscle i emerges from the "bone," with $\vec{m}_i^a$ being its point of attachment in the tissue. These two points specify a muscle vector $\vec{m}_i = \vec{m}_i^e - \vec{m}_i^a$. The displacement of node j in the fascia layer from $\vec{x}_j$ to $\vec{x}_j'$ due to muscle contraction is a weighted sum of m muscle activities acting on node j:

$$\vec{x}_j' = \vec{x}_j + \sum_{i=1}^{m} c_i b_{ij} \vec{m}_i, \qquad (8.13)$$

where $0 \leq c_i \leq 1$ is a contraction factor and b_{ij} is a muscle blend function that specifies a radial zone of influence for the muscle fiber. Defining $\vec{r}_{ij} = \vec{m}_i^a - \vec{x}_j$,

$$b_{ij} = \left\{ \begin{array}{ll} \cos\left(\frac{\|\vec{r}_{ij}\|}{r_i} \frac{\pi}{2} \right), & \text{for } \| \vec{r}_{ij} \| \leq r_i \\ 0; & \text{otherwise} \end{array} \right. , \qquad (8.14)$$

where r_i is the radius of influence of the cosine blend profile. Figure 8.28 illustrates a circular zone of muscle influence with an associated displacement falloff profile.

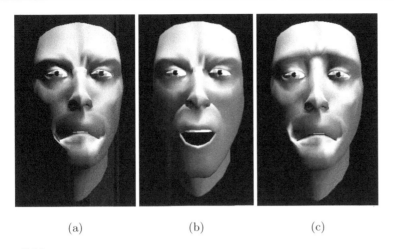

(a)   (b)   (c)

Figure 8.29.
Three examples of a physically based model under muscular control in both the upper and lower face. (a) The buckling deformation at the mouth corners under the influence of the anguli depressor muscles, (b) the furrowing of the brow and skin stretching surrounding the mouth when opened combined with the influence of the levator labii superioris alaeque nasi muscles, and (c) a combination of the mouth depressors and the frontalis inner brow raisers. See also Color Plate IV.

Once all the muscle interactions have been computed, the positions $\vec{x}_j$ of nodes that are subject to muscle actions are displaced to their new positions $\vec{x}_j'$. As a result, the nodes in the fatty, dermal, and epidermal layers that are not directly influenced by muscle contractions are in an unstable state, and unbalanced forces propagate through the lattice to establish a new equilibrium position.

8.6.6 Examples

By orchestrating muscle contractions, it is possible to create facial expressions that are superior to those created by purely geometric deformations. In particular, furrows on the brow can be pronounced by the contraction of the corrigator muscle, which draws the brows together as illustrated in Figure 8.29(a) and Color Plate IV. The same is true for the furrows around the mouth, which occur naturally as the physical model contracts, as illustrated in Figure 8.29(b).

8.6.7 Finite-Element Skin Tissue

The finite-element method (FEM) has a history in the application of structural analysis of materials and is used regularly in CAD/CAM, as well as nonstructural fields such as fluid mechanics, heat conduction, and biomedicine. A detailed description of finite elements is beyond the scope of this book; the reader is therefore referred to books on the subject, such as [Bathe 82].

Essentially, the finite-element method is a technique to approximate the solution of a continuous function with a series of trial shape functions. The finite-element method, like the discrete simulation approach described so far, also divides the geometry into regions (elements) that, taken together, approximate the behavior of the material being simulated. The difference between the two methods lies in the way information is passed from element to element as the material deforms. For a FEM, the material properties of the elements are combined into a global stiffness matrix that relates loads on the material at the nodal points to the nodal point displacements. This matrix then can be used directly to find the static solution. This is in contrast to the discrete simulation method, where the nodal points are iteratively displaced until the load contributions of all adjacent elements are in equilibrium.

8.6.8   Skin Flap Design

One of the first skin tissue models of skin tissue deformation using FEMs was constructed by Larrabee [Larrabee 86]. His approach attempted to model the effect of skin flap design for preoperative surgical simulation. His work was well motivated, because models of wound closure at that time were based almost completely on plane geometry or paper models. Furthermore, these geometric approaches ignored the elastic properties of skin and skin attachment.

Figure 8.30 illustrates the idealized elastic membrane that he created, with nodes spaced at regular intervals. Attached to each node is a small spring representing the subcutaneous attachments. The stress and strain properties of the skin are related by the standard equations of classical

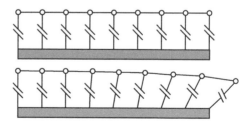

Figure 8.30.
Conceptualization of the finite-element model, where the skin is an elastic membrane divided by a series of nodes. The subcutaneous attachments are represented by springs that attach each node to an immobile surface.

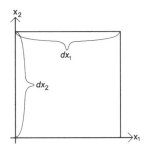

Figure 8.31.
Layout of a small square of skin dx_1, dx_2.

elasticity, with the following variables: (1) E or Young's modulus, which represents the slope of the stress/strain curve; (2) v or Poisson's ratio, which is 0.5 for an incompressible material; and (3) k, the spring constant of the subcutaneous attachment, assuming a linear relationship between nodal displacement and force. The equations of the model were as follows:

- σ_{11} = stress along the side perpendicular to the x_1-axis in the x_1-direction.

- σ_{12} = stress along the side perpendicular to the x_1-axis in the x_2-direction.

- σ_{21} = stress along the side perpendicular to the x_2-axis in the x_1-direction.

- σ_{22} = stress along the side perpendicular to the x_2-axis in the x_2-direction.

Force equilibrium for a small element of area $dxdy$, as in Figure 8.31, leads to the equations

$$\frac{\partial_{11}}{\partial \mathbf{x}_1} + \frac{\partial_{21}}{\partial \mathbf{x}_2} - ku_1 = 0, \qquad (8.15)$$

$$\frac{\partial_{12}}{\partial \mathbf{x}_1} + \frac{\partial_{22}}{\partial \mathbf{x}_2} - ku_2 = 0, \qquad (8.16)$$

where u_1 and u_2 are the displacements of the element in the x_1 and x_2 directions, respectively, and ku_i is the force per unit area in the x_i direction.

The stresses are related to the displacements by

$$\sigma_{11} = \frac{E}{1-v^2}\frac{\partial u_1}{\partial \mathbf{x}_1} + \frac{vE}{1-v^2}\frac{\partial u_2}{\partial \mathbf{x}_2}, \qquad (8.17)$$

$$\sigma_{22} = \frac{vE}{1-v^2}\frac{\partial u_1}{\partial \mathbf{x}_1} + \frac{E}{1-v^2}\frac{\partial u_2}{\partial \mathbf{x}_2}, \tag{8.18}$$

$$\sigma_{12} = \sigma_{21} = \frac{E}{2(1-v)}\left(\frac{\partial u_2}{\partial \mathbf{x}_1} + \frac{\partial u_1}{\partial \mathbf{x}_2}\right), \tag{8.19}$$

where E is Young's modulus and v is Poisson's ratio. To solve these equations for u_1 and u_2, triangular finite elements are used.

8.6.9   Surgical Tissue Simulation

Larrabee's approach was one of the first attempts to simulate the behavior of skin tissue. This method was soon followed by a more rigorous approach by Deng [Deng 88]. Her work attempted to simulate and analyze the closure of skin excisions on an idealized three-layer model of facial tissue. The computer simulation then minimizes *dog ears*, which are raised areas of skin that tend to form at the end of a closed wound, and closing of excisions traversing Langer's lines.

The model itself was constructed as a thick shell, as illustrated in Figure 8.32(a), consisting of three layers: a skin layer, a sliding layer, and a muscle layer. The model was then discretized into three layers of 16 node prism elements. Figure 8.32(b) illustrates a quarter of the model used in the skin excision simulations. The sliding layer was unique, since it facilitated sliding of the skin over the muscles by making the layer incompressible with a low shear moduli. The skin tissue moduli were defined from a variety of different experimental sources which were plugged into Automatic Dynamic Incremental Nonlinear Analysis (ADINA) to perform the numerical computations.

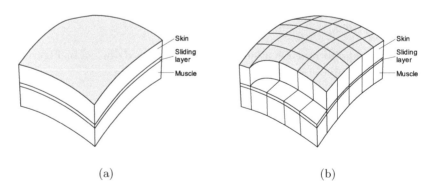

(a)   (b)

Figure 8.32.
(a) Facial tissue anatomy in three distinct layers. (b) The three layers are then discretized into sixteen node prisms, showing a quarter of the total model. The cutout on the skin layer represents a skin excision.

8.6.10 Increasing Facial Tissue Geometry Detail

The geometry of the tissue models described by Deng treats skin as an idealized slab of regularized elements. In reality, human face geometry is highly curved, varying in thickness and density. Furthermore, the mechanics of facial tissues are nonlinear and anisotropic. Consequently, it is challenging to create element configurations that accurately reflect facial tissue geometry and then animate successfully.

The availability of different data scanning technologies can be utilized to create accurate volumetric element configurations for FEM simulation. Computer tomography (CT) and magnetic resonance (MR) scanners reveal the internal hard and soft tissues, respectively. Laser and optical scanners can now provide highly detailed surface x, y, z and r, g, b data. The task of registring the different data types for an individual at a resolution for FEM simulation requires some additional effort.

As illustrated in Figure 8.33, both the surface and the skeletal surfaces can be extracted in perfect registration that provides accurate tissue depths. From such a representation, a simple regularized geometry can be created, much like a slab of tissue, but in this case, with varying subsurface depths. Before tissue simulation can begin, areas need to be identified as static, mobile, or sliding. This can be easily achieved with an interactive editor to simply mark the mobile nodes of the mouth, sliding nodes, and fixed nodes,

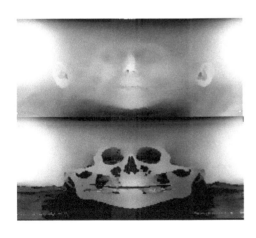 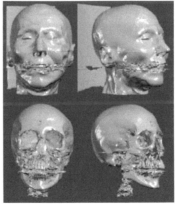

(a)   (b)

Figure 8.33.
(a) An example of computer tomography data cast into cylindrical coordinates [Waters 92]. The top image was extracted at a specific iso value for bone surfaces, while the bottom was extracted at the skin surface. (b) Iso surface rendering in Cartesian coordinates.

Figure 8.34.
The rectangular tissue layer lattice marked to be attached, mobile, or sliding for regions of the face [Waters 92]. In particular, the mouth region is unattached tissue that creates the mouth cavity.

as illustrated in Figure 8.34. Finally, muscles can be placed interactively and animated in an editor, as illustrated in Figure 8.35. While using CT data alone provides tissue depth information, it cannot provide accurate muscular information. As a result, the simulations treat muscles as if they have no mass or volume, when in reality the opposite is true.

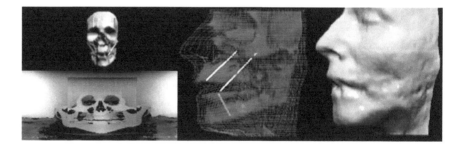

Figure 8.35.
Screens from an interactive CT scan editor capable of skin tissue modeling and muscle simulation [Waters 92]. The upper-left and center images show the placement of linear muscle vector fibers that are attached rigidly to the skull at one end and embedded into the soft tissues of the skin at the other.

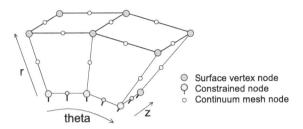

Figure 8.36.
An example of two elements from the continuum meshing process discretized into 16 node cuboids.

An outgrowth of Deng's work was Pieper's by the application of finite elements to facial data collected from scanners [Pieper 89]. The problem that Pieper addressed was how to map scanned facial data into a continuum mesh that could then be provided as input to a finite-element solver. The solution was to use laser-scanned data, as illustrated in Figure 4.11 and CT data. The next task was to provide a mapping between the source data and normalized cylindrical coordinates. In cylindrical coordinates, z represents the vertical axis, while θ is the angle from 0.0 to 360.0 degrees around the head. Here, r provides the distance from the z-axis to represent the skin surface at each point (θ, z).

The continuum meshing, necessary for the FEM computation, is created from the skin to the bone surface geometries along the r-axis. Triangles are extruded into wedge elements, and quadrilatrials are extruded into cuboid elements. Figure 8.36 illustrates a cross-section of the nodes and elements created by the continuum meshing. The FEM procedure employed by Pieper involved a home-grown static-displacement-based formulation of the finite-element method to solve elasticity equilibrium equations. This was closely based on procedures described in [Bathe 82]. The result was that he was able to demonstrate simple facial surgical simulations, for example, Z-plasty, a particular type of skin tissue excision and closure [Grabb et al. 86]. The use of CT and laser scan data still does not address muscle tissues. Pieper's work was focused on the dermis and epidermis behavior for surgical simuation and had no model of muscle.

A more complete representation of the face correlates scans that capture not only the surface, but also the subsurface bone, muscle and tissues. An anatomically accurate model can then be driven via simulations of tissue dynamics. Increasing the accuracy of the bone subsurface, muscle detail, and skin tissue resolution before simulating their behavior has been the subject of investigation by Kähler et. al [Kähler et al. 01]. The first stage of constructing a face model starts with a laser-scanned skull from which the

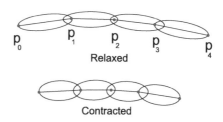

Figure 8.37.
An alternative volume model of muscle fibers constructed from per-segment ellipsoids [Kähler et al. 01]. The relaxed upper image shows the supporting polygons P_0–P_4. The lower configuration shows *bulging* of the ellipsoids when contracted.

geometry is fitted to the skin surface data through affine transformations. This provides a rough estimate of skin tissue depth [Kähler et al. 03]. Muscles are constructed from a piecewise linear representation [Lee et al. 95]. Such configurations allow fiber-based models of muscle to be complied into *sheet, linear* and *sphincter* bundles. For linear muscles, such as the zygomatic major, they can be replicated as a sequence of volume-preserving ellipsoids, as illustrated in Figure 8.37. Such configurations allow the geometry to maintain its volume and subsequently mimic *bulging* and *thinning* of real muscle under muscle activation.

The work of Sifakis [Sifakis et al. 06] creates a highly detailed face model from MRI data and high-resolution laser scans coupled with volumetric data from the visible human project [United States National Library of Medicine 94]. The intent of the model was to simulate speech via sequences of muscle activation. This technique, in particular the extraction of muscle parameters to drive the model, is discussed further in Chapter 9.

The MRI scan provided the basic tissue shapes, as well as indicating the interface with soft tissues and the facial skeleton. The high resolution surface data was aquired from a laser scan of a cast mask, as illustrated in Figure 8.38(a). This scan was produced at a resolution of 100 microns, to generate approximately 10 million polygons, and integrated into a volumetric flesh model, which resulted in a model with approximately 1.8 million elements. The model included 39 facial muscles, as illustrated in Figure 8.38(b), predominantly involved in speech (for details of the muscles of speech, see Chapter 9). These muscles were constructed with a fiber field for each muscle that was reflected in each element. The tempromandibular joint was represented as a rigid body rotation, and penalty forces were applied to avoid nodes penetrating into the skeletal surfaces. The nodal forces within the tetrahedral elements are

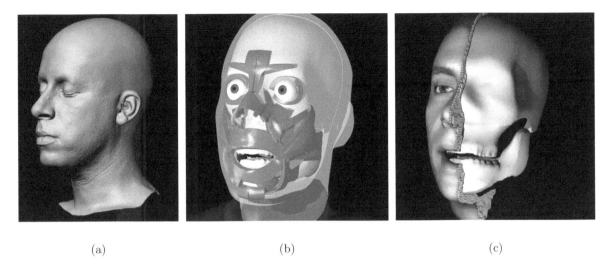

(a) (b) (c)

Figure 8.38.
A finite volume model (FVM) of facial tissues created from magnetic resonance data, a surface laser scan, and muscles created from the visible human project [Sifakis et al. 06]. (a) The surface laser scan, (b) the geometry of the facial muscles with the epidermis revealed transparently, and (c) the composite showing the skeletal subsurface and a cross-section of the skin and muscle tissues. (*Courtesy of R. Fedkiw and E. Sifakis.*) See also Color Plate VI.

$$\mathbf{f}(\mathbf{x}, \mathbf{a}) = \mathbf{f_0}(\mathbf{x}) + \sum_{i=1}^{M} a_i \mathbf{f_i}(\mathbf{x}),$$ (8.20)

where $\mathbf{f}$ and $\mathbf{x}$ are the forces and position of *all* nodes in the volume, and $\mathbf{a} = (a_1, a_2, \ldots, a_M)^T$ is the vector of activations of all M muscles. Here, $\mathbf{f_0}$ is the elastic properties of flesh. Each force component $\mathbf{f_i}$ is the contribution of a fully activated muscle modulated by a weighted level of activation $a_i \in [0, 1]$.

A quasistatic integration scheme was used to compute the equilbrium state of the model, based on the muscle activations and skeletal configuration. The intent was to generate face configurations defined by the input muscle control parameters, without a dependency on the deformation history. The steady state positions are defined by

$$\mathbf{f}(\mathbf{X}(\mathbf{a}, \mathbf{b}), \mathbf{a}) = \mathbf{0}.$$ (8.21)

Equation (8.21) is solved with an iterative Newton-Raphson solver; for more details, see [Sifakis et al. 05] and [Teran et al. 05].

8.7   A Dynamic Neck

The development of anatomically accurate models of face muscle and skin tissue can be applied to the neck. Face muscle differs from neck muscle in that neck muscles are *musculoskeletal*, with two bone attachments. These muscles play a significant role in coordinating movements that are critical for head pose control. The biomechanics of human motion has been the subject of much research and is beyond the scope of this book; however, an introduction to the subject is worth considering.

The muscles illustrated in Figure 3.26 represent only the superficial muscles of the neck. In reality there are three types of muscle that assist in head motion: *deep*, *intermediate*, and *superficial*, which represent 20 types of neck muscle with varying origins and insertions. Coupled to the seven cervical bones C1-C7, the complexity of the biomechanical system appears daunting. Nevertheless, it is possible to simplify the model to a series of musculoskeletal units controlling the rigid disks of the neck. The work of Sung [Lee and Terzopolous 06] develops a neck model based on seven 3-DOF joints of the neck controlled by a Hill muscle model (see Section 8.1.1 for more details on biological solids) that defines a uniaxial exponential spring:

$$ fp = \max(0, k_s(\exp(k_c e) - 1) + k_d \dot{e}), \tag{8.22} $$

where k_s and k_c are elastic coefficients, k_d is the damping coefficient, $e = (l - l_0)/l_0$ is the strain of the muscle with l and l_0 the length and slack length, respectively, and $\dot{e} = \dot{l}/l_0$ the strain rate of the muscle. The muscle is then controlled via the application of a simple linearized Hill-type activation. Once the muscles have been configured, the issue is one of control to affect head pose. This can be achieved through a number of different techniques to simulate voluntary control, as well as tone and gaze behavior.

9

Speech-Synchronized Animation

In traditional cell animation, synchronization between the drawn images and the speech track is usually achieved through the tedious process of reading the prerecorded speech track to find the frame times of significant speech events. Key frames with corresponding mouth positions and expressions are then drawn to match these key speech events. The mouth positions used are usually based on a canonical mapping of speech sounds into mouth positions [Blair 49].

Reading the track traditionally involves transferring the soundtrack to magnetic film with sprocket holes. This film is then manually analyzed by passing it back and forth over a magnetic playback head to locate the frame locations of speech events. Today, this task would most likely be done by converting the soundtrack to digital form and then locating the speech event times using a computer-based sound editor.

For a more realistic correspondence, a live actor is filmed or videotaped while speaking. These recorded frames are then rotoscoped to obtain the correct mouth positions for each frame or for each key frame.

Parke used both the speech track reading and the rotoscoping approaches in his early speech synchronized facial animation work [Parke 74]. Animation was created based on manually reading the speech track to determine the corresponding timed sequence of speech-related parameters. Animation was also created using parameter sequences determined by rotoscoping images of the actor reading the speech track. These timed parameter sequences were used to drive a parameterized face model.

The techniques outlined above assume that the speech track is created first and the animation images are then created to match. This production ordering is usually preferred. However, sometimes the reverse is required, where the speech track is created to match an existing animation sequence. And, as we shall see, computer-based speech animation allows a third possibility: speech and images created simultaneously.

9.1   Cartoon Lip Animation

According to Madsen, simplicity is the secret to successful cartoon character lip animation [Madsen 69]. For character animation, the goal is not to imitate realistic lip motions, but to create "a visual shorthand that passes unchallenged by the viewer." An effective approach is to use a visual pattern of vowel lip motions accented by consonants and pauses. Madsen provides the following lip animation steps, based on manually reading the speech track:

1. Determine the overall timing, and the number of frames within and between each word.

2. Find the accented words containing the sounds b, m, and p. Within these words, locate the frame times where the lips meet. These locations are the key frames that synchronize the lips with the consonants. Also locate the distinctive open vowels such as o and w.

3. Create the in-between frames with a simple visual pattern that approximates the rest of the spoken phrases.

Madsen also offers the following guidelines:

- Consonants are the accents of animated speech. Precision of the consonants gives credibility to the generalized patterns of the vowels. Perfect synchronization of each b, m, and p sharpens the animation.

- Letters like o and w require an oval mouth shape.

- The letters f and v require tucking the lower lip under the upper front teeth. This tuck tends to make the character look cute. Underanimate each f and v unless humor is desired.

- Pronunciations of a, c, d, e, g, h, i, j, k, l, n, q, r, s, t, x, y, and z are formed primarily by the tongue and do not require precise lip animation.

- When animating lip motions, the emotional qualities have to be created also. An angry "no" is different from a whispered "no."

The simplicity of this approach creates believable lip synchronization for cartoon characters. However, as the visual representation of the face becomes increasingly realistic, our human perception of synchronization is no longer as easily tricked, and we can quickly identify that there is something not quite right. To improve synchronization quality requires an understanding of how human speech is created. The following sections present a deeper understanding into speech production and how it relates to facial animation.

9.2   Speech Production

The production of speech is created though the increase and decrease of air pressure though the larynx and vocal tract out the nose and mouth by the action of the diaphragm, as illustrated in Figure 9.1(a) [Stevens 99]. The interaction of the various cavities, coupled to the vibration of the vocal cords, produce sounds. To create speech, the various parts of the larynx and mouth have to be in certain positions and must be moved in particular ways. Computer facial animation often focuses only on the outward appearance of speech, with the jaw position and the shape of the lips; however,

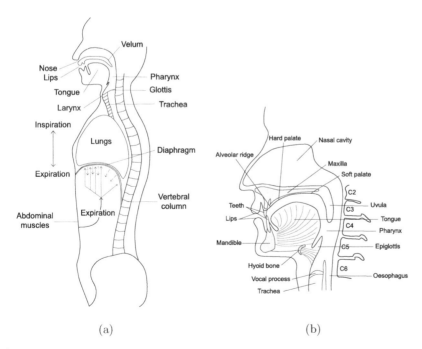

(a)   (b)

Figure 9.1.
(a) The anatomy involved speech production. (Adapted from [Stevens 99].)
(b) The speech organs of the vocal tract.

understanding what parts of the human anatomy are moving and why can provide a richer visual experience.

Figure 9.1(b) shows the human anatomy above the larynx, known as the vocal tract. The shape of the vocal tract is critical in the production of speech; when the airstream is constricted by the vocal cords, they vibrate. This vibration is known as *voiced*, in contrast to *voiceless*, when the airstream is unimpeded. For example, the long sound of *v* in the word "*vet*" causes the vocal cords to vibrate, while *f* in the word "*fish*" does not. In *voiceless* speech, turbulence in the air flow produces broadband noise. This is what we hear in whispered speech.

The parts of the vocal tract that form sounds are called *articulators*. Figure 9.2 illustrates positions of the tongue, lips, teeth, and other parts of the vocal tract during principal voiced sounds.

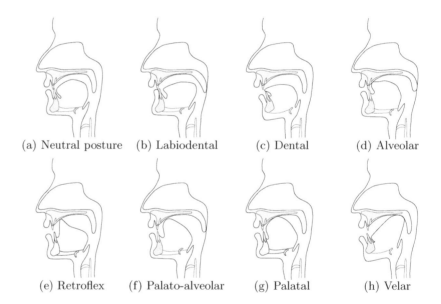

(a) Neutral posture   (b) Labiodental   (c) Dental   (d) Alveolar

(e) Retroflex   (f) Palato-alveolar   (g) Palatal   (h) Velar

Figure 9.2.
A mid-sagital view of the primary position of the articulators during speech: (a) Neutral posture. (b) Labiodental—the lower lip is raised and nearly touches the front teeth, as in the word "pie." (c) Dental—the tip of the tongue touches the front teeth and in some cases protrudes between the upper and lower teeth, as in the word "thigh." (d) Alveolar—with the tip of the tongue touching the alveolar ridge, as in the word "tie." (e) Retroflex—with the tip of the tongue and the back of the alveolar ridge, as in the word "rye." (f) Palato-alveolar—the blade of the tongue and the back of the avleolar ridge, as in the word "shy." (g) Palatal—the front of the tongue touches the hard palate, as in the word "you." (h) Velar—the back of the tongue touches the soft palate,, as in the word "hang."

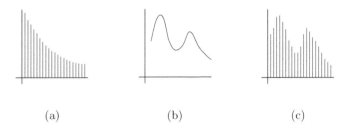

(a)   (b)   (c)

Figure 9.3.
Speech harmonic spectrum and the formants: (a) the vocal cord generated harmonic spectrum, (b) the vocal tract spectrum filter, (c) the resulting speech sound with resonant formant peaks [Lewis 91].

The vibrations of the vocal cords create the *voiced* sounds, where the periodic collision of the vocal cords produce a pitched buzzing sound, containing a spectrum of harmonic frequencies. The power in these harmonics falls off as the harmonic frequencies increase, as illustrated in Figure 9.3 and speech sounds may be modeled as a broadband sound source passed through a filter [Witten 82]. These sounds pass through the vocal tract into the mouth and nasal cavities, where the shape of the mouth cavity is modified by the position of the tongue, lips, and teeth. The energy in this noise is redistributed by the resonant properties of the vocal and nasal tracts. The vocal tract filters the sound, forming resonant energy peaks in the spectrum, called *formants*, as illustrated in Figure 9.3(b) and Figure 9.3(c).

The formant frequencies are changed by varying the position and shape of vocal tract articulators. The vowel sounds can be characterized by the frequencies of the first two formants. The formants change relatively slowly during vowels and change rapidly or disappear altogether during consonants and vowel-consonant transitions. This characteristic is especially true for sounds like *b, d, g, p, t,* and *k,* which are commonly called the *plosives* or the stop consonants.

The nasal sounds such as *m* and *n* are articulated much like the plosive sounds. These sounds involve rapid shifts in formant frequencies and rapid changes in general spectral quality when the vocal tract is quickly connected and disconnected to the nasal spaces by the velum, a valve in the back of the mouth formed by the soft palate.

Various hiss-like noises are associated with many consonants. During or just after the articulation of these consonants, air from the lungs rushes through a relatively narrow opening, in turbulent flow, generating the random hiss-like noises. Consonants are distinguished from vowels mainly by a higher degree of constriction in the vocal tract. It is completely stopped in the case of the stop consonants.

Whispered speech also involves turbulent airflow noise. But because this turbulence occurs in the initial part of the vocal tract, it is shaped by the vocal tract resonances and has many of the qualities of ordinarily spoken sounds.

9.2.1   Speech Phonetics

Understanding how sounds, utterances, words, and sentences map to articulations has been the subject of investigation for many years by phoneticians [Jones 18]. Clear imaging of the internal articulators of the mouth and vocal tract is awkward, and in the past, phoneticists have resorted to placing artificial palates in the mouth to observe the positions of the tongue, or to placing a small camera into the vocal tract. Techniques such as mid-sagital X-rays allow a view of how the jaw moves, with a rough indication of what is happening with respect to the soft tissues of the tongue and lips. More recently, real-time magnetic resonance imaging has revealed the motion of the soft tissues of the vocal tract during speech [Narayanan et al. 04].

There are of course more sounds that can be made by the human anatomy than there are letters in the English alphabet. Add to this the variety of distinct dialects within a language, and you end up with a problem of annotating the possible sounds found in languages. A solution has been developed by The International Phonetic Association with the creation of the *International Phonetic Alphabet* [The International Phonetic Association 99], where a set of symbols are used to represent the variety of sounds found in the languages of the world. The IPA is particularly useful when creating speech synchronization, as well as when mapping real speech components of a particular speaker—say an Englishman or an American—to an animated model of the face.

Figure 9.4 is the cardinal vowel chart, with the extremes at the four corners. The cardinal vowels are those that raise the tongue as far forward and as high as possible, as well as the opposite, as far back and as low as possible. The transition between the four postures is smooth, and the sound predominantly generated from the movement of the tongue, which modifies the shape of the mouth cavity. The lip activity is independent of tongue position, and is reflected in the closed "i" that spreads the lips, the "u" that has closely rounded lips, the "a" that is closed front unrounded, and the "ɒ" that has an open rounded shape.

Figure 9.5 and Table 9.1 are from the IPA Handbook and represent the vowel and consonant sounds. Effectively, they represent the constituent parts, or atomic units, of possible human generated sounds that make up the worlds' languages (the gray areas in the consonant chart in Table 9.1 represent sounds that are considered impossible to produce). Understanding the mapping between these sounds and the anatomy of speech mechanics can be valuable when animating the human face.

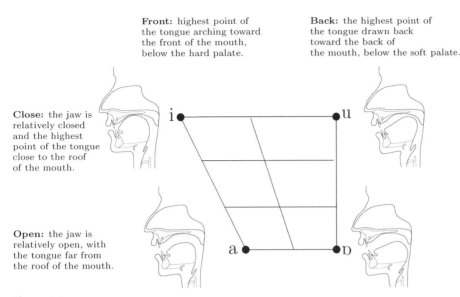

Front: highest point of the tongue arching toward the front of the mouth, below the hard palate.

Back: the highest point of the tongue drawn back toward the back of the mouth, below the soft palate.

Close: the jaw is relatively closed and the highest point of the tongue close to the roof of the mouth.

Open: the jaw is relatively open, with the tongue far from the roof of the mouth.

Figure 9.4.
Four extreme cardinal vowels, "i" close front unrounded, "a" open front unrounded, "ɑ" open back rounded, and "u" close back rounded with the approximate mid-sagital positions of the articulators. Note the location of the highest point of the tongue in each position, which approximately relates to the shape of the quadrilateral IPA chart.

	Bilabial	Labiodental	Dental	Alveolar	Postalveolar	Retroflex	Palatal	Velar	Uvular	Pharyngeal	Glotal
Plosive	p b			t d		ʈ ɖ	c ɟ	k ɡ	q ɢ		ʔ
Nasal	m	ɱ		n		ɳ	ɲ	ŋ	N		
Trill	ʙ			r					ʀ		
Tap or Flap				ɾ		ɽ					
Fricative	ɸ β	f v	θ ð	s z	ʃ ʒ	ʂ ʐ	ç ʝ	x ɣ	χ ʁ	ħ ʕ	h ɦ
Lateral fricative				ɬ ɮ							
Approximant		ʋ		ɹ		ɻ	j	ɰ			
Lateral approximant				l		ɭ	ʎ	L			

Table 9.1.
The complete IPA consonant chart. (From the *Handbook of the International Phonetic Association* [The International Phonetic Association 99].)

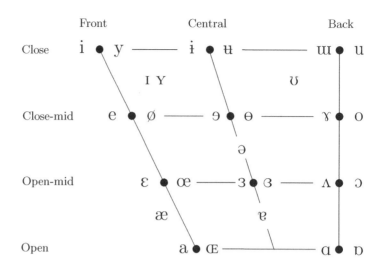

Figure 9.5.
The IPA vowel chart. (From the *Handbook of the International Phonetic Association* [The International Phonetic Association 99].)

The symbols on the IPA chart in Figure 9.5 provide a reference points in the vowel space. Importantly, the chart can represent the different sounds in different languages, for example, —IPA i can represent the English word *heed* and the French word *lit* (bed). For English, there are many different dialects spoken around the world. Consequently, care has to be taken when animating speech to take differences into account. For example, the

Bilabial and Labiodental	Dental Alveolar and Post-Alveolar	Palatal, Velar and Glottal
p "pie"	t "tie"	k "kite"
b "buy"	d "die"	g "guy"
m "my"	n "nigh"	ŋ "hang"
f "fie"	θ "thigh"	h "high"
v "vie"	ð "thy"	tʃ "chin"
	s "sigh"	dʒ "gin"
	z "zoo"	ʃ "shy"
w "why"	ɹ "rye"	ʒ "azure"
	l "lie"	j "you"

Table 9.2.
Example consonants for American English.

American English of a southern Californian has a different dialect from an individual from the East coast. Table 9.2 provides some American English examples from the IPA consonant chart. For mappings to additional languages, see [The International Phonetic Association 99].

9.2.2 Visemes

The phoneme is a basic unit of speech and has a visible equivalent in a *viseme*. Visemes are unique face, mouth, teeth and tongue movements corresponding to the voiced phonemes. The mapping between phonemes and visemes has been used extensively in facial animation [Waters and Levergood 93]. Figure 9.6 illustrates some key viseme postures. Correlating visemes to phonemes is known as visemetrics.

Not all voiced sounds create visibly distinct visemes. For example, the plosives *b, p* and *m* are visibly indistinct to lip readers [Jeffers and Barley 71]. This leads to some curious effects, where the perception of audio/visual in-

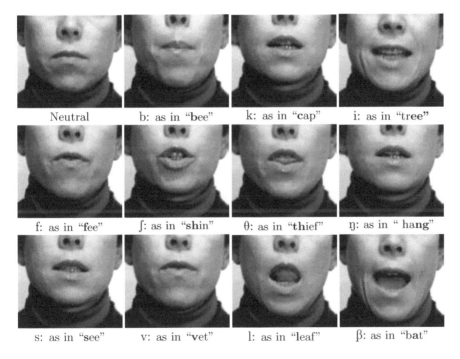

Neutral   b: as in "**bee**"   k: as in "**cap**"   i: as in "**tree**"

f: as in "**fee**"   ʃ: as in "**shin**"   θ: as in "**thief**"   ŋ: as in " **hang**"

s: as in "**see**"   v: as in "**vet**"   l: as in "**leaf**"   β: as in "**bat**"

Figure 9.6.
Nine example American English consonants and two vowel visemes
from [Waters and Levergood 93]. The lips and chin position provide the overall shape of the mouth posture. However, careful consideration should be given to the position of the teeth and tongue if the face is to be animated.

formation gets confussed. This perceptual phenomenon is known as the *McGurk effect* [McGurk and MacDonald 76]. For example, when individuals are presented with a visual /ga/ combined with an audible /ba/, the perception is of /da/.

Example American English visemes are illustrated in Figure 9.6. In the process of animating with distinct postures, careful consideration has to be given to the position of the teeth and tongue, as they provide vital clues as to perception of the viseme. The absence of the teeth and tongue has a measured degredation on lip readability [Brooke and Summerfield 82].

9.2.3   Visual Diphones and Triphones

Where visemes are the singular posture of the mouth parts, the combination of one or more postures can also be derived from their audible counterparts: diphones (two) and triphones (three). Diphones and triphones are used extensively in speech analysis and synthesis where it is necessary to label acoustic models to words in a language.

A *diphone* is the transition between adjacent phonemes, while *triphones* are a group of three phonemes. Such labeling defines a *coarticulation* that spans no more than two phonemes for diphones and three for triphones. If the number of phonemes in a language is P, the number of possible diphones is P^2 and is P^3 for triphones.

For visual labeling, the same concepts apply, and the database of transitions between diphone and triphone can be very large. The resulting visual coarticulation effects can improve the quality of the face synthesis and are described in more detail in Section 9.5.

9.2.4   Lip Reading Speech Postures

According to Walther, lip reading is based on observing the visemes associated with 45 English phonemes [Walther 82]. Visemes are the visually distinguishable phoneme classes. Nitchie discusses lip reading based on 18 visually distinct speech postures involving the lips, teeth, and tongue [Nitchie 79]. These are summarized in Table 9.3 and illustrated in Figure 9.4. The visible differences between similar speech postures may be quite subtle.

9.2.5   Coarticulation

As described, speech can be decomposed into a sequence of discrete units such as phonemes, diphones, and triphones. However, in actual speech production there is overlap in the production of these sounds. The boundaries between these discrete speech units are blurred.

The vocal tract motions associated with producing one phonetic segment overlap the motions for producing surrounding phonetic segments. This

Posture Name	Speech Sound	Posture Description
narrow	long *e* as in "we"	lips assume a narrow slit-like opening, mouth corners slightly drawn back and parted
lip to teeth	*f* and *v* sounds	lower lip rises and touches upper teeth
lips shut	*b*, *m*, and *p* sounds	lips naturally shut
puckered lips	long *oo* as in "moon"	lips are puckered, showing only a small mouth opening
small oval	short *oo* as in "good" *w* as in "we" *wh* as in "wharf"	lips form a small oval, lips less puckered than in puckered posture
widely open	*a* as in "farm"	mouth open widely, tongue drawn back slightly
elliptical	*u* as in "up" *u* as in "upon" *u* before *r* as in "fur"	intermediate open position with elliptical shape
elliptical puckered	*r* as in "free"	elliptical shape, but with mouth corners slightly puckered
relaxed narrow	*i* as in "pit" long *e* as in "believe" *y* as in "youth"	similar to narrow posture, but mouth corners are not drawn back and parted
front tongue	*th* as in "thin" and "then"	front of the tongue visible between the teeth
tongue to gum	*t* as in "time" *d* as in "dime" *n* as in "nine"	tongue touches the upper gum, while lips are in the relaxed narrow posture
tip to gum	*l* as in "leaf"	only the tip of the tongue touches the upper gum, while lips are in the elliptical posture
spherical triangle	*a* as in "all" *o* as in "form"	lips are open in the shape of a spherical triangle
tightened narrow	*s* as in "see" *z* as in "zebra"	narrow mouth opening with the muscles at the corner of the mouth slightly tightened, teeth close together
large oval	short *a* as in "mat"	lips form large oval, with corners slightly drawn up
protrusion	*sh* as in "ship" *s* as in "measure" *ch* as in "chip" *j* as in "jam" *g* as in "gentle"	mouth forms oval shape with lips protruding forward
medium oval	short *e* as in "let" *a* as in "care"	similar to the elliptical posture, but with mouth corners further apart
undefined open	*k* as in "keep" *g* as in "go" *nk* as in "rank" *ng* as in "rang"	mouth open with shape similar to the closest associated vowel

Table 9.3.
Speech postures from [Walther 82].

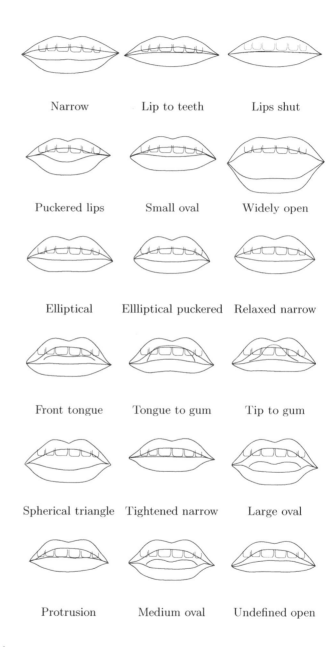

Table 9.4.
Visibly distinct lip postures from [Nitchie 79].

overlap is referred to as *coarticulation* [Kent and Minifie 77]. Coarticulation is the consequence of the physical dynamics of the vocal tract and the vocal tract postures required for various sounds. There are physical limits to how quickly the speech postures can change. Rapid sequences of speech sounds often require that the posture for one sound anticipate the posture for the next sound, or that the posture for the current sound is modified by the previous sound.

Coarticulation should be considered in speech animation, so that incorrect mouth positions can be avoided and smooth transitions generated. A simple approach to coarticulation is to look at the previous, the present, and the next phonemes to determine the current mouth position [Waters 87]. This examination is not always sufficient, since the correct mouth position can depend on phonemes up to five positions before or after the current phoneme [Kent and Minifie 77].

Forward coarticulation occurs when articulation of a speech segment depends on upcoming segments. The speech posture for one phonetic segment is anticipated in the formation of an earlier segment in the phonetic string. *Backward coarticulation* occurs when a speech segment depends on preceding segments. The speech posture for one segment is carried over to a later segment in the phonetic string.

Forward coarticulation can occur when a sequence of consonants is followed by a vowel. The lips can show the influence of the following vowel during the first consonant of the sequence. An example is the rounding of the lips at the beginning of the word "stew." The difference in articulation of the final consonant in a word depending on the preceding vowel occurs because of backward coarticulation.

Computing Coarticulation Effects

Pelachaud has proposed a three-step algorithm for determining the effects of coarticulation [Pelachaud 91]. This algorithm depends on the notion of clustering and ranking phoneme lip shapes based on how deformable they are. In this context, *deformability* refers to the extent that the lip shape for a phoneme cluster can be modified by surrounding phonemes. Ranking is from the least deformable, such as the *f, v* cluster, to the most deformable clusters, such as *s* and *m*. This deformability is also dependent on speech rate. A person talking slowly moves her lips much more than a person speaking rapidly.

The first step in this algorithm is to apply coarticulation rules to those highly deformable clusters that are context dependent. These forward and backward coarticulation rules consist of looking ahead to the next highly visible vowel and looking backward to the previous highly visible vowel. The lip shape for the current phoneme is adjusted to be consistent with the previous and next vowel shapes.

The next step is to consider the relaxation and contraction times of the mouth shape muscles [Bourne 73]. This step checks to see if each action has time to contract after the previous phoneme or to relax before the next phoneme. If the time between two consecutive phonemes is smaller than the contraction time of the muscles, the previous phoneme is influenced by the contraction of the current phoneme. Similarly, if the time between consecutive phonemes is smaller than the relaxation time, the current phoneme will influence the next one.

In the last step, geometric relationships between successive actions is taken into account. For example, closure of the lips is easier from a slightly parted position than from a puckered position. Also, the magnitude of speech actions is scaled, depending on phoneme and context.

Dominance and Blending

In their study of synthetic bimodal visual speech communication, Cohen and Massaro [Cohen and Massaro 93] implemented a model for coarticulation based on Lofqvist's [Lofqvist 90] gestural theory of speech production. This model uses the concepts of dominance and blending functions, as illustrated in Figure 9.7, where articulators move independently of one another over time.

In this model, each phoneme segment has an associated target set of facial control parameter values. Each phoneme segment also has a dominance function. Dominance is modeled using the following negative exponential function:

$$D_{sp} = \alpha_{sp} e^{-\theta_{sp}|\tau|^c}. \tag{9.1}$$

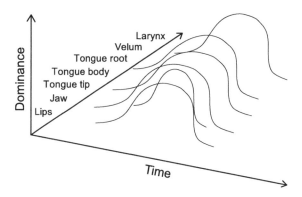

Figure 9.7.
A representation of a speech segment over time [Lofqvist 90].

The dominance of a phoneme segment parameter D_{sp} falls off exponentially according to the time distance τ from the segment center raised to the power c modified by a rate parameter θ_{sp}. The coefficient α_{sp} gives the magnitude of the dominance function for this parameter for this segment s. Different coefficients are generally used for θ_{sp} prior to the segment center and after the segment center. Here, τ is computed as follows:

$$\tau = t_{c_{sp}} + t_{o_{sp}} - t,$$

where $t_{c_{sp}}$ is the time center of the segment and $t_{o_{sp}}$ is a time offset for the dominance function peak and

$$t_{c_{sp}} = t_{\text{start}_s} + (\text{duration}_s/2).$$

The actual parameter value used at a given animation frame time is determined by blending the dominance functions for that parameter using a weighted average:

$$F_p(t) = \sum_{s=1}^{n}(D_{sp}(t)T_{sp})/\sum_{s=1}^{n}D_{sp}(t), \qquad (9.2)$$

where n is the number of phoneme segments in the utterance and the T_{sp} are the segment target parameter values. Figure 9.8 illustrates this approach for a simple two-segment utterance. The characteristics of the dominance functions and the blended results are controlled by the θ_{sp}, α_{sp}, and c values used.

The dominance function blending approach automatically incorporates the speech-rate-dependent aspects of coarticulation.

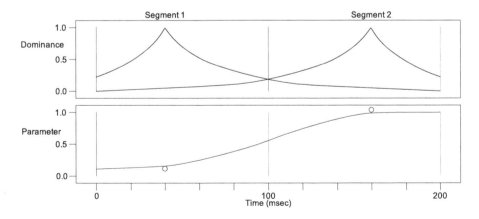

Figure 9.8.
Example dominance functions and a resulting blended control parameter.
From [Cohen and Massaro 93].

9.2.6   Intonation

Intonation is the melodic feature of an utterance. It is also the feature of speech most noticeably absent in synthetic speech. Intonation is important in conveying the emotions associated with a speaker's messages.

Intonation can be decomposed into three components: the type of utterance, such as interrogative or declarative; the attitude the speaker wants to show to the listener, such as politeness or irony; and finally, the involuntary emotional aspects of the speaker's speech [Scherer et al. 84]. The emotional component is differentiated by subjective pitch, perceived loudness, global pitch contour, speech tempo, and pauses. Anger, for example, is characterized by a high pitch level, wide pitch range, and large pitch variations. Angry speech is loud on average but has wide loudness fluctuations. Articulation is precise, and speech tempo is fast. Sadness, on the other hand, is characterized by low pitch level, narrow pitch range, and small pitch variations. Sad speech is soft, with small fluctuations in loudness. The tempo of sad speech is slow, with a number of long pauses [Cahn 89, Ladd et al. 85, Williams and Stevens 81].

9.2.7   Bimodal Communication

There has been considerable research indicating that multiple information sources are useful in human recognition and understanding of spoken language [Cohen and Massaro 93, Cohen and Massaro 94]. Being able to see a speaker's face seems to provide the listener with additional information valuable in understanding the speech. This concept is particularly true in noisy environments or other situations where the audio speech information is degraded. This research implies that both speech and accurate synchronized facial animation may be important components of human-computer interaction interfaces.

9.2.8   Speech as a Second-Level Parameterization

Any control parameterization for facial animation should support speech animation. Speech animation control is often a good example of *second-level* parameterized control. In these cases, speech animation is controlled by using a higher-level parameterization built on top of a lower-level basic parameterization.

The second-level parameterization used in speech animation is usually in terms of speech phonemes. The higher level control is specified in terms of phoneme transitions. The phoneme transitions are transformed into detailed lower level parameter transitions.

A fairly small number of visually distinct phonemes are needed to produce convincing animation. Since the same words may be spoken with different emotional overlays, the speech parameterization should be orthogonal to the emotional parameters.

The second-level phoneme parameterization approach has been used by Bergeron and Lachapelle [Bergeron and Lachapelle 85], Lewis and Parke [Lewis and Parke 87], Hill et al. [Hill et al. 88], and Magnenat-Thalmann et al. [Magnenat-Thalmann et al. 88] to produce successful speech animation.

9.3 Automated Synchronization

For automated synchronization, the visible speech postures, the positions of the lips and tongue, must be related in some identifiable way to the speech sounds. The source-filter speech model implies that lip and tongue positions are functions of the phonemes. Therefore, analyses that result in the representation of speech as timed phoneme sequences are suitable for creating synchronized animation.

9.3.1 Performance Measures

The viability of an automated synchronization method depends on the nature and purpose of the facial representation. Realistic or semirealistic characters offer the greatest challenge, demanding more precise speech postures and motions. They invite comparison with real people. The more fanciful the character, the more latitude we have in animating its speech and expressions.

Most people cannot read lips and cannot easily determine the sound corresponding to a given mouth position, but they can identify good and bad synchronization. Accurate rhythm in mouth movement is fundamental for acceptable speech synchronization, while accuracy of mouth positioning becomes necessary in close-up views of the realistic faces. Performance measures for speech synchronization are not well defined. There are probably several useful levels of performance. These levels include the performance level, useful for general character animation as described in Section 9.1, the performance level required for realistic animation, and the very high-quality standards necessary for lip-reading.

9.3.2 Taxonomy of Approaches

We would like computer-based systems that automatically synchronize facial animation with speech. Figure 9.9 illustrates a taxonomy of possible computer-based approaches. In this taxonomy, the primary differentiator is the initial form of the speech information. The speech may be available as text, prerecorded speech, both prerecorded speech and text, or as speech images.

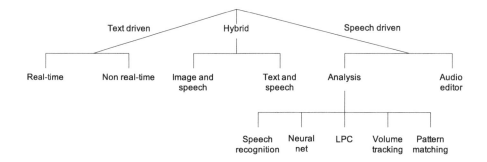

Figure 9.9.
Speech synchronization taxonomy.

Text-Driven

The idea here is to extract phoneme information from input text, then use a library of phoneme-based mouth shapes and durations to generate the synchronized facial animation. The text is also used to drive speech synthesis, which creates synthetic speech synchronized to the face animation. Examples of this approach are discussed in Section 9.4.

Speech-Driven

The idea here is to analyze the prerecorded speech on a frame-by-frame basis to determine speech information. This information is used to create facial animation that matches the speech segment. The complete animation is formed by merging the prerecorded speech with the generated animation. Speech-driven examples are discussed in Section 9.7.

Hybrid: Text-and-Speech-Driven

Morishima and Harashima developed a hybrid approach that depends on having both prerecorded speech and corresponding text information [Morishima and Harashima 93]. A bottoms-up speech analysis is used to identify vowels and speech segmentation, including pauses and speech component durations. Vowel recognition is done using pattern matching. Speech segmentation is based on speech waveform power changes and frame-to-frame changes in the speech spectrum. Top-down analysis of the text information is used to identify consonants.

The vowel and speech segmentation information is used to associate timing information with the phoneme information from the text input. The text and phoneme duration rules are used to determine consonants and the detailed timing used to drive the facial animation.

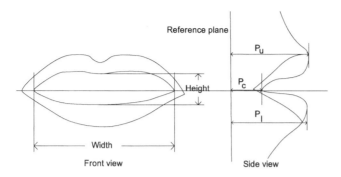

Figure 9.10.
Measured lip parameters [LeGoff et al. 94].

Hybrid: Image-and-Speech-Driven

Guiard-Marigny et al. [Guiard-Marigny et al. 94] and LeGoff et al. [LeGoff et al. 94] describe an approach to speech synchronization that is essentially automated rotoscoping. The shape of the generated mouth is determined by analyzing lip postures in a sequence of video images. The shape of the generated lips is computed using five parameters measured from real lip images. The five parameters are the height and width of the interior opening of the lips, plus the three lip protrusion values illustrated in Figure 9.10.

The generated lips are modeled using 320 polygons organized in four contour bands around the mouth. A set of continuous functions was devised that fits the shape of the lips to the viseme shapes. These functions are controlled by coefficients, derived from the five measured parameters, which specify the equations that best fit the viseme lip contours.

The complete synthetic face is created by superimposing the lips on a parametrically controlled polygonal face model [Parke 74, Cohen and Massaro 93, Cohen and Massaro 94]. For this animation one additional parameter is measured from the video images to control the jaw rotation of the synthesized face. The created animation is used to support visual speech synthesis research, where the generated facial animation is combined with the recorded speech.

9.4   Text-Driven Synchronized Speech

An appealing approach is to type in text and have both synthesized speech and synchronized facial animation created automatically. Synchronized synthetic visual speech is a general approach that lends itself to entirely automatic generation of speech animation.

This approach is reported by Pearce et al. [Pearce et al. 86] and Hill et al. [Hill et al. 88]. Waters and Levergood extended this approach to create the speech and animation simultaneously in real time [Waters and Levergood 93]. The major drawback is that current synthesized speech lacks many of the qualities of natural speech.

The user inputs text that is automatically translated into the corresponding phonetic symbols. The system may also use other information, such as models of spoken rhythm and intonation, and a set of composition rules that provide appropriate modeling of the natural movement from one target to the next.

9.4.1   Speech Synthesis

A full treatment of speech analysis and synthesis is given in [Witten 82]. The first speech synthesizer that modeled the vocal tract was the Parametric Artificial Talker, invented in the 1950s. This device modeled the various sound energy sources (periodic or random), the spectral characteristics of noise bursts and aspiration, and the resonances of the vocal tract. Only the three lowest resonances need to be variable for good modeling.

Speech may be produced from such a synthesizer by analyzing real speech to determine the appropriate parameter values needed to drive the synthesizer.

It is possible, given a specification of the sounds in an intended utterance, to algorithmically generate the parameters needed to drive the speech synthesizer. The target parameter values for all the sounds are stored in a table and a simple interpolation procedure is written to mimic variation from one sound target to the next. Appropriate sound energy source changes can also be computed.

9.4.2   Linear Prediction Speech Synthesis and Resynthesis

Linear prediction coding is an extremely effective formulation for synthetic speech and serves as the basis of many modern voice response systems. Linear prediction coding can be used to synthesize speech or to resynthesize natural speech. Variations of this form of analysis and resynthesis are commonly used for speech compression.

Robotic speech quality is obtained if the excitation signal is a synthetically generated pulse train or a random sequence. In the case of synthetic excitation, it is easy to speed up or slow down the speech. This change in speed is accomplished simply by accessing the coefficient frames at a faster or slower rate. Since the voice pitch is controlled by the excitation function, the speech rate can be changed without producing a shift in pitch.

In the most faithful resynthesis approach, the residual difference signal between the original speech and the output of the linear prediction filter is used as the synthesis excitation signal. The residual signal approximates an uncorrelated noise for consonants and whispered vowels, and approximates a pulse train for voiced vowels. The linear prediction analysis and the residual together encode most of the information in the original speech. Resynthesized speech is highly intelligible and retains the original inflection and rhythm, yet it has a subtle synthetic quality that may be appropriate for some computer animation.

9.4.3 Extending Synthesis to Include Faces

Voice sound changes result directly from movements of the vocal articulators, including the tongue, lips, and jaw rotation, which in turn cause changes in facial posture. As a result, programs for speech synthesis can be extended by adding information for each speech posture to control the relevant parameters for a face model.

In the approach described by Pearce et al., the phoneme script is specified directly by the animator [Pearce et al. 86]. For example, *Speak to me now, bad kangaroo* would be input as the following phonetic sequence:

s p ee k t u m in ah uu b aa d k aa ng g uh r uu

The implementation reported by Hill et al. starts with input text for the desired speech segment and transforms it into a phoneme sequence [Hill et al. 88].

It is difficult to achieve natural rhythm and articulation when speech is generated from a phoneme script. Synthetic speech quality can be improved somewhat by adding pitch, timing, and loudness annotations.

Using synthesis by rule algorithms, the phoneme sequence is used to control the speech generation. The phoneme sequence is also used to control a parameterized facial model. The speech synthesis algorithms are extended to produce not only the varying parameters needed for acoustic synthesis, but also the varying parameters needed to control the visible articulation attributes of a rendered synthetic face. This joint production process guarantees perfect synchronization between the facial speech expressions and the generated speech. The synthetic speech and the corresponding facial image sequences are generated separately and then merged in a post-process to form the final speech animation.

The extended speech algorithm outputs seventeen parameter values at successive two-millisecond intervals. The speech parameters are sent directly to the speech synthesizer to produce synthetic speech output. Nine face parameters controlling the jaw and lips are used to drive a version of the Parke parameterized face model [Parke 74]. The parameters may be interactively edited until the desired speech is obtained. All of the parameters are available for editing.

The facial parameter data is converted from the once-per-two-millisecond sampling rate to a once-per-frame time sampling rate, based on the desired number of frames per second. This conversion is done by resampling linear interpolation of the parameters. Hill observed that some form of temporal anti-aliasing might seem desirable. In practice, anti-aliasing did not appear to be needed. Indeed, the wrong kind of anti-aliasing could have a very negative effect, by suppressing facial movements altogether. It may be better to motion blur the images directly, rather than anti-aliasing the parameter track definitions.

The parameters used for speech articulation were those originally specified by Parke [Parke 74]. These parameters include jaw rotation, mouth width, mouth expression, lip protrusion, lower-lip tuck, upper-lip position, and mouth corner position offsets.

The tongue was not represented. High-quality speech animation requires that at least some parts of the mouth interior be included. At least the most visible part of the tongue and the more visible teeth should be included. Control of the tongue should be included in the low-level parameter set and reflected in the higher level phoneme parameterization.

9.4.4 Real-Time Text-to-Speech

Waters and Levergood developed a real-time synchronized visual speech system built around a software version of the DECtalk text-to-speech synthe-

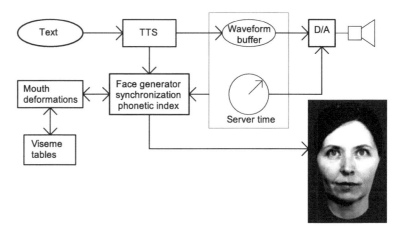

Figure 9.11.
Synchronized visual speech synthesis using a text-to-speech engine [Waters and Levergood 93].

sizer [Waters and Levergood 93]. In this system the text to be spoken was typed in and sent to the lexical analysis portion of the DECtalk synthesizer. This portion of the synthesizer produces a timed sequence of phonemes and control parameters that drive the speech output generation. The timed phoneme information is used to drive simultaneous real-time facial animation and automatically synchronized with the generated speech, as illustrated in the system diagram in Figure 9.11. For each phoneme there is a one-to-one mapping to its visible geometric equivalent viseme. Some of these visemes are illustrated in Figure 9.6. As a result, intermediate postures for the face are created from interpolating viseme postures.

9.5 Image-Based Visual Speech Synthesis

In contrast to generating realistic three-dimensional models of the head and face, an alternative is to use sequences of face images. A collection of images in a flip-book were some of the earliest examples of animation that used human persistence of vision to provide the appearance of face motion. This technique has been used to create face animation; however, is it limited to the sequence of images that have been recorded. So how can you develop new animated sequences from images that were not recorded? Such a technique is called image-based synthesis and has been the subject of recent investigation.

MikeTalk is an example of image-based visual speech synthesis [Ezzat and Poggio 00]. In many respects text-to-speech (TTS) has a visible equivalent in the visual domain, where text can be decomposed into phonemes with the visible component of a viseme. Words and sentences can then be re-constructed for both the sounds and the visual components.

First, a corpus of visemes is acquired for the speaker, from video speaking a set of enunciated words. In MikeTalk, this was a set of forty American English phonemes mapped to corresponding visemes. The second step is to construct a matrix of viseme morphs, transforming each viseme into every other viseme image, so that for N visemes there will be N^2 transformations, as illustrated in Figure 9.12. The third phase constructs a novel visual sequence by concatenating viseme morphs. A text-to-speech synthesizer generates phonemes and phoneme durations for an input set of words. The output phonemes, coupled to their corresponding visemes, provide the necessary key frames for the animated sequence, from which intermediate frames can be computed.

The morph construction of in-between key frames is a key aspect of MikeTalk. Morphing [Beier and Neely 92] provides a method to create an image-based transformation between two key frames; however, each posture requires features in each key frame to be manually created. In MikeTalk, a

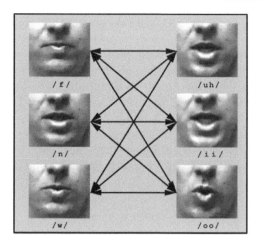

Figure 9.12.
MikeTalk's viseme transformation matrix from [Ezzat and Poggio 00]. The
transformation maps every viseme to every other viseme, such that if there are
40 visemes, there will be total of 40^2, or 1600, possible combinations.

correspondence map is generated using displacement vectors of pixels:

$$C_o(\mathbf{p_0}) = (d^{0\to1}(\mathbf{p_0}), \mathbf{d_y^{0\to1}}(\mathbf{p_0})), \qquad (9.3)$$
$$C_1(p_1) = (d^{0\to1}(p_1), d_y^{0\to1}(p_1)). \qquad (9.4)$$

A pixel in image I_0 at position $p_0 = (x, y)$ corresponds to a pixel in
image I_1 at position $(x + d_x^{0\to1}(x,y), y + d_y^{0\to1}(x,y))$. Likewise, a pixel in
image I_0 at postion $\mathbf{p_1} = (x, y)$ corresponds to a pixel image I_0 at position
$(x + d_x^{1\to0}(x,y), y + d_y^{1\to0}(x,y))$.

Estimating the correspondence vectors from images uses a well-
understood computer vision technique called *optical flow* [Horn and Schunck
81]. To create the inbetweens, a series of morphs based on the optical flow
vectors were created, as illustrated in Figure 9.13.

To generate audio-visual synchronization, a timeline of diphones—
generated from the TTS engine—and a matching viseme stream are generated from the procedure above. When played back, both the audio and
images appear synchronized.

Another complimentary image-based approach is to use existing video
footage of a speaker to create a new speech clip based on the original
footage [Bregler et al. 97]. This is a useful technique in movie dubbing
to an existing audio track and enables novel sequences to be generated from
new audio *from* existing video footage. Such a technique makes it possible
to "put words into people's mouths." Rewriting video leverages the same

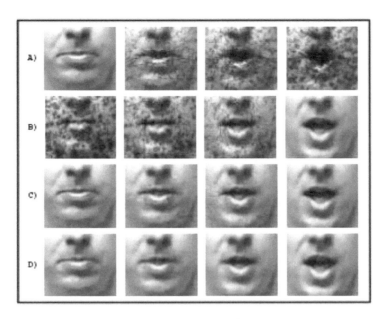

Figure 9.13.
The rows of the matrix: Row (A) illustrates the forward warping viseme I_0 towards I_1 from [Ezzat and Poggio 00]. Row (B) illustrates the forward warping of viseme I_1 toward I_0. Row (C) illustrates morphing I_0 and I_1 together. Row (D) illustrates the same images as in row (C) after hole-filling and median-filtering.

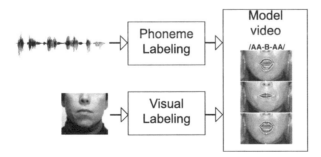

Figure 9.14.
Phase I: video-rewrite analysis adapted from [Bregler et al. 97]. The audio track segments the video into triphones. The orientation and pose of the head are resolved first, then the shape and position of the mouth in each image are determined.

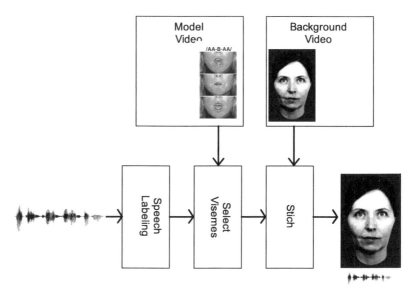

Figure 9.15.
Phase II: video-rewrite synthesis adapted from [Bregler et al. 97]. A new audio segment is used to select triphones from the video model. Based on labels from the analysis stage in Figure 9.14, the new mouth images are subsequently morphed into a new background face.

concepts as concatinative speech synthesis, where a speech corpus is segmented into triphone speech units, as illustrated in Figure 9.14, which can be recombined at playback time.

To create a new model and sequence there is a two-phase process. Phase I involves segmenting the audio and video sequence. At the same time as the audio is segmented, the corresponding video sequence is labeled and placed in a video model repository. Essentially, this builds unique video clips that are analogous to MikeTalk's diphone and DECface's phone model.

Phase II involves synchronizing the video to a new audio sequence, as illustrated in Figure 9.15. First the new sequence is segmented, then during playback, the appropriate video model is selected from Phase I, allowing a novel sequence to be generated.

9.6 Muscle-Driven Synchronization

During the production of speech, coordinated muscle contractions generate a variety of lip and mouth postures. These postures generate sounds based on orchestrated muscle contractions that position the vocal tract, teeth, tongue and lips. Theoretically, a holistic facial animation system could generate speech sounds by combining visual speech, also known as

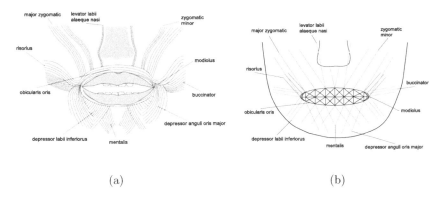

(a)   (b)

Figure 9.16.
The muscles of the lower face (a), and a simplified linear physical model of
muscles (b) [Waters and Frisbie 95]. The muscle fibers correspond to a small
number of linear vectors. The orbicularis oris, representing the lips, is
discretized into two cross braced bands.

visual-text-to-speech (VTTS), with a *text-to-speech* (TTS) system. Currently, simple parameters such as head size and vocal tract length are used
to create sounds in a TTS system. Such parameters could be extended to
involve detailed tongue, teeth, and lip positioning to drive a VTTS model.

Recent investigations attempt to model speech postures based on a
coordinated sequence of muscle contractions, with the goal of creating a
single coherent articulation model for facial expression and speech
[Waters and Frisbie 95, Sifakis et al. 06].

A simple physical model of the mouth under muscle control is illustrated in Figure 9.16(b). Each muscle is represented, as a discrete vector

Muscle	Origin	Insertion
Levator labii superioris	frontalis process	
alaeque nasii	of maxilla	upper lip
levator labii superioris	maxilla and zygomatic bone	upper lip
zygomatic major	zygomatic bone	angle of the mouth
zygomatic minor	zygomatic bone	angle of the mouth
risorius	masseteric facia	angle of the mouth
depressor anguli oris	oblique line of the mandible	angle of the lower lip
depressor labii inferioris	oblique line of the mandible	lower lip
obicularis oris	from other facial muscles	lips
buccinator	mandible	angle of the mouth
mentalis	incisive fossa of mandible	skin of the chin

Table 9.5.
Linear muscle origins and insertion around the mouth. The orbicularis oris is an
eliptical muscle that has no discrete origin or insertion.

with a contraction direction toward its static insertion as described in Table 9.5. The obicularis oris is a muscle surrounding the lips, as illustrated in Figure 3.20, and consists of several muscles, such as the buccinator, that converge on the mouth moduli and split to make up the upper and lower lip. A more detailed muscle model, which extends this approach in three dimensions to exploit muscle mass and alignment with an underlying skull, has been developed by Kähler et al. [Kähler et al. 03].

Once a geometry configuration has been established, a mass-spring system generates mouth postures, the details of which are described in Section 8.6.2. Essentially, the muscles supporting the obicularis act to modify the shape of the lips though a sequence of contraction and relaxation of the individual muscle vectors.

To animate the model, a sequence of images of a person talking were recorded, and key locations were identified, as illustrated in the top sequence of images in Figure 9.17. These key locations are then used to derive parameters for the muscle contractions by minimizing the corresponding location based on seven x, y pairs. A Nelder-Mead [Press et al. 86] optimization proceedure dertermined the input vector, which, when applied to the model, best matched the digitized data. "Best" was defined as the minimum total distance between the reference points on the digitized frame and the corresponding nodes of the model.

A similar, but more robust, alternative approach has been developed for the determination of muscle activations based on sparse three-dimensional motion capture data and highly detailed anatomical model by Sifakis et. al. [Sifakis et al. 06]:

$$c_{\text{opt}}(\mathbf{X}^T) = \arg\min_{c \in C_0} ||\mathbf{X}^L(c) - \mathbf{X}^T||, \tag{9.5}$$

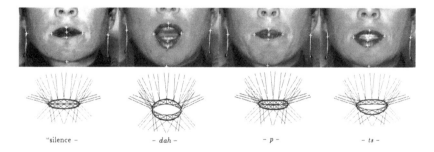

Figure 9.17.
Sample frames tracking the lip margins through a small number of discrete nodes (top) that in turn are used to drive the physical muscle model (below) [Waters and Frisbie 95].

where $\mathbf{X}^L(c)$ are the landmark positions, $\mathbf{X}^T$ are the motion capture marker data positions, and $c_{\mathrm{opt}}(\mathbf{X}^T)$ *stresses* that the optimal set of controls is a function of the target positions. The system is nonlinear and can be solved by least-squares optimization algorithms. For more details, see [Sifakis et al. 06] and Chapter 8.

9.7 Speech-Driven Synchronization

If the desired speech track has already been recorded, we would like automated techniques that analyze the speech track and produce the necessary timed control information to produce the synchronized facial animation. What we would like is a timed phoneme script that shows the sequence of speech phonemes and pauses, along with timing information for each phoneme. This timing information would include when each phoneme begins and its duration. We would also like additional information about speech rhythm and intonation, as well as indications of the speaker's emotional state. From the timed, and possibly annotated, phoneme script, detailed low-level parameters are derived to control a face model. The generated facial image sequence is merged with the original speech recording to form the final speech animation.

Using recorded natural speech avoids many of the problems associated with synthetic TTS, such as the lack of natural speech rhythm, prosody, and emotional content. However, using recorded speech presents its own challenges.

9.7.1 Simple Volume Tracking

A very simple approach to speech synchronization is to open the mouth and rotate the jaw in proportion to the loudness of the sounds. This approach requires only a simple analysis of the speech track. Summing the absolute values of all digital samples in each interval will provide a measure of the speech energy or loudness.

This approach has limitations. Real mouths do not just open and close. They assume a variety of visually distinct positions, or postures, during speech. In reality, such a simple approach is not even approximately correct. For example, nasal m sounds can be loud, even though the mouth is closed. However, when coupled with expressive animation, this approach works fairly well for very simple characters.

9.7.2 Speech Recognition Acoustic Preprocessor

Another analysis approach is to use the *front end* of a speech recognition system. Speech recognition involves transforming the speech into a representation in which the speech formant frequencies are emphasized and the pitch information is largely removed, and then parsing this representation to identify words. It is the parsing task that is most difficult. The acoustic preprocessing step is generally quite effective, and fortunately is all that is required for deriving a phonetic script.

The first part of a speech recognition system is to analyze the speech waveform to identify speech components such as phonemes and pauses. If this analysis phase is augmented to tag these speech components with timing information, the result is the phoneme script we need. However, most speech recognition systems do not provide output of this intermediate information.

The acoustic analysis portion of a speech recognition system is probably overkill for the synchronization task. We really do not need the high level of speech component accuracy required for speech recognition. What we really need is a system that will sample the speech waveform periodically and classify the current sample interval. This classification does not require the accuracy necessary for recognition. We just need to identify the viseme for each sample interval.

9.7.3   Linear Prediction Analysis

Lewis described such an automated method of analyzing recorded speech based on the *linear prediction* speech synthesis method [Lewis and Parke 87, Lewis 91]. In this approach, linear prediction is adapted to provide a fairly simple and reasonably accurate phoneme classification for each sample interval. The identified phonemes are then associated with mouth position parameters to produce synchronized speech animation.

This analysis approach uses the linear prediction speech synthesis model to obtain speech parameters that can be used to classify sample intervals into phoneme sets corresponding to visually distinctive mouth positions. This problem is considerably simpler than that of recognizing speech.

Linear Prediction Speech Model

Linear prediction models a speech signal s_t as a broadband excitation signal ax_t input to a linear autoregressive filter. This filter uses a weighted sum of the input and past output of the filter:

$$s_t = \alpha x_t + \sum_{k=1}^{p} a_k s_{t-k}. \tag{9.6}$$

This is a fairly accurate model of speech production. The filter models the vocal tract, including the mouth, tongue, and lip positions. The excitation signal approximates the acoustic signal produced by the vocal cords. This model is useful, since both human speech production and human perception separate pitch (determined by vocal cord tension) from phonetic information (determined by the vocal tract filtering). This separation can be illustrated by sounding a fixed vowel while varying the pitch. The mouth position and vowel are entirely independent of pitch.

In linear prediction speech *resynthesis*, the excitation signal is approximated as either a pulse sequence, resulting in pitched vowel sounds, or as uncorrelated noise, resulting in consonants or whispered vowels, depending on the filter. The filter coefficients a_k vary over time but are considered constant during the short time intervals used for analysis or synthesis. The analysis interval or frame time must be short enough to allow successive intervals to track perceptible speech events. However, the analysis interval needs to be longer than the voice pitch period. An analysis frame time of 15 to 20 milliseconds satisfies these conditions and corresponds to 50 to 65 sample intervals or frames per second. The fact that this sampling rate works well suggests that sampling mouth movements at the standard 24 or 30 frame per second animation rates may not be sufficient to accurately represent many speech events.

For speech animation, it is convenient to choose the analysis frame rate as twice the film or video playback frame rate. The resulting speech information can be reduced to the desired animation frame rate with a simple low-pass filter. Alternatively, animation images may be generated at the higher sample rate (e.g., 60 frames per second) and filtered across image frames, rather than across analysis frames. This supersampling approach reduces the temporal aliasing that can result from quantizing speech poses at the animation playback frame rate.

Solution Algorithm

Given an interval of digitized speech, the linear prediction coefficients a_k are determined by minimizing the squared error between the actual speech and predicted speech over some number of samples. Lewis points out that there are a number of approaches to determining this *least-squares* linear prediction.

Work by [Rabiner and Schafer 79] and [Witten 82] provide speech-oriented overviews of the autocorrelation approach and an additional covariance formulation, while [Markel and Gray 76] provides an exhaustive treatment of this subject.

Lewis uses the autocorrelation linear prediction method outlined below. This derivation views the speech signal as a random process that has stationary statistics over the analysis frame time. The expected squared estimation error

$$E = \mathbf{E}\{s_t - [\alpha x_t + \sum_{k=1}^{p} a_k s_{t-k}]\}^2 \qquad (9.7)$$

is minimized by setting

$$\partial \mathbf{E}/\partial a_k = 0.$$

Rewriting (9.7) in quadratic form leads to, for $1 \leq j \leq p$,

$$\mathbf{E} = \{s_t s_{t-j} - (\alpha x_t s_{t-j} + \sum_{k=1}^{p} a_k s_{t-k} s_{t-j})\} = 0. \tag{9.8}$$

Since the excitation at time t is uncorrelated with the previous speech signal, the expectation of the product $\alpha x_t s_{t-j}$ is zero. The expectation of terms $s_{t-j} s_{t-k}$ is the $(j-k)$th values of the autocorrelation function. These substitutions result in the following equation:

$$\sum_{k=1}^{p} a_k R(j - k) = R(j) \tag{9.9}$$

for $1 \leq j \leq p$, which can be solved for a_k, given the analysis frame autocorrelation function R. The function R can be estimated directly from the sampled speech signal using

$$R(t) \approx (1/L) \sum_{t=0}^{L-\tau-1} s_t s_{t+t} \tag{9.10}$$

for $0 \leq \tau \leq p$, where L is the length of the analysis interval in samples. The equations in Equation (9.8) can be written in matrix form and solved using efficient numerical techniques. See [Lewis 91] for a more detailed treatment.

Classifying the Speech Sample

We do not need to know the exact phoneme, but just the visually distinct phoneme class. We do so by comparing the results of the analysis with similar results for a set of *reference phonemes* representing the visually distinct phoneme classes.

The coefficients a_k resulting from the linear prediction analysis describe the speech spectrum over the sample interval, with the pitch information removed. A direct identification approach would be to compare the a_k coefficients for the interval with the a_k coefficients of the reference phonemes. However, least-squares identification directly on these coefficients performs poorly.

Lewis uses a classification scheme based on comparing the Euclidean distance of the interval spectrum with the spectra of the predetermined reference phonemes. This spectrum is obtained by evaluating the magnitude of the *z-transform* of Equation (9.6) at N points on the complex z-plane. Lewis determined that a resolution of $N = 32$ is sufficient. Here,

$$H(z) = \alpha/(1 - \sum_{k=1}^{p} a_k z^{-k}), \tag{9.11}$$

where $z = e^{-j\pi k/N}$.

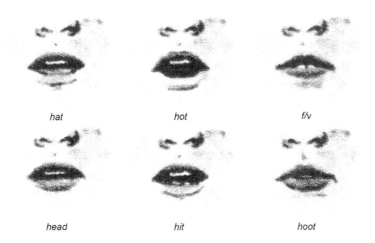

hat hot f/v

head hit hoot

Figure 9.18.
Lip shapes for several of the reference phonemes [Lewis 91].

The value for p, the number of a_k coefficients used, is determined based on the maximum frequency of the sampled audio signal. One coefficient is used for each kHz of the audio digital sampling rate, plus a few additional coefficients to model the overall spectrum shape.

Almost all of the semantically important information in speech lies below 5000 Hz, as demonstrated by the intelligibility of the telephone and AM radio. Therefore, if the signal has been low-pass filtered, an audio sampling rate of 10 kHz and a p of about 12 is sufficient for speech synchronization analysis applications.

Reference Phonemes

There are more than thirty phonemes in spoken English [Flanagan 65]. In most cases, the visually distinctive mouth positions correspond to vowels. The vowels are easily identified with the linear prediction speech model. Lewis found that very accurate vowel identification is possible using the linear prediction approach with 12 reference phonemes. The reference phoneme set he used consists of the vowels in the words *hate, hat, hot, heed, head, hit, hoe, hug,* and *hoot,* together with the consonant classes *m, s,* and *f.* The mouth shapes for several of these reference phonemes are shown in Figure 9.18.

Real-Time Implementations

In the system described by Lewis, the speech track analysis and the facial image generation were implemented as separate non-real-time tasks. The

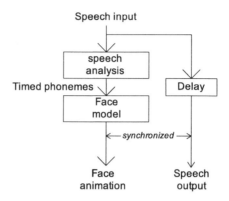

Figure 9.19.
Real-time synchronized speech animation.

timed phoneme information produced by the analysis task was saved and used as input to the face animation system.

It is now possible to analyze the speech and to output synchronized facial animation in real time. In this case, the speech analysis process feeds results directly into the facial animation process. The speech output is slightly delayed to compensate for the analysis processing time, as shown in Figure 9.19.

9.8   Expression Overlays

Complete communication between people takes place through the coordinated combination of spoken language, emotional voice qualities, facial expressions, and body language.

The face is an important and complex communication channel. While talking, a person is rarely still. The face changes expressions constantly. While talking, the lips move to help form the words, the eyebrows may raise, the eyes may move, the eyelids may blink, the head may turn, etc. Fully expressive automated character animation requires not only speech synchronization, but also automatic generation of the characteristic facial movements, such as expressions, prosodic nodding, and eye movements that occur during speech. The required expressions may be emotionally based or completely non-emotional.

9.8.1   Emotional Overlays

When people speak, there is almost always emotional information communicated along with the audible words. This emotional information is conveyed through multiple communication channels, including emotional qualities of the voice and visible facial expressions.

9.8.2 Emotions

Emotion combines visceral and muscular physiological responses, autonomic nervous system and brain responses, verbal responses, and facial expressions [Scherer et al. 84, Ekman 89]. Each emotion modifies physiology in particular ways. For example, anger is characterized by muscle tension, a decrease of salivation, a lowered brow, tense lips, and increased heart rate. Some of these physiological variations affect the vocal tract, while some muscle action variations affect facial expressions.

Several universal facial expressions are linked to emotions and attitudes. Anger, disgust, fear, happiness, sadness, and surprise are six emotions that have universal facial expressions [Ekman and Friesen 75]. Three main areas of the face are involved in visible expression changes: the upper part of the face with the brows and forehead, the eyes, and the lower part of the face with the mouth. Each emotion is characterized by specific facial changes. Fear is associated with tense, stretched lips, with the eyebrows raised and drawn together. Sadness has the inner side of the brows drawn up, the upper eyelid inner corner raised, and the corners of the lips down. The facial expressions of emotion are called *affect displays* [Ekman 89]. For more details on facial expression, see Chapter 2.

9.8.3 Non-emotional Overlays

Not all facial expressions are the result of emotion. Some facial movements are used as communication punctuation marks, similar to those used in written text. For example, eyebrow motions can punctuate a conversation. Ekman divides non-emotional facial expression into the following groups: *emblems, manipulators, conversational signals, punctuators*, and *regulators* [Ekman 89]. The repertory of such movements is elaborate.

Emblems are movements whose meanings are well known and culturally dependent. They are used to replace common verbal expressions. For example, instead of verbally agreeing, one can nod.

Manipulators correspond to the biological needs of the face, such as blinking the eyes to keep them wet and wetting the lips.

Conversational Signals

Conversational signals or *illustrators* are used to punctuate or emphasize speech. Conversational signals may occur on an accented item within a word or may stretch out over a portion of the sentence. These signals often involve actions of the eyebrows. Raised eyebrows often accompany accented vowels. Raised eyebrows can also signal a question. Head and eye motions can illustrate a word. An accented word is often accompanied by a rapid head movement [Hadar et al. 84, Bull and Connelly 85].

Conversational signals also depend on emotion. An angry or happy person will have more facial motions than a sad person. Emotion intensity affects the type and frequency of facial movements [Collier 85].

Punctuators

Punctuators are movements occurring at pauses. Punctuators appear at pauses due to hesitation, or to signal the pauses associated with the commas or exclamation marks of written text [Dittman 74]. The number of pauses affects speech rate. The rate of occurrence and the type of punctuators are emotion dependent. A frightened person's speech seldom shows pauses even of short duration [Cahn 89]. A sad person's slow speech is partly due to a large number of long pauses. A happy person tends to punctuate speech by smiling.

Certain types of head movements occur during pauses. A boundary between intermediate phrases will often be indicated by slow movement, while a final pause will often coincide with stillness [Hadar et al. 84]. Eye blinks can also occur during pauses [Condon and Osgton 71].

Regulators

Regulators are movements that help control how people take turns speaking in conversation. Duncan enumerated the regulators as follows [Duncan 74]:

- *Speaker-Turn-Signal* is used when the speaker wants to give up her speaking turn. It is composed of several intonation, paralanguage, body movement, and syntax clues. At the end of the utterance, the speaker turns her head to the listener, takes a more relaxed position, and ends any hand gestures and body motions.

- *Speaker-State-Signal* is used at the beginning of a speaking turn. It usually consists of the speaker turning his head away from the listener and beginning a hand or arm gesture.

- *Speaker-Within-Turn* is used when the speaker wants to keep his speaking turn, and to assure himself that the listener is following. It occurs at the completion of a grammatical clause. The speaker turns his head toward the listener.

- *Speaker-Continuation-Signal* often follows a Speaker-Within-Turn signal. The speaker turns her head and eyes away from the listener.

When people talk to each other, the listener's head motions and facial expressions are synchronized with the speaker's voice. This synchronization plays an important role in effective conversation. These responses help regulate the flow of the conversation by providing feedback to the speaker.

9.8.4   Eye Actions

Eye actions include eye blinks, changes in eye gaze, and changes in pupil size.

Eye Blinks

Blinking is an important characteristic that should be included in synthetic face models used in conversational interface modes. Speaker eye blinks are an important part of speech response systems that include synchronized facial visualizations.

Eyes blink not only to accentuate speech, but to address the physical need to keep the eyes wet. The eye blinks occur quite frequently. There is at least one eye blink per utterance.

The structure of an eye blink is synchronized with speech articulation. The eye might close over one syllable and start opening again over another word or syllable. Blinks can also occur on stressed vowels [Condon and Osgton 71].

Blink occurrence is also emotion dependent. During fear, tension, anger, excitement, and lying, the amount of blinking increases, while it decreases during concentrated thought [Collier 85].

Watanabe et al. proposed an eye blinking feedback model for synthetic faces [Watanabe 93]. This model estimates eye blinks and head nodding responses based on the on-off characteristics of the speaker's voice.

Observations based on face-to-face human interaction indicate that there is synchronization between the speaker's voice and the speaker's eye blinks. The speaker's eye blinks follow pauses in the speech. There is a slight delay between speech pauses and the corresponding blinks. This delay is about 0.5 seconds. Experimental results indicate that this is a fairly strong effect, occurring about 75 percent of the time.

Listener eye blinks and nods can be important user feedback in speech recognition contexts. There is synchronization between the speaker's voice and the listener's eye blinks, and also the listener's head nodding. Listener eye blinks also follow pauses in the speech. This effect is somewhat weaker, occurring about 50 percent of the time. The delay for the listener's blinks is about 0.4 seconds. Listener eye blinks frequently take place while nodding.

Changes in Eye Gaze

The eyes are almost always in motion. When looking at an object or person, the eyes will scan it from the most important features to the least important, in repeated cycles. When looking at a picture of a person, the eyes spend about 60 percent of the time looking at the picture's eyes and about 15 percent of the time looking at the mouth [Argyle and Cook 76]. In personal interactions, eye gaze is modified by social and cultural context.

Eye contact is important nonverbal communication. The amount of allowed and expected eye contact is culturally dependent. Eye contact increases with the degree of intimacy and friendship. Eye contact decreases when a person is lying or having difficulty speaking. Aversion to eye contact can be a sign of shame or sorrow.

Gaze can be used to communicate intentions and to modify another person's behavior. Gaze can be a function of power, aggression, and domination, especially when used contrary to normal cultural and social rules.

When a person is exasperated, or trying to solve a problem, or trying to remember something, the eyes will look up.

Changes in Pupil Size

The pupils constrict in bright light and dilate in dim light. Pupil size also reflects a person's judgmental attitude. Large pupil size accompanies a positive attitude, whereas constricted pupils are associated with negative judgments. Pupil dilation also changes during emotional experiences. Pupil dilation is followed by pupil constriction during happiness and anger, and remains dilated during fear and sadness [Hess 75].

9.9   Complete Speech Animation

As we have seen in the previous sections, complete speech animation of synthetic faces involves much more than simply manipulating the visible portions of the vocal tract. It involves the synchronized coordination of many facial actions. Pelachaud has proposed an approach to computing the sequence of the required facial poses that synchronize and coordinate these many actions to produce complete speech animation [Pelachaud 91].

This process is driven from an input script containing the desired speech, specified as phonemes, along with emotion and intonation information. Based on the input script, the following steps are applied to determine the complete facial posture for each phoneme of the animation. The computed complete postures are defined in terms of Ekman's facial action units (AUs) [Ekman and Friesen 78].

1. Compute lip shapes by applying rules that transform phonemes into action units. Computing the lip shapes takes into account coarticulation of the phoneme sequences.

2. Determine the action units for the desired emotion.

3. Compute eyebrow actions based on speech intonation accents, pauses, and emphasis.

4. Compute eye blinks, taking into account voluntary blinks associated with speech and emotion, and involuntary physiological eye blinks. Speech-related blinks are computed at the phoneme level.

5. Compute head motion based on emotion, speech accents and pauses, and conversational turn-taking rules.

6. Compute eye movements to scan the listener's face and to follow head motion.

7. Compute eye pupil size.

8. Collect and reconcile the facial action units generated by the previous steps. Concurrent actions can occur. The final face posture is the summation of all applied actions, modified to reconcile any conflicting actions.

9. Having computed the list of action units for each phoneme, in-between frames are obtained by spline interpolation of the phoneme values. Interpolation of the phoneme values takes into account the duration, onset, and offset characteristics of each action unit.

10. Generate the complete facial expression image for each frame, based on the interpolated action unit information.

10

Performance Animation

10.1 Background

The creation of facial animation control parameters is a tedious process at
best. Often, many dozens of parameters have to be specified and coordinated to create a short sequence. For the face, it is important to carefully
orchestrate these parameters, since actions have to be precisely timed to
create believable expressions. For example, surprise requires the onset and
duration to be correctly coordinated, or else the motion will look more like
a lazy yawn.

To alleviate the manual activity of creating animation parameters, it is
possible to capture an actor's performance and translate her motions into
a suite of control parameters. This has advantages for the director because
real-time motion capture can be created at low resolution, allowing performances to be blocked in and allowing subsequent high-fidelity rendering, in-
corporating all the capture data, to be completed offline. In many respects,
performance-based animation is a computer-based variation of traditional
rotoscoping, with "bells-and-whistles."

An early example of performance animation, or *expression mapping*,
was used to create the animated short film *Tony de Peltrie*, by Bergeron and Lachapelle [Bergeron and Lachapelle 85]. A polygon topology
drawn directly onto a person's face was photometrically digitized into a
data base of expressions. For details on photogrametry modeling tech-

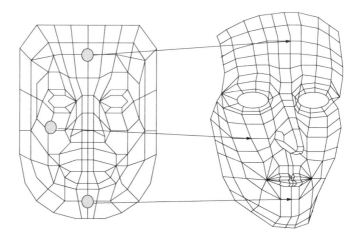

Figure 10.1.
A one-to-N correspondence mapping of the sampled face to a computer-generated counterpart. The mapping can be specified as a weighting function, which is often specified manually. Alternatively, a weighting function can be defined as a proportion of the distance d from the center of the vertex location. Such functions allow displacement fields to interact and overlap. Re-mapping, or *re-targeting*, to a target topology, is a fundamental technique in performance animation and is used in a wide range of systems.

niques see Chapter 4. A mapping was then specified between the individual's face and the very exaggerated "Tony" computer-generated caricature, as illustrated in Figure 10.1. Consequently, shape changes from the database of digitized expressions were correlated with the computer-generated model. A variation of *expression mapping* was developed by de-Graf and Wahrman [Parke 90]. Rather than slaving expressions, data collected from a series of Cyberware™ laser scans were used and interpolated in real time.

The use of an actor's performance to control a visual surrogate is essentially the same problem that was introduced in Chapter 2 with the concepts of video teleconferencing. While teleconferencing systems target the same encoding purposes as performance animation, there are significant limitations in the teleconferencing schema developed to date, with respect to the film industry. For instance, the eyes, eyelids, and eyebrows demand high-fidelity motion recording—sometimes at high speed—if a performance is to accurately portray an actor's emotions.

The precise capture of an actor's performance, and the playback of her performance as a computer-generated model, has become an important technique used in the film and game industries. The quality of today's capture sessions can now provide sufficient fidelity to accurately create an individual's motion nuances. Recognizable actors and character personalities, such as Jim Carrey (LifeF/X 1998), Hugo Weaving in *The Matrix Reloaded* (Warner Bros 2003), Tiger Woods (Electronic Arts 2005), Tom Hanks in *The Polar Express* (Sony Pictures Imageworks 2004) and the characters in *Monster House* (Sony Pictures Imageworks 2006), have been used in commercial production. To date, this requires specialized techniques, where the actor is marked and tracked in a controlled studio environment [Pighin and Lewis 06].

The interest in capturing performances from actors has led to a variety of different techniques, with varying degrees of success. As the area has developed, a number of terms are used that may not be familiar to the reader; therefore, the following terms are described and referred to in later sections:

- *MoCap* or motion capture refers to the recording of specific markers placed on the body or face during a performance. The motion data is then used to drive a computer-generated character. Systems often require reflectance markers to be carefully placed on the face, and for whole body systems, the performer wearing a body suit with markers strategically placed on the surface.

- *Blend shapes* are key face postures defined in a dataset, which can be used to define a linear space for facial expressions. As the name suggests, a new posture can be generated as a *blend* of two or more existing postures. Controlling the linear space can be specified through generalized functions, or determined automatically from capture sessions. Blend shaping is one of the most widespread techniques in facial animation and is controlled by *weights*—values on the *basis vector*— the geometry.

- *Re-targeting.* Here, the recorded source material is adapted to a target character. This is sometimes referred to as cross-mapping and is extensively used in performance-based systems, as illustrated in Figure 10.1. Re-targeting allows an actor's performance to be mapped onto characters that need not be a direct resemblance in themselves.

- *Rotoscoping* is a technique that has a long history in traditional animation [Thomas and Johnson 81]. A live performance is recorded and frame by frame the actor is traced to create a reference from which the animation sequence is generated. In many respects, computer-based performance animation is a versatile variant of rotoscoping, especially when the captured data of a three-dimensional model can be observed from a variety of novel viewpoints.

- *Expression cloning* is the ability to map vertex motion vectors from a source model to a new geometry having a different geometric proportions and topological layout. In many respects this is the same as re-targeting, with the variation of being more verstile.

- *PCA*, principal component analysis, is a mathematical technique capable of reducing multi-dimensional data sets to lower dimensions for analysis. Within the context of faces, PCA is capable of capturing all the geometric variations of a performance in a single dataset. Such analysis is useful when considering playback compression techniques on devices with low computational resources, such as game consoles and video-teleconferencing systems. PCA is particularly effective for face data where there is a high level of correlated geometric structure and texture map motion over long sequences.

- *Dense motion capture* refers to tracking multiple markers at high density. To create high density markers, reflective elements in phosphorescence paint are applied to the face, like makeup. The markers can be seen under ultraviolet light and tracked. Whereas single large markers are placed at strategic locations on the face and tracked frame to frame in most MoCap systems, dense marker patches are uniquely identified and tracked over time.

The ultimate performance-based systems will be unobtrusive and markerless. Such systems will operate with unconstrained actors, who then can perform in sets with props, as well as with other actors, both indoors and outside. This is in contrast to current state-of-the-art systems, where performances are typically captured in controlled environments. For example, high-fidelity data capture sessions often require high luminosity, physical restraints for the head, or even clumsy headgear. Hardly a conducive environment to generate best performances from actors. Nevertheless, much progress has been achieved in the recent past and has extended the quality of facial animation. Indeed, the levels of realism demanded by the film industry have come close to fooling the observer into thinking that the final virtual actor is real.

A majority of techniques developed using performance systems combine modeling, animation and control. As a result, adjusting the geometry of the face and modifying the captured performances can be awkward. Therefore, systems that separate geometry capture from animation control are likely to be more successful, because they will allow flexibility for modelers and animators.

The following sections outline some of the basic techniques and systems that have been successfully used in the commercial film and game industries. It is noted that there has been a great deal of additional research reported on performance-driven animation; however, they tend to target niche areas and are often hard to scale to production levels. For a more comprehensive view, see [Pighin and Lewis 06].

10.1.1 Mechanical Performance Systems

Historically, mechanical devices provided the first performance-driven systems. Devices such as six-degrees-of-freedom trackers, keyboards, joysticks, and DataGloves™ captured the actions of a performer, which were subsequently converted into time-varying control parameters. A computer-generated character can then animated in real time, or used to drive an animated character at a later date.

10.1.2 Animatronics

Animatronics is a mechanical precursor of computer-based performance animation. Animatronics has been extensively used in special effects, especially when it is impossible for a puppeteer to insert a hand into the puppet. In such a situation, the performer is placed off camera and provided with a remote interface through which he can manipulate the character.

The most common animatronic puppets are radio controlled. Motors, mounted inside the puppet, move various features of the faces, such as opening and closing the mouth. The puppeteer is given a number of physical controls, which transmit radio signals to the motors mounted inside the puppet. As the puppeteer moves the controls, the puppet reacts accordingly. These interfaces often resemble the puppets they are designed to control, and the manner in which the performer manipulates them is very similar to the way he or she would manipulate the real puppet. A term commonly used to refer to the skeleton type of interface is a *Waldo*.

A classic example of a Waldo is the bicycle scene from *The Muppet Movie*. In this scene, Kermit and Piggy are riding bicycles through a park while singing a song. Lip synchronization requires the puppeteer to have direct real-time control. As one can imagine, it is difficult to hide a person on a bicycle built for a three-foot puppet; hence the use of Waldos. Each Waldo consists of a glove, much like the inside of a puppet, mounted on the end of a rod. The performer places one hand in the glove and holds the end of the rod in the other. Consequently, as the puppeteer's hand is opened and closed, the mouth of the puppet opens and closes accordingly.

Computer-Aided Animatronics

The next step for animatronics involves replacing the mechanical puppet by a computer-generated model. Instead of transmitting controls to a mechanical device, the parameters control a computer-generated character.

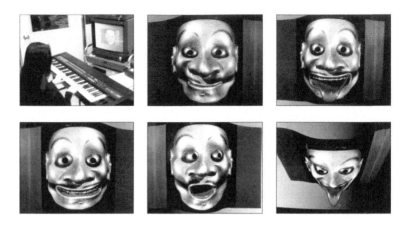

Figure 10.2.
Example expressions of a real-time performance Kabuki mask developed at the
Sony Research laboratory.

An example of a real-time system is illustrated in Figure 10.2. The
system, called System G, is a real-time 30-frames-a-second animation and
texture mapper. The Kabuki mask originated as a flat image and was
warped into a three-dimensional model, and, by means of predefined macros,

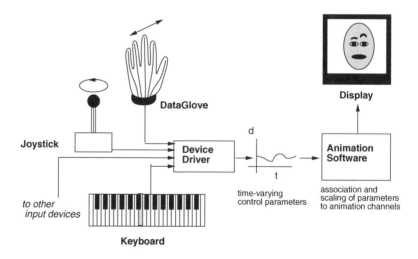

Figure 10.3.
Manual performance-based animation control. In this example, one of the input
device channels is associated with the raising of an eyebrow. The animation
software associates and scales the parameters for the virtual computer character.

the face can be transitioned between a variety facial postures. To control the system, a keyboard acts as a user interface, as illustrated in Figure 10.3, such that when a key is depressed a facial posture is displayed.

Mixing Animatronics and a Computer-Generated Waldo

The next step for animatonics is integrating the computer-generated puppets with their real, physical counterparts.

Creating a scene with a computer-generated Waldo takes place in three phases. The first phase involves a live session with an interactive wireframe Waldo operating in concert with other characters, as illustrated in Figure 10.4. This system outputs a low-resolution image of the character and, at the same time, records its movements. This procedure is referred to as *interactive rotoscoping*. In the second phase of the production process, the recorded motion data are input to an animation system. Within the animation system, secondary motion can be added, for example, a pseudodynamic simulation to generate a flexible motion of the body and appendages. In the final phase, a fully rendered version of the Waldo is composited with the live-action puppets, and special effects are added and recorded to tape.

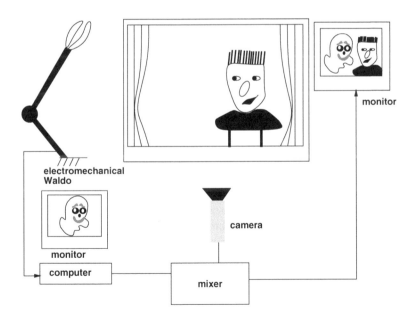

Figure 10.4.
The production of a computer-generated Waldo. The camera captures the live action of the puppeteer, which is then mixed with a computer-generated image for display on a monitor for both the Waldo operator and the real puppeteer.

Phase 1: Interactive Rotoscoping

Interactive rotoscoping, which captures the Waldo's movements, is based on an electromechanical armature. The armature, resembling an upside-down luxo lamp, with optical encoders mounted at the joints and "clam-shell" gloves mounted at one end, records the puppeteer's motions, as illustrated in Figure 10.4. The output of the animated character subsequently is fed to a video system and used to record the performance of the handmade puppets. The Waldo's performer places his hand in the glove, and in real time he can manipulate a low-resolution image of the Waldo on the screen. This image is then composited on top of the regular puppet's performance [Graves 89].

The fact that the live performance of a Waldo can be seen on the same screen as that for the regular puppets is significant. When puppeteers perform, they do not gauge their performance by looking at the puppets above their heads, but rather by looking at the monitors that display the image being recorded by the camera. Thus, from the performer's point of view, seeing a Waldo on the screen is the same as having it float around in front of the camera. This means that in terms of eye contact, lip synchronization and blocking, a Waldo can interact with the other characters as they interact with each other.

Phase 2: Secondary Action

The second phase creates the high-resolution images of the Waldo, which involves building any new models required for the Waldo's costumes, designing any secondary animation needed to affect the Waldo's transformations, and finally specifying the parameters for the pseudo-dynamic simulation system.

Geometric models are constructed and reused as much as possible, so much so that modeling on the Waldo project is referred to as "wardrobe." Secondary animation is kept to a minimum, and the bulk of the character's personality is brought out through dynamics.

The pseudo-dynamic simulation is performed by examining the motion of an object and, based on a description of its flexibility, deforming its shape accordingly. An object can be made to appear flexible and dynamic. For example, components of the wardrobe may be deformable and may be automatically animated to flex and bend to automatically generate squash-and-stretch and follow-through motions.

Phase 3: Compositing

In the final step, the high-resolution animation is recomposited on top of the image of the puppets as performed. Careful consideration has to be given to ensure that the animation is perfectly synchronized with the original performance. The slightest deviation will cause glaring problems in lip synchronization, eye contact, and simple blocking.

Full Computer-Generated Waldo

Mixing live action with puppeteers is a cumbersome production process, so with the advent of real-time graphics hardware, the physical puppet could be replaced with a computer generated Waldo. Mike Normal is an example of a virtual Waldo and was constructed from a series of Cyberware^{TM} laser scans of actor Mike Gribble [deGraf and Wahrman 88]. In addition to a static pose, two dozen or so key postures were captured, including round- and close-mouth postures for speech mapping. Each scan was subsequently re-sampled to reduce the resolution from 40,000 polygons to approximately 2,000 polygons.

Animating a Virtual Mike Normal

Digitizing all the face postures to be topologically equivalent was the key to animating a Mike, because any intermediate poses could be generated by interpolation functions. See Chapter 5 for more details.

In addition to interpolating the whole face configuration, regions of the face could be harnessed to particular actions. For example, the eyebrow region could be extracted from one scan and blended onto another. By grouping specific regions of the face to particular actions, a variety of channels could control the facial model. Each face unit was controlled by a single channel in real time, allowing the layering of new animation with predefined animation clips. The fundamental creation of a new face posture could be described by the following shorthand notation:

$$\text{NewFace} = \text{Channel}A * \text{FaceUnit1} + \text{Channel}B * \text{FaceUnit2} + ... \quad (10.1)$$

Some channels could be driven automatically, akin to the human nervous system, such as nostril flares, blinking, breathing, and babbling. Alternatively, units could be associated, such that the brows rose when the mouth opened beyond a certain point.

Skilled puppeteers simultaneously controlled a number of the Mike's degrees of freedom, allowing them to transparently translate their refined hand-eye coordination. It was crucial that the interface provided an interactive performance (10–12 Hz) to allow the puppeteer to observe the actions of the Mike with the real puppets. The first puppeteer to use the system embedded amazing life into Mike in his first hour of use.

10.2 The Envelope for Face Deformations

The interpolation of postures, described in Equation (10.1), requires *topological equivalence* and is widely used in modeling and animation, as described in Chapters 4 and 5. In addition to topological equivalence, the transformation between poses requires *feature correspondance*, and in many respects this is the *feature morphing* problem, as described by Beier and Neely [Beier and Neely 92]. Feature morphing has been extended in a variety of different face animation techniques, such as speech mapping [Ezzat and Poggio 00]. See Chapter 9 for more details. However, before describing how to track feature points, it is worth reviewing some observations of the three-dimensional space in which faces can possibly move. Such a space can be considered a *dynamic envelope* for the face.

A rich set of topologically equivalent face shapes in a wide variety of postures results in a data set that defines the possible motions for that data set. As a result, a face pose can be constructed from a combination of n basis vectors, where each vector is one of the potential shapes, and a vertex of the face $\vec{v}$ belonging to the intermediate face shape can be written as follows:

$$\vec{v} = \sum_{i=1}^{n} \alpha_i \vec{v}_i, \qquad (10.2)$$

where the scalars α_i are the blending weights, $\vec{v}_i$ is the location of the vertex in the blend shape i, and n is the number of blend shapes. The assumption is that the data set is normalized such that $\alpha_i \geq 0$, for all i and sums to 1 for rotation and translational invariance [Pushkar et al. 03].

The concept expressed in Equation (10.2) has been leveraged in several original modeling and animation systems [Pighin et al. 98, Blanz and Vetter 99, Pushkar et al. 03]. In addition, extensions and research into the model and animation concepts have grown in the past few years, to the extent that a SIGGRAPH course was dedicated to performance-driven animation systems and techniques [Pighin and Lewis 06].

While the creation of whole face targets through blend functions generates a wide range of possible expressions, it is still desirable to generate regional, or local blend shapes, such of those found in the upper and lower face. The ability to mask regions and weight other target areas allows novel localized expressions, such as raising the corner of the mouth or raising the eyebrow. By tracking face motions, it is possible to create a set of parameters from a blend shape model [Choe et al. 01]. This is in contrast to determining the parameters manually.

The creation of localized blend shape parameters can be correlated to the action units described in the Facial Action Coding System [Ekman and Friesen 78] to create a versatile and powerful animation system. Once the parameters for the data set are determined, the face can be animated as a selection and summation of the desired shape weighting functions for a new posture geometry,

$$N\text{posture} = \alpha AU12 + \alpha AU24 + \alpha AU4... + \alpha AUn, \qquad (10.3)$$

and for a new texture color,

$$N\text{texture} = \beta AU1 + \beta AU2 + \beta AU3... + \beta AUn, \qquad (10.4)$$

or more generally,

$$\vec{v} = \sum_{1=0}^{n} w_i E_i, \qquad (10.5)$$

where w_i is the weighting function, E_i the expression basis, and n the number of expressions.

The ability to create a blend shape data set is determined not only by the static capture of the face, but also by the ability to track the features of the performer's face making expressive poses. Tracking surface features can be achieved through a number of techniques, from marks to optical flow, which are described in more detail in the following sections.

10.3   Feature Tracking and Correspondence

The problem of identifying salient features, such as the outermost point of the eyebrow, observing its location from frame-to-frame, then mapping that point to a corresponding vertex of the geometry model, is the essence of all performance animation systems. Importantly this is a *feature correspondence* problem, and many of today's performance-driven systems solve this issue by the explicit mapping of tracked feature points placed on the head and face. Alternatively, when markers are not used, small features of the face are identified and tracked over time to achieve the same result.

10.3.1   Automated Marker Tracking

The simplest approach to tracking face features is to track markers placed directly on the subject at salient points. This technique is appropriate for one-time performances in which the actor is placed in an artificial environment and recorded. The actions can then be processed in an offline process to extract the x, y location of the markers in the image plane. The resulting displacements of these points then can be used to control a face geometry and texture map. This technique was first demonstrated by Williams and has been repeated in many other systems to date [Williams 90b, Guenter et al. 98, Pighin and Lewis 06].

The process involves sticking retroreflective markers directly onto the performer's face. A beam-splitter (a plate glass), set at 45 degrees between the camera and the performer, and a slide projector, set at right angles to the camera position, ensure that the direction of the light and the camera are coaxial, as illustrated in Figure 10.5. By adjusting the light intensity and

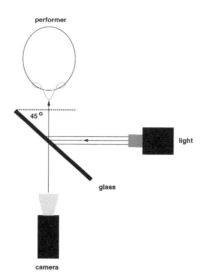

Figure 10.5.
The configuration of the camera, light, and glass plate during the video recording process. This configuration ensures that the light and camera are coaxial.

camera aperture, it is possible to generate views on which the retroreflective markers—and little else—are visible.

Digitizing the actor's performance now becomes a problem of tracking a set of bright spots in a dark field. By placing the markers carefully to avoid occlusion and by ignoring global head translation and rotation, it is reduced to a planar x, y tracking problem.

The basis of the spot tracking algorithm is solved as follows.

1 The centroid of a marker is selected manually from the first video frame.
2 A window a few pixels larger than the spot is positioned around the selected pixel.
3 The x, y coordinates of each pixel are multiplied by the intensity of the current pixel.
4 The window's center of gravity (c_x, c_y), based on light intensity, is then calculated using the following equations:

$$S = \sum_x \sum_y I(x,y), \tag{10.6}$$

$$C_x = \sum_y \sum_x x * I(x,y)/S, \tag{10.7}$$

$$C_y = \sum_y \sum_x y * I(x,y)/S. \tag{10.8}$$

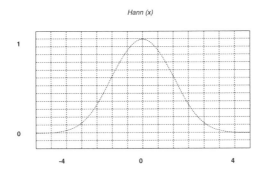

Figure 10.6.
Hann window.

5 To refine the location of the pixel intensities first moment, the process is iterated a few times.

6 Finally, the next frame and the subsequent motion of the spot are introduced, and the process is repeated, using the old window position as a starting point. The result is a new center of gravity, and the window moves accordingly.

To apply the locator displacements to the facial model, a variation of a Hanning function was used [Wolberg 91]. A Hanning function is specified as follows (see Figure 10.6):

$$\text{Hann}(x) = \begin{cases} \alpha + (1 - \alpha) \cos \frac{2\Pi x}{N-1}, & x < \frac{N-1}{2}, \\ 0, & \text{otherwise.} \end{cases}$$

In three dimensions, the Hanning function is described to be radially symmetric and is scaled to 1.0 in the center, diminishing smoothly to 0.0 at the edges, with no negative values.

Marker tracking is effective, provided that there are discrete spots to track, and that they remain in view at all times. There have been commercialized versions of this type of approach. Adaptive Optics developed a device that the actor wears on her head in combination with reflective markers placed on her face, as illustrated in Figure 10.7(a). When the person moves, the head-mounted camera moves in unison, as illustrated in Figure 10.7(b); as a result, the markers remain in view at all times, which obviates the need to compensate for head rotation, tilting, and looming. The obvious limitations of this approach are that it requires a subject to wear head attire and to have his or her face marked or painted. While these limitations are fine in many situations, the ability to capture facial motion in an unconstrained environment is a more significant problem.

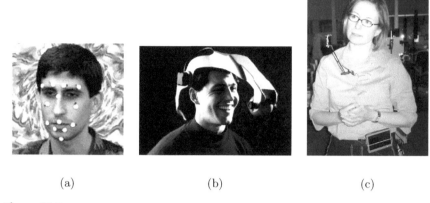

(a)   (b)   (c)

Figure 10.7.
Two types of face tracking systems. A head-mounted optical face tracker,
involving (a) the placement of reflective marker on the face and (b) a
head-mounted device. (c) *Self-Cam*, a small, lightweight portable camera device
capable of detecting facial motions and then determining emotional states. ((a)
and (b) *Courtesy of Adaptive Optics.* (c) *Courtesy of R. Picard.*)

More recently, the ability to use lightweight portable cameras and belt-
mounted handtops, as illustrated in Figure 10.7(c), can be used in a less
intrusive way to observe and analyze head and face motions. This system,
known as *Self-Cam*, tracks head and facial features to determine emotional
states during social interaction [Teeters et al. 06].

The technique described above reduces the issue to a simplified two-
dimensional tracking problem. Improvements can be made to track the
three-dimensional features points from two or more cameras. This is commonly referred to as *pose recovery* and is described in Section 4.12.3 from a
pair of photographs.

Computer vision algorithms can estimate the viewing parameters (position, orientation, and focal length) for each of the input frames. From these
estimates it is possible to recover the three-dimensional coordinates from a
set of feature points. A good example of face pose recovery from sequences
of images is presented in [Pighin et al. 98]. With more input viewpoints, the
finer the three-dimensional resolution; for example, Guenter et al. present
a video tracking system with six synchronized cameras capturing 182 face
markers that were used to drive a face model [Guenter et al. 98].

10.3.2   Markers and Video Texture Capture

In addition to tracking markers and using them to control a corresponding
thee-dimensional model, there is the opportunity to capture the video of
the performer as a dynamic texture map. Such techniques allow both the

three-dimensional deformation of a model and a registered texture image to be captured simultaneously [Guenter et al. 98].

By placing a number of bright colored dots on the face, in view of multiple cameras, their three-dimensional location can be tracked and used to control a corresponding facial model. Each vertex of the face geometry can be moved by a linear combination of the offset of the nearest dot. The linear combination for each vertex v_j is expressed as a set of blending coefficients α_k^j, one for each dot, and normalized. The new location p_j^i of the vertex v_j at frame i is

$$p_j^i = p_j + \sum_k \alpha_k^j ||d_k^i - d_k||, \qquad (10.9)$$

where p_j is the initial location of the vertex v_j.

For the texture map the dots placed on the face need to be removed from the texture map and can be achieved by substituting nearest-neighbor skin texture pixels. The texture maps can then be re-parameterized into a more convenient form from storage, retrieval, and compression over sequences.

Separating the texture map from the geometry allows high-levels of compression, using PCA for the geometry and image compression using MPEG video codecs for the texture maps. As a result, the playback can be achieved at low data rates without much loss of image fidelity.

10.3.3 Dense Marker Motion Capture

Tracking spots requires the careful placement of markers on the face and can take a significant amount of preparation time with an actor. More recent advances leverage a large number of markers distributed randomly

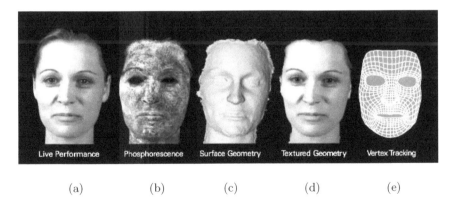

(a)   (b)   (c)   (d)   (e)

Figure 10.8.
Five steps in dense motion capture: (a) live actor, (b) phosphorescence paint, (c) surface geometry, (d) texture map, and (e) polygon topology. (*Courtesy of Mova Contour Reality Capture system.*)

over the surface of the face in the form of elements in retroreflective paint. The phosphorescent paint is applied like makeup and matches normal flesh-tones, such that the actor does not appear "spotted." Not only is the paint easy to apply, it can be seen under florescent light, as illustrated in Figure 10.8(b).

The elements in the paint, while distributed randomly, can also be uniquely identified once the capture session is complete and a small group of markers define a unique pattern that can be tracked using computer vision techniques. To capture a performance, the actor stands in an operational volume, as shown in Figure 10.9, and from the known camera positions the face geometry can be reconstructed.

One of the advantages of dense motion capture systems is that the performer is not so severely constrained or *locked down*; instead, the actor can perform within a capture space in proximity to the sensors.

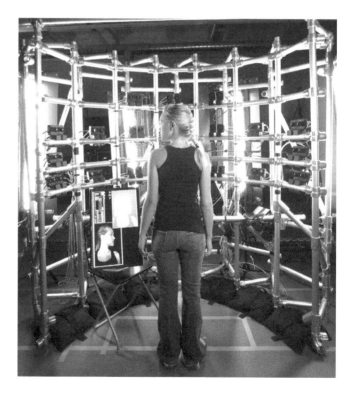

Figure 10.9.
A performer standing in a dense capture rig containing multiple synchronized cameras and specialized florescent lights. (*Courtesy of Mova Contour Reality Capture system.*)

10.3.4 Generalized Face Image Analysis and Tracking

The concept of automatically tracking the face and its features has drawn the attention of the computer vision community over the past few years. Much of this attention has been focused on the general problem of tracking the face in everyday environments under general lighting conditions. To *reliably* perform these tasks is hard to achieve at sufficient resolution for film quality production. Nevertheless, low resolution systems may be sufficient for video-teleconferencing or games systems, as described in Section 1.3.3.

Despite the complexity of the problem, there has been some success in both model-based and image-based analysis. Model-based analysis assumes that there is an underlying geometry to which the image can be matched. This method is in contrast to image-based approaches, which deal with fundamental transformations of the image or parts of the image. Several examples follow.

10.3.5 Deformable Templates

A deformable template makes the assumption that the face consists of features (such as the eyes, nose, and mouth) that are uniquely identifiable in the image under analysis. Therefore, a model, called a *template*, can define the shape under observation by modifying the parameters that describe the geometry of the template. An example of an eye-deformable template was developed by Yuille [Yuille et al. 89]. The template, as illustrated in Figure 10.10, consists of the following features:

- A circle of radius r, centered on a point $\vec{x}_c$. This circle corresponds to the boundary between the iris and the whites of the eye.

- A bounding contour of the eye, attracted to edges. This contour is modeled by two parabolic sections representing the upper and lower parts of the boundary. It has a center $\vec{x}_e$, with eye width $2b$, maximum height c for the boundary below the center, and an angle of orientation θ.

- Two points, corresponding to the centers of the whites of the eyes, which are attracted to peaks in the image intensity. These points are specified by $\vec{x}_e + p_1(\cos\theta, \sin\theta)$ and $\vec{x}_e + p_2(\cos\theta, sin\theta)$, where $p_1 \geq 0$ and $p_2 \leq 0$. The point $\vec{x}_e$ lies at the center of the eye, and θ corresponds to the orientation of the eye.

- The regions between the bounding contour and the iris also correspond to the whites of the eyes. These regions will be associated with large values in the image intensity function. These components are linked together by three types of forces: (1) forces that encourage $\vec{x}_c$ and $\vec{x}_e$ to be close together, (2) forces that make the width $2b$ of the

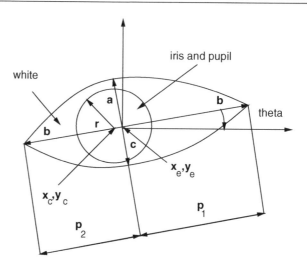

Figure 10.10.
A deformable template for an archetypal human eye. (Adapted
from [Yuille et al. 89].)

eye roughly four times the radius r of the iris, and (3) forces that
encourage the centers of the whites of the eyes to be roughly midway
from the center of the eye to the boundary.

In total, the eye template has nine parameters represented by

$$\vec{g} = (\vec{x}_c, \vec{x}_e, p_1, p_2, r, a, b, c, \theta).$$

All of these parameters are allowed to vary during matching.

Image Intensities

The deformable template acts on the representation of the image. The
representation is chosen to extract properties of the image, such as peaks
or troughs in the image intensity. In turn, the intensities act as potential
fields, attracting components of the template. An image edge Φ_e, valley Φ_v,
and peak Φ_p potential functions can be computed as follows:

$$\Phi_e(x,y) = e^{-\rho(x^2+y^2)^{1/2}} * \Psi_e(x,y),$$

$$\Phi_v(x,y) = e^{-\rho(x^2+y^2)^{1/2}} * \Psi_v(x,y), \qquad (10.10)$$

$$\Phi_p(x,y) = e^{-\rho(x^2+y^2)^{1/2}} * \Psi_p(x,y),$$

where $-\rho(x^2 + y^2)^{1/2}$ is an exponent smoothing function that enables interactions to be effective over longer distances.

Energy Function

At the heart of the algorithm is a potential energy function for the image, which is minimized as a function of the parameters of the template. The complete energy function is given as a combination of terms due to valley, edge, peak, image, and internal potentials:

$$E_c = E_v + E_e + E_i + E_p + E_{\text{prior}}.\qquad(10.11)$$

As an example, the edge potentials E_e are given by the integrals over the boundaries of the circle divided by its length and over the parabola divided by their lengths:

$$E_e = -\frac{c_2}{|\partial R_w|}\int_{\partial R_w}\Phi_e(\vec{x})ds - \frac{c_3}{|\partial R_w|}\int_{\partial R_w}\Phi_e(\vec{x})ds.\qquad(10.12)$$

For the complete set of edge potentials described in Equation (10.11), the reader is referred to the original paper [Yuille et al. 89].

One of the limitations of this approach is that the template can become brittle and unstable. For instance, the feature has to be apparent in the image under observation; if not, the template will continue to fit to the data with which it is presented, even though the feature may not be present. Another limitation is that although eyes usually appear to have an iris, a pupil, and distinct boundaries, under variable lighting conditions and observation angles, the features can be misinterpreted.

10.3.6 Active Contour Models

By relaxing the feature-based template constraint to a single two-dimensional curve or spline, it becomes possible to track feature lines and boundaries in the image. This ability is particularly interesting because the face has many such features, such as brows, furrows, and lip margins. A technique commonly referred to as *active contour* or *snake* can be used to track features over time [Kass et al. 88] (see Figure 10.11).

10.3.7 A Discrete Deformable Contour

A discrete deformable contour is defined as a set of nodes indexed by $i = 1, \ldots, n$ that are connected in series by springs [Terzopoulos and Waters 90]. Associated with these nodes are time-varying positions $\vec{x}_i(t) = [x_i(t), y_i(t)]'$ in the image plane. An interactive deformable contour results from numerically simulating the first-order dynamical system

$$\gamma\frac{d\vec{x}_i}{dt} + \boldsymbol{\alpha}_i + \boldsymbol{\beta}_i = \vec{f}_i; \qquad i = 1, \ldots, n,\qquad(10.13)$$

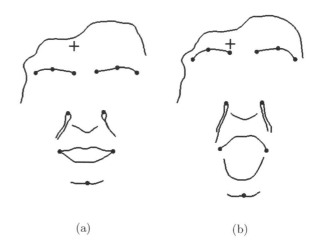

(a)   (b)

Figure 10.11.
Snakes and control points used for muscle contraction estimation on two key
frames: (a) a relaxed face and (b) a surprised expression.

where γ is a velocity-dependent damping constant, $\boldsymbol{\alpha}_i$ and $\boldsymbol{\beta}_i(t)$ are "tension" and "rigidity" forces internal to the contour, and $\vec{f}_i(t)$ are external forces acting in the image plane.

By following the formulation of a basic spring lattice, as described in Equation (8.9), we can describe a chain of nodes connected together by springs where l_i is the natural length of the spring connecting node i to node $i + 1$. Let $\vec{r}_i = \vec{x}_{i+1} - \vec{x}_i$ be the separation of the nodes, and let $e_i = ||\vec{r}_i|| - l_i$ be the deformation. Hence,

$$\boldsymbol{\alpha}_i = \frac{a_i e_i}{||\vec{r}_i||}\vec{r}_i, \qquad (10.14)$$

where $a_i(t)$ is a tension variable. A viscoelastic contour may be obtained by letting $dl_i/dt = \nu_i e_i$, where ν_i is a coefficient of viscoelasticity. Next,

$$\boldsymbol{\beta}_i = b_{i+1}(\vec{x}_{i+2} - 2\vec{x}_{i+1} + \vec{x}_i) - 2b_i(\vec{x}_{i+1} - 2\vec{x}_i + \vec{x}_{i-1}) + b_{i-1}(\vec{x}_i - 2\vec{x}_{i-1} + \vec{x}_{i-2}),$$
$$(10.15)$$

where b_i are rigidity variables. Tension, rigidity, and viscoelasticity are locally adjustable though the a_i, b_i, and ν_i variables.

The deformable contour is responsive to a force field, derived from the image, that influences its shape and motion. It is convenient to express the force field though a time-varying potential function $P(x, y, t)$:

$$\vec{f}_i = p\nabla P(\vec{x}_i), \qquad (10.16)$$

where p is the strength of the image forces and $\nabla = [\partial/\partial x, \partial/\partial y]'$ is the gradient operator in the image plane.

10.3.8 Tracking Features with Active Contours

The human face has many feature lines and feature boundaries that an active contour can track. By placing the contours on or close to specific features, such as an eyebrow or a lip boundary, it is possible not only to track the feature but also to estimate face muscle contraction parameters from image sequences. In turn, these parameters can be used to drive a facial animation model [Terzopoulos and Waters 93].

To apply deformable contours to facial image analysis, the image intensity function $I(x, y, t)$ at time t is transformed into a planar force field using image processing techniques. The procedure is illustrated in Figure 10.12. From the facial image in Figure 10.12(a), a two-dimensional potential func-

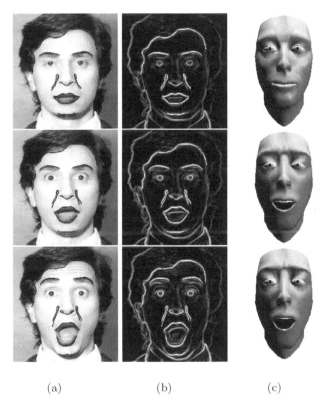

(a)   (b)   (c)

Figure 10.12.
Dynamic facial image analysis using deformable contours (a) and (b), and the resulting facial mimic (c) from muscle contraction estimates.

tion $P(x, y, t)$ is created, whose ravines (extended local minima) coincide with the significant intensity changes associated with facial features such as the eyebrows, mouth, and chin. This action is accomplished by computing the magnitude of the gradient of the image intensity:

$$P(x, y, t) = -||\nabla G_\sigma * I(x, y, t)||, \qquad (10.17)$$

where $G_\sigma*$ denotes convolution with a Gaussian smoothing filter of width σ that broadens the ravines so that they attract the contours from a distance. Figure 10.12(b) shows the negative of $P(x, y)$ computed from the frame in Figure 10.12(a).

The contours "slide downhill" in $P(x, y, t)$ (for fixed t) and come to equilibrium at the bottoms of the nearest ravines, thus conforming to the shapes of the facial features of interest. Once the contours have settled into ravines of the current image, the next image is introduced, and the contours again slide into the displaced ravines, so long as the movement of facial features is small. This procedure is repeated on subsequent frames to track the nonrigid motions of the facial features. As the deformable contours evolve, their dynamic-state variables $\vec{x}_i^t$ provide quantitative information about the nonrigid shapes and motions of the facial features.

10.3.9   A Facial Image Analysis Example

Figure 10.12 illustrates the analysis of one of the frames in the sequence, showing nine deformable contours, the black curves in Figure 10.12(a) and the white curves in Figure 10.12(b), in their final equilibrium positions, locked onto the left and right eyebrows, the left and right nasolabial furrows, the tip of the nose, the upper and lower lips, and the chin boss. Highlighter, applied to the brows and lips, enhanced the image feature boundary contrasts, making them easier to track from frame to frame. From the state variables of the deformable contours, the following are automatically estimated:

- Head reference point from the average position of the hairline contour;

- Contractions of the left and right zygomaticus major from the position of the endpoints of the upper-lip contour;

- Contraction of the left and right levator labii superioris alaeque nasi from the positions of the uppermost points of the associated nasolabial furrow contours;

- Contractions of the left and right inner, major, and outer occipito-frontalis, respectively, from the positions of the innermost, center, and outermost points of the associated eyebrow contours; and

- Jaw rotation from the average position of the chin boss contour.

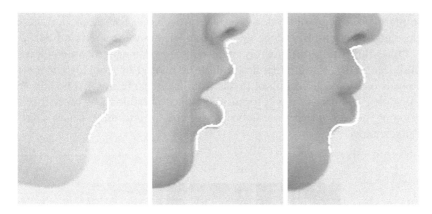

Figure 10.13.
Three example tracked key-frame lip postures. A weighted sum of these key frames are added to the formulation of the basic rigid motion tracker. (*Courtesy of A. Blake and M. Isard.*)

The estimated muscle contractions may be converted to dynamic contraction factors and input to the face model to reconstruct the expression. A sequence of frames from the reconstructed motion of surprise is illustrated in Figure 10.12(c).

The spline-based approach to tracking facial features in images was improved by [Blake and Isard 94]. In their model, the snake was a B-spline with time-varying control points. The most significant enhancement was the ability to sensitize the spline to various affine transformations, in particular with zooming, translation, and rotation. This ability was achieved with a slightly modified steady-state Kalman filter [Press et al. 86]. This basic rigid motion tracker was further enhanced to capture nonrigid motions, such as the shape of the lips during speaking. To achieve a profile lip tracker, as illustrated in Figure 10.13, additional lip posture key frames were added to the fundamental matrix formulation such that nonrigid motion and rigid motion could be monitored independently [Blake and Isard 94].

Progress in active contours, for the purpose of tracking complex nonrigid bodies at real-time rates, has been further developed by Blake and Isard [Blake and Isard 98]. Clearly, the reliability of such techniques, leveraging splines and probabilistic modeling, holds much promise for the general problem of head and face tracking with low quality camera input and general illumination conditions.

10.3.10   Local Parametric Models of Face Motion

Image motion parameters that correspond to various facial expressions can be recovered from image sequences. These techniques exploit both the template-based and optic-flow-based approaches. For more details, see [Mase and Pentland 91, Black and Yacoob 95, Essa and Pentland 94].

Optic-flow computations rely on a sequence of images at a pixel level of detail [Singh 91]. Essentially, flow can be estimated by tracking the motion of pixels or of a small group of pixels from frame to frame. To be effective, optical flow requires as much textural detail as possible to be present in the region of interest; otherwise, it becomes hard to determine where a group of pixels move.

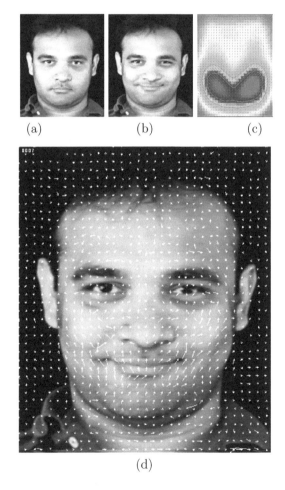

Figure 10.14.
Optical flow estimation images. Two poses of the face, (a) static and (b) smiling. (c) The pattern of motion energy for the expression. (d) The flow estimates of the face for the transition between (a) and (b). (*Courtesy of I. Essa.*)

An example of an image flow field can be seen in Figure 10.14(d), where flow vectors have been overlayed on the face image [Essa and Pentland 94]. The resulting facial image flow patterns make it possible to estimate muscle activation and subsequently classify facial expressions. This ability to capture the dynamic characteristics of facial expression is particularly significant because facial coding systems, such as FACS, ignore the temporal aspects of an expression, which undoubtedly plays a significant role in the recognition of emotions [Darwin 72]. Furthermore, it is being argued that the dynamics of expressions, rather than the detailed spatial deformations, are more significant for facial expression recognition [Bassili 82]. By generating patterns of motion energy, as illustrated in Figure 10.14(c) from optical flow examples of facial expression, Essa and Pentland were able to construct a simple expression detector that identifies motion energy associated with a particular facial expression [Essa and Pentland 94].

In more general terms, two principal motions for the head and face have to be accounted for if we are to track and identify expressions on the face: rigid head motions and nonrigid motions associated with the facial features, as illustrated in Figure 10.15. Figure 10.16 illustrates the

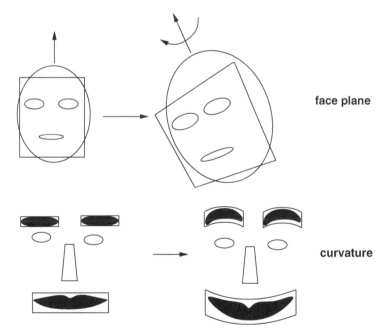

Figure 10.15.
The top row illustrates the basic affine transformations: divergence, deformation, and curl. The principal assumption is that the face is a planar surface. The bottom row illustrates the curvature transformations for the face, the brows, and the lips.

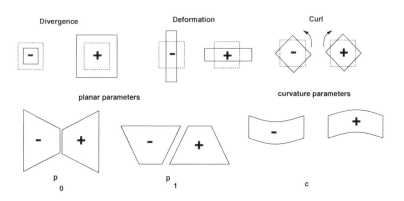

Figure 10.16.
A graphical representation of the motions captured by the various parameters or various regions.

various parameters that can be used to represent the motion of image regions [Black and Yacoob 95]. The first two, divergence and deformation, are affine transformations; the last, curl, is a bending of the image. This type of parameterization can be captured in a low-order polynomial:

$$u(x,y) = a_0 + a_1 x + a_2 y,$$
$$v(x,y) = a_3 + a_4 x + a_5 y, \qquad (10.18)$$

where a_i are constants and where $u(x,y)$ and $v(x,y)$ are the horizontal and vertical components of the flow at an image point $\mathbf{x} = (x, y)$.

The parameters a_i have simple interpretations in terms of image motion, as illustrated in Figure 10.16. For example, a_0 and a_3 represent horizontal and vertical translation, respectively. These parameters take care of the planar motions. Divergence (isotropic expansion), curl (rotation), and deformation (squashing) can be created by the following combinations:

$$\text{divergence} = a_1 - a_5,$$
$$\text{curl} = -a_2 + a_4, \qquad (10.19)$$
$$\text{deformation} = a_1 - a_3.$$

The affine transformations are not sufficient to capture the motion of a face when it occupies a significant proportion of the field of view. To accommodate these characteristics, the face can be approximated as a single plane viewed under perspective projection. As a result, it is possible to describe the image by the following eight-parameter model:

$$u(x,y) = a_0 + a_1 x + a_2 y + p_0 x^2 + p_1 xy,$$
$$v(x,y) = a_3 + a_4 x + a_5 y + p_0 xy + p_1 y^2. \qquad (10.20)$$

The two additional terms p_0 and p_1 are added to correspond to "yaw" and "pitch." The nonrigid motions of facial features such as the eyebrows and mouth cannot be captured by the affine transformations. The basic curvature characteristics can be captured by the addition of a parameter c to the affine transformation:

$$u(x,y) = a_0 + a_1 x + a_2 y,$$
$$v(x,y) = a_3 + a_4 x + a_5 y + cx^2. \tag{10.21}$$

The c parameter captures the gross curvature of the features. In combination with the basic affine transformation, the seven parameters can capture the essential image motion of the mouth and eyebrows.

A generalized variation of the Black and Yacoob approach has resulted in the *Active Appearance Model* (AAM) developed by Cootes et. al. [Cootes et al. 98]. In an Active Appearance Model, statistical appearance models are generated by combining a model of *shape variation* with a model of *texture variation*, for the purpose of image matching. The end results are more robust solutions that can be used to match face models to images of faces. Such an approach is promising in situations where the quality and resolution of the face images are poor, for example in low-cost video teleconferencing.

10.3.11 Optical Flow Performance Capture

The practical implementation of markerless optical flow at film production levels is possible and has been successfully used in the making of the film sequel *The Matrix Reloaded.* The first stage in the production process involved recording actor Hugo Weaving from five synchronized high-definition cameras and capturing a u, v texture map from stitching together multiple camera views. Figure 10.17 illustrates three different expressions captured from five cameras. Optical flow was used at a pixel-level resolution to track the motion of features. The three-dimensional location of feature points was also calculated using to deform a geometry created from a Cyberware^{TM} scan of the actor. Figure 10.18 illustrates the re-projection of the geometry back onto the captured expression frame. Figure 10.19 illustrates the final rendered frames of Agent Smith for the movie.

Optical flow techniques are prone to errors in both the two-dimensional pixel level drift, as well as the corresponding three-dimensional reconstruction. These are well understood issues in the computer vision community and are related to the *aperture problem* [Klaus and Horn 86]. Such errors resulting in modeling and animation artifacts cannot be tolerated for movie production. Therefore, high-resolution capture and modeling were required where some of the errors could be alleviated [Borshukov et al. 03].

Figure 10.20 illustrates how multiple synchronized cameras provide wide angular coverage, thereby reducing errors when estimating three-dimensional pixel locations. The three-dimensional location of a pixel can be recovered through several well-defined techniques involving base-line stereo and stereo epipolar geometry. Such techniques are based on the observation that the projection of a point onto one camera's projection plane has a corresponding point in the other camera's projection plane and is constrained to lie on a line. This line is called the *epipolar line*, and the correspondence between one projected point and this line is described by the *fundamental matrix*. Introducing a third camera means that the point is uniquely defined through a *trifocal tensor*. Describing such techniques is beyond the scope of this chapter; however, such techniques are well understood and are excellently described by Faugeras and Luong [Faugeras and Luong 01].

Re-projection from a limited number of camera viewpoints can result in poor three-dimensional estimates. Additional viewpoints, at increasingly further separation, can improve the three-dimensional reconstruction accuracy. Figure 10.17 illustrates three expressions t_1, t_2, t_3 captured from five different viewpoints A, B, C, D, and E at a single frame for the performance.

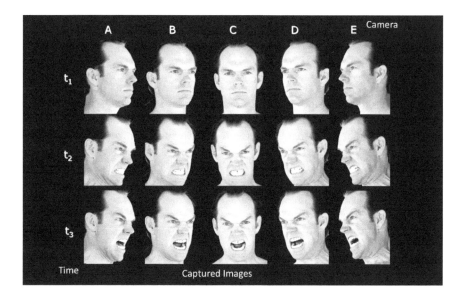

Figure 10.17.
The actor Hugo Weaving during the capture session in 2000 for the Matrix sequel *The Matrix Reloaded* as Agent Smith. Five high-definition cameras capture synchronized views of the performance over time. The result was a reconstruction of the path for each vertex over time. Illustrated is a neutral pose, t_1, and two expressions, t_2 and t_3. (*Courtesy of G. Borshukov. Copyright ESC Entertainment 2003.*)

Figure 10.18.
A re-projection of the three-dimensional wireframe geometry (blue) onto the original capture frames. Pixel-level tracking in the image plane was performed, where each three-dimensional position was estimates using triangulation. See also Color Plate VII (*Courtesy of G. Borshukov. Copyright ESC Entertainment 2003.*)

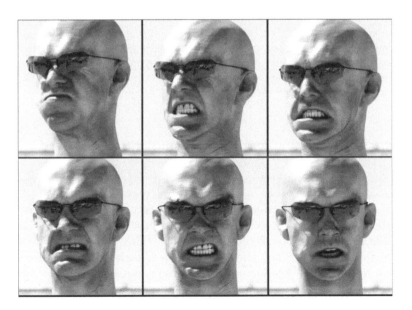

Figure 10.19.
Final rendered frames of Agent Smith for the Matrix sequel *The Matrix Reloaded.* (*Courtesy of G. Borshukov. Copyright ESC Entertainment 2003.*)

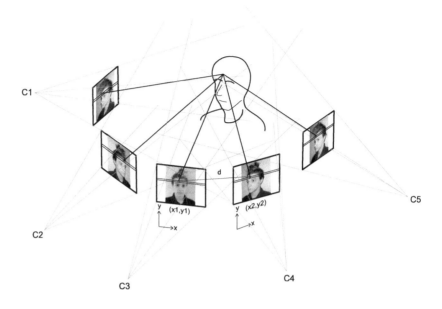

Figure 10.20.
Multiple cameras C1, C2, C3, C4, and C5 set up for optimal separation to maximize view coverage and therefore depth accuracy, as well as correlated pixel motion estimates from multiple frames. Epipolar geometry constraints, based on the camera parameters, can be used to determine the three-dimensional depth for each pixel projected in each image plane (x_n, y_n) projection.

10.4   Directions for Performance Animation

Tracking an actor's actions is the essence of performance-based animation. For facial animation, this is particularly relevant because we are highly tuned to subtle facial actions that are extremely difficult to mimic using traditional hand-crafted techniques. In the case of studio performances, invasive markers can be tolerated for a short while. However, in situations where the actions are not known in advance, such as a teleconferencing system, markers and head-mounted devices cannot be effectively worn all the time. Therefore, automated, robust and non-invasive feature tracking techniques need to developed.

The task of automatically tracking heads and facial motion without invasive markers or special lighting conditions remains an active and challenging area of research. As a result, what has been covered in this chapter is neither inclusive nor complete, but provides an insight into current trends; no

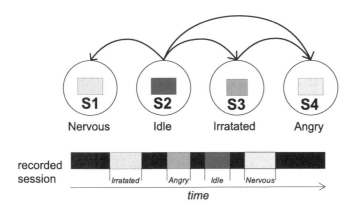

Figure 10.21.
An example of a performance session recording, extraction, and transition state
motion modeling. The recorded sequence is segmented into discrete temporal
expression units (EUs) from which *states* are created. The task is then to
establish transitions between $S1, S2, S3$ and $S4$.

doubt we will see the most rapid development in the areas that will have
commercial impact: for example, performance animation for the film industry, and the ability to develop synthetic characters in games, avatars for the
Internet, and video conferencing.

High-resolution facial performance capture from multiple synchronized
cameras is computationally and storage intensive. For example, uncom-
pressed high-definition images from five cameras can easily result in a storage capacity of 1 Gb/sec and processing to recover shape and texture takes
many hours. Clearly, optimization to recover and process high-fidelity images at real-time rates requires careful consideration. Encoding and decoding geometry and texture using PCA techniques shows promise; however,
they come with control and adaptability problems that make systems brittle
and nonintuitive for animators.

Recording a performance is a linear activity that inherently introduces
the problem of how to segment the recording into re-usable chunks, in alternative sequences. A logical approach is to manually segment sequences
into *expression units* (EUs) and then define transitions between these EUs
as a state transition model, as illustrated in Figure 10.21. Such animation
techniques provide easy reuse of the recorded session; however, they are
still restrictive to the animator who requires a freedom beyond what was
recorded.

As mentioned at the beginning of this chapter, the most successful systems will separate geometry modeling from the animation capture processes,
because this allows a separation of concerns between modelers, renderers
and animators. Tightly coupling all three processes can hinder the overall

production task and can be awkward, especially when a section of the animation or the geometry needs to be "tweaked." The following are a few outstanding issues that need to be addressed:

- Given that we can capture live performance, what kinds of editing tools are appropriate for refining these performances?

- At what point can a performance be abandoned in favor of more script-oriented animation systems?

- Blending a live performance with a script-orientated animation is challenging. Is it possible to create novel sequences beyond the captured performance?

- Well-defined expression units are building blocks for creating a sequence; how can these be created from data that never existed? How can eye motions and behaviors be easily integrated? Speech mapping for the mouth, lips, tongue, and teeth is problematic for all animation systems. Can a performance sequence capture the subtleties of features such as the tongue, which barely appear to be accurately animated?

- How can a performance be *"sweetened"*? A performance may not sufficiently fall into the performance dynamic envelope. Can a performance be extrapolated and extended?

- Is it possible to re-target onto recognizable personalities with recognizable behaviors? Can an actor who was never recorded in a capture session be re-created?

11

Modeling and Animating Hair

Hair is an important aspect of creating believable facial models. Realistic synthetic human images need realistic hair models and realistic hair motion. Such representations of human hair present challenges to all aspects of computer graphics, including shape modeling, animation, and rendering.

11.1 Hair Structure

Hair is composed of fibrous protein structures originating in follicle structures integrated into the skin, as shown in Figure 3.28. Hair follicles are tubular epidermal structures. The wall of the follicle forms an inner and outer sheath for the hair. The inner sheath grows up with the hair and has two layers: the outer Henle layer and the inner Huxley layer. It also has a thin cuticle of cells that interlock with the scales of the hair cuticle. From the base of the follicle up to the skin, the hair has three regions: the rounded bulb containing the papilla, then a region where the hair is enclosed by the inner sheath, and finally the neck of the follicle [Ryder 73].

In cross-section, hair is composed of a thin outer cuticle and an inner cortex. Some hairs also have a central medulla. The medulla is usually not present in the tip or the base of the hair. Growing hair receives nutrients from blood vessels in the papilla and surrounding the follicle. Hair cells are rounded near the base of the follicle, but stretch out to be much longer than they are wide near the top of the follicle. This change of shape is associated with a keratinization process, where the cells gradually harden and die. This process starts about one-third of the way up the follicle.

The cortex forms most of the hair mass. It consists of spindle-shaped cells that align along the hair direction. The cortical hair cells are about 100 micrometers long and 1 to 6 micrometers thick. The cortical cells contain macrofibrils, which are in turn composed of microfibrils. These microfibrils have a diameter of 0.1 to 0.4 nanometers. The microfibrils are composed of multiple protofibrils which are in turn composed of multiple molecular chains [Robbins 02].

The cuticle is a thin covering of the hair made up of overlapping flat cells known as *scales*. These scales are only about 0.5 micrometers thick, with about 5 micrometers of exposed surface each. The scales point toward the tip of the hair. The shape and orientation of these cells account for the differential friction effects of hair. Coarser hair tends to have a thicker cuticle. The detailed shape and arrangement of the scales vary between types of hair. There is also a fourth hair component, the epicuticle, only 50 to 100 angstroms thick, which covers the cuticle.

11.1.1 Hair Characteristics

Hair is very fine in infancy and increases in diameter with increasing age, until early adulthood. Hair again becomes thinner with advancing age. Infant hair generally does not exceed 15 cm in length. Children's hair does not usually exceed 60 cm. Adult hair can be much longer. With advancing age, maximum hair length tends to decrease [Robbins 02].

There are typically 100,000 to 150,000 individual hair strands on the average person's head. The diameter of a human hair is from 40 to 120 microns. The shape of each of these thin hair strands can be quite complex.

Curvature, thickness, cross-section shape (the ratio of maximum diameter to minimum diameter) and color of hair are genetically controlled and vary across population groups. For example, the cross-section ratios vary from about 1.25 for Asian groups to about 1.75 for Black groups, with Caucasian hair having a ratio of about 1.35 [Robbins 02]. There is considerable variation in these properties within groups, as well. And, for example, the diameter of hair strands from the same person can vary by more than a factor of two.

11.1.2 Properties of Hair

Hair has complex dynamic and optical properties. Friction, static, strand-to-strand interactions, and hair-to-head interactions contribute to its dynamic complexity. Hair can have a wide variety of colors and mixtures of colors. It has anisotropic reflection properties. It is self-shadowing. Its color, optical, and dynamic properties may be altered by wetting, and by a variety of cosmetic products.

Elastic and Tensile Deformations

For every *strain* (deformation) of an elastic substance, there is a corresponding *stress* (tendency to return to its normal condition). The units of stress are in force per unit area. The most common forms of strain are stretching or elongation, linear compression (or decrease in length), shear (ratio of displacement in one plane relative to an adjacent plane), bending, and torsion. Each type of stress and strain has a ratio of stress to strain, its modulus. This modulus is in terms of force per unit area. The stretching modulus is called Young's modulus. The bending modulus is called Young's modulus of bending. Torsional modulus is the modulus of rigidity [Robbins 02].

When a hair fiber is stretched, the relationship relating elongation to load has three regions. The first of these is the Hookean region, where strain (elongation) is linearly related to stress (load). The ratio of stress to strain in this region is the Young's modulus. The middle region is the *yield* region, where strain increases substantially with relatively little increase in stress. The third region is the *post yield* region, where strain is again linearly related to stress, but with a different modulus. *Tensile strength* is a measure of the stress needed to break the hair fiber. The tensile strength of hair is linearly related to its diameter.

The *extensibility* (elongation under load) of hair is dependent on humidity. Young's modulus for hair at 100% relative humidity is less than half that of hair at 65% relative humidity. With higher humidity, hair can be stretched more before it breaks. Hair that is stretched, but not broken, tends to return to its original length. Varying humidity also influences the dimensions of hair. At 100% humidity, the diameter of hair increases by about 14% over that of dry hair. Cross-sectional area increases by about 30% at 100% humidity [Robbins 02].

When a hair fiber is bent, the layers on the outside of the bending arc are stretched, while the layers on the inside of the bend are compressed. Stiffness is simply the resistance to bending. The stiffness coefficient is related to hair fiber density and to fiber diameter. Stiffness is also related to humidity. Stiffness decreases with increased humidity.

Resistance to hair fiber twisting is called *torsional rigidity*. This rigidity is in terms of the torque required to produce a certain amount of twist per unit length, usually a twist of one turn per centimeter. The torsional modulus for human hair is lower than either the stretching or bending modulus. Water has a greater effect on torsional properties than on stretching or bending properties.

Hair Friction

The force that resists motion when one surface slides over another is called *friction*. The magnitude of this force is proportional to the normal force pressing the two surfaces together. The proportion between these forces is called the *coefficient of friction*. The force needed to initiate motion determines the *static* friction coefficient. The force needed to maintain motion determines the *kinetic* friction coefficient and is usually less than the static coefficient. In hair, friction is influenced by moisture and by the forces pressing the hair strands together. Wet hair friction is higher than dry hair friction. Friction effects in hair are directional. It is easier to move along a hair strand from root to tip than from tip to root [Robbins 02]. Friction is influenced by cosmetic products that lubricate the hair, reducing friction effects. Bleaching and permanent waving increase hair friction.

Static Electricity in Hair

Hair strands can accumulate static electric charge, through combing or brushing for example. Static charge causes the hair strands to repel each other, causing *flyaway* hair. Dry hair is more prone to static charge than damp hair. Some cosmetic products decrease static charge accumulation, making the hair easier to groom [Robbins 02].

Cosmetic Effects

If wet hair is held in a given shape while drying, it will tend to hold that shape. This is called a *water-set*. This effect is associated with hydrogen bonds in the hair. High humidity, which also affects the hydrogen bonds, will usually cause a loss of this set.

In permanent waving or hair straightening, hair is *stressed* (curled or combed) while hair molecules are reoriented through chemical reactions that modify disulfide bonds within the hair. This effect is relatively immune to moisture changes in the hair.

Hair conditioning products generally involve lubricating the surface of hair fibers. This is accomplished by the binding of lubricating materials to the surface of the hair—the first few cuticle layers.

There are two ways to change the color of hair. It may be made lighter in color by bleaching, or artificial color may be added. The artificial color may be introduced using various kinds of temporary or permanent dyes [Robbins 02].

11.2   Representing Hair

We want hair models that allow realistic rendering, easy specification of hairstyles, and natural hair motion due to head movements and air flow. Modeling simplicity, controllability, realistic motion, and realistic rendered images, and having reasonable computational demands is the goal. Various simplifications have been made to produce effective results, within the limitations of current computing technology.

Modeling, animating, and rendering hair is difficult primarily because of the very large number of hair strands on the head. Since the hair is such a complex system to model, animate, simulate, and render, all modeling approaches make simplifying assumptions. Different approaches have made different simplifications. The simplifying choices made determine the quality of the resulting animation and rendered images, and also the range of hair styles that they can successfully address.

The past ten years have seen much research devoted to the representation of human hair [Ward et al. 07]. However, modeling, animating and rendering hair are all still open problems in search of better solutions. There currently exists no unified approach that addresses all aspects of all possible hair, hair styles, and hair dynamics. Each approach has strengths that address some aspects of hair, but usually simplifies or ignores other aspects.

When the head moves or the winds blows, each individual hair moves, creating a complex changing of shape and appearance. Accurately simulating the motion of hair is difficult. As the head moves or as the wind blows the hair, there are complex interactions of the hair strands with the head, and even more complex strand-to-strand interactions. Friction, static charge, and various cosmetic products may also affect the way hair moves.

11.2.1   Hair Rendering

Rendering hair has both local and global aspects. Local hair properties include the way hair strands are illuminated and shaded. Global properties include how the hair strands interact, especially how the strands shadow each other.

Kajiya and Kay have proposed a hair reflectance model that is composed of an anisotropic specular component, as well as a diffuse component [Kajiya and Kay 89]. Marschner et al. have measured the scattering from real hair strands and proposed a model that accounts for subtle scattering effects such as multiple specular highlights that are observed from real hair [Marschner et al. 03].

11.2.2   Hair Self-Shadowing

Much of the visual character of hair is due to self-shadowing. Exterior hair strands tend to be fully illuminated, while interior strands tend to be in shadow because of intervening hair strands. Variations of shadow maps and ray casting through volume densities are the two principal approaches to hair self-shadowing. See Section 11.14.4.

11.3   Hair Modeling

Many hair modeling approaches make use of methods where hair is represented as a large collection of geometric primitives, such as surfaces, polylines, parametric curves, or cylinders.

One simple way to represent hair is through the use of colored or textured surfaces, such as polygons. This approach is widely used in real-time applications such as computer games. This technique allows little opportunity to represent the dynamic behavior or complex shading of hair.

11.3.1   Polygon-Based Hair

The simplest, and also probably the least satisfying, approach to approximating hair is to assign the desired hair color to some of the polygons on the existing head or face surfaces. The shape of these colored polygons should approximate the shape of the desired hair areas. Parke used this technique to include eyebrows and eyelashes, as shown in Figure 7.13 [Parke 74].

11.3.2   Polygon Hair Shapes

The next level of complexity is to explicitly model the overall shape of hair areas with polygon surfaces and then render these polygons with the desired hair color. Of course, this approach is not limited to polygonal surfaces. Other surface description primitives, such as bicubic patches, could be used to model the hair shapes.

DiPaola modeled facial hair (eyebrows, mustaches, and beards) using what he called *hair globs* [DiPaola 89]. These globs were small irregular polygonally modeled shapes. A mustache, for example, was modeled as an overlapping collection of these globs arranged along an *attachment path* above the upper lip. The globs were flexibly *attached* to the face at defined points. When the surface of the face changed shape, these attachment points moved along with the shape changes. As the attachment points moved, the path through the points also changed. The globs were procedurally repositioned along the changed path. As a result, the mustache moved with the upper-lip surface. Similar glob collections may be used to form eyebrows and even beards. Facial hair created using this technique is shown in Figure 11.1.

Csuri et al. used a massive number of polygons to form static representations of hair [Csuri et al. 79]. Csuri et al. were among the first to model fur-like surfaces. In their approach, each fur strand was modeled by a triangle on the surface. The surface with a multitude of these fur strand triangles was rendered using a z-buffer algorithm.

Figure 11.1.
Use of hair globs. (*Courtesy of S. DiPaola.*)

11.3.3 Hair as Surface Textures

An obvious extension is to map hair textures onto hair-shaped surfaces. This technique can produce considerable static realism, but it lacks the dynamics of real hair and does not faithfully mimic the reflective properties of real hair. Another approach would be to model the hair using a set of polygon *ribbons*, with or without texture mapping.

Yamana and Suenaga used a hair model that treated hair as a texture, with anisotropic reflection mapped on the head surface [Yamana and Suenaga 87]. This approach assumes that adjacent hair strands are nearly parallel to each other and have anisotropic reflectance properties. It also assumes that precise rendering of each hair is not necessary. Their rendering was based on ray tracing that incorporated an anisotropic reflection table. Hair images created with this technique have a somewhat metallic appearance.

11.3.4 Special Shading and Special Shapes

Miller used anisotropic shading of multiple hair *sticks*, modeled as tall triangular pyramids, to create images with hair and fur [Miller 88a]. A *pseudoreflectance map* was used to efficiently compute the reflection intensities of the anisotropically shaded sticks. This implementation was limited to relatively thick, straight hairs.

Perlin and Hoffert's *hypertexture* used generalized Boolean shape operators and volume rendering to create visually realistic representations of shape and texture phenomena such as glass, fluid flow, erosion effects, *and hair* [Perlin and Hoffert 89]. Specification and control of dynamic hair based on hypertextures seems difficult.

Texels

Kajiya and Kay [Kajiya and Kay 89] developed three-dimensional texture elements called *texels* to create a photorealistic furry teddy bear image. Texels are suitable for short straight hair or fur.

Texels are a particular kind of solid texture stored as a three-dimensional array of volume elements. Each element of the array contains a value corresponding to the density of the element, a vector corresponding to an alignment direction, and information used to describe light interaction with the element.

These texels are applied to the surfaces to be rendered. Each texel has a rectangular base of elements that lie directly on the surface. Each texel has a number of volume element layers that stack on top of the base layer elements. Kajiya and Kay used a texel that was 40x40x10 volume elements. They describe creating a single fur texel and then repeatedly applying it across the surfaces of interest. To accommodate surface curvature, the texels were distorted so that the sides of adjacent texels would coincide. The result was a tiled set of distorted texels covering the surfaces.

Images are produced by ray tracing through the collection of texels representing the furry surfaces. Each ray tracing operation finds the world space entry and exit points of the ray through each texel it intersects. Once these intersection points are found, a ray marching algorithm is used to sample along the line between these intersections. The ray marching is done in the undistorted texel space. The ray marching operation successively accumulates shading values based on the volume attributes stored in the texel elements along the line path.

Fake Fur

Goldman introduced a probabilistic model, called *fake fur*, to approximate the lighting and shading properties of a furry surface [Goldman 97]. It is very efficient, but is only suitable for short hair or fur viewed from some distance.

11.4   Cluster Hair Model

Motivated by the hypertexture [Perlin and Hoffert 89] and texel [Kajiya and kay 89] concepts, Yang et al. introduced the *cluster* hair model [Yang et al. 00], which extends the notion of modeling hair using volume density to include hair styles with long strands. The cluster hair model combines the use of volume density with the use of an explicit geometry model.

Complete hair styles are modeled using a collection of hair clusters. Each of these clusters is intended to embody a bundle of individual hair strands. Each hair cluster is explicitly modeled as a generalized cylinder. This approach easily supports hair styles such as braids and ponytails.

Each generalized cylinder is formed around a space curve that is parameterized with respect to its arc length S. The generalized cylinder has a shape function R, which is parameterized in both S and a radial angle α.

This means that at every S location along the space curve, there is a perpendicular cross-section that has a radially defined shape contour based on the α angle around the curve. These contours can have arbitrary shape.

In this model, the generalized cylinder forms the boundary of a defined volume density function. The density function is created as follows. Where the cluster originates from the scalp, a set of randomly distributed points is created in the base cross-section of the cylinder. Each of these points corresponds to the center of a hair strand in the cluster bundle. A two-dimensional Gaussian distribution function defines density around each of these center points. This density cross-section is then, in essence, swept along the space curve to form a volume density function. As the cross-section density is swept down the curve, compensations are made to account for cross-section variation, such that the resulting density corresponds to hair strands of uniform thickness.

Rather than actually sweeping the cross-section density down the cylinder curve, the algorithm actually projects specific cross-section points back into their corresponding locations in the base density cross-section. This projection is based on the radial and angular values of the point in its specific cross-section. These values are transformed into the corresponding radial and angular point in the base cross-section. This transformation takes into account varying contour shape along the cylinder. The resulting point density value is computed by summing the contributions at the projected point from all individual hair density functions in the base cross-section.

An additional function of arc length, $K(s)$, can be used to modulate volume density along the hair. This function can be used to trim the length of hair strands and to vary thickness, such as at the strand tips. This function in effect multiplies the computed hair density at each evaluated point. This function could be based on an additional variable W, defined across the base cross-section. When the density function for a projected point is computed, the value for W is also determined. If, for example, the length s were greater than a threshold length $S_o + W$, $K(s)$ would be set to 0, effectively trimming the strand at that length. Then, S_o would be set for each cluster, while W would likely be based on random values. Similarly, if s was between S_o and $S_o + W$, the value of $K(s)$ would be $1 - (S - S_o)/W$, tapering the strand tip density down to zero.

This model utilizes volume rendering techniques to create hair images. The basic idea is to find intersections of rays from the view position with the generalized cylinder boundaries of the hair clusters and then apply volume rendering to ray segments that intersect the clusters. The first step is to find the intersections of rays with the hair clusters. Computing these intersections with generalized cylinders is complex. Therefore, each generalized cylinder boundary is approximated by a polygonal surface. This is done by first approximating the space curve defining the generalized cylinder with a polyline. At each vertex of the polyline, a polygon approximating the generalized cylinder cross-section is used. Connecting the vertices of two adjacent cross-section polygons forms a polyhedron approximating a section of the generalized cylinder. The collection of these polyhedron sections approximates the hair cluster. Rays are tested for intersections with these segments. Intersections for each ray are found and stored in a list sorted by distance from the viewpoint.

Using the intersection list, ray marching is used to sample cluster volumes along the path of the ray. Each sample point is converted into cluster coordinates and projected back to the base cross-section to find the sample point density, as described above.

Shading is done similar to that by [Perlin and Hoffert 89]. This approach assumes constant light intensity and involves the density and density gradient at each sample point. The density gradient is not analytically available for the hair clusters. It is computed using density differences. In addition to the density at the sample point, density at three additional points is evaluated. These points are offset from the sample point in three orthogonal directions, u, v, and w, where the u direction is in the ray direction. The density differences between the sample point and these three offset points form the components of the gradient vector.

At each sample point, opacity and color values are computed. These color and opacity values are accumulated as the sample point is marched along the ray. The accumulated opacity is used to determine visibility. Iteration along the ray within a cluster continues until the accumulated opacity reaches unity or the ray leaves the cluster. This accumulation is determined based on

$$t = \alpha_k(1 - \alpha),$$
$$\text{color} = \text{color} + t\text{color}_k,$$
$$\alpha = \alpha + t,$$

where color_k and α_k are the sample color and opacity, respectively.

This shading approach does not include shadowing between hair strands. This self-shadowing could be added by casting secondary rays toward the light sources from each sample point. However, these secondary rays would add considerable computational cost. It was observed that the cluster model provided information allowing additional shading information to be computed at relatively little cost. The surface model for the generalized cylinder can be rendered as a grayscale image by a surface renderer. The grayscale values in this image can be used to modulate the shading values derived from the ray marching algorithm.

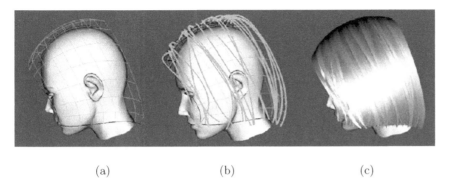

(a)   (b)   (c)

Figure 11.2.
The thin shell volume model: (a) the base surfaces used to define the hair, (b)
the combing paths, and (c) the resulting combed hair. (Adapted
from [Kim and Neumann 00].)

11.5   The Thin Shell Volume Model

At the macro scale, some long hair styles can be viewed as relatively smooth
hair strand collections that can be approximated by an appropriate set of
surfaces. At the micro scale, each hair strand is a long, thin curved cylinder.

The *thin shell volume* model, introduced by Kim and Neumann
[Kim and Neumann 00], is useful for long hair styles that can be modeled
using thin volumes based on hair surfaces surrounding the head. The thin
shell volume approach begins by defining the hair as a set of surfaces, usually
bi-parametric surfaces such as NURBS. Figure 11.2(a) shows an example of
these surfaces.

A thin three-dimensional parametric volume is constructed corresponding to each hair surface by extending it in the direction of the surface normals. The u parameter of this volume corresponds to *thickness* (the surface
normal direction). The t parameter corresponds to the length direction of
the hair strands. The s parameter is orthogonal to u and t and goes across
the hair strands (see Figure 11.3(a–b)). The s, t, and u parameters have a
range from 0.0 to 1.0. The innermost hair strands have u values near 0.0.
The outermost hair strands have u values near 1.0.

This volume is divided into a grid of cells indexed by i, j, and k.
These indices range from 0 to L, M, and N respectively, where L, M,
and N are the resolution of the grid. Inside this volume, a number of hair
strands are evenly distributed. Initially, n uniformly distributed straight
hair strands are created. Each of these strands has M particles that lie
along its path. These hair strands lie along the t direction. Values of t near
0.0 are near the start of a strand, while values of t near 1.0 are at the end

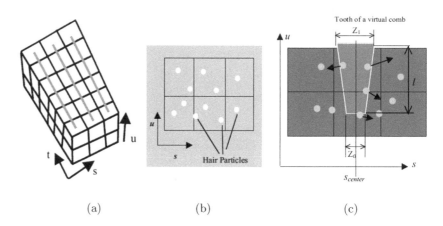

(a) (b) (c)

Figure 11.3.
The thin shell volume model structure: (a) the parametric coordinate system and the distribution of hair strands, (b) a cross-section view, and (c) a virtual comb tooth. (Adapted from [Kim and Neumann 00].)

of strands. Each grid cell has a list of the hair particles that lie within it. The density of particles defines the hair opacity that is used to determine shadowing.

Particle sets associated with the hair strands can move under certain constraints. This model allows the individual hair particle sets to be *combed*. This combing action represents a particular kind of constrained hair-to-hair interaction. The curved hair volume is warped into a rectilinear grid prior to the combing operation.

Combing actions have the effect of redistributing the hair strand particles. Combing is accomplished by moving *comb teeth* through the thin shell volume. Comb teeth are modeled as trapezoidal radial influence functions in the s, u plane. This is shown in Figure 11.3(c). As a comb tooth moves along its path through the hair volume, particles hit by the tooth are affected. Each affected particles moves away from the center of the tooth's influence. Each affected particle attempts to follow the path of the comb. Combed particles move upward to lie on top of unaffected particles. Various hair patterns result from varying the comb path, and changing tooth shape and tooth distribution.

Each particle is tested to see if it is affected by a comb tooth. The path of a tooth is modeled as a parametric curve on the s,t plane. The influence zone of the tooth is modeled as a function of s and u. For each particle, the nearest influence zone, based on t, is evaluated. A random number is compared to the evaluated influence value to determine whether the tooth affects that particle. Particles closer to the center of the tooth are more likely to be affected. The affected particles are randomly repositioned within the range of the influence zone. The sign of the evaluated influence determines whether affected particles are moved in the positive s or the negative s direction.

The combed hair strands follow the path of the comb tooth. This is accomplished by finding the first particle in each hair strand affected by the tooth. The new s coordinate for this particle is calculated. The s distance of this new particle position from the tooth center is calculated. For subsequent particles going down the length of the strand, the new s positions are computed by adding this distance to the tooth path center position at that t value.

Combed strands are moved above the uncombed strands. This is done by exchanging a combed particle with a particle from an upper cell. If there are no upper particles, the u value of the combed particle is incremented by a small amount. Care is taken to insure that particles do not move outside the hair volume. This virtual combing can be performed multiple times, each with varying comb paths, tooth shapes, and tooth influence functions. This virtual hair combing embodies a particular constrained hair-to-hair interaction model.

Hair strands are reconstructed by connecting the strand particles with smooth interpolation curves. The resulting curves are passed to the rendering process.

For rendering, each hair strand is approximated by a series of line segments, each about 10 pixels in length. These segments are drawn using a standard z-buffer algorithm, making use of supersampling with an accumulation buffer. Local shading is computed at each node in the strand. This shading uses the illumination model developed by [Kajiya and Kay 89]. These shading values are multiplied by shadow values based on extending the method used in [Kong and Nakajima 99]. Shadow generation is based on the assumption that inner strands are more likely to be in shadow than the outer strands. The opacity of each cell is proportional to the number of particles in the cell. The shadowing due to each cell is based on hair strand optical thickness and the opacity of the cell. The shadowing at each cell is the sum of the shadowing due to the cells directly above it. Figure 11.2(c) shows a rendered version of combed hair.

With this model, animation of hair styles is achieved by animating the reference surfaces for the thin shell volumes. This surface animation may include dynamics based deformations and collision detection.

11.6 Loosely Connected Particles Model

Bando et al. introduced an approach that models hair as a set of connected particles [Bando et al. 03]. These particles act as sample points that track the motion of the hair volume. Each particle represents a certain volume of the hair. The particles are *loosely* connected to their neighboring particles. Hair dynamics, including hair-to-hair interactions, are simulated using the interactions of the particles.

Each particle has a mass, a location, and a velocity. The mass of each particle represents the mass of the hair volume in its region. In addition, each particle has a unit vector that represents hair direction.

The scalp area of the head is bounded by four spline curves. These curves are mapped into a unit square. A hair volume is created by adding a third dimension based on the arc length of hair strands in the volume. Particles representing the hair are distributed in this volume. Since the arc length dimension can be slightly negative, some of the particles will be below the scalp level. These particles are considered to be embedded or *rooted* in the scalp and move with the head. The rooted particles are mapped back to the world space scalp. The root particle directions are based on scalp surface normals. The other particles are initially positioned and directed in world space using the cantilevered beam simulation method discussed in Section 11.10.

To simulate hair dynamics, connections are established between neighboring particles. The strength of the connection between each particle pair is influenced by the distance between them and their direction vector alignment. The hair volume is viewed as a deformable body that can be animated by connecting neighboring particles with damped springs. Since hair is difficult to stretch but can move freely from side to side, high tensile stiffness and low bending stiffness are used.

Hair-to-hair interactions are modeled with attractive, repulsive, collision, and friction forces. The effect of attraction and repulsion is to maintain average hair density. Forces are calculated to maintain this hair density. Collision and friction forces are calculated to reduce the relative velocity of particles that approach each other.

Gravity is modeled as a downward force that is proportional to particle mass. Air friction is modeled as a damping force that is proportional to

Figure 11.4.
Shaken hair modeled with the particle model. See also Color Plate X. (*Courtesy of Y. Bando.*)

Figure 11.5.
Wind blown hair modeled with the particle model. See also Color Plate IX.
(*Courtesy of Y. Bando.*)

particle velocity. Wind is modeled as an additional set of particles that interact with the hair particles, producing drag forces. Inertial forces due to head motions are included in the calculations. Collisions between the hair particles and the head and body are detected and modeled using repulsive forces to counter the relative velocities between the particles and the body. See [Bando et al. 03] for a detailed presentation of the mathematics involved in the simulations used for this model.

For rendering, each hair particle is replaced by a small rectangle or *billboard*, which has a hair texture mapped on it. This texture is oriented according to the particle direction. Self-shadowing is achieved by using the hair particle distribution as a density function that attenuates incoming light. An anisotropic function is also used to approximate the directional reflection and transmission properties of hair. The results of this modeling and rendering approach are shown in Figure 11.4 and Figure 11.5.

11.7 Strand-Based Hair Models

The creation of individual computer-modeled hair strands can be fairly simple. A strand of hair can be viewed as just a thin, string-like, three-dimensional object with a cylindrical cross-section. The major difficulties are to control and realistically render a large collection of such thin objects. Three of the reported *strand*-based approaches to modeling and animating hair are [Rosenblum et al. 91, Anjyo et al. 92, Watanabe and Suenaga 92]. These approaches vary in many details, but have much in common.

They all model the hair as a large collection of thin hair strands, each strand being approximated as a connected set of straight segments. If each hair-like strand is modeled with 32 linear cylinders, with each cylinder approximated by a 16-sided prism (32 triangles), then the 100,000 hair strands would require over 100,000,000 triangles. This is an unreasonable number of triangles to render for animation sequences. Therefore, various simplifications have been used to reduce the necessary computation to reasonable levels.

All three approaches include techniques to approximate real hair motion based on reasonably simple dynamics and control parameters. And each approach takes into account the special problems of rendering hair, including hair lighting effects. Each of these approaches includes techniques for specifying and controlling hair shape and hairstyles.

These approaches can also be effective for modeling and rendering facial hair such as eyebrows, eyelashes, beards, and mustaches.

11.7.1   Strand Modeling

Watanabe and Suenaga developed a hair model in which each hair strand is approximated as a connected series of short cylinders [Watanabe and Suenaga 92].

However, to minimize the number of rendered polygons, each of these cylinders is represented as a prism with only three sides, referred to as a *trigonal* prism. These are the simplest possible prism approximations to the hair segment cylinders. Figure 11.6(a) shows a single segment of a *trigonal* hair strand, while Figure 11.6(b) shows an example trigonal hair strand made up of six connected prisms. Strand characteristics are defined by controlling the length l, direction vector v, thickness d, and twist angle t of each trigonal prism, while n represents the number of trigonal prisms per strand. In this example, the hair strand segments have constant thickness. Straight, wavy, or curly hair strand types can be specified by controlling these segment parameters.

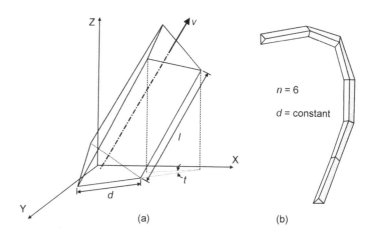

Figure 11.6.
(a) Trigonal prism, and (b) trigonal hair strand. (Adapted from [Watanabe and Suenaga 92].)

Anjyo et al. [Anjyo et al. 92] and Rosenblum et al. [Rosenblum et al. 91] geometrically model each hair strand simply as a linearly connected point set. Anjyo et al. also developed a method for modeling hair dynamics, which employs the simple ordinary differential equations used to describe cantilever beam deformation, along with appropriate simplifying heuristics. Rather than emphasizing a rigorous physical model, several intuitive simplifying ideas are employed to speed computations, while producing visually satisfactory results. Simple differential equations of one-dimensional angular momenta are used for describing the dynamic behavior of the hair strands. Collision detection of hair strands with the head is also incorporated.

Rosenblum et al. used a mass-spring-hinge system to control each strand's position and orientation. This technique is simple in concept and produces fairly realistic hair motion simulations. This implementation also included an interactive system for defining the position of hair strands on the head. Special attention was paid to self-shadowing of the hair strands.

11.7.2   Hairstyling

Many techniques are used to shape real hair, such as wetting, combing, cutting, and cosmetic preparations, for making hair more attractive. Important physical properties of hair include hair color, strand width, and pliability.

A necessary condition for a hair modeling method is that it represent the intrinsic properties of hair. This representation may be partially achieved through rendering techniques. However, efficient and effective techniques are desired for modeling the shape of hair.

11.8   Wisp-Based Hair

Watanabe and Suenaga introduced the concept of hair *wisps* [Watanabe and Suenaga 92]. Using wisps is one approach to forming and controlling hairstyles. In this approach, a head of hair contains many wisps, where wisps are groups of individual hair strands. Hairstyles are not created by controlling individual hairs, but by cutting and forming wisps or sets of hair strands.

Wisps are used as template units to efficiently create and control the total hair set. Wisps consist of many instances of the same string-like hair model. Using wisps drastically reduces the number of control parameters needed to obtain complete hair images. The details of each wisp are controlled by its own parameters.

The wisp model is illustrated in Figure 11.7, where each hair is defined as a connected sequence of trigonal prisms. In addition to the parameters controlling each strand, wisps are defined by the randomness, r, in their

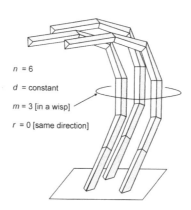

Figure 11.7.
Wisp model hair strands. (Adapted from [Watanabe and Suenaga 92].)

initial direction vectors, and by the density of strands, m. Figure 11.8(a) shows a wisp model defined by a large r, while Figure 11.8(b) shows a wisp model defined by almost parallel vectors, a small r. The hair density is typically 100 hairs per wisp.

Hairstyles are created by controlling a small number of additional parameters, including hair color, the total number of wisps, and the kind of wisps. Different kinds of wisps may be used to vary hair shape on the forehead, side, and back of the head. Specifying more wisps produces heavier hair, and using more hairs per wisp produces denser hair. Eyebrows and eyelashes have also been created using the wisp model.

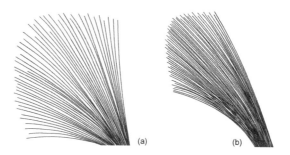

Figure 11.8.
Effect of wisp randomness: (a) large r, and (b) small r. (Adapted from [Watanabe and Suenaga 92].)

11.8.1   Animation Based on Wisps

Real hair motion is determined by the physical characteristics of each hair strand and the hair environment. When hair flows in the wind, each strand moves individually. When the head moves, the hair also moves.

In the wisp approach, hairstyle is determined by controlling the shape and characteristics of the wisps. Control of individual wisp shapes and motions is also used to approximate realistic hair motion. Generating the hair motion requires controlling only a small number of wisp parameters. For example, as the head turns rapidly from a profile view to a full face view, the hair first flies out, continues to move as the head stops, and then slowly settles back down.

An approximating parabolic trajectory is used to control the motion of each wisp. These wisp trajectories are determined using initial velocity vectors and acceleration vectors, such as the acceleration of gravity.

11.9   Mass-Spring-Hinge Hair Model

In the Rosenblum et al. approach, each strand of hair is represented as a series of connected straight strand segments [Rosenblum et al. 91]. The position of each strand segment is determined by simple dynamic simulation. Each strand is modeled as a linearly connected series of point masses, springs, and hinges. The strand point masses have direct correspondences with the segment end-points used in rendering. Stiff connecting springs maintain relatively constant distances between the masses. Spring hinges placed between the strand segments allow the hair strands to bend.

11.9.1   Hair Dynamics

Each strand of hair is modeled as a series of interconnected masses, springs, and hinges, as shown in Figure 11.9. Each strand segment is modeled as two point masses held a nearly fixed distance apart by a strong spring. Since hair does not stretch very much, this spring is stiff. A hinge spring is located between segments at the point mass locations. These hinges apply forces to the outlying masses. In this implementation, adjacent hair strands do not interact.

Forces applied to each point mass by the *interconnecting* springs are determined from Hooke's law:

$$F_s = k_s d, \tag{11.1}$$

where F_s is the magnitude of the force, k_s is the spring constant, and d is the displacement of the spring. The direction of this force is always along the line connecting the two point masses. If the spring is stretched, the force

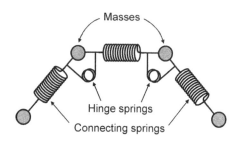

Figure 11.9.
Mass-spring-hinge model. (Adapted from [Rosenblum et al. 91].)

vectors at each mass point toward each other. If the spring is compressed, the forces point away from each other. When simple damping is included, the equation becomes

$$F_s = (1 - D_s)(k_s d), \tag{11.2}$$

where D_s is the spring damping constant.

Similarly, a force is applied to each mass by its associated hinge spring,

$$F_h = (1 - D_h)(k_h \alpha), \tag{11.3}$$

where F_h is the hinge force magnitude, α is the hinge angular displacement, k_h is the hinge spring constant, and D_h is the hinge damping constant. This force is applied in three places. It is applied at the two outlying masses in the direction necessary to cause the strand to straighten. The negative sum of these two is also applied to the mass at the hinge location.

The force of gravity is included in the form

$$F_g = mg, \tag{11.4}$$

where F_g is the force of gravity, m is the mass of the point, and g is the acceleration of gravity.

Finally, an *aerodynamic* drag force is determined as

$$F_d = v D_d, \tag{11.5}$$

where v is the current velocity of the mass and D_d is an aerodynamic drag coefficient.

All of the force components are summed and used to compute the acceleration of the mass based on Newton's second law:

$$a = F_{\text{sum}}/m, \tag{11.6}$$

where

$$F_{\text{sum}} = F_s + F_h + F_g + F_d.$$

The acceleration a is used to update the mass velocity, which in turn is used to compute the new mass position.

To calculate the motion for a single animation frame, the frame time is subdivided into smaller time steps. For each of these small time steps, these equations are used to compute new mass positions, based on the sum of forces applied to each mass point.

Strand-to-Head Collisions

Simple strand-to-head collision detection and response is supported as follows. The head is modeled as a sphere. Whenever a strand point mass lies inside the radius of this sphere, an outward spring force is applied to the mass. This force is applied only when the mass is moving closer to the head, and not when the mass is moving away from the head. This simulates inelastic collisions and allows strands to rest on the surface of the head.

Dynamic Simplifications

This model makes several simplifying assumptions. The aerodynamic drag does not take into account strand orientation relative to the current velocity vectors. The hinge model does not calculate torque, which would take into account the distance of the outlying masses from the hinge in the force calculations. And, the damping coefficients are entirely ad hoc. The simplified drag, damping, and hinge force calculations reduce the computational load. Figure 11.10 shows an animation frame with two views of the same hair. For this animation, about 1,100 hair strands were used, each strand having

Figure 11.10.
Two views of the dynamic hair [Rosenblum et al. 91].

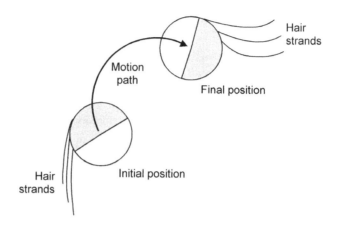

Figure 11.11.
Motion used to flip the hair. (Adapted from [Rosenblum et al. 91].)

14 segments. The first segment of each strand is embedded in the scalp and moves with the head. As Figure 11.11 shows, the head was initially tilted forward and then quickly flipped back. The simulation was calculated at 60 steps per second.

These simulations are subject to oscillations and instabilities. Reducing the time step size and increasing the number of steps per frame reduced these problems. These simulations also required experimentation to empirically determine the mass, spring, and damping constant values that produced the desired results.

11.10   Beam Bending Hair

Anjyo et al. [Anjyo et al. 92] developed a hair modeling approach that consists of the following:

1. Define an ellipsoid that roughly approximates the desired three-dimensional head model (see Figure 11.12).

2. On this ellipsoid, specify the desired hair follicle regions. One hair strand will originate from each follicle location.

3. For each strand, calculate its bent shape, based on a simplified cantilever beam simulation. This shape calculation includes collision detection between each hair and the approximating head ellipsoid.

4. Adjust or cut hair strand lengths for various follicle regions and apply shaping forces to achieve the desired overall hair shape.

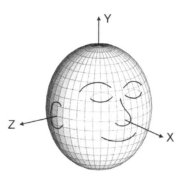

Figure 11.12.
Ellipsoid model for the head. (Adapted from [Anjyo et al. 92].)

While the head ellipsoid is not a completely accurate representation of the head, follicle positions are more easily specified on it than on a polygonal head model. A polar coordinate system is used for explicit follicle positioning on the ellipsoid. Collision detection between the approximating ellipsoid and the hair strands has lower computational cost than between a polygonal head model and the strands.

In a physically faithful simulation, the number of functions appearing in the derived differential equations will be large. In particular, it would be very difficult to numerically treat self-interaction or collision detection for the very large number of hair strands. The desire is for techniques that are physically faithful to the true dynamics of hair and that are also computationally tractable. This model uses a differential-equation-based approach that employs easy-to-solve equations to approximate the physical aspects of hair.

11.10.1   Cantilever Beam Simulation for Hair Bending

This hair modeling method involves a process to bend the hair, which is based on the numerical simulation of cantilever beam deformation. To describe the simulation technique, the simpler two-dimensional case is treated first.

Suppose that the two-dimensional cantilever beam is in an initial state as shown in Figure 11.13(a) where one end of the beam is fixed. This fixed end corresponds to the follicle end of a hair. In a typical case, the beam is loaded by an external force such as gravity, uniformly distributed along the length of the beam. Two types of deformation actually occur; one caused by the bending momentum and one caused by the shearing force. Only the bending moment of deformation is considered. The x-axis is defined to

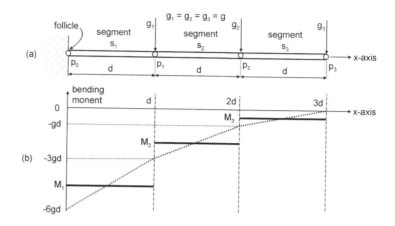

Figure 11.13.
(a) Cantilever beam hair model load distribution. (b) Beam bending moment
diagram. (Adapted from [Anjyo et al. 92].)

be along the initial beam direction, and the y-axis is perpendicular to this
direction. The beam deflection y is in the y-axis direction. Assuming elastic
materials, the following equation describes this deformation:

$$d^2y/dx^2 = -M/(EI), \tag{11.7}$$

where M is the bending moment, E is Young's modulus for the hair material, and I denotes the cross-sectional second moment of inertia about the
neutral axis of the beam. The term EI usually is referred to as the *flex-
ural rigidity* and depends on the beam material properties. This equation
is actually only valid for small deformations. It is considered valid for this
model since the deflection of each segment is relatively small. The calculation method for the bending moment M is illustrated in Figure 11.13(b).

In this simulation, the distributed load $\mathbf{g}$ is approximated by the sum
of segmentally averaged concentrated segment loads. The cantilever beam
is considered to consist of a number of linear segments, each with the same
length. Let $\mathbf{p}_0, \mathbf{p}_1, \ldots, \mathbf{p}_k$ be the node vectors of the segments, where $\mathbf{p}_0$
is the follicle end and $\mathbf{p}_k$ is the free end of the beam. The simplified beam
shown in Figure 11.13 (a) consists of three segments s_1, s_2, and s_3, such
that s_i corresponds to the vector $\mathbf{p}_{i-1}\mathbf{p}_i$ and the length of each segment
$\| \mathbf{p}_{i-1}\mathbf{p}_i \|$ is d, for $1 \leq i \leq 3$. Let $\mathbf{g}_1, \mathbf{g}_2$, and $\mathbf{g}_3$ be the node forces, where
$\mathbf{g}_i$ is a concentrated load at the node $\mathbf{p}_i$. The bending moment at point
x on the beam is represented by the dotted line shown in Figure 11.13(b).
For simplicity, the bending moment is assumed constant on each segment.

The constant bending moment values M_i for the segments s_i are defined as

$$M_i = - \parallel \mathbf{g} \parallel d(\sum_{n=1}^{k-i+1} n + \sum_{n=1}^{k-i} n)/2 = - \parallel \mathbf{g} \parallel d(k-i+1)^2/2. \qquad (11.8)$$

The displacement y_i of the node $\mathbf{p}_i$ can be determined using the following equation:

$$y_i = -((M_i/EI)d^2)/2, \qquad (11.9)$$

which is derived from Equation (11.7). Suppose that node positions $\mathbf{p}_{i-2}$ and $\mathbf{p}_{i-1}$ have been computed. Then we can obtain the new position of the node $\mathbf{p}_i$. To do so, we determine the vector $\mathbf{e}_i$ such that

$$\mathbf{e}_i = \mathbf{p}_{i-2}\mathbf{p}_{i-1} + \mathbf{y}_i \qquad (11.10)$$

where the x-axis for this calculation is defined as being along the segment vector $\mathbf{p}_{i-2}\mathbf{p}_{i-1}$, and the vector $\mathbf{y}_i$ is in the deflection direction, with its magnitude being equal to y_i in Equation (11.9). The new node position $\mathbf{p}_i$ is defined as

$$\mathbf{p}_i = \mathbf{p}_{i-1} + (d/\parallel \mathbf{e}_i \parallel)\mathbf{e}_i \qquad (11.11)$$

where $d = \parallel \mathbf{p}_{i-1}\mathbf{p}_i \parallel$. The deflection vectors and node positions are calculated successively, working from $\mathbf{p}_1$ to $\mathbf{p}_k$.

Deflection in Three Dimensions

The deflection calculation is extended to three dimensions as follows. First, a suitable coordinate system is defined. The $a0$-axis in Figure 11.14 corresponds to the x-axis used in the two-dimensional case. The $a0$-axis is defined

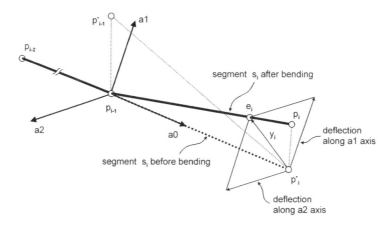

Figure 11.14.
Three-dimensional beam deflection. (Adapted from [Anjyo et al. 92].)

as being along the segment vector $\mathbf{p}_{i-2}\mathbf{p}_{i-1}$. Let $\mathbf{p}_i^*$ be a point which is a distance d from $\mathbf{p}_{i-1}$ along the $a0$-axis. Also let $\mathbf{p}_{i-1}^*$ denote a point which is positioned relative to $\mathbf{p}_{i-1}$, such that the three points $\mathbf{p}_{i-1}, \mathbf{p}_{i-1}^*$, and $\mathbf{p}_i^*$ define a plane. The $a1$-axis is perpendicular to the $a0$-axis and on the defined plane. The $a2$-axis is orthogonal to both the $a0$- and $a1$-axes. The two-dimensional method is applied to obtain the deflection component y_1 along the $a1$-axis and the deflection component y_2 along the $a2$-axis, using the respective components of the applied force. Assuming no compression of the beam, the composite deflection vector is $y_1\mathbf{a}_1 + y_2\mathbf{a}_2$, where $\mathbf{a}_1$ and $\mathbf{a}_2$ are unit vectors parallel to the $a1$- and $a2$-axes. As in the two-dimensional case, the new beam node positions are obtained by working sequentially from the follicle end to the free end, successively applying the computed deflection vectors.

Collision Detection

As in the previously described strand models, hair-to-hair strand collisions are ignored. A simplified collision detection is used to prevent the hair strands from intersecting the head. Collision detection is limited to checking for intersections between the approximating head ellipsoid and the hair strand segments. Collision detection and avoidance are performed as part of computing the deflected positions of the $\mathbf{p}_i$ nodes. Suppose that two deflected beam nodes $\mathbf{p}_{i-2}, \mathbf{p}_{i-1}$ have been computed. Then, it is easy to determine whether the next node $\mathbf{p}_i$, computed using the beam deflection simulation, intersects the ellipsoid. This determination is done by checking the signature of the quadric equation $E(\mathbf{p}_i)$, which defines the ellipsoid: $E(\mathbf{p}) = 0$. If the node $\mathbf{p}_i$ is inside the ellipsoid, it is moved outside the ellipsoid, such that it is near the original computed position $\mathbf{p}_i$ and lies on the plane formed by the points $\mathbf{p}_{i-2}, \mathbf{p}_{i-1}$, and $\mathbf{p}_i$.

Examples

Typically, 10,000 to 20,000 individual hair strands are used to model the hair, each hair strand having less than 20 segments. The initial state of the hair strands is as shown in Figure 11.15(a), where the follicle positions and the initial length of the hair are specified. Since there are no external forces or gravity applied to the initial hair strands, they stand straight out radially. By adding gravity, the hair strands are bent down, as illustrated in Figure 11.15(b). The hair strands near the top of the head are not bent much because these strands are essentially parallel to the gravity vector, and their bending moments are small. Undulations of the hair in front of the face shown in Figure 11.15(c) are caused by the collision avoidance calculations.

Cutting, combing, or brushing makes real hair more attractive. These techniques can be used to give short bangs, parting of the hair at the middle

Figure 11.15.
Beam bending example: (a) initial state, (b) adding gravity, (c) undulations of the hair in front of the face, and (d) final result. (*Courtesy of K. Anjyo.*)

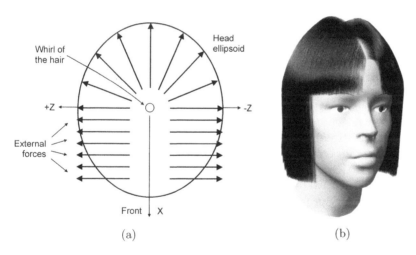

Figure 11.16.
(a) Top view of additional forces. (Adapted from [Anjyo et al. 92].) (b) Resulting hairstyle. (*Courtesy of K. Anjyo.*)

of the head, and so on. Instead of using shears and a brush or comb, in this approach, cutting operations and the addition of external forces to the bending calculations are used for hairstyle modeling. Specification of the hair strands to be cut is performed using the polar coordinate system of the head ellipsoid and length thresholds. For instance, the follicle positions of the hair strands to be cut are specified using ranges of azimuth ϕ and elevation θ angles such that $\phi_0 < \phi < \phi_1$ and $\theta < \theta_0$.

The segments of hair strands whose follicles are within the specified ranges are displayed only if the distance of their nodes from the follicle, along the strand, is less than the designated length threshold. This cutting is done as a postprocess after the beam bending calculations. Each hair strand is displayed as a polyline connecting the strand segment nodes.

To create various hairstyles, different external forces may be applied to selected regions of the head. To *comb* or shape the hair, external forces in addition to gravity are specified. To illustrate, the external force field shown in Figure 11.16(a) is applied to the hair segments that are located higher than the eyes. Figure 11.15(c) shows the result of using the external force field to simulate the hair segments in the positive z-region. The hair shown in Figure 11.15(d) is obtained by using the external forces for hair in both the positive and negative z-regions. By cutting the back hair in Figure 11.15(d), the hairstyle shown in Figure 11.16(b) is created.

11.10.2   Dynamic Behavior of Bending Beam Hair

One aesthetic feature of hair motion occurs where long hair is gently blowing in the wind or is swaying according to head movements. Animating each individual strand of hair is not difficult. However, to create truly realistic motion requires that the hair strands interact with each other and with the head, and that physical properties such as friction and static charge are included. Heuristic techniques are used to roughly approximate solutions to this difficult problem.

Some aspects of hair motion are the result of inertia and applied forces. The motion equations used should at least include the inertial properties of hair. To do so, simple ordinary differential equations were used, as follows.

One-Dimensional Projective Equations for Hair Dynamics

As described above, each hair strand is represented as a deformed beam composed of linked linear segments. The technique used for the dynamic behavior of the hair is based on solving simple one-dimensional differential equations of angular momentum for each hair. Collision and interaction of the hair strands with themselves and with the head are not explicitly considered. However, heuristic techniques are used in conjunction with the solution of these differential equations to give approximate solutions to these difficult problems. One heuristic is to use a pseudoforce field, described

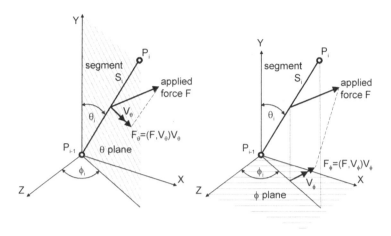

Figure 11.17.
Hair dynamics coordinate systems. (Adapted from [Anjyo et al. 92].)

below, in solving the differential equations. In addition, pliability of the
hair is included, using a parameter for limiting the angles between adjacent
hair segments.

Consider the dynamics of a single hair. Using the polar coordinate
system as shown in Figure 11.17, the behavior of the zenith angle θ_i and
the azimuth ϕ_i of the ith segment s_i of the hair are observed. Particular
consideration is given to the projections of the segment on the θ and ϕ
planes, which are defined as shown in Figure 11.17. The θ plane is the
plane spanned by the y-axis and the segment s_i. If s_i is almost parallel
to the y-axis, the θ plane is defined using the y-axis and the applied force
F instead of s_i. The ϕ plane is defined as the xz-plane. On these planes,
the variables $\theta_i(t)$ and $\phi_i(t)$, as functions of time, t, are governed by the
ordinary differential equations

$$d^2\theta_i/dt^2 = c_i u_i F_\theta, \tag{11.12}$$

$$d^2\phi_i/dt^2 = c_i v_i F_\phi, \tag{11.13}$$

where c_i corresponds to the reciprocal of the inertia moment of s_i, $u_i =
(1/2) \parallel s_i \parallel$, v_i is half the length of the projection of s_i onto the ϕ plane,
and F_θ and F_ϕ are the components of the applied force **F** in the respective
planes as shown in Figure 11.17.

The idea is to use the *one-dimensional projective equations*,
Equations (11.12) and (11.13), for describing hair dynamics, even though
these equations originally described the *projective* behaviors of the hair
model.

The component F_θ of the applied force field $\mathbf{F}$ is the scalar value defined by the inner product $(\mathbf{F}, \mathbf{V}_\theta) = \| \mathbf{F}_\theta \| = F_\theta$, where $\mathbf{V}_\theta$ is the unit vector on the θ plane that is perpendicular to the segment s_i. Similarly the F_ϕ component is defined by $(\mathbf{F}, \mathbf{V}_\phi) = \| \mathbf{F}_\phi \| = F_\phi$, where $\mathbf{V}_\phi$ is the unit vector on the ϕ plane that is perpendicular to the projection segment of s_i onto the ϕ plane.

For numerical simulation, these equations are the basis for simple second order recurrence formulas shown below. Using the known values θ_i^{n-1}, θ_i^n, ϕ_i^{n-1} and ϕ_i^n, the new values θ_i^{n+1} and ϕ_i^{n+1} at time $(n+1)\Delta t$ are obtained from

$$\theta_i^{n+1} - 2\theta_i^n + \theta_i^{n-1} = (\Delta t)2c_i u_i F_\theta, \tag{11.14}$$

$$\phi_i^{n+1} - 2\phi_i^n + \phi_i^{n-1} = (\Delta t)2c_i v_i F_\phi. \tag{11.15}$$

The calculation starts with segment s_1, and the new position of each s_i is successively determined using Equations (11.14) and (11.15).

11.10.3   Inertia Moments and Heuristic Modifications

Consider a straight stick S with length kd and density ρ. Then its inertia moment I_s is given by $I_s = (1/3)\rho(kd)^2$. For this hair model, the terms $c_i v_i$ and $c_i u_i$ in Equations (11.14) and (11.15) are closely related to I_s. For example, suppose that the inertia moment I_i of s_i is proportional to $1/i$ $(1 \leq i \leq k)$ and that I_k is equal to I_s. Then I_i is given as $I_i = (\rho/3i)k^3 d^2$. The term $(\Delta t)^2 c_i u_i$ in Equation (11.14) may be rewritten as $(3(\Delta t)^2 i)/(2k_3 \rho d)$. A similar expression may be obtained for the term $(\Delta t)^2 c_i v_i$ in Equation (11.15). These expressions may be used for numerically estimating the magnitude of the right-hand side of Equations (11.14) and (11.15).

Strand-to-strand interaction effects can be approximated by modifying the c_i values actually used. For example, if the c_i values used are relatively small for the segments near the top of the head, then the hair near the top will move relatively slowly, when affected by an applied force field. This reault can be thought of as a rough approximation of frictional hair effects. Therefore, the c_i coefficients are heuristically modified to achieve the desired results.

Pseudoforce Field

Another conceptually simple technique is used for avoiding hair collisions with the head. The technique consists of using a heuristically determined pseudoforce field, instead of the specified force field. The pseudoforce field is based on $\mathbf{F}$, the force field specified by a user.

A segment direction $\mathbf{D}_i$ for each hair segment s_i is obtained using the head-defining ellipsoid equation $E(\mathbf{p})$. Here, $\mathbf{D}_i = (E_x(\mathbf{p}_i), E_y(\mathbf{p}_i), E_z(\mathbf{p}_i))$, where E_x, E_y, and E_z are partial derivatives of the ellipsoid polynomial. The inner product $(\mathbf{D}_i, \mathbf{F})$ is compared with $\alpha \parallel \mathbf{D}_i \parallel \parallel \mathbf{F} \parallel$, where α is a selected value such that $\mid \alpha \mid \leq 1$. If the inner product is smaller, it means that the segment direction is roughly opposite the direction of $\mathbf{F}$. If the segment is near the head, then $\mathbf{F}$ is replaced by the pseudoforce $\epsilon_i \mathbf{F}$, where $0 \leq \epsilon_i \leq 1$. The pseudoforce constants ϵ_i for the segments near the follicle are usually assigned smaller values, whereas those for the segments near the endpoint p_k are equal to one. The pseudoforce $\epsilon_i \mathbf{F}$ near the follicle can be viewed as the simplification of compositing the force $\mathbf{F}$ with an opposite repulsive force away from the head.

Joint Angle Adjustment

The joint angle ν_i at the node $\mathbf{p}_i$ is the angle between $\mathbf{p}_i \mathbf{p}_{i-1}$ and $\mathbf{p}_i \mathbf{p}_{i+1}$. Then the *stiffness* of the hair strand is determined by the parameters $\sigma_i (0 \leq \sigma_i \leq \pi)$. The ith stiffness parameter σ_i is applied after the new $\mathbf{p}_{i+1}$ is determined using the recurrence formulas in Equations (11.14) and (11.15). If ν_i is greater than σ_i, the node $\mathbf{p}_{i+1}$ is adjusted, such that the joint angle is equal to σ_i. Usually, the stiffness parameters for nodes near a follicle are set at 180 degrees, so that no adjustments of the nodes are done. For smooth curved hair strands, the parameters σ_i would be small, 10 to 15 degrees, for nodes far from the follicle.

Figure 11.18.
Results of beam bending hair dynamics. (*Courtesy of K. Anjyo.*)

Randomness

Small hair strand fluctuations were created using uniform random values. The random perturbations were applied after calculating the new node positions. Then, using the stiffness parameters, the hair strand nodes were adjusted to maintain smooth strand curvature. Figure 11.18 illustrates the effectiveness of the bending beam approach to hair dynamics.

11.11   Hair-to-Hair Interaction

An important aspect of many hair styles is the dynamic behavior of hair strands as they collide with each other. Chang et al. describe an approach to hair-to-hair collision that depends on simulating the dynamic behavior of a sparse set of *guide* hairs and then interpolating them across a dense hair model [Chang et al. 02].

The input to their simulation is a sparse hair model with a few hundred strands. Each of these strands has multiple segments connected at vertices. Each of these strands represents a cluster of hair strands in the dense hair model.

Each strand vertex is treated as a rotational joint with a hinge. Triangular polygon meshes are constructed, connecting adjacent guide strand vertices. These meshes are used in the simulation of hair-to-hair interactions. Animation sequences are produced by simulating hair behavior based on this sparse model.

Figure 11.19.
Results of hair-to-hair interaction simulation. See also Color Plate VIII. (*Courtesy of Y. Yu.*)

For rendering, a high-quality dense hair model is obtained by transforming and interpolating the sparse model guide strands to form hair strand clusters. Hair strand rendering uses diffuse and specular reflection, as well as hair volume translucency, to achieve self-shadowed hair. The translucency is based on a modified version of the opacity shadow buffer algorithm [Kim and Neumann 01]. Figure 11.19 shows an example hair behavior created with this approach.

11.12 Interactive Hair Modeling Tools

This section describes the interactive hair modeling tools developed to support the wisp model described in Section 11.8 and the Rosenblum et al. model.

11.12.1 The Wisp Model

Watanabe and Suenaga described an interactive hair-modeling system [Watanabe and Suenaga 92]. Their system had two modes: a wisp-modeling mode and a hair-drawing mode. Wisps were controlled by interactively selecting the desired parameter values in the wisp-modeling mode. Then hair images using these wisps were created in the hair-drawing mode. This system provided a number of default wisp types, which could be selected from a hairstyle menu. When selected, 12 wisp-modeling parameters were set as a group. These parameters included angle, bend, ratio, thickness, length, fold, density, direction randomness, color, and two wave control values. A screen window was used to show the wisp shape and location generated by the selected parameters. The simplified wisps were shown in real time, superimposed on the human head model. An overall hairstyle menu was used to specify the set of wisps types to be used.

In the hair-drawing mode, all the hair strands in the specified wisps were drawn on a human head model. The head model consisted of about 800 triangles. The hair strand root positions were located within about 300 triangles of the head model that formed the scalp area. In these triangles, several positions are selected as the hair orientation points for the wisps. Representing the hair strands required about 700,000 trigonal prisms.

11.12.2 The Mass-Spring-Hinge Model

Rosenblum et al. described the development of an interactive graphical *follicle map editor*, used to place hair follicles onto a polygonally defined head model [Rosenblum et al. 91]. In their system, the user interactively drew the follicle positions in two dimensions. These positions were then spherically mapped onto the head object. Several additional screen windows were used to display orthogonal views of the resulting three-dimensional follicle

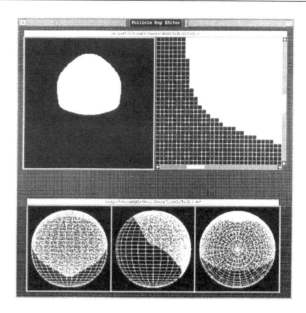

Figure 11.20.
Follicle map editor [Rosenblum et al. 91].

placement. The follicle editor also had an option to randomly jitter the follicle placement to remove patterns caused by the mapping process. See Figure 11.20.

11.13   Super-Helices Hair Model

Bertails et al. have developed an approach to computing natural hair shapes [Bertails et al. 05a] and an approach to simulating the dynamics of human hair [Bertails et al. 06], based on the *Kirchhoff* equations for *Cosserat* rods. This mechanically based approach models the curvatures and twist of deformable elastic rods [Pai 02]. In these approaches, hair strands are represented as Cosserat rods or as piecewise helical rods called *super-helices*.

The configuration of a Cosserat rod is defined by a centerline space curve $\mathbf{r}(s)$ where s denotes the location along the curvilinear axis of the rod. A *material* frame $\mathbf{F}(s) = (\mathbf{n}_1(s), \mathbf{n}_2(s), \mathbf{t}(s))$ is attached to each point on this curve (see Figure 11.21(b)). Usually, the vector $\mathbf{t}$ is the local tangent of the centerline, and the vectors $\mathbf{n}_1$ and $\mathbf{n}_2$ lie in the local cross-section plane. In this case, $\mathbf{n}_1$ and $\mathbf{n}_2$ are the elliptical axes of the cross-section.

The Cosserat rod can locally bend in directions $\mathbf{n}_1$ and $\mathbf{n}_2$ and twist about the centerline. The amount of bending or twisting is determined by curvatures $\mathbf{k}_1$ and $\mathbf{k}_2$ and torsion τ, which are properties of the rod material.

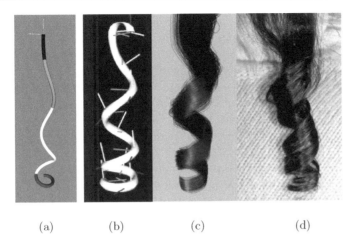

(a)   (b)   (c)   (d)

Figure 11.21.
(a) An example of a super-helix. (b) A Cosserat rod model. (c) A computed hair curl. (d) A real hair curl. (*Courtesy of F. Bertails.*)

In the static case, the shape of the hair strand, modeled as a Cosserat rod, is computed by finding the equilibrium form of the strand in a gravity field. The approach here is to find the minimum potential energy of the strand. The strand has a potential energy component due to its internal elastic deformation and a potential energy component due to the gravity field. As the strand stretches, its internal elastic energy increases, while

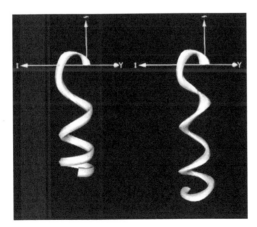

Figure 11.22.
Equilibrium hair strand shapes. The left strand has $\mathbf{e} = 0.0$, while the right strand has $\mathbf{e} = 0.2$. (*Courtesy of F. Bertails.*)

its gravitational potential energy decreases. The internal elastic energy depends on a number of material properties, including $\mathbf{k}_1$, $\mathbf{k}_2$, τ, and the eccentricity $\mathbf{e}$ of its elliptical cross-section. See [Bertails et al. 05a] for a detailed discussion of the potential energy calculations.

Figure 11.22 shows the equilibrium shape for two hair strands. The left strand has an eccentricity of $\mathbf{e} = 0.0$, while the right strand has an eccentricity of $\mathbf{e} = 0.2$. Figure 11.21(c) shows a simulated hair curl created using this approach. Compare this result with the real hair curl shown in Figure 11.21(d).

Wetting hair changes several of its physical properties, including its radius, its mass, and its stiffness. All of these properties are included in the potential energy calculations above. Adjusting these properties to correspond to wet hair values produces changes in computed hair shape corresponding to the changes we see when wetting real hair.

Figure 11.23 shows several hair styles created by varying the eccentricity $\mathbf{e}$ and the natural curvatures $\mathbf{k}_i^0$ of the hair strands. The natural curvatures correspond to the case where no forces are applied. The left-most hair style has $\mathbf{e} = 0.2$, and $\mathbf{k}_i^0$ is much greater than 1.0. The center hair style has $\mathbf{e} = 0.1$ and $\mathbf{k}_i^0$ approximately equal to 1.0. The right-most hair style has $\mathbf{e} = 0.0$ and $\mathbf{k}_i^0 = 0.0$. The generated hair images are rendered using the physically accurate scattering model described in [Marschner et al. 03].

This general approach is is extended in [Bertails et al. 06] to include the representation of the hair strands as super-helices. Super-helices are C^1 continuous piecewise representations of hair strands. Figure 11.21(a) shows an example super-helix. Each section of the strand is a helical rod with its own discrete properties, such as curvature and twist. By using this piecewise representation for the hair strands and by applying Lagrangian mechanics to the resulting system, simulation of the dynamic behavior of

Figure 11.23.
Several hair styles created using a model based on Cosserat rods. (*Courtesy of F. Bertails.*)

the hair strands is enabled. See [Bertails et al. 06] for a detailed discussion of the simulation process.

11.14   Strand Rendering

Hair has complex optical properties. It is not completely opaque, and the strands actually have two specular highlights. One is reflected directly off the surface of the strand, while the other is a reflection of transmitted light off the strand's back wall. The surface of hair is not smooth, but is covered with layers of scales. The properties of these scales strongly influence light reflection. The optical and dynamic properties of hair are also influenced by oil on the hair and by various cosmetic hair products.

Techniques for rendering cylinders are well known. However, the very small diameter of human hair makes it difficult to realistically render using traditional rendering techniques. Because of the small size and the very large number of strands to be rendered, several specialized strand rendering techniques have been developed.

11.14.1   Mass and Spring Hair Rendering

Rosenblum et al. used z-buffer-based techniques for efficient rendering of these high complexity scenes [Rosenblum et al. 91]. The very thin hair strand segments make anti-aliased rendering especially important; therefore, stochastic supersampling [Crow 81, Cook 86] was used; see Section 6.6.

A polygon mesh could be used to approximate each segment cylinder; however, this would not be efficient for cylinders that are at most a few pixels wide. The fact that each strand segment has a small rectangular profile after transformation into screen space can be exploited. Containment within the projected strand segment can be determined by testing the distance between a sample point and the center line of the strand.

The total number of samples used to scan convert each segment should be minimized. This reduction is done by only sampling the immediate region containing the segment. To test if a sample falls within a segment, the distance from the sample point to the center line of the segment is compared to the strand width.

If P_1 and P_2 are the two endpoints that define the segment in screen space, then the parametric form of the line that passes through these points is

$$P(t) = P_1 - (P_2 - P_1)t. \qquad (11.16)$$

The parameter t for the point on $P(t)$ that has minimum distance to a given sample point P_0 is given by

$$t = (\Delta x(x_1 - x_0) + \Delta y(y_1 - y_0))/(\Delta x^2 + \Delta y^2). \qquad (11.17)$$

If this t value is between 0.0 and 1.0, it is used to calculate x and y of the nearest point. If the square of the distance between P_0 and $P(t)$ is less than or equal to half the strand width then the sample is inside the segment.

For each segment, the Δx and Δy values are constant and only need to be computed once. Rewriting this equation results in a computationally efficient form for t:

$$t = AC + BD, \tag{11.18}$$

where $C = x_1 - x_0$, and $D = y_1 - y_0$.

The square of the distance between $P(t)$ and P_0 becomes

$$(C + \Delta x t)^2 + (D + \Delta y t)^2. \tag{11.19}$$

An estimate of the segment z depth at the sample point can be computed as

$$z = z_1 + (z_2 - z_1)t, \tag{11.20}$$

where z_1 and z_2 are the depths of P_1 and P_2 in screen space. This z depth value is used by the supersampled z-buffer to determine sample visibility.

An approximate *ad hoc* shading technique for small cylinders as reported by Kajiya [Kajiya and Kay 89] was used for shading the strand segments. The shading components are defined as

$$\begin{aligned}
\text{diffuse} &= k_d \sin \theta_{vi}, \\
\text{specular} &= k_s \cos^p \phi_{ee},
\end{aligned} \tag{11.21}$$

where k_d is the diffuse coefficient, k_s is the specular coefficient, θ_{vi} is the angle between the tangent vector at the sample and the light vector, ϕ_{ee} is the angle between the eye vector and the specular reflection vector, and p is an exponent to control highlight sharpness.

For each segment, the tangent vector is parallel to the line defined by its endpoints. For adjacent segments, a vertex tangent vector is the vector sum of the adjacent tangent vectors. These vertex tangent vectors are interpolated to smoothly shade along the length of the strand.

Since for this approximate shading, the tangent vector is the basis for the calculations, shading will change as the tangent vector is interpolated along the length of the strand. Shading changes across the width of the strand are ignored. The net result is that the strands are rendered as anti-aliased lines with smooth interpolated shading along their lengths.

Shadows were used to enhance perceived depth and realism, and to minimize unwanted lighting effects. Without the use of shadows, unwanted specular highlights appear, causing the hair to *glow* [Kajiya and Kay 89]. A high resolution shadow depth buffer was used to determine shadows [Williams 78]. In the shadow algorithm, a small, experimentally determined bias value was added to the depth values to avoid incorrect self shadowing caused by precision problems. This bias was adjusted to eliminate incorrect self-shadowing while still allowing strands to shadow each other.

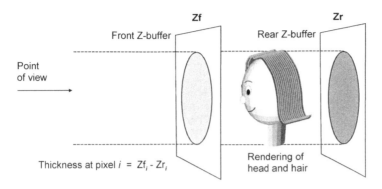

Figure 11.24.
Use of double z-buffer. Adapted from [Watanabe and Suenaga 92].

11.14.2 Backlighting Effects

Producing realistic renderings of the back lighting effects commonly seen on natural hair is also a challenge.

In backlit situations, the silhouette hair strands seem to shine. Reproducing this effect is important for realistic hair images. Watanabe and Suenaga [Watanabe and Suenaga 92] used an extension to the conventional z-buffer approach to support this effect. This method identifies the areas for the backlighting effect, during image generation, using a *double* z-buffer.

A z-buffer is generally used to determine which portions of an object are visible from a particular viewpoint. The contents of the z-buffer are the depth values for pixels from that viewpoint. Depth values can also be used to compute object thickness. The difference between front surface and rear surface depth values defines object thickness. See Figure 11.24.

The pixel-by-pixel z depth difference corresponds to object thickness at each pixel. Using these depth differences, thin areas can easily be identified. Backlighting effects are obtained by giving higher shading intensities to pixels in *thin* areas.

11.14.3 Anisotropic Reflection Model for a Three-Dimensional Curve

At the rendering stage, the geometry of the bent strand hair model [Anjyo et al. 92] is a collection of piecewise-linear three-dimensional curves, drawn as polylines. A standard illumination equation involves ambient, diffuse, and specular components. The hair treated by this approach was mainly straight, relatively dark, and glossy. For this hair, the specular component seemed dominant. The diffuse term was eliminated for simplicity. The resulting hair shading was based on the sum of an ambient constant and specular components. When hair strands are represented as polylines

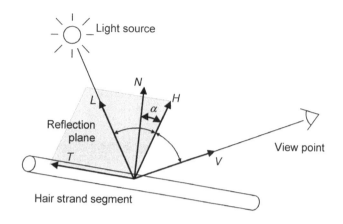

Figure 11.25.
Anisotropic reflection. (Adapted from [Anjyo et al. 92].)

with no volume, they have ill-defined normal vectors. For shading purposes, each hair strand segment is modeled as a cylinder with a very small radius. An accurate calculation of the specular reflection would involve integration around the circumference of the hair. However, a simple approximate technique for calculating the specular shading term was developed. Referring to Figure 11.25, we see the specular term ϕ_s at the point $\mathbf{P}$ on a surface is defined by

$$\phi_s = k_s(\mathbf{N}, \mathbf{H})^n, \tag{11.22}$$

where k_s is the specular reflection coefficient, $\mathbf{N}$ is the surface normal at point $\mathbf{P}$, $\mathbf{H}$ is the vector halfway between the light vector $\mathbf{L}$ and the vector $\mathbf{V}$ toward the eye, and n is the exponent indicating the sharpness of the specular highlight. The normal $\mathbf{N}$ used lies in the plane defined by the vector $\mathbf{H}$ and the hair direction vector $\mathbf{T}$ at point $\mathbf{P}$. The inner product $(\mathbf{N}, \mathbf{H})$ can be rewritten as

$$(\mathbf{N}, \mathbf{H}) = \cos\alpha = (1 - (\mathbf{T}, \mathbf{H})^2)^{1/2}. \tag{11.23}$$

The total shading intensity at a point $\mathbf{P}$ on the hair strand is then

$$I(\mathbf{P}) = I_a k_a + I_s \phi_s(\mathbf{P}), \tag{11.24}$$

where I_a is the intensity of the ambient light, k_a is the ambient reflection coefficient, and I_s is the intensity of the light source. The ambient reflection coefficient k_a is a hair material property that plays an important role. In this model, the k_a values have a normal random distribution. That is, k_a has the same value for each segment in a given hair strand, but randomly differs between strands.

Figure 11.26.
"Wind-blown" beam bending hair with anisotropic shading. (*Courtesy of K. Anjyo.*)

Let $\mathbf{p}_0, \mathbf{p}_1, \ldots$, and $\mathbf{p}_k$ be the nodes of the hair segments $s_1, s_2, \ldots$, and s_k. The shading value or color at each node $\mathbf{p}_i$ is defined by $I(\mathbf{p}_i)$ as in Equation (11.22), where the direction vector $\mathbf{T}$ is defined as $\mathbf{p}_{i-1}\mathbf{p}_i / \parallel \mathbf{p}_{i-1}\mathbf{p}_i \parallel$. Then the color at each point on the segment is linearly interpolated between the node colors.

This approach can take advantage of the hardware z-buffer, anti-aliased line drawing, and linear color interpolation support of high-end graphics workstations. Anti-aliasing is needed, since the hair strands are typically about 1/4 of a pixel wide when transformed into screen space. The anti-aliasing can be done by supersampling. Figure 11.26 illustrates the effectiveness of this shading approach; about 50,000 hair strands were used, whose screen width is about 1/4 pixel size.

11.14.4 Hair Self-Shadowing

Many hair self-shadowing techniques rely on extensions to the shadow map concept [Williams 78]. A *shadow map* is created by rendering a scene from the point of view of a light. Depth values for the visible surfaces in the scene are stored into the corresponding two-dimensional pixel array. This depth map is referred to as a shadow map, since scene elements that are farther away from the light than the depth value at each pixel are in shadow. Since shadow maps only contain one depth value for each pixel, they are not well suited for shadowing partially transparent hair strands.

Deep shadow maps. Lokovic and Veach extended the shadow map concept to create *deep shadow maps* [Lokovic and Veach 00]. Rather than a single depth value for each shadow map pixel, a transmittance or visibility function is stored at each pixel location. This map is usually created by intersecting many rays from the light through the scene for each pixel. The visibility information from each of these rays is used to compute visibility as a function of depth for each pixel. The resulting functions give the fraction of light penetration as a function of depth.

Opacity shadow maps. Kim and Neumann proposed a specific implementation of this idea, called *opacity shadow maps* and applied it to hair rendering [Kim and Neumann 01]. In their approach, the hair volume is sliced into many sections along the direction of the light. The portions of the hair volume between two consecutive slices are rendered, from the light's point of view, into consecutive alpha maps. This set of alpha maps forms the opacity shadow map. When rendering a segment of hair, the opacity information from the two slices bounding the segment is interpolated to determine shadowing at that location in the hair volume.

Density clustering. Another variation of the opacity shadow map idea is proposed by Mertens et al. [Mertens et al. 04]. Their version is intended for implementation on a GPU. In this approach, hair is viewed as a clustered density field, resulting in a piecewise linear opacity function for each pixel of an opacity map. To determine the density field, the hair primitives, usually line segments, are rendered from the point of view of the light. The generated rasterized fragments each have depth and opacity information. The fragment information for each pixel is grouped into a specified number of clusters or depth ranges. The number of depth clusters is usually set to four to make best use of the specialized hardware in most graphics processors. The opacity information for the fragments within each cluster

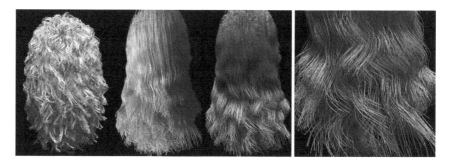

Figure 11.27.
Several examples of hair rendered with *density clustering* self-shadowing. The right-most image is a closeup view. (*Courtesy of T. Mertens.*)

is accumulated. The accumulated opacity is assumed to be uniformly distributed across the depth of the cluster. The depth *width* of each cluster is chosen to be proportional to the standard deviation of the cluster. By depth integration across these uniform opacity clusters, a piece-wise linear opacity function is computed for each pixel. Figure 11.27 shows several examples, including a closeup, of hair rendered using this density clustering self-shadowing technique.

Density maps. Bertails, et al. introduced the use of use of *light-oriented density maps* as the basis for hair self-shadowing [Bertails et al. 05b]. These density maps may also be used to optimize hair self-collisions.

A

A Face Model

This appendix briefly outlines a program that constructs a face model from three input data files, articulates the face geometry with muscles, and displays the results. The underlying muscle model algorithms are described in Chapter 6 and represent the code used to generate some of the illustrations in this book. The code should be viewed as a basic boiler plate for muscle modeling, with the distinct advantage that the muscles are not "hardwired" into a specific facial geometry. Therefore, with a little effort, it is possible to use your favorite facial geometry with this version of the muscle model.

This version of the code uses simple keyboard bindings to drive the face and was written in C using OpenGL display commands. The data structures are more complex than necessary; however, they do provide a certain amount of design flexibility and scope for further development. The geometry is based on a discrete triangle representation documented in the header files. Once you have understood this simple geometry configuration, it should be straightforward to convert your face data into this representation. As a final step, the muscle geometry file will have to be adapted to the face geometry you provide. This step simply involves the specification of the head and tail of each muscle as a pair of three-space vectors. A copy of the code can be obtained at the following site: http://www.faceanimation.com.

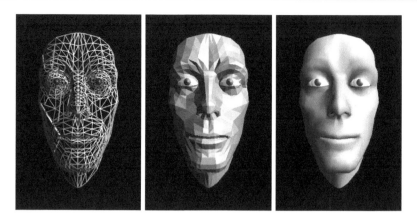

Figure A.1.
Wireframe, flat shading, and Gouraud shaded model of the geometry.

A.1   The Data Files

There are three basic input files: `faceline.dat`, `index.dat`, and `muscle.dat`. The polygon index list provides unique indexes into the three-dimensional node list file that constructs the facial geometry as a collection of triangular polygons that can be displayed and rendered. In addition, predetermined indices are defined for the jaw and eyelid pointers, so they can be opened and closed.

The muscle data file contains a list of muscle descriptions in the form of a head and tail three-space vector, two zones of influence, an angular zone, and a muscle bias factor. In this version there are 18 paired muscle types: the *zygomatic majors*, *depressor anguli oris*, inner portion of the *frontalis majors*, mid portion of the *frontalis majors*, outer portion of the *frontalis majors*, *levator labii superioris alaeque nasi*, *levator anguli oris*, and the *corrugators supercilli*.

A.2   Control

Simple keyboard bindings are used to control the face. The principle controls are for individual muscle activation. For example, the "a" key will progressively increment the activation of the current muscle, while "A" progressively decrements the current muscle activation. To select another muscle, the "n" key is used, which cycles through the muscle list. The full listing of the binds is in the "readme" file provided with the source code. Figure A.1 illustrates the end result of rendering the static face geometry in wireframe, flat, and smooth.

B

Simple Parameterized Face Program

The following is brief documentation for a simple interactive parameterized three-dimensional face model implemented in the C language. It runs on systems using the OpenGL graphics programming interface. Input to the model consists of three data files and user keyboard commands. Output consists of facial images in an OpenGL screen window. This version uses a very simple keyboard-driven user interface. This simple command interface was used to avoid as much OpenGL-specific code as possible. This should make it relatively easy to port to your favorite system and your favorite user interface. This program is a fairly primitive direct descendent of the original Parke parameterized face model developed at the University of Utah. It and its associated data files should be viewed as a *starter kit* for parameterized facial modeling. You will undoubtedly find many ways to improve and enhance the model, its user interface, and its associated data files.

B.1   Input Data

The input data files consist of two three-dimensional vertex data files and one polygon topology file. The two vertex files describe the basic face vertex positions and the extreme position values for those points, which are computed using interpolation. The program asks for the two vertex file names. The standard topology file name is assumed. The standard files used are:

st1.pts The first vertex data set.

st2.pts The second vertex data set.

stt.top The face topology file.

The face topology used is shown in Figure B.1. You are certainly free to construct and use your own data files. Brief study of these standard files will give you the required file formats.

Warning: The face polygon topology, as specified in the topology file, is intimately related to the parameterized manipulation of the face. Changes in this topology will usually require corresponding changes in the *points* procedure of the program.

Hints: In the topology file, vertices specified in the form $n.m$ have the following interpretation. the variable n refers to the vertex number, and m

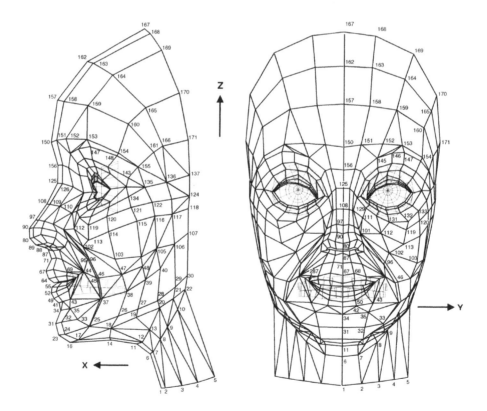

Figure B.1.
The polygon topology used for the simple parameterized face model.

refers to the normal number to be used for this instance. Multiple normals are used for vertices along creases. The first value on each line is a surface attribute (primarily color) index for that polygon. In the first vertices file, points not specified are part of the eyelid and are computed by the program. For vertices 184 through 221, which form most of the eyelid, the first value is a radius value used to fit the eyelid to the eyeball.

In the second vertices file, points not specified are at the same position as in the first vertices file. Positions consist of X, Y, Z values in the face coordinate system—X forward, Y to the face's left, and Z up.

B.2   Running the Program

The program first asks for the vertices data file names and reads in the desired data. It then prompts with a ">". At the prompt, it is expecting a command. Commands consist of single characters followed by a "carriage return." The following commands are valid:

"p" Change a parameter value. The program asks for a parameter number and then the new parameter value. The valid parameters and their initial values are indicated in the source code.

"d" Display a new face image.

"r" Read and output a current parameter value.

"q" Quit and exit the program.

B.3   Source and Data Files

These files are slight modifications of those included in the SIGGRAPH '90 *State of the Art in Facial Animation* tutorial notes [Parke 90]. A copy of the code can be obtained at the following site: http://www.faceanimation.com.

Bibliography

[Allan et al. 89] J. B. Allan, B. Wyvill, and I. H. Witten. "A Methodology for Direct Manipulation of Polygon Meshes." *Proc. CG International 89*, pp. 451–469. Berlin: Spinger, 1989.

[Allen et al. 87] J. Allen, M. S. Hunnicutt, and D. Klatt. *From Text to Speech: The MITalk System.* Cambridge, UK: Cambridge University Press, 1987.

[Anjyo et al. 92] K. Anjyo, Y. Usami, and T. Kurihara. "A Simple Method for Extracting the Natural Beauty of Hair." *Proc. SIGGRAPH '92, Computer Graphics* 26:2 (1992), 111-120.

[Apodaca and Gritz 00] A. Apodaca and L. Gritz. *Advanced RenderMan: Creating CGI for Motion Pictures.* San Francisco: Morgan-Kaufmann, 2000.

[Appel 67] A. Appel. "The Notion of Quantitative Invisibility and the Machine Rendering of Solids." In *Proc. ACM National Conference* 14, pp. 387–393. New York: ACM, 1967.

[Argyle and Cook 76] M. Argyle and M. Cook. *Gaze and Mutual Gaze.* Cambridge, UK: Cambridge University Press, 1976.

[Arijon 76] D. Arijon. *Grammar of the Film Language.* Los Angeles: Silman-James Press, 1976.

[Atkin 80] R. J. Atkin. *An Introduction to the Theory of Elasticity.* London: Longman Group, 1980.

[Bando et al. 03] Y. Bando, B-Y. Chen, and T. Nishita. "Animating Hair with Loosely Connected Particles." *Computer Graphics Forum* 22:3 (2003), 411–418.

[Bartles et al. 87] R. Bartles, J. Beatty, and B. Barsky. *Introduction to Splines for Use in Computer Graphics and Geometric Modeling.* Los Altos: Morgan Kaufmann, 1987.

413

[Bassili 82] J. N. Bassili. "Facial Motion in the Perception of Faces and of Emotional Expressions." *Journal of Experimental Psychology: Human Perception and Performance* 4 (1982), 373–379.

[Bates et al. 83] R. H. Bates, K. L. Garden, and T. M. Peters. "Overview of Computerized Tomography with Emphasis on Future Developments." *Proc. IEEE* 71:3 (1983), 356–372.

[Bathe 82] K. J. Bathe. *Finite Element Procedures in Engineering Analysis.* Englewood Cliffs, NJ: Prentice-Hall, 1982.

[Beier and Neely 92] T. Beier and S. Neely. "Feature-Based Images Metamorphosis." *Proc. SIGGRAPH '92, Computer Graphics* 26:2 (1992), 35–42.

[Bell 33] C Bell. *The Hand Its Mechanism and Vital Endowments as Evincing Design.* London: W. Pickering, 1833.

[Bergeron and Lachapelle 85] P. Bergeron and P. Lachapelle. "Controlling Facial Expressions and Body Movements." In *Advanced Computer Animation,* SIGGRAPH '85 Tutorials, pp. 61–79. New York: ACM, 1985.

[Bertails et al. 05a] F. Bertails, B. Audoly, B. Querleux, F. Leroy, J-L. Leveque, and M-P. Cani. "Predicting Natural Hair Shapes by Solving the Statics of Flexible Rods." In *Eurographics '05 (short papers),* Aire-la-Ville, Switzerland: Eurographics Association, 2005.

[Bertails et al. 05b] F. Bertails, C. Menier, and M-P. Cani. "A Practical Self-Shadowing Algorithm for Interactive Hair Animation." In *GI '05: Proceedings of Graphics Interface 2005,* pp. 71–78. Waterloo: Canadian Human-Computer Communications Society, 2005.

[Bertails et al. 06] F. Bertails, B. Audoly, M-P. Cani, B. Querleux, F. Leroy, and J-L. Leveque. "Super-Helices for Predicting the Dynamics of Natural Hair." *ACM Transactions on Graphics* 25:3 (2006), 1180–1187.

[Bierling 88] M. Bierling. "Displacement Estimation by Hierarchical Block Matching." In *SPIE Conf. Visual Communications and Image Processing.* Belingham, WA: SPIE, 1988.

[Bizzi et al. 82] E. Bizzi, W. Chapple, and N. Hogan. "Mechanical Properties of Muscles." *TINS* 5:11 (1982), 395–398.

[Black and Yacoob 95] M. J. Black and Y. Yacoob. "Tracking and Recognizing Rigid and Non-Rigid Facial Motions using Local Parametric Models of Image Motion." In *IEEE International Conference on Computer Vision,* pp. 374–381. Los Alamitos, CA: IEEE Computer, 1995.

[Blair 49] P. Blair. *Animation: Learning How to Draw Animated Cartoons.* Laguna Beach, CA: Walter T. Foster Art Books, 1949.

[Blake and Isard 94] A. Blake and M. Isard. "3D Position, Attitude and Shape Input using Video Tracking of Hands and Lips." In *Proceedings of SIGGRAPH 94, Computer Graphics Proceedings, Annual Conference Series,* edited by Andrew Glassner, pp. 185–192, New York: ACM Press, 1994.

[Blake and Isard 98] A. Blake and M. Isard. *Active Contours.* London: Springer-Verlag, 1998.

[Blanz and Vetter 99] V. Blanz and T. Vetter. "A Morphable Model for the Synthesis of 3D Faces." In *Proceedings of SIGGRAPH 99, Computer Graphics Proceedings, Annual Conference Series*, edited by Alyn Rockwood, pp. 187–194, Reading, MA: Addison Wesley Longman, 1999.

[Blinn and Newell 76] J. F. Blinn and M. E. Newell. "Texture and Reflection in Computer Generated Images." *CACM* 19:10 (1976), 542–547.

[Blinn 78] J. Blinn. "Simulation of Wrinkled Surfaces." *Proc. SIGGRAPH '78, Computer Graphics* 12:3 (1978), 286–292.

[Blinn 82] J. F. Blinn. "A Generalization of Algebraic Surface Drawing." *ACM Trans. on Graphics* 1:3 (1982), 235–256.

[Bloomenthal and Wyvill 93] J. Bloomenthal and B. Wyvill. "Interactive Techniques for Implicit Modeling." In *Modeling, Visualizing and Animating Implicit Surfaces, SIGGRAPH '93 Course Notes # 25.* New York: ACM Press, 1993.

[Borshukov et al. 03] B. Borshukov, D. Piponi, O. Larsen, J.P. Lewis, and C. Tempelaar-Lietz. "Universal Capture—Image-Based Facial Animation for "The Matrix Reloaded"." In *SIGGRAPH '03: ACM SIGGRAPH 2003 Sketches & Applications*, pp.1–1. New York: ACM Press, 2003.

[Bouknight and Kelley 70] W. Bouknight and K. Kelley. "An Algorithm for Producing Half-Tone Computer Graphics Presentations with Shadows and Movable Light Sources." In *Proc. AFIPS Spring Joint Computer Conf.* 36 pp. 1–10, Washington, D.C.:AFIPS, 1970.

[Bouknight 70] W. Bouknight. "A Procedure for Generation of Three-Dimensional Half-Tone Computer Graphics Presentations." *CACM* 9:3 (1970), 527–536.

[Bourne 73] G. H. Bourne. "Structure and Function of Muscle." In *Physiology and Biochemistry*, 2nd edition. New York: Academic Press, 1973.

[Breazeal and Foerst 99] C. L. Breazeal and A. Foerst. "Schmoozing with Robots: Exploring the Original Wireless Network." In *Proceedings of Cognitive Technology*, pp. 375–390. Los Alamitos, IEEE Press, 1999.

[Breazeal 02] C. L. Breazeal. *Designing Sociable Robots.* Cambridge, MA: The MIT Press, 2002.

[Bregler et al. 97] C. Bregler, M. Covell, and M. Slaney. "Video Rewrite: Driving Visual Speech with Audio." In *Proceedings of SIGGRAPH 97, Computer Graphics Proceedings, Annual Conferenece Series*, edited by Turner Whitted, pp.353–360, Reading, MA: Addison Wesley, 1997. (Proc. SIGGRAPH '97).

[Breitmeyer and Ganz 76] B. G. Breitmeyer and L. Ganz. "Implications of Sustained and Transient Channels for Theories of Visual Pattern Masking, Saccadic Suppression, and Information Processing." *Psychological Review* 23:1 (1976), 1–36.

[Brennan 82] S. E. Brennan. "Caricature Generator." Master's thesis, Massachusetts Institute of Technology, Cambridge, MA, 1982.

[Brewster et al. 84] L. J. Brewster, S. S. Trivedi, H. K. Tut, and J. K. Udupa. "Interactive Surgical Planning." *IEEE Computer Graphics and Applications* 4:3 (1984), 31–40.

[Brooke and Summerfield 82] M. Brooke and Q. Summerfield. "Analysis, Synthesis and Perception of Visible Articulatory Movements." *Journal of Phonetics* 11 (1982), 63–76.

[Bull and Connelly 85] P. Bull and G. Connelly. "Body Movement and Emphasis in Speech." *Journal of Nonverbal Behavior* 9:3 (1985), 169–187.

[Bulwer 48] J. Bulwer. *Philocopus, or the Deaf and Dumbe Mans Friend.* London: Humphrey and Moseley, 1648.

[Bulwer 49] J. Bulwer. *Pathomyotamia, or, A dissection of the significtive muscles of the affections of the minde.* London: Humphrey and Moseley, 1649.

[Cahn 89] J. Cahn. "Generating Expression in Synthesized Speech." Master's thesis, Massachusetts Institute of Technology, Cambridge, MA, 1989.

[Carpenter 84] L. Carpenter. "The A-Buffer, An Antialiased Hidden Surface Method." *Proc. SIGGRAPH '84, Computer Graphics* 18:3 (1984), 103–108.

[Catmull and Rom 74] E. Catmull and R. Rom. "A Class of Local Interpolating Splines." In *Computer Aided Geometric Design*, edited by Robert Barnhill, Richard Reisenfeld, pp. 317–326, New York: Academic Press, 1974.

[Catmull 74] E. Catmull. "A Subdivision Algorithm for Computer Display of Curved Surfaces." Ph.D. thesis, University of Utah, Salt Lake City, Utah, 1974.

[Catmull 78] E. Catmull. "A Hidden-Surface Algorithm with Anti-Aliasing." *Proc. SIGGRAPH '78, Computer Graphics* 12:3 (1978), 6–11.

[Chadwick et al. 89] J. Chadwick, D. Haumann, and R. Parent. "Layered Construction for Deformable Animated Characters." *Proc. SIGGRAPH '89, Computer Graphics* 23:3 (1989), 234–243.

[Chang et al. 02] J. Chang, J. Jin, and Y. Yu. "A Practical Model for Hair Mutual Interaction." In *Symposium on Computer Animation*, pp. 73–80, Aire-la-Ville, Switzerland: Eurographics Association, 2002.

[Cheney and Kincaid 80] W. Cheney and D. Kincaid. *Numerical Mathematics and Computing.* Monterey, CA: Brooks-Cole, 1980.

[Chernoff 71] H. Chernoff. "The Use of Faces to Represent Points in *N*-Dimensional Space Graphically." Technical Report Project NR-042-993, Office of Naval Research, 1971.

[Choe et al. 01] B. Choe, H Lee, and H-S. Ko. "Performance-Driven Muscle-Based Facial Animation." *The Journal of Visualization and Computer Animation* 12:2 (2001), 67–79.

[Choi et al. 90] C. S. Choi, H. Harashima, and T. Takebe. "Highly Accurate Estimation of Head Motion and Facial Action Information on Knowledge-Based Image Coding." Technical Report PRU90-68, Tokyo: Institute of Electronics, Information and Communication Engineers of Japan, 1990.

[Clayton 92] M. Clayton. *Leonardo da Vinci, the Anatomy of Man.* Boston: Bulfinch Press, 1992.

[Cline et al. 87] H. E. Cline, C. L. Dumoulin, H. R. Hart, W. E. Lorensen, and S. Ludke. "3D Reconstruction of the Brain from Magnetic Resonance Images using a Connectivity Algorithm." *Magnetic Resonance Imaging* 5:5 (1987), 345–352.

[Cohen and Massaro 90] M. Cohen and D. Massaro. "Synthesis of Visible Speech." *Behavioral Research Methods and Instrumentation* 22:2 (1990), 260–263.

[Cohen and Massaro 93] M. Cohen and D. Massaro. "Modeling Coarticulation in Synthetic Visual Speech." In *Models and Techniques in Computer Animation,* edited by N. M. Thalmann and D. Thalmann. Tokyo: Springer-Verlag, 1993.

[Cohen and Massaro 94] M. Cohen and D. Massaro. "Development and Experimentation with Synthetic Visual Speech." *Behavioral Research Methods, Instrumentation, and Computers,* 26 (1994), pp. 260–265.

[Collier 85] G. Collier. *Emotional Expression.* Hillsdale, NJ: L. Erlbaum Associates, 1985.

[Condon and Osgton 71] W. S. Condon and W. D. Osgton. "Speech and Body Motion Synchrony of the Speaker-Hearer." In *The Perception of Language,* edited by D. Horton and J. Jenkins, New York: Charles E. Merrill Co., 1971.

[Cook et al. 84] R. Cook, T. Porter, and L. Carpenter. "Distributed Ray Tracing." *Proc. SIGGRAPH '84, Computer Graphics* 18:3 (1984), 137–145.

[Cook 84] R. Cook. "Shade Trees." *Proc. SIGGRAPH '84, Computer Graphics* 18 (1984), 223-231.

[Cook 86] R. Cook. "Stochastic Sampling in Computer Graphics." *ACM Transactions on Graphics* 5:1 (1986), 51–72.

[Cootes et al. 98] T.F. Cootes, G.J. Edwards, and C.J. Taylor. "Active Appearance Models." In *Proc. European Conference on Computer Vision 1998,* Vol. 2, edited by H. Burkhardt and B. Neumann, pp. 484–498. Berlin: Springer, 1998.

[Coquillart 90] S. Coquillart. "Extended Free-Form Deformation: A Sculpturing Tool for 3D Geometric Modeling." *Proc. SIGGRAPH '90, Computer Graphics* 24:4 (1990), 187–196.

[Crow 76] F. C. Crow. "The Aliasing Problem in Computer Synthesized Images." Ph.D. thesis, University of Utah, Salt Lake City, Utah, 1976. Technical Report, UTEC-CSc-76-015.

[Crow 81] F. Crow. "A Comparison of Anti Aliasing Techniques." *IEEE Computer Graphics and Animation* 1:1 (1981), 40–48.

[Csuri et al. 79] C. Csuri, R. Hakathorn, R. Parent, W. Carlson, and M. Howard. "Towards an Interactive High Visual Complexity Animation System." *Proc. SIGGRAPH '79, Computer Graphics* 13:2 (1979), 289–299.

[Cyberware Laboratory Inc. 90] Cyberware Laboratory Inc. *4020/RGB 3D Scanner with Color Digitizer.* Monterey, CA, 1990.

[Darwin 72] Charles Darwin. *Expression of the Emotions in Man and Animals.* London: J. Murray, 1872.

[Darwin 04] Charles Darwin. *Expression of the Emotions in Man and Animals,* Second edition. Aylesbury, UK: Hazell, Watson and Viney, Ltd., 1904.

[DeCarlo et al. 98] D. DeCarlo, D. Metaxas, and M. Stone. "An Anthropometric Face Model Using Variational Techniques." In *Proceedings of SIGGRAPH 98, Computer Graphics Proceedings, Annual Conference Series,* edited by Michael Cohen, pp. 67–74, Reading, MA: Addison Wesley, 1998.

[deGraf 89] B. deGraf. "Notes on Facial Animation." In *State of the Art in Facial Animation, SIGGRAPH '89 Tutorials,* pp. 10–11. New York: ACM, 1989.

[deGraf and Wahrman 88] B. deGraf and M. Wahrman. "Mike, the Talking Head." *SIGGRAPH 88 Film and Video Show,* 1988.

[Deng and Neumann 08] Z. Deng and U. Neumann. *Data-Driven 3D Facial Animation.* New York: Springer Verlag, 2008.

[Deng 88] X. Q. Deng. "A Finite Element Analysis of Surgery of the Human Facial Tissue." Ph.D. thesis, Columbia University, New York, 1988.

[DeRose and Barsky 88] T. DeRose and B. Barsky, editors. *Geometric Splines.* San Mateo, California: Morgan Kaufmann, 1988.

[DiPaola 89] S. DiPaola. "Implementation and Use of a 3D Parameterized Facial Modeling and Animation System." In *State of the Art in Facial Animation,* SIGGRAPH '89 Tutorials. New York: ACM, 1989.

[DiPaola 91] S. DiPaola. "Extending the Range of Facial Types." *J. of Visualization and Computer Animation* 2:4 (1991), 129–131.

[Dittman 74] A. T. Dittman. "The Body Movement-Speech Rhythm Relationship as a Cue to Speech Encoding." In *Nonverbal Communications.* Oxford, UK: Oxford University Press, 1974.

[Duchenne 62] G. B. Duchenne. *The Mechanism of Human Facial Expression.* Paris: Jules Renard, 1862.

[Duchenne 90] G. B. Duchenne. *The Mechanism of Human Facial Expression.* New York: Cambridge University Press, 1990.

[Duncan 74] S. Duncan. "On the Structure of Speaker-Auditor Interaction During Speaking Turns." *Language in Society* 3 (1974), 161–180.

[Ekman and Friesen 75] P. Ekman and W. V. Friesen. *Unmasking the Face.* Palo Alto, CA: Consulting Psychologists Press, Inc., 1975.

[Ekman and Friesen 78] P. Ekman and W. V. Friesen. *Facial Action Coding System: A Technique for the Measurement of Facial Movement.* Palo Alto, CA: Consulting Psychologists Press, Inc. 1978.

[Ekman et al. 72] P. Ekman, W. V. Friesen, and P. Ellsworth. *Emotion in the Human Face: Guidelines for Research and a Review of Findings.* New York: Pergamon Press, 1972.

[Ekman 73] P. Ekman. *Darwin and Facial Expressions.* New York: Academic Press, 1973.

[Ekman 77] P. Ekman. *Facial Signals*. Bloomington, IN: Indiana University Press, 1977.

[Ekman 89] P. Ekman. "The Argument and Evidence About Universals in Facial Expressions of Emotion." In *Handbook of Social Psychophysiology*. New York: Wiley, 1989.

[Ekman et al. 02] Paul Ekman, Wallace V. Friesen, and Joseph C. Hager. *FACS Manual*, 2002. Available online (www.face-and-emotion.com/dataface/facs/new_version.jsp)

[Elsenaar and Scha 02] A. Elsenaar and R. Scha. "Electric Body Manipulation as Performance Art: A Historical Perspective." *Leonardo Music Journal* 12 (2002), 17–28.

[Elson 90] M. Elson. "Displacement Facial Animation Techniques." In *SIGGRAPH State of the Art in Facial Animation: Course #26 Notes*, pp. 21–42. New York: ACM, 1990.

[Essa and Pentland 94] I. Essa and A. Pentland. "A Vision System for Observing and Extracting Facial Action Parameters." Technical Report 247, Cambridge, MA: MIT Perceptual Computing Section, 1994.

[Ezzat and Poggio 00] T. Ezzat and T. Poggio. "Visual Speech Synthesis by Morphing Visemes." *International Journal of Computer Vision* 38:1 (2000), 45–57.

[Faigin 90] G. Faigin. *The Artist's Complete Guide to Facial Expressions*. New York: Watson-Guptill, 1990.

[Farkas 94] L. G. Farkas. *Anthropometry of the Head and Face*, Second edition. New York: Raven Press, 1994.

[Farrell et al. 84] E. J. Farrell, R. Zappulla, and W. C. Yang. "Color 3D Imaging of Normal and Pathological Intracranial Structures." *IEEE Computer Graphics and Applications* 4:7 (1984), 5–17.

[Faugeras and Luong 01] O. Faugeras and Q-T. Luong. *The Geometry of Multiple Images*. Cambridge, MA: MIT Press, 2001.

[Ferner and Staubesand 83] H. Ferner and J. Staubesand. *Sobotta Atlas of Human Anatomy Vol.1: Head, Neck, Upper Extremities*. Munich: Urban and Schwarzenberg, 1983.

[Flanagan 65] J. Flanagan. *Speech Analysis, Synthesis, and Perception*. New York: Springer-Verlag, 1965.

[Foley et al. 90] J. Foley, A. van Dam, S. Feiner, and J Hughes. *Computer Graphics: Principles and Practice*. Reading, MA: Addison-Wesley, 1990. 2nd Edition.

[Forsey and Bartels 88] D. Forsey and R. Bartels. "Hierarchical B-spline Refinement." *Proc. SIGGRAPH '88, Computer Graphics* 22:4 (1988), 205–212.

[FPC 63] Famous Photographers School, Inc., Westport, Conn. *Famous Photographers Course*, 1963. Lesson 10.

[Fridlund 94] J. A. Fridlund. *Human Facial Expression An Evolutionary View.* San Diego, CA: Academic Press, 1994.

[Fried 76] L. A. Fried. *Anatomy of the Head, Neck, Face, and Jaws.* Philadelphia: Lea and Febiger, 1976.

[Fuchs et al. 77] H. Fuchs, Z. Kedem, and S. Uselton. "Optimal Surface Reconstruction from Planar Contours." *CACM* 20:10 (1977), 693–702.

[Fuchs et al. 80] H. Fuchs, Z. Kedem, and B. Naylor. "On Visible Surface Generation by A Priori Tree Structures." *Proc, SIGGRAPH '80, Computer Graphics* 14:3 (1980), 124–133.

[Fuchs et al. 83] H. Fuchs, G. Abram, and E. Grant. "Near Real-Time Shaded Display of Rigid Objects." *Proc, SIGGRAPH '83, Computer Graphics* 17:3 (1983), 65–72.

[Gasser and Hill 24] H.S. Gasser and A.V. Hill. "The Dynamics of Muscular Contraction." *Royal Society of London Proceedings* 96 (1924), 398–437.

[Geiger et al. 03] G. Geiger, T. Ezzat, and T. Poggio. "AI Memo 2003-003: Perceptual Evaluation of Video-Realistic Speech." Technical report, MIT, 2003.

[Gillenson 74] M. L. Gillenson. "The Interactive Generation of Facial Images on a CRT Using a Heuristic Strategy." Ph.D. thesis, Ohio State University, Computer Graphics Research Group, Columbus, Ohio, 1974.

[Glassner 84] A. Glassner. "Space Subdivision for Fast Ray Tracing." *IEEE Computer Graphics and Applications* 4:10 (1984), 15–22.

[Glassner 89] A. Glassner, editor. *An Introduction to Ray Tracing.* London: Academic Press, 1989.

[Glenn et al. 85] W. E. Glenn, K. G. Glenn, and C. J. Bastian. "Imaging System Designed Based on Psychophysical Data." *Proc. Society of Information Display* 26:1 (1985), 71–78.

[Goldman 97] D. Goldman. "Fake Fur Rendering." In *Proceedings of SIGGRAPH 97, Computer Graphics Proceedings, Annual COnference Series,* edited by Turner Whitted, pp. 127–134, Reading, MA: Addison Wesley, 1997.

[Gonzales and Wintz 87] R. C. Gonzales and P. Wintz. *Digital Image Processing,* 2nd Edition. Reading, MA: Addison-Wesley, 1987.

[Gonzalez-Ulloa and Flores 65] M. Gonzalez-Ulloa and S. E. Flores. "Senility of the Face: Basic Study to Understand its Causes and Effects." *Plastic and Reconstructive Surgery* 36:2 (1965), 239–246.

[Goral et al. 84] C. Goral, K. Tottance, and D. Greenberg. "Modeling the Interaction of Light Between Diffuse Surfaces." *Proc. SIGGRAPH '84, Computer Graphics* 18:3 (1984), 213–222.

[Gouraud 71] H. Gouraud. "Continuous Shading of Curved Surfaces." *IEEE Trans on Computers* 20:6 (1971), 623–629.

[Grabb et al. 86] M.D. Grabb, C. William, W. James, and M.D. Smith. *Plastic Surgery.* Boston: Little, Brown and Company, 1986.

[Grant 88] C. W. Grant. "Introduction to Image Synthesis." In *Image Synthesis*, SIGGRAPH '88 Tutorial, pp. 1–12, New York: ACM, 1988.

[Graves 89] G. Graves. "The Dynamics of Waldo." *The IRIS Universe* (1989), 6–9.

[Greenspan 73] D. Greenspan. *Discrete Models*. Reading MA: Addison Wesley, 1973.

[Guenter et al. 98] B. Guenter, C. Grimm, D. Wood, D. Malvar, and F. Pighin. "Making Faces." In *Proceedings of SIGGRAPH 98, Computer Graphics Proceedings, Annual Conference Series*, edited by Michael Cohen, pp. 55–66, Reading, MA: Addison Wesley, 1998.

[Guiard-Marigny et al. 94] T. Guiard-Marigny, A. Adjoudani, and C. Benoit. "A 3D Model of the Lips for Visual Speech Synthesis." In *Proceedings of 2nd ETRW on Speech Synthesis*, pp. 49–52, 1994.

[Hadar et al. 84] U. Hadar, T. J. Steiner, E. C. Grant, and F. C. Rose. "The Timing of Shifts in Head Postures During Conversation." *Human Movement Science* 3 (1984), 237–245.

[Hale et al. 85] J. D. Hale, P. E. Valk, and J. C. Watts. "MR Imaging of Blood Vessels Using Three-Dimensional Reconstruction Methodology." *Radiology* 157:3 (1985), 727–733.

[Halton 65] R.G. Halton. *Figure Drawing*. New York: Dover Publishing, 1965.

[Hanrahan and Krueger 93] P. Hanrahan and W. Krueger. "Reflection from Layered Surfaces Due to Subsurface Scattering." In *Proceedings of SIGGRAPH 93, Computer Graphics Proceedings, Annual Conference Series*, edited by James T. Kajiya, pp. 165–174, New York: ACM Press, 1993.

[Hanrahan and Lawson 90] P. Hanrahan and J. Lawson. "A Language for Shading and Lighting Calculations." *Proc. SIGGRAPH '90, Computer Graphics* 24:4 (1990), 289–298.

[Hanrahan and Sturman 85] P. Hanrahan and D. Sturman. "Interactive Animation of Parametric Models." *The Visual Computer* 1:4 (1985), 260–266.

[Harkness 77] R. D. Harkness. *Mechanical Properties of Skin in Relation to its Biological Function and its Chemical Components*. New York: Wiley-Interscience, 1977.

[Hemmy et al. 83] D. C. Hemmy, D. J. David, and G. T. Herman. "Three-Dimensional Reconstruction of Cranial Deformity Using Computed Tomography." *Neurosurgery* 13:5 (1983), 534–541.

[Hess 75] E. H. Hess. "The Role of Pupil Size in Communication." *Scientific American* 223 (1975), 110–119.

[Hill et al. 88] D. R. Hill, A. Pearce, and B. Wyvill. "Animating Speech: An Automated Approach using Speech Synthesis by Rules." *The Visual Computer* 3 (1988), 277–289.

[Hinshaw and Lent 83] W. S. Hinshaw and A. H. Lent. "An Introduction to NMR Imaging from Bloch Equation to the Imaging Equation." *Proc. IEEE* 71:3 (1983), 338–350.

[Hjortsjö 70] C-H Hjortsjö. *Man's Face and Mimic Language*. Malm: Nordens Boktryckeri, 1970.

[Hogarth 81] B. Hogarth. *Drawing the Human Head*. New York: Watson-Guptill, 1981.

[Horn and Schunck 81] B. K. P. Horn and B. G. Schunck. "Determining Optical Flow." *Artificial Intelligence* 17 (1981), 185–203.

[Huxley and Niedergerke 54] A.F. Huxley and R. Niedergerke. "Structural Changes in Muscle during Contraction." *Nature* 173 (1954), 971–973.

[Ishii et al. 93] T. Ishii, T. Yasuda, and J. Toriwaki. "A Generation Model for Human Skin Texture." In *Proc. CG International '93: Communicating with Virtual Worlds*, edited by N. M. Thalmann and D. Thalmann, pp. 139–150. Tokyo: Springer-Verlag, 1993.

[Jeffers and Barley 71] J. Jeffers and M. Barley. *Speachreading (Lipreading)*. Springfield, Illinois: Charles C. Thomas, 1971.

[Jensen 01] H. W. Jensen. *Realistic Image Synthesis using Photon Mapping*. Wellesley, MA: A K Peters, 2001.

[Jones 18] D. Jones. *An Outline of English Phonetics: First Edition*. London: W. Heffer, 1918.

[Joy et al. 88] K. Joy, C. Grant, and N. Max. *Image Synthesis, SIGGRAPH Course Notes*. New York, ACM, 1988.

[Kähler et al. 01] K. Kähler, J. Haber, and H. Seidel. "Geometry-Based Muscle Modeling for Facial Animation." In *Graphics Interface 2001*, pp. 37–46. Ottawa: Canadian Information Processing Society, 2001.

[Kähler et al. 03] K. Kähler, J. Haber, and H-S. Seidel. "Reanimating the Dead: Reconstruction of Exressive Faces from Skull Data." *ACM Trans. Graph* 22:3 (2003), 554–561.

[Kajiya and Kay 89] J. T. Kajiya and T. L. Kay. "Rendering Fur with Three-Dimensional Textures." *Proc. SIGGRAPH 89, Computer Graphics* 23:3 (1989), 271–280.

[Kalra and Magnenat-Thalmann 94] P. Kalra and N. Magnenat-Thalmann. "Modeling Vascular Expressions in Facial Animation." In *Computer Animation '94*, pp. 50–58. Los Alamitos, CA: IEEE Computer Society Press.

[Kalra et al. 91] P. Kalra, A. Mangili, N. Magnenat-Thalmann, and D. Thalmann. "SMILE: A Multi Layered Facial Animation System." In *Modeling in Computer Graphics*, edited by T. L. Kuni, pp. 189–198. New York: Springer, 1991.

[Kalra et al. 92] P. Kalra, A. Mangili, N. Magnenat-Thalmann, and D. Thalmann. "Simulation of Facial Muscle Actions Based on Rational Free Form Deformations." In *Proc. Eurographics 92*, pp. 59–69. Aire-la-Ville, Switzerland: Eurographics Association, 1992.

[Kass et al. 88] M. Kass, A. Witkin, and D. Terzopoulos. "Snakes: Active Contour Models." *International Journal of Computer Vision* 1:4 (1988), 321–331.

[Katz 91] S. Katz. *Shot by Shot*. Michael Wiese Productions, 1991.

[Kaufman 88] A. Kaufman. "TSL—A Texture Synthesis Language." *Visual Computer* 4:3 (1988), 148–158.

[Kay 79] D. Kay. "Transparency, Reflection and Ray Tracing for Computer Synthesized Images." Master's thesis, Cornell University, 1979.

[Kay and Kajiya 86] T. Kay and J. Kajiya. "Ray Tracing Complex Scenes." *Proc. SIGGRAPH '86, Computer Graphics* 20:4 (1986), 269–278.

[Kenedi et al. 75] R. M. Kenedi, T. Gibson, J. H. Evans, and J. C. Barbenel. "Tissue Mechanics." *Physics in Medicine and Biology* 20:5 (1975), 699–717.

[Kent and Minifie 77] R. D. Kent and F. D. Minifie. "Coarticulation in Recent Speech Production Models." *Journal of Phonetics* 5 (1977), 115–135.

[Kim and Neumann 00] T-Y. Kim and U. Neumann. "A Thin Shell Volume for Modeling Human Hair." In *Computer Animation 2000*, pp. 121–128. Los Alamitos, CA: IEEE Computer Society, 2000.

[Kim and Neumann 01] T-Y. Kim and U. Neumann. "Opacity Shadow Maps." In *Proceedings of the 12th Eurographics Workshop on Rendering Techniques*, pp. 177–182. London: Springer, 2001.

[Klaus and Horn 86] B. Klaus and P. Horn. *Robot Vision*. Boston: MIT Press, 1986.

[Kleiser 89] J. Kleiser. "A Fast, Efficient, Accurate Way to Represent the Human Face." In *State of the Art in Facial Animation*, SIGGRAPH '89 Tutorials, pp. 37–40. New York: ACM, 1989.

[Knuth 69] D. Knuth. *The Art of Computer Programming, Volume 2: Seminumerical Algorithms*. Reading, MA: Addison-Wesley, 1969.

[Kochanek and Bartels 84] H. D. Kochanek and R. H. Bartels. "Interpolating Splines with Local Tension, Continuity and Bias Control." *Computer Graphics* 3:18 (1984), 33–41.

[Kodak 61] Eastman Kodak Company. *Studio Techniques for Portrait Photography*, Kodak Publication No. O-4, Rochester, NY, 1961.

[Kong and Nakajima 99] W. Kong and M. Nakajima. "Visible Volume Buffer for Efficient Hair Expression and Shadow Generation." In *Proc. of Computer Animation '99*, pp. 58–68. Los Alamitos, CA: IEEE Press, 1999.

[Kulikowski and Tolhurst 73] J. J. Kulikowski and D. J. Tolhurst. "Psychophysical Evidence for Sustained and Transient Detectors in Human Vision." *Journal of Physiology* 232 (1973), 149–162.

[Kunz 89] J. Kunz. "Painting Portraits in Watercolor: Part 1, Facial Features." *The Artist's Magazine* 6:6 (1989), 62–71.

[Kurihara and Arai 91] T. Kurihara and K. Arai. "A Transformation Method for Modeling and Animation of the Human Face from Photographs." In *Computer Animation '91*, edited by N. Magnenat-Thalmann and D. Thalmann, pp. 45–58. Berlin: Springer-Verlag, 1991.

[Ladd et al. 85] D. R. Ladd, K. Scherer, and K. E. Silverman. "An Integrated Approach to Studying Intonation and Attitude." In *Intonation in Discourse*, edited by C. Johns-Lewis. London: Croom Helm, 1985.

[Ladefoged 75] P. Ladefoged. *A Course In Phonetics*. Orlando, FL: Hardcourt Brace College Publishers, 1975.

[Larrabee 86] W. Larrabee. "A Finite Element Model of Skin Deformation. I. Biomechanics of Skin and Soft Tissue: A Review." *Laryngoscope* 96 (1986), 399–405.

[Lassiter 87] J. Lassiter. "Principles of Traditional Animation Applied to 3D Computer Animation." In *SIGGRAPH '87 Tutorials, Course 21*, pp. 35–44. New York: ACM, 1987

[Lee and Terzopolous 06] S-H. Lee and D. Terzopolous. "Heads Up! Biomechnanical Modeling and Neuromuscular Control of the Neck." *Transactions on Graphics (TOG)* 25:3 (2006), 1188–1198.

[Lee et al. 93] Y. Lee, D. Terzopoulos, and K. Waters. "Constructing Physics-Based Facial Models of Individuals." In *Graphics Interface '93*, pp. 1–8. Tornoto, ON: Canadian Human-Computer Communications Society, 1993.

[Lee et al. 95] Y. Lee, D. Terzopoulos, and K. Waters. "Realistic Modeling for Facial Animation." *Computer Graphics* 29:4 (1995), 55–62.

[LeGoff et al. 94] B. LeGoff, T. Guiard-Marigny, M. Cohen, and C. Benoit. "Real-Time Analysis-Synthesis and Intelligibility of Talking Faces." In *Proceedings of the Second ESCA/IEEE Workshop on Speech Synthesis*, pp. 53–56. Los Alamitos, CA: IEEE Press, 1994.

[Lennie 80] P. Lennie. "Parallel Visual Pathways; A Review." *Vision Research* 20 (1980), 561–594.

[Lewis and Parke 87] J. P. Lewis and F. I. Parke. "Automatic Lip-Synch and Speech Synthesis for Character Animation." In *Proceedings Human Factors in Computing Systems and Graphics Interface '87*, pp. 143–147. Toronto, ON: Canadian Human-Computer Communications Society, 1987.

[Lewis 89] J. P. Lewis. "Algorithms for Solid Noise Synthesis." *Proc. SIGGRAPH '89, Computer Graphics* 23:3 (1989), 263–270.

[Lewis 91] J. P. Lewis. "Automated Lip-Sync: Background and Techniques." *Journal of Visualization and Computer Animation* 2:4 (1991), 118–122.

[Lofqvist 90] A. Lofqvist. "Speech as Audible Gestures." In *Speech Production and Speech Modeling*, edited by W.J. Hardcastle and A. Marchal, pp. 289–322. Dordrecht: Kluwer Academic Publishers, 1990.

[Lokovic and Veach 00] T. Lokovic and E. Veach. "Deep Shadow Maps." In *Proc. Proceedings of SIGGRAPH 2000, Computer Graphics Proceedings, Annual Conference Series*, edited by Kurt Akeley, pp. 385–392. Reading, MA: Addison Wesley, 2000.

[Lorensen and Cline 87] W. E. Lorensen and H. E. Cline. "Marching Cubes: High Resolution 3D Surface Construction Algorithm." *Proc. SIGGRAPH '87, Computer Graphics* 21:4 (1987), 163–169.

[Madsen 69] R. Madsen. *Animated Film: Concepts, Methods, Uses.* New York: Interland, 1969.

[Magnenat-Thalmann and Thalmann 87] N. Magnenat-Thalmann and D. Thalmann, editors. *Synthetic Actors in Computer-Generated 3D Films.* Tokyo: Springer-Verlag, 1987.

[Magnenat-Thalmann et al. 88] N. Magnenat-Thalmann, N. E. Primeau, and D. Thalmann. "Abstract Muscle Actions Procedures for Human Face Animation." *Visual Computer* 3:5 (1988), 290–297.

[Magnenat-Thalmann et al. 89] N. Magnenat-Thalmann, H. Minh, M. deAngelis, and D. Thalmann. "Design, Transformation and Animation of Human Faces." *The Visual Computer* 5 (1989), 32–39.

[Markel and Gray 76] J. Markel and A. Gray. *Linear Prediction of Speech.* New York: Springer-Verlag, 1976.

[Marschner et al. 03] S. Marschner, H. Jensen, M. Cammarano, S. Worley, and P. Hanrahan. "Light Scattering from Human Hair Fibers." *ACM Transactions on Graphics* 22:3 (2003), 780–791.

[Mase and Pentland 91] K. Mase and A. Pentland. "Automatic Lipreading by Optical-Flow Analysis." *Systems and Computers in Japan* 22 (1991), N06.

[McGurk and MacDonald 76] H. McGurk and J. MacDonald. "Hearing Lips and Seeing Voices." *Nature* 264 (1976), 746–748.

[Mertens et al. 04] T. Mertens, J. Kautz, P. Bekaert, and F. Van Reeth. "A Self-Shadow Algorithm for Dynamic Hair Using Density Clustering." In *Proceedings of Eurographics Symposium on Rendering*, pp. 173–178. Aire-la-Ville, Switzerland: Eurographics Association, 2004.

[Miller 88a] G. Miller. "From Wireframes to Furry Animals." In *Graphics Interface '88*, pp. 138–145. Toronto: CIPS, 1988.

[Miller 88b] G. Miller. "The Motion Dynamics of Snakes and Worms." *Proc. SIGGRAPH '88, Computer Graphics* 22:4 (1988), 169–178.

[Mori 70] M. Mori. "The Uncanny Valley." *Engery* 7:4 (1970), 33–35.

[Morishima and Harashima 93] S. Morishima and H. Harashima. "Facial Animation Synthesis for a Human-Machine Communication System." In *Proceeding of the 5th International Conf. on Human-Computer Interaction*, pp. 1085–1090. New York: ACM, 1993.

[Morishima et al. 89] S. Morishima, K. Aiwaza, and H. Harashima. "An Intelligent Facial Image Coding Driven by Speech and Phoneme." In *Proceedings of IEEE ICASSP89*, pp. 1795–1798. Los Alamitos, CA: IEEE Press, 1989.

[MPEG 97] Motion Picture Expert Group. "ISO/IEC 14496-1 FBA", International Organization for Standardization, 1997.

[Nagao 72] M. Nagao. "Picture Recognition and Data Structure." In *Graphics Languages*, edited by Nake and Rosenfeld. Amsterdam: North-Holland, 1972.

[Nahas et al. 88] M. Nahas, H. Huitric, and M. Sanintourens. "Animation of a B-Spline Figure." *The Visual Computer* 3:5 (1988), 272–276.

[Nahas et al. 90] M. Nahas, H. Huitric, M. Rioux, and J. Domey. "Facial Image Synthesis using Texture Recording." *The Visual Computer* 6:6 (1990), 337–343.

[Narayanan et al. 04] S. Narayanan, K. Nayak, S. Lee, A. Sethy, and D. Byrd. "An Approach to Real-Time Magnetic Resonance Imaging from Speech Production." *Acoustical Society of America* 4:115 (2004), 1771–1776.

[Neider et al. 93] J. Neider, T. Davis, and M. Woo. *OpenGL Programming Guide: The Official Guide to Learning OpenGL.* Reading, MA: Addison Wesley, 1993.

[Newell et al. 72] M. Newell, R. Newell, and T. Sancha. "A New Approach to the Shaded Picture Problem." In *Proc. ACM National Conf.*, pp. 443–450. New York, ACM 1972.

[Newman and Sproull 79] W. Newman and R. Sproull. *Principles of Interactive Computer Graphics*, Second edition. New York: McGraw-Hill, 1979.

[Nishimura et al. 85] H. Nishimura, A. Hirai, T. Kawai, T. Kawata, I. Shirakawa, and K. Omura. "Object Modeling by Distribution Function and Method of Image Generation." In *Electronic Communications Conf., J68-D(4)*, 1985. (in Japanese).

[Nishita and Nakamae 85] T. Nishita and E. Nakamae. "Continuous Tone Representation of Three-Dimensional Objects Taking Account of Shadows and Interreflection." *Proc. SIGGRAPH '85, Computer Graphics* 19:3 (1985), 23–30.

[Nitchie 79] E. B. Nitchie. *How to Read Lips for Fun and Profit.* New York: Hawthorne Books, 1979.

[Osipa 03] J. Osipa. *Stop Staring: Facial Modeling and Animation Done Right.* San Francisco: Sybex, 2003.

[Pai 02] D. Pai. "Strands: Interactive Simulation of Thin Solids Using Cosserat Models." *Proc. Eurographics '02, Computer Graphics Forum* 21:3 (2002), 347–352.

[Parke 72] F. I. Parke. "Computer Generated Animation of Faces." Master's thesis, University of Utah, Salt Lake City, 1972. UTEC-CSc-72-120.

[Parke 74] F. I. Parke. "A Parametric Model for Human Faces." Ph.D. thesis, University of Utah, Salt Lake City, Utah, 1974. UTEC-CSc-75-047.

[Parke 82] F. I. Parke. "Parameterized Models for Facial Animation." *IEEE Computer Graphics and Applications* 2:9 (1982), 61–68.

[Parke 90] F. I. Parke, editor. *State of the Art in Facial Animation, SIGGRAPH Course Notes 26.* New York: ACM, 1990.

[Parke 91a] F. I. Parke. "Perception-Based Animation Rendering." *Journal of Visualization and Computer Animation* 2 (1991), 44–51.

[Parke 91b] F. I. Parke. "Techniques for Facial Animation." In *New Trends in Animation and Visualization*, edited by N. Magnenat-Thalmann and D. Thalmann, pp. 229–241. New York: John Wiley and Sons, 1991.

[Patel 95] M. Patel. "Colouration Issues in Computer Generated Facial Animation." *Computer Graphics Forum* 14:2 (1995), 117–126.

[Peachey 85] D. Peachey. "Solid Texturing of Complex Surfaces." *Proc. SIGGRAPH '85, Computer Graphics* 19:3 (1985), 279–286.

[Pearce et al. 86] A. Pearce, B. Wyvill, G. Wyvill, and D. Hill. "Speech and Expression: A Computer Solution to Face Animation." In *Proceedings of Graphics Interface '86*, pp. 136–140. Toronto: Canadian Information Processing Society, 1986.

[Pearson and Robinson 85] D. Pearson and J. Robinson. "Visual Communication at Very Low Data Rates." *Proc. IEEE* 73 (1985), 795–812.

[Pelachaud 91] C. Pelachaud. "Communication and Coarticulation in Facial Animation." Ph.D. thesis, University of Pennsylvania, 1991. Technical Report MS-CIS-91-77.

[Perlin 85] K. Perlin. "An Image Synthesizer." *Computer Graphics* 19:3 (1985), 287–296. Proc. SIGGRAPH '85.

[Perlin and Hoffert 89] K. Perlin and E. Hoffert. "HyperTexture." *Proc. SIGGRAPH '89, Computer Graphics* 23:3 (1989), 253–262.

[Peterson and Richmond 88] B. W. Peterson and F. J. Richmond. *Control of Head Movement.* Oxford: Oxford University Press, 1988.

[Phillips and Smuts 96] V. M. Phillips and N. A. Smuts. "Facial Reconstruction: Utilization of Computerized Tomography to Measure Facial Tissue Thickness in Mixed Racial Population." *Forensic Science International* 83 (1996), 51–59.

[Phong 76] B. T. Phong. "Illumination for Computer Generated Pictures." *CACM* 18:6 (1976), 311–317.

[Pieper 89] S. D. Pieper. "More Than Skin Deep: Physical Modeling of Facial Tissue." Master's thesis, Massachusetts Institute of Technology, Media Arts and Sciences, 1989.

[Pieper 91] S. D. Pieper. "CAPS: Computer-Aided Plastic Surgery." Ph.D. thesis, Massachusetts Institute of Technology, Media Arts and Sciences, 1991.

[Pighin and Lewis 06] Frédéric Pighin and John P. Lewis, editors. *Performance-Driven Facial Animation, SIGGRAPH Course Notes 30.* New York: ACM, 2006.

[Pighin et al. 98] F. Pighin, J. Hecker, D. Lischinski, R. Szeliski, and D. Salesin. "Synthesizing Realistic Facial Expressions from Photographs." In *Proceedings of SIGGRAPH 98, Computer Graphics Proceedings, Annual Conference Series*, edited by Michael Cohen, pp. 75–84. Reading, MA: Addison Wesley, 1998.

[Pixar 88] Pixar. *Tin Toy*, Short Animated Film. San Rafael, CA: Pixar, 1998.

[Platt 80] S. M. Platt. "A System for Computer Simulation of the Human Face." Master's thesis, The Moore School, University of Pennsylvania, 1980.

[Platt and Badler 81] S. M. Platt and N. I. Badler. "Animating Facial Expressions." *Proc. SIGGRAPH '81, Computer Graphics* 15:3 (1981), 245–252.

[Pol 87] Polhemus Navigations Sciences. *3Space Isotrack Users Manual*, Colchester, VT: Polhemus Navigations Sciences, 1987.

[Press et al. 86] W. Press, B. Flanney, S. Teukolsky, and W. Verttering. *Numerical Recipes: The Art of Scientific Computing*. Cambridge: Cambridge University Press, 1986.

[Pushkar et al. 03] J. Pushkar, W. Tien, M. Desbrun, and F. Pighin. "Learning Controls for Blend Shape Based Realistic Facial Animation." In *Eurographics/SIGGRAPH Symposium on Computer Animation*, pp. 187–192. Aire-la-Ville, Switzerland: Eurographics Association, 2003.

[Rabiner and Schafer 79] L. Rabiner and R. Schafer. *Digital Processing of Speech Signals*. Englewood Cliffs, NJ: Prentice-Hall, 1979.

[Reeves 90] W. T. Reeves. "Simple and Complex Facial Animation: Case Studies." In *State of the Art in Facial Animation: SIGGRAPH Course 26*, pp. 88–106. New York: ACM, 1990.

[Ricci 73] A. A. Ricci. "A Constructive Geometry for Computer Graphics." *The Computer Journal* 16:2 (1973), 157–160.

[Riewe 07] J. L. Riewe. "A Virtual Sculpture Based Morphable Face Model." Master's thesis, Texas A&M University, 2007.

[Robbins 02] C. R. Robbins. *Chemical and Physical Behavior of Human Hair*, Fourth edition. Berlin: Springer-Verlag, 2002.

[Roberts 63] L. Roberts. "Machine Perception of Three Dimensional Solids." Technical Report TR 315, Cambridge, MA: MIT, 1963.

[Romanes 67] G. J. Romanes. *Cunningham's Manual of Practical Anatomy, Vol 3: Head, Neck, and Brain*. Oxford, UK: Oxford Medical Publications, 1967.

[Romney et al. 69] G. Romney, G. Watkins, and D. Evans. "Real Time Display of Computer Generated Half-Tone Perspective Pictures." In *Proc. 1968 IFIP Congress*, pp. 973–978. Amsterdam: North Holland, 1969.

[Rose et al. 78] E.H. Rose, L.M. Vistnes, and G.A. Ksander. "A Microarchitectural Model of Regional Variations in Hypodermal Mobility in Porcine and Human Skin." *Annals of Plastic Surgery* 1:3 (1978), 252–266.

[Rosenblum et al. 91] R. Rosenblum, W. Carlson, and E. Tripp III. "Simulating the Structure and Dynamics of Human Hair: Modelling, Rendering and Animation." *J. Visualization and Computer Animation* 2:4 (1991), 141–148.

[Russell and Fernandez-Dols 79] J. Russell and J. Fernandez-Dols,editors. *The Psychology of Facial Expression*. Cambridge, UK: Cambridge University Press, 1979.

[Ryder 73] M Ryder. *Hair*. London: Edward Arnold, 1973.

[Sagar et al. 94] M. A. Sagar, D. Bullivant, G. D. Mallinson, and P. J. Hunter. "A Virtual Environment and Model of the Eye for Surgical Simulation." In *Proceedings of SIGGRAPH 94, Computer Graphics Proceedings, Annual Conference Series*, edited by Andrew Glassner, pp. 205–212. New York: ACM Press, 1994.

[Scherer et al. 84] K. Scherer, D. R. Ladd, and K. Silverman. "Vocal Cues to Speaker Affect: Testing Two Models." *Journal Acoustical Society of America* 76 (1984), 1346–1356.

[Sederberg and Parry 86] T. W. Sederberg and S. R. Parry. "Free-form Deformation of Solid Geometry Models." *SIGGRAPH '86, Computer Graphics* 20:4 (1986), 151–160.

[Serkis 03] A. Serkis. *The Lord of the Rings: Gollum, How We Made Movie Magic.* Boston: Houghton Mifflin Company, 2003.

[Sibson 78] R. Sibson. "Locally Equiangular Triangulations." *The Computer Journal* 21:3 (1978), 243–245.

[Sifakis et al. 05] E. Sifakis, I. Neverov, and R. Fedkiw. "Automatic Determination of Facial Muscle Activations from Sparse Motion Capture Marker Data." *Trans. on Graphics* 24:3 (2005), 417–425. 2005.

[Sifakis et al. 06] E. Sifakis, A. Selle, A. Robinson-Mosher, and R. Fedkiw. "Simulating Speech with a Physics-Based Facial Muscle Model." In *ACM SIG-GRAPH/Eurographics Symposium on Computer Animation (SCA)*, pp. 261–270. Aire-la-Ville, Switzerland: Eurographics Association, 2006.

[Singh 91] A. Singh. *Optical Flow Computation: A Unified Perspective.* Los Alamitos, CA: IEEE Computer Society Press, 1991.

[Smith 78] A. Smith. "Color Gamut Transform Pairs." *Proc. SIGGRAPH '78, Computer Graphics* 12:3 (1978), 12–19.

[Steele and Bramblett 88] D. G. Steele and C. A. Bramblett. *The Anatomy and Biology of the Human Skeleton.* College Station, TX: Texas A&M University Press, 1988.

[Stevens 99] K. N. Stevens. *Acoustic Phonetics.* Cambridge, MA: The MIT Press, 1999.

[Sutherland 74] I. E. Sutherland. "Three-Dimensional Data Input by Tablet." *Proceedings of the IEEE* 62 (1974), 453–461.

[Sutherland et al. 74] I. Sutherland, R. Sproull, and R. Schumacker. "A Characterization of Ten Hidden-surface Algorithms." *Computing Surveys* 6:1 (1974), 1–55.

[Takashima et al. 87] Y. Takashima, H. Shimazu, and M. Tomono. "Story Driven Animation." In *CHI+CG '87*, pp. 149–153. Toronto: Canadian Information Processing Society, 1987.

[Teeters et al. 06] T. Teeters, E. Kaliouby, and P. Picard. "Self-Cam: Feedback From What Would Be Your Social Partner." In *SIGGRAPH '06: ACM SIGGRAPH 2006 Research posters*, p. 138. New York: ACM, 2006.

[Teran et al. 05] J. Teran, E. Sifakis, S. Salinas-Blemker, V. Ng-Thow-Hing, C. Lau, and R. Fedkiw. "Creating and Simulating Skeletal Muscle from the Visible Human Data Set." *IEEE Transactions on Vision and Computer Graphics* 11:3 (2005), 317–328.

[Terzopoulos and Fleischer 88a] D. Terzopoulos and K. Fleischer. "Deformable Models." *The Visual Computer* 4:6 (1988), 306–331.

[Terzopoulos and Fleischer 88b] D. Terzopoulos and K. Fleischer. "Viscoelasticity, Plasticity and Fracture." *Computer Graphics* 22:4 (1988), 269–278.

[Terzopoulos and Waters 90] D. Terzopoulos and K. Waters. "Physically-Based Facial Modeling, Analysis, and Animation." *J. of Visualization and Computer Animation* 1:4 (1990), 73–80.

[Terzopoulos and Waters 93] D. Terzopoulos and K. Waters. "Analysis and Synthesis of Facial Image Sequences using Physical and Anatomical Models." *IEEE Transactions on Pattern Analysis and Machine Intelligence* 15:6 (1993), 569–579.

[Terzopoulos 88] D. Terzopoulos. "The Computation of Visible-Surface Representations." *IEEE Transactions on Pattern Analysis and Machine Intelligence* PAMI-10:4 (1988), 417–438.

[Terzopoulous and Waters 91] D. Terzopoulous and K. Waters. "Techniques for Realistic Facial Modeling and Animation." In *Computer Animation '91*, edited by N. Magnenat-Thalmann and D. Thalmann, pp. 59–74. Tokyo: Springer-Verlag, 1991.

[The International Phonetic Association 99] The International Phonetic Association. *Handbook of the International Phonetic Association*. Cambridge, UK: Cambridge University Press, 1999.

[Thomas and Johnson 81] F. Thomas and O. Johnson. *Disney Animation: The Illusion of Life*. New York: Abbeville Press, 1981.

[Todd et al. 80] J. T. Todd, S. M. Leonard, R. E. Shaw, and J. B. Pittenger. "The Perception of Human Growth." *Scientific American* 242 (1980), 106–114.

[Todd 80] J. T. Todd. Private Communication, 1980.

[Tolhurst 75] D. J. Tolhurst. "Sustained and Transient Channels in Human Vision." *Vision Research* 15 (1975), 1151–1155.

[Turing 50] A. M. Turing. "Computing Machinery and Intelligence." *Mind* 59:236 (1950), 433–460.

[United States National Library of Medicine 94] United States National Library of Medicine. *The Visible Human Project*, 1994.

[Vannier et al. 83] M. W. Vannier, J. F. Marsch, and J. O. Warren. "Three-Dimensional Computer Graphics for Craniofacial Surgical Planning and Evaluation." *Proc. SIGGRAPH '83, Computer Graphics* 17:3 (1983), 263–273.

[Waite 89] C. T. Waite. "The Facial Action Control Editor, Face: A Parametric Facial Expression Editor for Computer Generated Animation." Master's thesis, Massachusetts Institute of Technology, Media Arts and Sciences, Cambridge, MA., 1989.

[Waite and Welsh 90] J. Waite and W. Welsh. "Head Boundary Location Using Snakes." *British Telcom Technology Journal* 8:3 (1990), 127–136.

[Walther 82] E. F. Walther. *Lipreading*. Chicago: Nelson-Hall Inc., 1982.

[Wang 93] C. L. Wang. "Langwidere: Hierarchical Spline Based Facial Animation System with Simulated Muscles." Master's thesis, University of Calgary, Calgary, Alberta, 1993.

[Ward et al. 07] K. Ward, F. Bertails, T-Y. Kim, S. Marschner, and M-P. Cani. "A Survey on Hair Modeling: Styling, Simulation, and Rendering." *IEEE Transactions on Visualization and Computer Graphics* 13:2 (2007), 213–234.

[Warfel 73] J. H. Warfel. *The Head, Neck and Trunk*. Philadelphia: Lea and Febiger, 1973.

[Warnock 69] J. Warnock. "A Hidden Line Algorithm for Halftone Picture Representation." Technical Report TR 4-15, University of Utah, 1969.

[Warwick 73] R. Warwick. *Grey's Anatomy, 35th Edition*. Loondon: Longman, 1973.

[Watanabe and Suenaga 92] Y. Watanabe and Y. Suenaga. "A Trigonal Prism-Based Method for Hair Image Generation." *IEEE Computer Graphics and Applications* 12:1 (1992), 47–53.

[Watanabe 93] T. Watanabe. "Voice-Responsive Eye-Blinking Feedback for Improved Human-to-Machine Speech Input." In *Proceedings of the 5th International Conf. on Human-Computer Interaction*, pp. 1091–1096. New york: ACM Press, 1993.

[Waters and Frisbie 95] K. Waters and J. Frisbie. "A Coordinated Muscle Model for Speech Animation." In *Graphics Interface 95*, edited by W. Davis and P. Prusinkiewicz, pp. 163–170. Toronto: Canadian Information Processing Society, 1995.

[Waters and Levergood 93] K. Waters and T. M. Levergood. "DECface: An Automatic Lip Synchronization Algorithm for Synthetic Faces." Technical Report CRL 93/4, DEC Cambridge Research Laboratory, Cambridge, MA., 1993.

[Waters and Terzopoulos 91] K. Waters and D. Terzopoulos. "Modeling and Animating Faces Using Scanned Data." *J. of Visualization and Computer Animation* 2:4 (1991), 123–128.

[Waters 87] K. Waters. "A Muscle Model for Animating Three-Dimensional Facial Expressions." *SIGGRAPH '87, Computer Graphics* 21:4 (1987), 17–24.

[Waters 92] K. Waters. "A Physical Model of Facial Tissue and Muscle Articulation Derived from Computer Tomography Data." *SPIE Proceedings of Visualization in Biomedical Computing* 1808 (1992), 574–583.

[Watkins 70] G. Watkins. "A Real Time Hidden Surface Algorithm." Ph.D. thesis, University of Utah, 1970. Technical Report UTEC-CSc-70-101.

[Weil 82] P. Weil. "About Face." Master's thesis, Massachusetts Institute of Technology, Architecture Group, 1982.

[Welsh et al. 90] W. Welsh, S. Searby, and J. Waite. "Nodel-Based Image Coding." *British Telcom Technology Journal* 8:3 (1990), 94–106.

[Welsh 91] W. Welsh. "Model-Based Coding of Images." Ph.D. thesis, Electronic System Engineering, Essex University, 1991.

[Whitted 80] T. Whitted. "An Improved Illumimation Model for Shaded Display." *CACM* 23:6 (1980), 343–349.

[Williams and Stevens 81] C. Williams and K. Stevens. "Vocal Correlates of Emotional States." In *Speech Evaluation in Psychiatry*. New York: Grune and Stratton, 1981.

[Williams et al. 89] P. L. Williams, R. Warwick, M. Dyson, and L. H. Bannister. *Grey's Anatomy, 37th Edition*. London: Churchill Livingstone, 1989.

[Williams 78] L. Williams. "Casting Curved Shadows on Curved Surfaces." *SIGGRAPH '78, Computer Graphics* 12:3 (1978), 270–274.

[Williams 83] L. Williams. "Pyramidal Parametrics." *SIGGRAPH '83, Computer Graphics* 17:3 (1983) 1–11.

[Williams 90a] L. Williams. "3D Paint." *Computer Graphics* 24:2 (1990), 225–233.

[Williams 90b] L. Williams. "Performace Driven Facial Animation." *SIGGRAPH '90, Computer Graphics* 24:4 (1990), 235–242.

[Witten 82] I. Witten. *Principles of Computer Speech*. London: Academic Press, 1982.

[Wolberg 91] G. Wolberg. *Digital Image Warping*. Los Alamitos, CA: IEEE Computer Society Press, 1991.

[Woodwark 86] J. R. Woodwark. "Blends in Geometric Modeling." In *Proceedings on Mathematics of surfaces II*. New York: Clarendon Press, 1986.

[Wright 77] V. Wright. "Elasticity and Deformation of the Skin." In *Biophysical Properties of Skin*, edited by H. R. Elden. New York: Wiley-Interscience, 1977.

[Wylie et al. 67] C. Wylie, G. Romney, D. Evans, and A. Erdahl. "Halftone Perspective Drawing by Computer." In *Proc. Fall Joint Computer Conf.*, pp. 49–58, 1967.

[Wyvill et al. 86] B. Wyvill, C. McPheeters, and G. Wyvill. "Animating Soft Objects." *Visual Computer* 2:4 (1986), 235–242.

[Wyvill et al. 88] B. Wyvill, D. R. Hill, and A. Pearce. "Animating Speech: An Automated Approach Using Speech Synthesized by Rules." *The Visual Computer* 3:5 (1988), 277–289.

[Yamana and Suenaga 87] T. Yamana and Y. Suenaga. "A Method of Hair Representation Using Anisotropic Reflection." *IECEJ Technical Report PRU87-3*, pp. 15-20, Tokyo: Institute of Electronics, Information, and Communications Engineers of Japan, 1987.

[Yang et al. 00] X. Yang, Z. Xu, J. Yang, and T. Wang. "The Cluster Hair Model." *Graphics Models and Image Processing* 62:2 (2000), 85–103.

[Yuille et al. 89] A. L. Yuille, D. S. Cohen, and P. W. Hallinan. "Feature Extraction from Faces Using Deformable Templates." In *IEEE Computer Society Conference on Computer Vision and Pattern Recognition (CVPR'89)*, pp. 104–109. San Diego: IEEE Computer Society Press, 1989.

Index

Plate I.
A complete rendered frame of Gollum from The Lord of the Rings^{TM}. (*"The Lord of the Rings: The Two Towers"* Copyright MMII, New Line Productions, Inc, TM The Saul Zaentz Company d/b/a Tolkien Enterprises under license to New Line Productions, Inc. All rights reserved. Photo by Pierre Vinet. Photo appears courtesy of New Line Productions, Inc.)

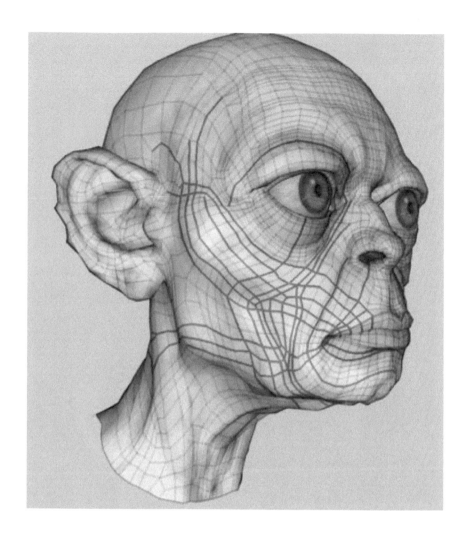

Plate II.
The geometry of Gollum from *The Lord of the Rings*^{TM}. (*"The Lord of the Rings: The Two Towers" Copyright MMII, New Line Productions, Inc, TM The Saul Zaentz Company d/b/a Tolkien Enterprises under license to New Line Productions, Inc. All rights reserved. Photo by Pierre Vinet. Photo appears courtesy of New Line Productions, Inc.*)

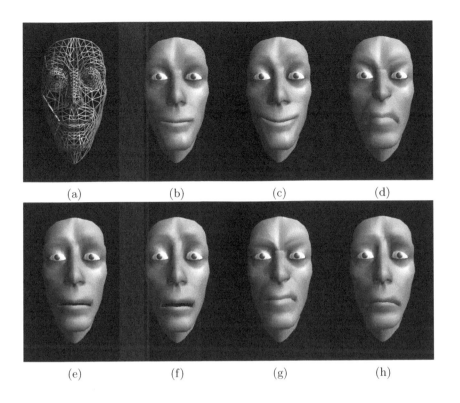

(a)   (b)   (c)   (d)

(e)   (f)   (g)   (h)

Plate III.
Images (a) and (b) illustrate the static geometry. Images (c)-(h) illustrate the
six primary expression created by the muscle model process. (a) static wire
frame, (b) static shaded, (c) happiness, (d) anger, (e) fear, (f) surprise (g)
disgust, (h) sadness.

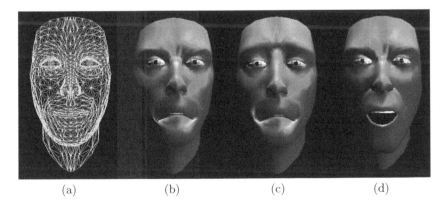

(a)   (b)   (c)   (d)

Plate IV.
Images (a)–(d) illustrate facia action created by the physical model. (a) the
wireframe geometry, (b) anger, (c) worry, (d) jaw drop and brows furrowed.

Plate V.
Four images from an animated sequence using a physically based model. The individual was modeled using Cyberware^{TM} range data.

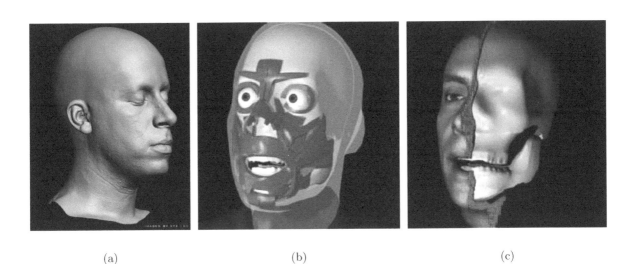

(a)   (b)   (c)

Plate VI.
A finite volume model (FVM) of facial tissues created from magnetic resonance data, a surface laser scan, and muscles created from the visible human project [Sifakis et al. 06]. (a) The surface laser scan, (b) the geometry of the facial muscles with the epidermis revealed transparently, and (c) the composite showing the skeletal subsurface and a cross-section of the skin and muscle tissues. (*Courtesy of R. Fedkiw and E. Sifakis.*)

Plate VII.
A re-projection of the three-dimensional wireframe geometry (blue) onto the original captures frames. Pixel level tracking in the image plane was performed where each three-dimensional position is estimates using triangulation. (*Courtesy of G. Borshukov. Copyright ESC Entertainment 2003.*)

Plate VIII.
The results of hair-to-hair interaction simulation. (*Courtesy of Y. Yu.*)

Plate IX.
Wind blown hair modeled with the particle model. (*Courtesy of Y. Bando.*)

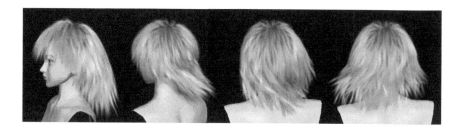

Plate X.
Shaken hair modeing with the particle model. (*Courtesy of Y. Bando.*)

T - #0054 - 101024 - C6 - 235/191/25 [27] - CB - 9781568814483 - Gloss Lamination